4,90

Paul Erker, Nils Fehlhaber
150 Years Continental

Paul Erker, Nils Fehlhaber

150 Years Continental

The Skill of Transformation

DE GRUYTER
OLDENBOURG

Paul Erker is an associate professor at the Ludwig Maximilian University of Munich. The focus of his teaching and research is economic and business history. He is author of many historical works on companies, and for Continental's 125th company anniversary was commissioned to write its first historical study: "Wachsen im Wettbewerb. Eine Zeitgeschichte der Continental AG" ("Growth and Competition. A Contemporary History of Continental AG"), Düsseldorf 1996. Recently he wrote "Zulieferer für Hitlers Krieg. Der Continental-Konzern in der NS-Zeit" (Suppliers for Hitler's War. The Continental Company in the Nazi Era"), Munich/Berlin 2020.

Nils Fehlhaber holds a doctorate in history. Since September 2016, he has run Continental AG's company archive.

ISBN 978-3-11-073695-3
ISBN (PDF) 978-3-11-073237-5
ISBN (Epub) 978-3-11-073239-9

Library of Congress Number: 2021937492

Bibliographic information published by the Deutsche Nationalbibliothek
The Deutsche Nationalbibliothek lists this publication in the Deutsche Nationalbibliografie; detailed bibliographic data are available in the Internet at http://dnb.dnb.de.

© 2021 Walter de Gruyter GmbH, Berlin/Boston
Cover illustration: A collage of photographs and advertising graphics from different media and eras in Continental's history
Typesetting: Michael Peschke, Berlin
Printing: CPI books GmbH, Leck

www.degruyter.com

Content

1   Anniversary dates and transformation phases in the company's history —— 1

2   Founder Consortia, Major Investors and Key Shareholders Corporate Governance and Prominent Figures in Continental's History —— 49
        Siegmund Seligmann: The Rise to Become a Large Modern Enterprise —— 49
        Willy Tischbein and the Americanization of Continental in the 1920s —— 60
        The Major Shareholder between the Weimar Republic and the Era of the Economic Miracle: Continental and the Opel Family —— 73
        Alfred Herrhausen and Carl H. Hahn: Steering Continental through the Major Crisis —— 83
        Two Takeover Attempts and the Search for a Key Shareholder: Turbulent Corporate Governance Structures Between 1990 and 2010 —— 93

3   The People of Continental Identities and Interests in Times of Upheaval in the Working World —— 99
        The Development of the Continental Workforce Through the Lens of Corporate Social and Welfare Policy (1871 to 1918) —— 101
        Self-confident Continental Employees and an Instrumentalized Company Community. Working Worlds, Conflicts and Identity (1918 to 1945) —— 110
        Cold War and Class Struggles at Continental. Collective Bargaining Conflicts, disputes about production sites and Solidarity (1945/48 to 1990/91) —— 118
        The Globalization of Continental in the Context of Production Relocations and Transformations in the World of Working (1990s to the Present) —— 140

4   Rubber—Resource Management, Sustainability and Environment, or: the Metamorphosis of a Key Raw Material
     Global Conflicts over Natural Rubber and a Sunken Rubber Steamer Named "Continental" in Brazil (1870s to 1920s) —— 162
     Mobilization of Resources During the Nazi Era: German Rubber and the Radical Upheaval of Raw Materials —— 171
     Raw Material Management in the Context of the Korean War and Oil Price Crises (1950s to Early 1980s) —— 175
     Sustainable Supply Chain Management, "Dandelion Rubber" and "Smart Rubber." Upheavals in the Raw Materials World from the Early 1980s to Today —— 181

5   A Brief History of the Continental Tire, or: the Metamorphoses of a High-tech Product and the Continental Product Portfolio —— 191
     The Eternal Search to Square a Circle, or: "A Tire for Well-being" —— 194
     Conti Inside. A Changing Product Portfolio, or: Aspects of a history of experience with Continental products —— 217

6   The Continental Shares
     The Life Cycle of a Security in a Changing Capital Market —— 228
     The Varied Career of Continental Shares, from a "Dividend Behemoth" to a "Widow-and-Orphan Stock" in Times of Crisis: 1879 to the Early 1930s —— 228
     From the Economic "Miracle Years" to a Long Period of Crisis: the Boom and Bust of Continental Shares from 1948 to the mid-1980s —— 240
     Continental Shares in the Era of Financial Market Capitalism (1985 to 2020): From the Soaring Flight of a Stock Market Darling to the Stall in the Wake of the Corona Crisis —— 251

7   From Local Trademark to Global Brand
     The Brand and its Marketing in Continental's History —— 269
     The Horse's Importance for the "Continental" Brand —— 269
     The Continental Color and Brand Strategy —— 276
     The customer magazine *Echo Continental* was a reflection of the company's progressive image —— 280

Talking tires and travelling workers: Characters in Continental advertisements —— **289**
Modern advertising formats and repositioning the company as a mobility service provider —— **294**

8 Continental as a Global Company
The Long Road Toward Internationalization —— 306

The internationalization at the heart of the company's early strategy —— **306**
Collaborations and establishing an international network (1889–1914) —— **310**
Collapse of the network abroad and re-internationalization during the 1920s —— **316**
Export strategy in the Nazi era and focussing on the domestic market until well into the 1970s —— **325**
The four phases of internationalization at Continental (1979 to present) —— **331**

9 Between Vision and Speculation
Continental in 2046, or: The History of Past and Present Expectations for the Future within the Company —— 339

The Invention of New Mobility as a Result of Mastering the Raw Material of the Future. Continental's Long "Rubber Age" (1870s to 1930s) —— **340**
No Visions, or: The Key to the Future is Managing the Present (1930s to 1970s) —— **344**
Visions of an Integrated Supplier and Technology Corporation and of "Intelligent Tires" (1980s to 2001) —— **349**
The Future Seems Plannable. Orientation Toward the "Mobility of the Future" (2002 to 2020) —— **352**
Operating System Provider of Software-supported Mobility: Continental in 2046 —— **358**

Annex

Annex 1 Member of the Executive Board —— **365**
Annex 2 Number of Continental Employees —— **369**
Annex 3 Sales Development —— **371**

Annex 4a   Members of the Supervisory Board
(Shareholder Representatives) —— **373**
Annex 4b   Members of the Supervisory Board
(Employee representatives) —— **378**

Image credits —— 381

1 Anniversary dates and transformation phases in the company's history

At the age of 150, Continental is a success story. One that is based on the constant transformation and reinvention of the organization. However, Continental's anniversaries have never been accompanied by good fortune. A look back at the history of the company reveals that its anniversary celebrations were rarely good omens for outstanding commercial success. Frequently, a veritable economic crisis, industrial upheaval or radical organizational change had just been overcome or was imminent, with the cumulative effect of external and internal factors often having a profound impact and sometimes even threatening the company's survival. In 1896, at the time of its 25th anniversary—which the company explicitly did not celebrate—Continental was just coming out of its first major crisis, in which it suffered a capital shortage and was still in the final phase of the depression that started with the Panic of 1873. Called the Great Depression until the 1930s, this far-reaching global crisis consisting of a stock market crash and economic collapse followed the economic boom of the *Gründerjahre* ("founder's years") in Germany, which was still a fledgling industrial country at the time. The anniversaries marking 50 and 75 years of business—in 1921 and 1946—fell in the immediate aftermath of World War I and II respectively. Until 1914, Continental had been actively advancing globalization, but the war subsequently laid waste to the success the company had amassed. In 1921, Continental's Executive Board was instead confronted with destroyed, lost or expropriated foreign subsidiaries, as well as an alarming rise in inflation. In 1946, the company's management and workforce were faced with a Continental that literally lay in ruins. Bombs from the war in the skies had destroyed the majority of the company, and having been politically discredited on many levels due to its support of the Nazi regime, it had to fundamentally reinvent itself and replace its severely warped corporate culture. Global political events did not play a role in its centennial in 1971, yet Continental's continued survival was highly uncertain. The *Wirtschaftswunderjahre* ("miracle years"—West Germany's period of rapid economic recovery after World War II) were at their end, and management had slept through a revolution in tire technology, as well as making other operational errors. 1996 did not bring clear skies either. On the 125th anniversary of its founding, the company was still licking its wounds from a hostile takeover attempt by Pirelli and, in particular, from the internal fragility that had made it vulnerable in the first place. Continental was in the middle of a radical reorganization and restructuring process, while facing intensifying global competition for survival in the tire industry. After a long period of success and expansion, Continental is now celebrating its 150th anniversary. And once more, the company's ability to confront a crisis with resolve and to compete in the market is being seriously tested by a period of fundamental transformation which requires it to adapt. The situation Continental faces in 2021 is particularly pervasive because it is accompanied by various economic, technological and internal factors exacerbating the crisis. Between the company's numerous phases of upheaval, however, it has continued to reach new heights of success, demonstrating not only its immense inner robustness and cultural vitality but also the importance it places on the autonomy and entrepreneurial spirit of its people and the organization itself.

Its anniversaries, whether counted decade by decade or every 25 years, only tell part of the story of the larger transformation phases that the company was going through at the time. In many cases, the people of the time were aware of the changes that were in progress. But often, the transformations could only be identified in retrospect. This held true in particular when determining who or what was the driving factor behind the transformation and understanding the multidimensional factors that set it in motion. Were they offensive or defensive? Was the transformation planned and part of a strategy? Or was it unplanned and epitomized by incrementalism, with those involved simply muddling through and riding it out? And was there a vision that drove the change, or was it the result of pragmatic short-term goals defined by corporate policy?

In Continental's history, there have been at least nine transformation phases, some overlapping and some more or less conspicuous than others. These are briefly described below. Contemporary terms used to describe and analyze the respective corporate developments were often used prescriptively, in the sense that they expressed characteristics that were considered desirable or necessary for a modern company, and they thus differed accordingly. However, they frequently had the same meaning—even if not explicitly used at the time and redefined later. In many cases, they were simply catchphrases or management terms in a new guise which, on closer inspection, form a common thread running through the company's history. Not least, this applies to the concept of transformation itself, which has been used in the business world as of late whenever companies want to avoid referring to a crisis, restructuring or a reorganization. Terms such as "agile companies" and "transforming corporations" have replaced former watchwords like "adaptable companies" and "change management," which meant the same thing. Even before 1900, corporate culture was employed as a control instrument and management model. Company managers such as Siegmund Seligmann and Willy Tischbein faced volatility, uncertainty, complexity and ambiguity prior to World War I—long before these seemingly new challenges were combined into the modern-day acronym VUCA. "Purpose," "CSR (corporate social responsibility)" or "stakeholder value" as an expression of newly discovered corporate responsibility for society as a whole—frequently demanded by external forces—is another concept that has its roots in the 19th century, in the voluntary commitment to corporate social policy for employees and toward the company's location. The key difference to the contemporary definition lies, firstly, in the increasing scale of these tasks, and secondly, in their increasing complexity on a global level and, above all, in the quest to shape the ever-shorter cycles of upheaval on a continual basis and anticipate these accordingly. For a corporate transformation does not simply occur—it is driven, encouraged and harnessed by the organization itself and its staff, with the latter defining their terminology accordingly.

As early as the 1870s and especially in the 1920s and 1930s, Continental was forced to develop a substantial degree of resilience, even though back then nobody had heard of crisis-proofing or developing the skills necessary to survive a crisis well. Interestingly, a "new Continental" was declared again and again, before or after each transformation phase. Rather than just changes in the technology used or developed or a new organizational or strategic direction for the company, this also referred to an associated change in positioning within the relevant industry sector and market. Correlations can therefore also be drawn between the company's phases of upheaval and the history of mobility and its specific forms.

Continental underwent its *first* transformation phase between 1871 and 1895/96. During these 25 years, the company evolved from a flawed start-up that was fraught with risks into an established business, braving an economic slump, lack of capital and management errors along the way. When the nine private bankers and entrepreneurs who formed the founding consortium launched Continental Caoutchouc- und Gutta-Percha Compagnie, the timing was in fact favorable. Having been victorious in the war against France, the German Reich was experiencing a massive surge in the founding of companies and a strong push toward industrialization, during which thousands of companies were created as public corporations—a comparatively new company type at the time. The economy and society of the day were very much defined by the age of the railway. Rubber was still a new and promising raw material, but its material properties and nearly limitless market potential were largely unknown. Nonetheless, it offered access to a highly lucrative business area in the future. Just as prescient as the choice of raw material was the choice of company name, which indicated its transnational character. The founders also conducted a thorough market analysis and investigated future sales opportunities, a task made easier by the fact that several of them also held functions and investments in the Hannoversche Gummi-Kamm-Compagnie, founded nine years earlier in 1862. Whereas this company manufactured trinkets and combs from hard rubber, the broad sector of soft rubber products was earmarked for Continental—from rubber balls and other toys to hoses for water, steam and gas pipes, hot water bottles and medical items. In addition, there was the potential to produce countless consumer items from rubber, such as preserving rings, gaskets, rubber mats, perfume sprayers, travel air cushions and waterproof clothing. Founding the company was not without its risks, however, with numerous insolvencies having occurred since the emergence of the rubber industry in Germany at the end of the 1850s.

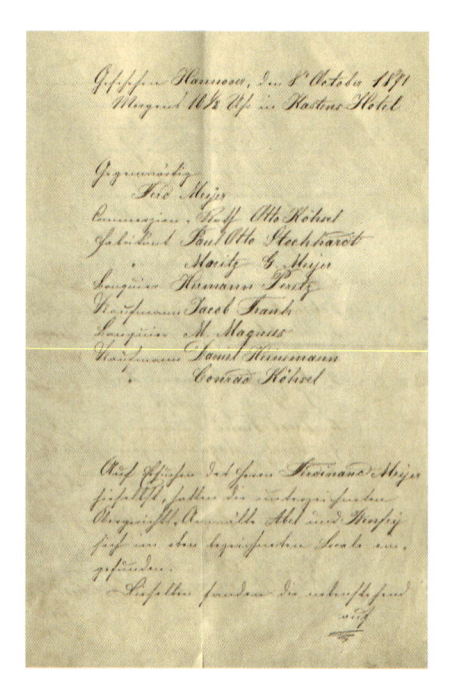

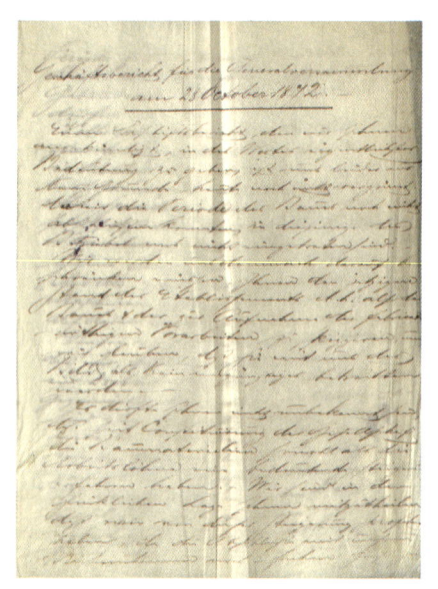

Fig. 1: Certificate of incorporation dated October 8, 1871, and first annual report of October 1872.

And indeed, the outlook for Continental soon turned gloomy, starting with delays in the construction of its factory and facilities. When, in the fall of 1873, production did finally commence in Vahrenwald, the economy was hit by the *Gründerkrach* ("founder's crash") followed by a prolonged period of deflation and economic downturn. So it was that Continental, barely having been founded, suffered its first global economic crisis—followed by numerous others. Company management changed frequently. In the brief period up to 1876 alone, four factory and company managers were replaced due to a lack of necessary know-how in the fields of business, engineering or chemistry. To add to the problems, there were internal conflicts. Technological convergence in the rubber industry soon rendered the distinction between hard and soft rubber obsolete, with the result that Continental and the Gummi-Kamm-Compagnie increasingly encroached on each other's business territory. This initially led to close cooperation in the 1880s, followed by talks of a merger, but these ultimately broke down and negotiations would not prove successful until more than 40 years later under different conditions. By 1875/76, most of the founding capital of 300 thousand thalers (equivalent to approximately 6.3 million euros today)—a substantial amount at the time—had already been used up, so that the shareholders had to inject fresh capital into the company. In the run-up to this, however, a restructuring report was drawn up which, on the one hand, predicted the imminent collapse of the company without new capital, but on the other envisaged flourishing sales for Continental in the future if various restructuring measures were carried out.

As a result, the company slowly recovered and reestablished itself from the late 1870s onward, employing around 300 people and essentially presenting itself as the "new Continental." Management was replaced, and from 1876 the company became profitable again. A dividend was also paid out for the first time, amounting to 5 percent of the share capital. Germany, already highly industrialized, was rapidly turning into a mobilized and urbanized society. Although Continental was unable to profit from the railway boom, it benefited from this economic backdrop by producing hoof buffers for horses, which were frequently used to pull streetcars and droshky carriages, and, from 1883, offered solid rubber tires for carriages and bicycles. Sales reached 1.37 million marks and increased—albeit with considerable fluctuations—to no less than 3.26 million marks in 1884, before tending to stagnate until the beginning of the 1890s. Only then did a significant upward trend set in, thanks to the brightening economy and the gradually increasing momentum in the pneumatic tire business. In 1874, the company appointed the chemist Adolf Prinzhorn and created its own research laboratory.

Continental thus became a member of the ever-growing circle of science-based high-tech industry, which, led by chemical and electrical corporations, was now shaping the landscape of the German industrial economy and was soon to gain prominence on the world stage.

The development of air-filled tires from 1890 onward was a key breakthrough. At the same time, bicycles became a mass means of transport and mobility for the general population, as well as being at the heart of the burgeoning sport of cycle racing. In 1892, Continental became the first German company to introduce pneumatic tires for bicycles. Just two years later, it proudly announced to shareholders in its annual general report that the "Continental Pneumatic" had acquired a leading position on the market. Behind the success of the bicycle tire business lay Willy Tischbein, then European champion in men's tricycle racing. Tischbein was both a competitor and friend of fellow racing athlete Georg von Opel, the grandson of the Opel founder, whose sewing machine factory broadened its scope in 1886 and started to produce bicycles as well. Tischbein joined Continental in 1894 and pushed for business with the growing plethora of bicycle companies such as Adlerwerke, formerly Heinrich Kleyer AG in Frankfurt and soon to become one of Continental's most important customers.

The *second* transformation phase can be discerned from the mid-1890s to 1913. During these 23 years, Continental experienced its breakthrough as an automotive tire manufacturer, whose numerous innovations during the short first globalization phase of the German economy up to 1913/1914 also made it successful internationally. In 1897, production commenced on air-filled (or pneumatic) tires for automobiles, which were invented by Michelin in France only two years earlier and had been developed to maturity for mass production. "The expectations we held for the past year," states the annual report for the general shareholders' meeting on March 24, 1897,

> have been fulfilled in every way, and profits even exceed those of the year before. This success is the result of the continuously increasing popularity of our brands, which enabled us to increase our sales by around another 2 million marks in 1896. This considerable sum is distributed evenly across all of our production items. Our Continental Pneumatic tire has retained its leading position on the global market.

At the time, the bicycle tire business still accounted for the main share of profits outside of technical products. However, by the turn of the century at the latest, automobile tire business became dominant. A glance at the abrupt rise in sales shows just how successful this new main business sector was. Between 1897, which already saw sizeable sales of 10.4 million marks, and 1913, the figures kept climbing by two to three million marks every year until 1904, after which the annual sales growth amounted to 20 million or more, reaching 119.33 million marks in 1913. The policy of diversifying into technical rubber products and consumer items made of rubber significantly contributed to business success. In 1908, for example, the company started producing products for shoemakers. With the rubber sole, which was created in 1912, Continental not only developed a widely known brand product but also spearheaded a revolution in shoe manufacturing.

Besides this, new business areas opened up due to developments in mobility in the German Reich, such as the manufacturing of balloon material and canvas for aircraft skins and the first pneumatic aircraft tires, ensuring further sustained growth. Back then, not a single Zeppelin airship took to the air without gas cells from Continental, and, in 1909, the Frenchman Louis Blériot became the first person to cross the English Channel in an aircraft covered with Continental material. However, there were also causes for caution. The bicycle was gradually being replaced by motorcycles and automobiles as a means of mass mobility, which led to crises in the bicycle industry around the turn of the century that were also felt by Continental. Business in the pneumatic tires segment could be highly cyclical and was sensitive to economic fluctuations. Last but not least, there was the risk of being dependent on automotive manufacturers such as Opel, the largest carmaker at the time. Nevertheless, for many years, Continental was able to carve out a position as Opel's OEM of choice and continuously break new records for sales and profit growth. The number of staff also increased rapidly, from just under 500 workers and employees at the beginning of the 1890s to more than 7,000 in 1913—an analyst's report of 1932 even claims that the total number of people on the Continental payroll domestically and abroad already amounted to 13,000 in 1913. By 1929, it had risen to almost 16,800. Dividends increased at the same pace. As of 1893, they had risen to 30 percent, and then to 40 and 50 percent, until the highest level of 55 percent was attained in 1896. Thereafter, they stabilized for the years up to 1913 in the region of 40 to 45 percent.

During this phase, Continental also gained wide acclaim for its numerous innovations. In 1904, it manufactured the world's first profiled tires for automobiles, followed in 1905 by the production launch of rivet anti-skid tires, which were similar to the studded tires introduced 70 years later. In 1908, the detachable wheel rim was invented, greatly simplifying the painstaking and exhausting process of changing a tire. At automobile races, which were rapidly gaining in popularity across Europe, all the famous drivers—including those in Daimler-Benz cars from 1901 onward—won using Continental tires. The tires of the Hanover-based company shaped international motorsports like no other manufacturer, deeply engraining its image among large sections of the general public. The company also pushed ahead with the internationalization and globalization of its business during this period. By 1913, it had established a dense network of sales branches and subsidiaries across all continents as well as its own manufacturing plants in France and Australia, thereby avoiding the customs restrictions prevalent in international trade. Approximately 60 percent of total sales were attributable to foreign exports, with North America alone accounting for around a third of this figure. By now Continental had become a global enterprise, and at the world exhibitions of the time, such as Paris in 1900 or St. Louis in 1904, the company won one award after another.

Fig. 2: Postcard with news about the awards for Continental at the 1904 World's Fair in St. Louis, USA.

"At the 1910 International Exposition in Brussels, we were awarded three Grand Prix, one for automobile and bicycle tires, one for materials for steerable airships and airplanes, and one for technical rubber items," stated the annual report for 1910. "We also won a Grand Prize at the International Railway and Overland Transport Exhibition held in Buenos Aires in 1910." Without a doubt, Continental had become a large, internationally renowned brand.

Fig. 3: The Continental stand at the International Motor Show in St. Petersburg in 1913. At these exhibitions, a common method for determining market share was to count how many Continental tires were used on the exhibits of the automotive manufacturers—in this case, 691 of 1,677 tires, i.e. a 41 percent share of the market.

However, another reason for Continental's international success and its rampant export business was the fact that, together with Excelsior AG (as the Gummi-Kamm-Compagnie was called from 1912 onward), Continental was one of the world's largest producers of toys. Rubber dolls and balls as well as countless replicas of animals, mythical creatures and fairytale figures of all kinds replaced the earlier wooden toys and became bestsellers. A Cupid doll that resembled a chubby newborn with squinting eyes, a pointed head of hair and short wings—a popular talisman among men and women in the USA at the time—was a particular sales hit. Continental became one of the key contributors to contemporary mobility in 19th century society, which was characterized by the spread of the motorcycle and automobile. By this time, the company had long since developed into a provider of mobility services too, even if this term did not exist at the time. Shortly after the turn of the century, the company started publishing an annual handbook for motorists and motorcyclists, the "Continental Handbook for Automobilists," as well as the "Continental Atlas" with city maps, round trips and tour routes. In 1912, Continental also set up a touring office to promote the "art of travel." Against a background of intense pro-automobile propaganda ("Where the railroad was a despot that belittled us, taking away our right to determine a route [...], the car has returned our freedom to decide for ourselves. It allows us to think autonomously and create our own itinerary, according to our own needs but also at our own risk."), dozens of employees devised travel plans for automotive tourists free of charge, including precise distance information, sightseeing tips and recommended hotels. The ADAC (Germany's automobile association) did not offer services like this until much later.

Fig. 4: A view of Continental's touring office in 1913.

The company's newly erected, highly prestigious administrative building also reflected its unwavering self-confidence, while mergers and external growth additionally contributed to its transformation into a modern, bureaucratically organized, major corporation with a divisional orientation, as evidenced for example by the subdivision of its branches: 21 were devoted to the tire business, eight sold technical products, and seven other branches handled Continental's sports and weatherproof clothing business. As early as 1912/13, the company boasted no less than five accounts departments, sophisticated reporting and comprehensive quarterly data compilations for the Supervisory Board, including all key figures on production, raw material consumption and the various costs, as well as an internationally orientated finance department that was to prove its worth during the later years of inflation and beyond, all of which were testimonies to its highly efficient, bureaucratic organization.

But this development was abruptly interrupted by World War I and subsequently inflation. Sales fell to 33.6 million marks in 1916, which was just one-third of the pre-war level. Additionally, the export business completely collapsed; the company's foreign companies were expropriated and assets held there seized. The scale of the material loss alone was massive, as illustrated by the fact that Continental was later granted 40 million gold marks in compensation by the German Reich, of which the company ultimately received only 3 million. This all took place during the *third* transformation phase, which only lasted around 14 years. Despite all efforts, Continental failed to continue seamlessly from its pre-war success, even with Tischbein subjecting the company to a thorough process of Americanization. Due to the efforts of key shareholder, B.F. Goodrich, which incorporated the latest American tire technology as well as US rationalization concepts by introducing the Bedaux system and ultimately forged a modern group structure with strong divisional elements modelled on large American corporate groups, Continental became one of the most "Americanized" German companies of the time. In the 1950s and 1990s, further "Americanization phases" of a completely different nature were to follow within the overarching transformation phases. Nevertheless, Continental still achieved success in the 1920s.

Soon after 1918, inflation started to soar, which initially led to a sharp rise in figures without this being backed up by real business success. In 1923, the year of hyperinflation, Continental recorded an astronomically high revenue of 2,052 quadrillion marks; in its annual report of April 10, 1924, after-tax profit alone is listed as 294 quadrillion marks—with 15 zeros. As a key shareholder against the threat of a hostile takeover by competitors, a cooperation, consulting and participation agreement was concluded with the friendly American tire and rubber company B.F. Goodrich, which acquired about 20 percent of the shares in 1920. This deal also enabled Continental to acquire the latest tire technology know-how from the USA. In 1921, on the 50th anniversary of its founding, Continental subsequently became the first German company to present the new cord tire, which was considerably superior to the previous square-woven fabric tire. Another premiere was the development of giant tires—low-pressure balloon tires for trucks— for which solid rubber tires had previously been the only option due to the high stress loads. As a result, the company was responsible for boosting innovation in tire technology.

Fig. 5: Tire advertisement from 1927.

Continental also broke new ground with its innovations in the technical sector. Conveyor belts with ever-increasing widths and higher load capacities contributed to significant productivity gains in the mining industry. And the invention of the endless V-belt, which replaced the prevailing leather belts and chains, was a decisive step in motorization, improving both the power transmission and the operating safety of cars. During these years, Continental itself also went through several phases of rationalization. Machines were increasingly used for tire wrapping, which had been a strenuous manual task for many years, and in the mid-1920s Continental introduced what was known as the Bedaux system, making it a pioneer in the use of modern work performance and remuneration systems in Germany (although many staff also perceived it as a system devised to hasten their labor). Intensive research and development efforts led to an ever better understanding of high-tech materials and enabled new applications in manufacturing technology. In this way, new products arose for the sophisticated leisure and consumer society of the Weimar Republic in the 1920s, such as sports equipment, bathing caps, floating rubber animals, football bladders and tennis balls, and last but not least, rubber dinghies for collapsible boat sport popular at that time. In response to the considerable sports boom of the 1920s, which Continental itself helped to fuel by donating 50,000 marks for the training of sports instructors and promotion of sport in general in April 1921, sports items and clothing were added to its range. Furthermore, the company profited from municipal and public healthcare driven by the setup of the welfare state as well as society's growing use of home-based medical products during this period. The number of these products, such as transfusion hoses, hygiene showers, rubber gloves and rubber bed underlays, increased significantly. In a dedicated hall for the sewing of raincoats, hundreds of women tailored state-of-the-art clothing, which customers could then view and try on in a separate clothing department as well as at a number of special branches across Germany. Along with the rubber perfume sprayer, fashionable shoe heels and other cosmetic items such as combs and hair clips, Continental was also a fashion company of sorts during this period. In an advertising brochure, Continental's main competitor Michelin made fun of the former's diversification policy, alleging this was a symptom of fragmented development efforts at the Hanover-based company, while praising its own commitment to just one goal: "to produce the best tire possible." Continental's success both in the automotive tire sector and in technical products and rubber products for consumers was proof the company had adopted the right strategy, however, and also made it considerably less dependent on economic fluctuations and potential crises in the German automotive industry.

In 1924, revenue was reported using the new Reichsmark currency for the first time and amounted to 77.9 million. This was doubled the very next year, before 1926 brought a significant drop. By 1930, however, it had increased again to 145.4 million reichsmarks. One contributing factor was the further systematic expansion of the export business, aided by the Internationale Continental-Caoutchouc-Compagnie, which was founded in 1923 in Amsterdam and acted as a central controlling company. In 1929, Continental had 24 branches in European countries and 40 outside of Europe. After Continental acquired four tire and rubber factories in 1929—Hannoversche Gummiwerke Excelsior (Hanover), Peters Union (Frankfurt a.M.), Polack-Titan (Waltershausen) and Liga-Gummiwerke Heinrich Peter (Frankfurt a.M.)—a significant centralization of its internal administration ensued. Once again, a "new Continental" was proclaimed and it renamed itself Continental Gummi-Werke AG. The company combined the four factories it had taken over (located in the Limmer district of Hanover and in Korbach) and the factory headquarters (in the Vahrenwald district of Hanover) into one production network. In September 1929, around 165,000 tires and hoses were manufactured for motor cars, 38,000 for motorcycles and 410,000 for bicycles. More than 1,200 trademarks in Germany and abroad, as well as 58 patents, 13 registered designs (design samples) and 190 utility models safeguarded the market and brand success of Continental products. Shortly thereafter, however, the next global economic crisis of 1930/31 brought this dynamic transformation to a standstill. Sales fell by half, from 145.4 million reichsmarks (1930) to 72.5 million reichsmarks (1932), but the company still remained profitable. Its competitors suffered far more as a result of the crisis.

Fig. 6: 50-year anniversary celebrations in 1921. There was no great party. Instead, Continental donated 10 million marks to employees, workers and welfare institutions. Managing director Willy Tischbein is at center left, with privy councilor Siegmund Seligmann next to him on the right.

Continental's *fourth* transformation phase took place between 1933 and 1945. This was a comparatively short period, yet the changes had severe consequences. The company developed into an armaments manufacturer and a model enterprise of the Nazi era, becoming one of the most important suppliers for Hitler's war. Indeed, as mentioned above, it had weathered the global economic crisis comparatively well, particularly because managing director Tischbein had cut down on costs and expenses. Thereafter, however, the ailing economy and, above all, the political erosion in society—characterized by the seizure of power by Hitler and the National Socialist German Workers' Party (NSDAP)—led to a dictatorship which changed the political and economic environment of the company in many ways. Now there was central government regulation and economic control to cope with, as well as the obligation to a racially nationalist state and its ideological goals as a new "stakeholder." However, the company also subjugated itself to this new system and its rules in a program of voluntary self-adjustment, particularly when the conditions to do so became favorable for business on a broader scale. Automobilization gained new impetus with the "National Socialist economic wonder," as the National Socialists themselves declared it, and the tire business soon boomed again. Continental's other products were also in great demand in the leisure and consumer society of Nazi Germany, something ideologically encouraged by those now in power.

Within a short space of time, the principles of democratic values and capitalist competition, on which the corporate culture had previously been based, were done away with. The *Führer* principle and National Socialist concept of a *Betriebsgemeinschaft* ("collective") quickly permeated the company, although the exclusion of dissidents and racial vilification of "non-Aryans" within the workforce and Supervisory Board only occurred gradually and lasted until 1938. The ideology of the "operational collective" pursued by the new National Socialist consultative council, which had replaced the works council, certainly appealed to the workforce and management, not least because its cross-factory orientation made it easier for the Continental corporation, which had only recently come into existence, to grow closer together. The National Socialist policy of self-sufficiency and armament also fundamentally changed the basic principles of the company's policy, in particular through the obligation to use Buna, a synthetic rubber developed in Germany, as the new raw material basis. Use of this material for the manufacturing and development of new "Buna tires" for the war effort, a policy which was soon to be openly pursued, presented Continental engineers with significant challenges, which they ultimately overcame with their usual persistence and creativity. By no later than 1938, the company again presented itself as a "new Continental," this time in the guise of a model National Socialist company. With 16,500 workers and employees, its workforce had never been greater and, in the eyes of management, it was a prime example of a "National Socialist collective," both inwardly and outwardly. Sales also rocketed from 76 million reichsmarks (1933) to 262 million reichsmarks, a figure that the company would never again be able to match, not even with the resultant geographical expansion during the war.

Fig. 7: Swastika flags at the Continental administration building in 1938.

The war fundamentally changed the company's political plight and scope for maneuver once again, which contributed to its wholesale radicalization on various levels. This started with the tailoring of its production processes toward the war economy, the heterogenization of the workforce through the increased employment of women, conscripted Germans and, above all, forced foreign labor, and included the expansion of the business area and sales territory to the occupied territories and countries. With the help of its Buna know-how—and steered by the National Socialist state—a diverse and complex large-scale war production network was created across allied and occupied countries in a short time. It extended over large parts of Europe and encompassed newly founded foreign subsidiaries and Continental-controlled partner factories, leased factories, as well as supervised and consultant factories. The company also built new plants in this period: the Hanover-Stöcken plant, on which construction began in 1938 but which was never finished, and the Posen (Poznan) and Krainburg (Kranj) plants in the former Polish and Slovenian territories that were now part of the German Reich. Continental also became a model of the various manifestations and stages in the use of foreign and forced labor in this era, ultimately culminating in the use of concentration camp prisoners at various production sites—a clear reflection of how deeply the company had by now become entangled in the crimes of the Nazi state. By the end of 1943, almost 5,500 forced laborers and war refugees from 22 countries were toiling away at Continental, to which approximately 1,200 concentration camp prisoners were added in 1944. However, the actual total number of laborers forced to work at Continental is likely to be considerably higher, on account of the significant level of fluctuation. By the end, it was not only the Nazi regime and National Socialist war economy that imploded but Continental's extensive manufacturing network too, until the main plant in Vahrenwald was reduced to rubble as a result of bomb attacks. However, the factories in Limmer and Korbach remained largely intact, as did the still uncompleted Stöcken plant, which was planned and designed to be the largest and most sophisticated tire factory in Europe but was still only a shell before the bombings.

Many were keen to quickly forget these years, but they cast a long shadow, which time and time again and for many years has forced Continental to deal with what is the darkest chapter in its corporate history and confront its own past—a process that continues into the present day.

The *fifth* transformation phase lasted approximately 35 years, although it can in some ways be regarded as two periods. It stretches from 1945/46 to the beginning of the 1980s, including the "miracle years" and also the subsequent crisis of Germany's "long seventies," which were characterized by the rise in oil prices. Both of these periods were closely linked, as the history of Continental clearly shows. After the end of the war, a "new Continental" was created, which, on the one hand, demonstrated much continuity with the years before, for example at management level and due to its major shareholder Opel. On the other hand, however, there was no attempt on the part of the company to return to the pre-war era and the 1920s. Instead it "reinvented" itself to a certain extent within the context of the newly created Federal Republic of Germany, driven by the strong tailwind of the years of reconstruction and the "miracle years," thereby integrating itself into the new market-based liberal economic system. This new sense of self-confidence was based, among other things, on having attained the production capacity of 1938 again as early as November 1950, and was reflected symbolically by the newly erected headquarters from which the company started to operate in 1953. At the time, the Continental tower block at Königsworther Platz was the tallest office building in Germany and a visible statement. The development of the "new Continental" was a reflection of the mobility of those years and is closely linked with the wave of motorization that occurred in the 1950s and

1960s, which finally turned the passenger car and, above all, the Volkswagen, into a true means of mass motorization.

Fig. 8: Press conference on April 11, 1961, at the Stöcken plant, during the presentation of "The New Continental" round-shoulder tire.

At the time, however, the future of mobility was highly controversial, and the question of whether priority should be placed on rail or road was a major topic of debate. Continental naturally sided with motorization lobbies from the automotive, tire and oil industries, which touted motorization in large-scale advertisements, deployed a range of measures designed to make the railway unattractive as a mobility competitor and demanded the reallocation of tax resources toward the expansion of road traffic. Thereafter, the company did indeed attain gilt-edged balance sheets again thanks to the endless demand, a seller's market in which tires were more allocated than sold, exploding sales (from 242 million German marks in 1949 to 1.1 billion German marks in 1965/66) and a rapid increase in employment figures (from 6,733 in 1945 to 28,000 in 1969, with the company's previous highest staff count already having been exceeded in 1954, at 17,116). Last but not least, the company paid out substantial dividends of 16 to 18 percent on its share capital, which amounted to 140 million German marks at the time. This was reminiscent of the "old" Continental. But there was nothing left of the cosmopolitan company of the 1920s with its charismatic managing directors. In the 1950s and 1960s, Continental focused on its domestic market and came across as stuffy and conservative. It was managed by a collective executive board, at times numbering up to eight men who were barely seen in public and whose names were unfamiliar even to many of their contemporaries.

The attempt to form a new company under the conditions of the post-war boom years was steered by corporate policy—even if this was never pursued as an explicit strategy. A return to the global market was initiated, albeit hesitantly, and was primarily aimed at tapping the European tire markets by building a new tire factory in Sarreguemines in France in 1961. In the end, however, the export share of the total revenue was a modest 15 percent. As recently as 1957, the credo behind the company's corporate policy was: "A consensus exists among us not to pursue expansionist policies and therefore not to aspire to achieve the tire market shares of the pre-war era." In the early 1960s, the Executive Board also first initiated a policy of "beyond rubber" by venturing into plastics processing and heavily investing in this second main material. No fewer than three new plants—in Dannenberg, Northeim and Babenhausen—were built or bought, in which new products such as PVC floors, polyurethane foams, plastic inflatable boats and other plastic items were manufactured from the competing and much cheaper material, which could also be perfectly tailored to its application and brightly colored. At the original production facilities in the Vahrenweld and Stöcken districts of Hanover, departments for plastics processing and foam rubber manufacture were also established. In Hanover, the goal of the company was to be prepared should the new plastics era replace the old "rubber era." The thinking behind this new policy was: "If products that are part of our standard manufacturing program can be manufactured better, more expediently and, in particular, more economically using plastic instead of rubber, we will convert our production accordingly. And if new items made from sophisticated plastics expand the range of applications of our current manufacturing program, we will then commence this production." The new innovations had names like "Contipren," "Contilan," "Contiplast" and "Conticell," and were sold as hoses, molded products, films, and floor coverings.

However, the new "plastics policy" proved successful only to a limited extent. In the case of some lucrative mass-market products, for example hula hoops, it was only after the fad had passed and the boom was over that the Executive Board started to produce these using expensive machines. Proudly and unyieldingly,

Fig. 9: The Continental Executive Board in 1966, from left to right: Dr. Oskar Müller, Richard Beckadolph, Karl H. Braudorn, Dr. Georg Göbel (Executive Board spokesperson), Hans Christian Pauck, Hans Stark, Adolf D. Niemeyer.

the board clung to the Continental tradition of being a full-range provider. In an advertising brochure from 1956, the 730-page product catalog listing Continental's 35,000 different items is referenced right at the beginning. From the cradle to the grave, every hour of the day, Continental products had a ubiquitous presence in everyday life with varying degrees of visibility—from bus tires and "tasteful and decorative" Continental floor covering materials to seating upholstered with Continental foam, Latex foam pads, Continental household gloves, preserving rings, rubber end caps, garden hoses and balls, and last but not least, the famous Continental hot-water bottle. The product range mirrored the needs of the working, leisure and consumer society of the young Federal Republic of Germany. In this respect, the new Continental was still very much the one of old. Finally, extensive efforts were made to modernize its research and development activities. The age of plastic brought with it new requirements: a high degree of expertise in the new field of elastomers, the development, application and processing of new types of synthetic rubber, laboratories for fabric and wire cord research and, last

Fig. 10: The plastic products section of the Continental trade fair booth, 1967.

but not least, the Contidrom tire testing center built in 1967 in the south of the Lüneburg Heath. Yet much expertise was acquired from the company's policy of cooperation with US tire firms, whose ideas about tire technology strongly influenced Continental's own philosophy.

The managers at Continental's helm during Germany's "economic miracle" years had apparently led the company to new heights. They also benefited from guaranteed tire prices (known as resale price maintenance) and were virtually without competitors. At the end of the 1960s, however, they steered the company into its biggest existential crisis to date. Continental was still in the process of transitioning to a modern post-war corporation when Michelin's technological revolution, the radial ply tire, caused the customary business model in the tire sector to collapse, thereby putting Continental's survival at risk. The crisis, which had already made itself felt in 1967 with declining sales and profits as well as rising costs, heralded the end of the "miracle years." For far too long, however, the Executive Board had turned a blind eye to the looming issues and—vindicated by the professional public and financial press—instead distracted itself from the dark clouds on the horizon by focusing on its seemingly relentless, above-average profitability, "which is equal to the much-praised profitability of the Volkswagen plant," as the German newspaper FAZ wrote in May 1967. Excessive wages were considered to be the only problem factor, and all measures were therefore focused on cutting costs. The fact that the wind had by now radically changed for OEMs was also deliberately overlooked. For example, in the fall of 1965, the Volkswagen factory had set up a new costing group within its purchasing department. In order to determine the tire prices to be paid, the group demanded documents breaking down costing from suppliers such as Continental. "Prospects for the future arise from keeping pace," was the slogan of Continental's Executive Board. And at the Annual Shareholders' Meeting in June 1968, Georg Göbel, then the spokesperson of the Executive Board, announced: "The crisis is behind us!" Even analysts at the Institut für Bilanzanalysen, a highly renowned institute for financial analysis at the time, casually stated that the 1969 balance sheets for Continental's rubber business had "lost some of [their] usual shine." But then, in addition to the economic downturn and growing competitive pressure, the situation was exacerbated both by misjudgments regarding the new Michelin tire technology, the steel radial tire and also adherence to Continental's plans to develop its own belted tire, until demand massively collapsed and, for the first time in the company's history, profits were tens of millions in the red.

Continental's competitors were not much better off. In 1967 and 1975, there were hectic attempts at collaboration, strategic alliances and mergers of various kinds, including an alliance between Continental, Dunlop and Pirelli, and a merger with Metzler and (predominantly) Phoenix. All of these attempts failed, however. During these years, a "new Continental" was proclaimed several times, first in October 1971, when the old Executive Board justified this to the Supervisory Board while the crisis was still in progress by stating that "for the past three years, our procurement programs and activities have been aimed at building what might be termed a 'new Continental.' We now need to have the courage to continue along this path until we reach the finishing line, despite all the difficulties." Only a short time later, in the fall of 1973, Carl H. Hahn, then the incumbent chairman of the Executive Board, announced his vision of a "new Continental" as part of a radical restructuring program. The company's core area, more than ever before, was the tire business, and during its preceding, desperate efforts to survive the crisis, the question of whether this focus should be maintained had been a topic of discussion among the Supervisory Board. The dry spell and the crisis years, which brought with them the uncertainties of not knowing when they would end and whether Continental would survive, continued until 1983. Regardless of the specific circumstances, these years were a textbook example of how, after a long period of profitable growth and lack of competitive pressure, a company can quickly lose its sensibility for impending crises if it ignores problem factors. In doing so, a company can very quickly find itself in a position where its survival is threatened. The situation can become particularly critical if the company's diminished perceptiveness and resulting errors of judgment not only relate to economic and industry-specific upheavals but also to disruptive changes necessary from a technological point of view.

In retrospect, the mere 10 years between 1981 and 1991 that make up the *sixth* transformation phase constitute more of an episode. From the perspective of the people at the time, however, this was when Continental rose to become a modern and truly international corporation in the dawning age of financial market capitalism. During these years, Continental—like all major German companies—bid farewell to the "bureaucratic corporation" model that had been in place since the 1870s (W. Plumpe). New guiding principles for corporate development started to spread, with the flexibilization of organizational structures, the global alignment of business models and the permeation of the principles of financial market capitalism into corporate processes being the top priorities. After the company's expensive lesson of playing catch-up in mastering new tire technology, something it managed in the nick of time, the Executive Board in essence deployed attack as the best form of defense to survive on the increasingly competitive but stagnating markets. This started with the purchase of the European division of US tire company Uniroyal in July 1979, which was something of a coup at the time, and its subsequent integration in the years that followed. In this, the decades-long friendly relations with Belgian company Englebert, which formed the core of Uniroyal Europe, came full circle. Back in the 1890s, Continental had owned Englebert shares for some years. This was followed by a failed takeover of what was then French tire company Kléber and a series of collaborations in the USA and Japan, but these resembled a "poor man's policy" more than an offensive strategy of internationalization. It was not until the end of 1983 that Continental's earnings also started to improve, when all of the company's business units returned to the black for the first time in many years. "Continental has achieved a turnaround," the Austrian credit institution Creditanstalt wrote in an analyst report in 1985. "The company is recommended for a medium to long-term investment." In the same year, Continental also purchased the tire division of Austrian rubber group Semperit. Finally, in 1987, it landed its biggest coup to date: the takeover of General Tire, one of the "big five" of the American tire industry, for the then-enormous sum of 1.2 billion German marks. At the time, however, General

Tire was only a shadow of its former self and had lost its dominance. In the subsequent period, the management in Hanover was engaged in the task of integrating and networking the dozens of plants worldwide that had become part of the corporation due to all these acquisitions, as well as the more than 24,000 workers and employees who now joined the 18,000-strong Continental workforce. The multitude of different tire brands and company cultures had to be managed and merged, and the required restructuring measures, which only became apparent little by little, had to be implemented and funded. The precarious inner structure of the company could also be discerned by its external organization: the Technical Products division (renamed ContiTech from 1989), which had shrunk, stood alongside the powerful Tires division (with Continental, Uniroyal and Semperit) and General Tire, which formed a division of its own. Rather than being integrated into Continental's Tires division, it instead remained an independent US company with strong in-house management—and therefore a permanent foreign body within the corporation. Not even the guidance and control exercised from Hanover within the scope of monthly board meetings could alleviate this—quite the contrary in fact. Nevertheless, as a result of its acquisition phase, Continental was now a player to be taken seriously in the international rubber and tire industries; in Europe, it ranked second behind Michelin, and worldwide it was fourth—albeit by a considerable margin. In the course of this internationalization, Continental also intensively concerned itself with the characteristics of global mobility for the first time. For example, Europe and the USA had very different demands and expectations in terms of the mode and manner of individual mobility and road traffic, which in turn affected the construction of cars, road surfaces and highway infrastructure. This made developing an "American" tire a necessity.

The "new Continental" of the 1980s resulted not only in a new look but also a new name. In 1987, it was renamed "Continental Aktiengesellschaft," and the addition "Gummi-Werke" (rubber plants) was dropped in recognition of the company's greater internationalization. There was also a new logo: instead of the old yellow and orange font and trademark, turquoise/green was now introduced to the corporate identity for the holding and central functions of the corporation. For international investors and capital market stakeholders, now operating on the basis of the shareholder value ideology, Continental appeared to represent a new growth story, as reflected not least by the corporation's revenue performance, with sales tripling from 2.6 billion German marks (1979) to 9.7 billion German marks (1992). However, a look at the sales structure also reveals that, in the course of its growth strategy, the company had shifted far away from its former status as a multi-industry corporation and was now almost exclusively a tire manufacturer. In 1978, the tire business still accounted for 57.5 percent of sales, whereas technical products brought in 40 percent; ten years later, it was 80.5 percent tires to 19.5 percent technical products, which, significantly, now had simply became the "non-tires" division within the company. For the first time, the company also held roadshows and analysts' conferences, where it communicated its new self-image with confidence: it regarded itself as a globally active rubber company that was reliable, in excellent financial health, innovative and growth-oriented. In short, it was a company with a future. The upheavals on the financial and capital markets also opened up new corporate financing opportunities everywhere, something Continental had already taken advantage of when it made use of convertible bonds in the Uniroyal takeover. The company soon caused a stir with highly creative measures to increase its equity and liquidity, using diverse financial innovations such as zero bonds denominated in German marks issued by Intercontinental Rubber Finance BV, which was founded specifically for this purpose. Very quickly, then CFO Horst W. Urban perfectly mastered the finer skills and regulations of global financial market capitalism.

Fig. 11: Press conference in Akron, Ohio, on the occasion of the General Tire acquisition in November 1987.

In terms of products too, Continental was likewise able to make a name for itself as a modern, future-oriented technology corporation, thanks to a range of innovations. The research and development departments had been working intensively on get-you-home tire systems and, in November 1983, at a large-scale world premiere, presented the "Conti Tire System." This new tire invention (in the words of the company) made waves in the tire world—if only for a short time. Another innovation, the EOT (energy-optimized tire) was launched soon after. It turned the company into a pioneer in reconciling economy and ecology, a topic that was much discussed at the time, by providing an answer to the greater environmental awareness in society. However, neither of these innovations was ultimately successful in the long term, in part due to technical manufacturing problems that could not be overcome. The subsequent phase of severe recession in the automotive and tire industries, combined with a hostile takeover attempt by Italian tire company Pirelli in September 1990, put an abrupt end to Continental's run of success. The confrontation between the two companies soon developed into a public takeover battle and dragged on until the end of 1992, culminating in an extraordinary Annual Shareholders' Meeting on March 13, 1991, at which the merger was rejected by a majority of votes. The conflict tied up a considerable amount of management capacity on both sides, permanently shattered the relationship of trust between the Supervisory Board and the Executive Board in Hanover, and led to a change in the company's management. Above all, the attack caused a deep sense of uncertainty within the company and destroyed the illusions it had about its own strength, having showed the world how vulnerable and exposed Continental really was, despite its new, international and innovative appearance.

The *seventh* transformation phase comprised an 18-year span from 1991 to 2008/09. It was the longest to date but also the most hectic in Continental's corporate development, with the company pressing ahead at a breathtaking pace and experiencing highly dynamic development—sometimes excessively so. This affected all business areas and divisions: tires, technical products (which had been combined into ContiTech) as well as the third and completely new automotive business area, which was in permanent upheaval itself. No stone would be left unturned, as Mr. Kessel, then chairman of the Executive Board, stressed with confidence. For many employees, however, this sounded like a threat and triggered uncertainty. The fundamental corporate restructuring and rapid forging of a "new Continental" also had its downsides. It was a strategy that came with risks and last but not least, incurred high costs. The blend of non-simultaneity and the cumulative effect of change processes severely tested the culture and organization of the company. In 1991 and 2001, Continental was beset by two far-reaching waves of restructuring and rehabilitation, which penetrated to the core of the corporation.

Fig. 12: Staff demonstration prior to the extraordinary Annual Shareholders' Meeting on March 13, 1991.

This transformation phase was heavily influenced by individuals, especially Hubertus von Grünberg, who was initially chairman of the Executive Board from July 1991, and then chairman of the Supervisory Board from June 1999 to March 2009. It was he who also introduced a new management and decision-making style, characterized by American management methods. This and the pace that Grünberg was now setting frequently overwhelmed his colleagues on the Executive Board, who were still accustomed to the leadership style of the old Continental. This phase was also influenced by three economic crises, in 1991, 2001 and 2008, which shook the company significantly, as well as a rapid technological transformation that not only affected the automotive industry but also fundamentally changed the mobility of society as a whole. In the end, however, the economic lows were followed by rapid recovery phases, during which Continental continued its growth and trajectory of expansion. Its transition from tire manufacturer to automotive system supplier beyond tires was largely complete and now formed the basis for the company's activities. This raised Continental's market and competitive position, as well as its revenue potential, to a completely new level.

After von Grünberg took over as chairman of the Executive Board in July 1991, his first task was to eliminate Continental's weaknesses and problems, which were in evidence everywhere. In the ensuing period, five central corporate policy and strategic measures were initiated and largely implemented. First, further internationalization was promoted. In 1992, for example, Swedish tire manufacturer Nivis with its Gislaved brand was acquired, and in 1993, a share of Czech tire company Barum was purchased. Later, in 2007, another takeover was completed for Slovakian tire company Matador. This was backed by the second measure: relocating tire production to "low-cost locations" and abandoning comparatively expensive production locations, a radical policy which was consistently implemented yet highly controversial and a cause of conflict. Third, the loss-making core business area, Tires, became the focus of the company's restructuring efforts. This arduous process, which continued almost endlessly until around 2006, suffered repeated setbacks and presented a number of responsible Executive Board members with headaches over the years. Fourth, the new Vehicle Systems division was established in 1994, and although it was initially extremely rudimentary and comparatively small, this ushered in a period of great strategic change that Continental underwent in the von Grünberg era. Fifth and finally, a policy of large-scale acquisitions and corporate takeovers was pursued from 1998, focusing almost exclusively on establishing and expanding the new Continental Automotive Systems (CAS) business area, with the aim of turning CAS into the corporation's future core business. Of these five measures, the restructuring of the tire business was the most urgent, as not only Continental's European OEM segment had been in the red for many years, but also General Tire and the tire business in North America were highly unprofitable too. In 1991 alone, the European passenger car and light truck tire original equipment business unit was 115 million German marks in the red. All in the industry had become accustomed to these practically traditional losses, which affected them likewise. However, this also triggered a spiral that further weakened the company, as the need to compensate for the constant OEM losses on the replacement market posed the risk of becoming vulnerable in this sector, especially to attacks by cheap tire suppliers from Southeast Asia. In the USA, General Tire recorded a loss of 200 million German marks over the same period. The severe recession that hit the automotive industry in 1993, particularly in Europe, did not make a change of direction any easier. Even in 1995, the Executive Board was seriously considering whether Continental still needed the Truck Tires business area and whether it was even possible to restructure it or run it without losses in the long term. Ultimately, the tire business and its organizational structures underwent a fundamental redesign. The passenger car and commercial vehicle areas became independent divisions, and the Tires division was temporarily managed by von Grünberg himself, who also took on the task of restructuring it. Within this sector, an OEM division was also created, with its own research and development, production and sales departments. Later on, a "Conti International" department was also set up in an attempt to develop the tire business globally. These measures were accompanied by a series of site closures, as well as a reduction in production capacity and relocation to the order of 2 million tires per year on average, something which affected sites from the Irish plant in Dublin to Traiskirchen in Austria, Herstal in Belgium and plants in Canada, and even locations with long traditions such as the Stöcken site in Hanover. The beneficiaries were low-cost plants in Portugal, Czechia, the French Alsace region, and Slovakia. In the USA, similar plant closures and production relocations were carried out, while the tire activities in Mexico were sold. Some of the production relocations to non-European countries were also planned as joint ventures with domestic tire companies and failed to achieve success even after many years of efforts, such as in India or Russia. Nevertheless, the bottom-line goal of long-term reductions in the production costs of tires was achieved. It took many more years to reduce the losses, however. Time and again, the responsible managers promised they would break even by a certain year, and time and again, these dates had to be postponed. Not until 1997 did Continental enter the black in the OEM sector for passenger car and light truck tires, a milestone that also made Continental one of the first major tire manufacturers to break free from the traditional dictates of automotive companies toward their suppliers. However, the reorganization of its US tire business turned out to be quite protracted. On several occasions, the "recovery" of General Tire was proclaimed. To "better exploit synergy potential," Continental now proceeded to strategically and operationally integrate the division into the two European sectors for passenger car and commercial vehicle tires until, by the end of March 2002, the US tire business, which had been operating as Continental Tire North America, was dissolved and correspondingly assigned to the two tire business areas, now operating as divisions. However, even after this, the situation improved only slowly. The turnaround originally expected for the end of 2005 once again failed to materialize, and it was not until 2006 that the US tire business permanently got back in the black. By then, restructuring expenses had cost Continental at least twice what it had originally paid to acquire General Tire in 1987.

At the beginning of 1994, a new "Vehicle Systems" division was set up and a separate Executive Board position created for manager Hans Albert Beller, who had recently been persuaded to join from brakes specialist Teves. The vision behind this was to open up new business areas with high growth potential beyond the conventional tire business, such as innovative system solutions for the development of new motor vehicles, from complete air spring systems including air bellows, sensor technology and control electronics, to rear axle level control systems, semi-active suspensions, systems for active and passive sound absorption, vehicle dynamics systems and tire pressure monitoring. In addition, Continental started supplying the automotive industry with complete wheel systems, assuming responsibility for scheduling, assembly and logistics. The new products and services, touted as "future-oriented" system solutions for the automotive industry, were soon known to at least the professional public and among original equipment manufacturers by their abbreviations IWS (Integrated Wheel System), CASS (Continental Air Suspension System), PANC (Passive and Active Noise Cancellation), CEEC (Continental Electronic Chassis Control), SWT (Sidewall Torsion Sensor System) and TPMS (Tire Pressure Monitoring System). Although the sales generated from these solutions were initially marginal, they helped change Continental's image from a conventional tire company to a modern high-tech corporation. The starter module known as an ISAD (Integrated Starter Alternator Damper) acquired a certain notoriety as a "new energy management method for cars." It enabled automatic switch-on and switch-off functions and replaced numerous components required previously, or rather integrated them in a single module. In 1997, Continental received the renowned German Industry Innovation Award for this product. However, establishing the new Automotive Systems sector, as it was soon named, also meant abandoning the dream of joining the powerful trinity of the global tire industry, comprising Michelin of France, Goodyear of the USA and Bridgestone of Japan. Each held around a 20 percent share of the market, whereas Continental held around 8 percent. "Structures between the automotive industry and suppliers are changing," stated a presentation by the Executive Board for the Supervisory Board in April 1996. "We see this realignment as an opportunity for our company to break new ground."

In 1997, the new self-confidence and self-image were also indicated inwardly and outwardly by a seemingly contradictory measure. The turquoise/green logo

Fig. 13: The Continental Executive Board in April 1996, from left to right: Hans Albert Beller, Dr. Jens P. Howaldt, Dr. Hubertus von Grünberg (Executive Board chairman), Dr. Peter Haverbeck, Dr. Klaus-Dieter Röker.

used in the corporate design was replaced by the traditional yellow/orange logo of Continental's leading brand. With this step, the company seemed to be returning to its roots, but in fact was signaling that it was moving away from its old policy of having multiple tire brands and instead establishing Continental as its core brand not only for tires but also for new technological products and systems. "We are pursuing a systematic course from rubber products to electronics, in order to achieve complete systems for vehicles [...] Our conversion to a globally operational high-tech company is proceeding apace [...]" the Executive Board was quoted as saying of the ongoing transformation process. But at least this time, the value of the tire business, which was more dominant than ever in terms of both sales and profit, was remembered. "Continental must expand its systems capability in tires; ContiTech must extend its activities to embrace the entire automotive chassis," said von Grünberg in 1997. "But I must warn against any strategy of high-tech diversification that causes us to neglect our core business." The transition initiated between 1991 and 1997 was initially a transformation of Continental from the inside, basing the Automotive Systems business on the development of its own future technologies, without external acquisitions.

In 1998, however, the opportunity for a takeover arose which would prove to be a coup. The September acquisition of ITT Automotive Brake & Chassis, as Teves was now called, significantly accelerated the transformation process. The takeover saw a company join the corporation that had been heavily influenced by the American parent company and its cost controlling culture. At 3.47 billion German marks, the purchase price for Teves far exceeded all previous Continental acquisitions. As a result, Continental gained 16 plants worldwide, 10,700 employees and, above all, dozens of new technologies, products and systems, particularly in the field of brakes. Alongside Bosch, Teves was a global market leader in ABS (anti-lock braking systems), TCS (traction control systems) and ESC, i.e. electronically controlled brake and chassis stability control systems. This acquisition thereby expanded Continental's core competencies to include expertise in the field of chassis and vehicle dynamics control, subsequently reshaping the company. At last, Continental was no longer seen by analysts, investors and even the automotive industry as a "tire manufacturer that was too small worldwide." The business and technological synergies of both companies promised the development and market penetration of highly profitable, new "Continental technologies." The Hanover company had thus maneuvered itself into a unique position, not only on the global tire market, where it had succeeded at least partly in freeing itself from the dominant ideology and constraints, but also in the global supplier industry. However, it also faced new, no less powerful competitors in the automotive supplier industry, such as Bosch, ZF, Denso, Delphi and Magna, with whom it had previously had virtually no contact in its operating business.

The acquisition of Teves in 1998 also caused the self-confidence of large parts of the management to soar. The "new Continental," which was still in the process of being formed, was already touted as fact and the end of the transformation process announced. The year 1998 was celebrated as the most successful in the company's history, and the now seemingly definitive "new Continental" was proclaimed. The heading of the agenda for the Executive Board strategy meeting in March 1999 reflected this sentiment. "Continental joins the Champions League of automotive suppliers," it stated proudly; along with lauding its own tires as the "ultimate in mobility." The euphoria about the "new Continental" was unmistakably tinged with a derogatory view of the "old Continental." The importance of the historical relativity was absent from the seemingly new business areas and company acquisitions. In view of the history of Continental, the simple catchphrase "from tire manufacturer to high-tech corporation" coined by the company during this phase to describe the transformation process is skewed at best and misleading, as the tire had been a complicated "high-tech" product since its invention, both with regard to the use of rubber as a material and its numerous individual components. Continental had therefore been a science and research-based company since the 1890s at the latest. A new vision was touted on the road to technology leadership: the "30-meter car." With its significantly reduced braking distances, thanks to innovative brake solutions and improved tire technology, it made Continental a pioneer of a new mobility world geared toward comfort and safety.

Fig. 14: The Continental flag is raised at the Rödelheim site in Frankfurt to symbolize the integration of the new Continental Teves subsector.

This new positioning and the strategy pursued were fueled by seemingly favorable and serendipitous acquisition opportunities. In February 2001, the former DaimlerChrysler AG sold the Temic Group, the electronics division of the Stuttgart-based automotive corporation, to Continental for just under 650 million euros. Initial talks and negotiations on this deal already took place in 1998, but it was only gradually that Daimler became prepared to help turn Continental into a "second Bosch" by selling Temic and thus reducing its own dependency on the neighboring supplier group. For Continental, the acquisition of Temic meant expanding its expertise in the field of vehicle electronics and yet again accelerating its transformation into an integrated system provider. However, some concerns were also raised within the Supervisory Board. "Price too high for the expected results: destruction of assets" and "mixed goods store: very little fits with chassis strategy" were just some of the notes made by a member of the Supervisory Board in the margin of the draft resolution from February 2001. In addition, the revenue was highly dependent on the two main customers, Daimler and Teves. On the other hand, Continental knew the new member of its corporate family well, as a cooperation agreement for the development of electronic chassis systems had previously been concluded with Temic a number of years before. With the acquisition of the 25 production, development and sales locations worldwide, 6,000 Temic employees now became Continental staff. No sooner had the purchase been decided than the next opportunity arose to take Continental into another new dimension through further acquisitions. In June 2001, damper and clutch specialist Sachs, which was part of the dissolved Mannesmann conglomerate's huge investment portfolio at the time, was put up for sale for just under 1 billion euros. Additionally, Continental had the opportunity to take over the American automotive supplier TRW Automotive for 2 billion euros. The Executive Board of the time intended to bid for both companies and embark on serious purchasing negotiations. This would before long have turned Continental into one of the world's three largest suppliers. At the same time, however, the transformation process had taken on a momentum of its own that was proving difficult to control. In this new Continental, there no longer seemed to be space for the ContiTech division, though it had been thoroughly rehabilitated after several restructurings, was also geared to the global market and had by now become profitable. The division was put up for sale.

The lofty announcements were soon followed by great disillusionment. The Supervisory Board refused to approve the planned acquisitions of TRW and Sachs. In fact, it stepped on the brakes just in time to prevent Continental coming under the wheels of the Executive Board's freewheeling plans and being crushed by the resulting debt. For subsequently, in September 2001, one of the most severe financial and economic crises to date followed. When Manfred Wennemer was appointed new chairman of the Executive Board, he implemented a combination of tough restructuring measures and a strict austerity policy, while also continuing to pursue Continental's offensive transformation into an "automotive systems" corporation, by concluding further major acquisitions.

Initially, the work of the new Executive Board was dominated by restructuring measures and a policy of "resolute cost management." This put an end to the expansive transformation process for the time being. In North America, the tire business was suffering a crisis again and entered the red, and costs were scrutinized at all production sites. A new wave of change rippled through the company: production sites were closed in Europe and North America, particularly in Mexico, additional production capacity was relocated to Eastern Europe, and new tire plants were built on green pastures, for example in Brazil. According to an internal forecast from spring 2004, Continental did not expect there to be any tire factories left in Germany in 30 years' time. The economic crisis was therefore an opportunity to not only resume but also intensify the long-term restructuring course that was necessary on an almost ongoing basis. At first, no one explicitly spoke of a transformation into an automotive systems corporation, but where the old core business, tires, was concerned, the Executive Board members toyed with ideas and considered restructuring the portfolio (as the divisions and business areas were called in management parlance). Once again, the future of the tire business was questioned. The agricultural tire sector was put up for sale, and a withdrawal from the bicycle tire business was also considered, even though, beyond the profit aspect, it was of significant importance to Continental's image, as well as its brand identification and awareness. At the same time, however, the first steps were taken to enter the Chinese tire market in September 2004 with the help of a joint venture. Ideas and possible scenarios for the future tire business pursued in 2002 ranged from close cooperation with Bridgestone in the USA to a "major solution" with Japanese global market leader Bridgestone, i.e. selling and thus exiting from the tire business or spinning off the tire divisions as an independent listed company.

Following the restructuring phase, Continental switched back to a more offensive corporate policy only gradually. The vision of a "30-meter car" was shelved and replaced by the new corporate goal of "making individual mobility safer and more convenient." Figures such as von Grünberg ensured that the transformation did not lose momentum. In spring 2003, he announced that the company would be stepping up a gear again. The metaphorical slogan was that Continental had "left the freeway and was back on the interstate" and would soon be switching to the fast lane. Initially, this affected technical products. The plan to sell Conti-Tech was scrapped, based on the rationale that it would be unwise to "kill such a cash cow." Instead, the business area was reinforced and aggressively expanded, among other measures by acquiring a majority share in a Chinese manufacturer of air conditioning and power steering hoses and a establishing a joint venture with a Korean company for air spring production. In spring 2004, Continental landed a major coup by making a public takeover bid for Phoenix AG. The idea of a merger between Phoenix and ContiTech, followed by an IPO, had been mooted since 2002 under the code name "Universe." Now, two years later—after 80 years of mutual cooperation and competition as well as numerous takeover attempts—the two companies finally joined forces. This significantly strengthened the core business areas of hoses and hose assemblies, conveyor belt systems and air spring systems, as well as compounding technology, but also turned out to be a thorn in the side of the European Commission as the responsible antitrust authority. As part of the protracted takeover process, which took until spring 2007, an "in-depth audit process" was initiated on the grounds of suspicion that Continental would be in a position to dominate the future market. Phoenix saw 47 production sites in 20 countries and 9,700 employees join the Continental corporation.

Shortly after the Phoenix takeover, however, further acquisitions followed, facilitating the further expansion of the Automotive Systems business and representing another quantum leap in the growth of what had now become a strong third business area for the corporation. In spring 2006, under the code name "Apollo," Continental decided to purchase the automotive electronics business of the US Motorola Group. For around 1 billion euros, Continental obtained six factories in the USA and Europe with a total workforce of just under 5,500. With this acquisition, Continental strengthened its automotive electronics expertise in the powertrain, telematics, body electronics, chassis controls and sensor technology areas. The telematics business in particular meant entering a technology area in which the CAS division had never before operated.

Barely a year later, Continental's next and by far largest takeover coup followed: the acquisition of Siemens VDO Automotive AG. This had been set up in the course of the Munich-based electronics group's own plans to diversify into the automotive sector and create a "second Bosch" in its supply business, and was ultimately born from the breakup of the Mannesmann conglomerate and the merger of Mannesmann-VDO with Siemens Automotive in 2001. Continental and Siemens had been contemplating a mutual takeover of each other's automotive business or collaboration and investigating strategic options since 2002, but these plans had initially come to nothing. For Hubertus von Grünberg, the acquisition was not only an "outstanding strategic addition to Continental's portfolio," but also the fulfillment of a 14-year dream and vision of Continental as an integrated global supplier. In the eyes of Continental's management team, this was ample reason to look beyond the exorbitant purchase price of 11.3 billion euros and the resulting long-term financial burden. The "excellent prospects for the future" were the overwhelming argument, particularly as the deal could seemingly be financed without any problems, even though the market environment was getting tougher.

Siemens VDO contributed upwards of 50,000 employees at more than 100 locations worldwide and meant that Continental was now fifth among the world's largest automotive suppliers. With this deal, Continental's second major growth phase characterized by acquisitions drew to a close. It had lasted from 1998 to 2007 but, compared with the previous phase in the 1970s and 1980s, it had taken a completely different direction in corporate policy terms—automotive instead of tires—and both the acquired business areas and the purchasing prices were on a whole different level. "A traditional manufacturer of tires and technical products is developing at full speed into a high-tech corporation with a wide range of complex supplier parts for the automotive industry," is how Hubertus von Grünberg, who played a pivotal role in initiating the transformation, described the process in 1996. At the time, Continental was only just getting started and the dynamics of change were to really pick up speed in the years that followed, even if there was also the risk that the company would skid and fly off course.

A look at the figures further illustrates the new dimensions into which Continental had been catapulted in purely quantitative terms. The total workforce, which had numbered around 50,000 in 1991, had grown to 148,000 workers and employees by 2008, i.e. three times as many. Although there had been years of stagnation and job cuts in between, these were quickly more than compensated for by the acquisitions. Revenue, which amounted to the equivalent of 4.8 billion euros in 1991, exploded to first 11.4 billion euros (2001) and then 24.2 billion euros (2008). Even during the years of the 2000/01 major economic crisis, there was no decline in sales due to the strong external growth resulting from the acquisitions. However, where profit and earnings were concerned, the picture was a lot more mixed. In 1991, Continental started off with a loss equivalent to 65.5 million euros, followed by a rapid increase to a net income of €234.7 million, before sharply dropping in 2001 to a shortfall of €257.6 million. By 2007, profit had shot up to 1.02 billion euros, but this was followed by a further rapid slump, with a reported loss of 1.12 billion euros and 1.65 billion euros respectively in the years of the 2008 and 2009 crisis. During this phase, Continental made more profit than ever before in its history, but it also never had to record such big losses. The new Automotive sector developed to become a real profit machine. Between 1999 and 2005, net income increased tenfold to 570 million euros (with the exception of the slump in the 2001 crisis), although this was against the backdrop of the Rubber sector as a whole having been highly profitable. However, an unmistakable warning signal was the fact that the dramatically high losses in the crisis year 2008 had been generated exclusively by the Automotive sector—in particular in the business areas that dealt with system solutions for the vehicle powertrain. Here, the product portfolio ranged from gasoline and diesel injection systems to engine and transmission control units and solutions for semi-electric hybrid drives.

After the Siemens VDO acquisition, another "new Continental" was proclaimed, presenting itself in a new organizational structure consisting of six divisions. Alongside the three old divisions Passenger and Light Truck Tires, Commercial Vehicle Tires and ContiTech, the former Continental Automotive Systems division, which had already undergone numerous restructuring and reorganization processes in terms of both the number and operational structure of its business units, was dissolved and replaced by three new, independent divisions: Chassis & Safety, Interior and Powertrain. Most of Siemens VDO was absorbed into the latter. For some Continental employees, the acquisition and integration of Siemens VDO posed a risk of having to relinquish the culture and tradition of the tire divisions and ContiTech, i.e. Continental's rubber business, and adjusting to a new, completely different "automotive systems" culture. A look at the sales structure with the significant changes that occurred between 1991 and 2008 appears to confirm this. In 1998, the rubber sector still contributed more than 90 percent of sales (65.3 percent Tires, 25.3 percent ContiTech), while the young automotive business represented only 9.4 percent of sales. This ratio changed fundamentally in 2008, with Rubber accounting for 39 percent (Tires 26.8 percent, ContiTech 12.4 percent) and Automotive Systems 61.5 percent. However, the stronger its automotive business became, the more Continental would again become dependent on the automotive industry—despite its declared intention in 1991 to better decouple itself from the latter's economic fluctuations. The 60 percent maximum limit specified for the automotive industry's share of total sales had long since been exceeded. What the skeptics and advocates of the "old Continental Rubber culture" overlooked, though, was the fact that ContiTech in particular already consisted of a wide variety of companies and cultures, and this was even more true of the Automotive sector, which was far from homogeneous. Nevertheless, during this transformation phase, Continental had already developed a highly heterogeneous corporate culture and had become a highly diverse corporation in terms of its workforce composition. Only a short time later, a fundamental reorganization seemed to confirm the fears of the "traditionalists" and further highlighted the new division of the Continental corporation into an Automotive Group and a Rubber Group. The process thus initiated for an organizationally and legally independent rubber sector in the guise of a newly formed Rubber Group confirmed the assumption among many employees that its separation was intentional and would sooner or later become an independent company listed separately on the stock exchange. However, this reorganization was closely associated with another event.

This phase ended the way it started—with a takeover attempt that was perceived as hostile in the eyes of Continental's Executive Board, this time by the Schaeffler Group from Herzogenaurach in Germany, which was likewise active in the automotive supplier business. However, the situation resulting from the various contradictory and overlapping interests of the different actors involved was highly complex this time, and not at all as clear-cut as the Pirelli case. Between the summers of 2008 and 2009, the future of Continental was completely uncertain. No one could say to what degree the company would be able to develop independently, not to mention the prospects for its financial viability and the pace of the economic recovery everyone was hoping for. On top of this, Manfred Wennemer stepped down as chairman of the Executive Board, followed by the sudden departure of Hubertus von Grünberg as chairman of the Supervisory Board in early March 2009. The Siemens VDO purchase had resulted in credit obligations and financial demands by the banks that were now heavily burdening the company, and the operating results of the Siemens VDO business areas were sobering, particularly as it quickly became apparent that some of them required a considerable amount of restructuring and rehabilitation. "In starting off the first year of the 'new' Continental, we were filled with energy," wrote the Executive Board to shareholders. "We finished off the year with just as much energy—but much differently than expected. Instead of being in a position to concentrate on the VDO integration and the restructuring of the Powertrain division [...], in the second half of the year we suddenly had to refocus the company to weather the automotive industry's worst crisis in decades." Among other measures, the "greatest cost-containment program in the history of the company" was set in motion. However, the long-term strategy and corporate policy path on which the company had fundamentally embarked remained unchanged. In the following years, these continued to represent the basic pillars and framework, so to speak, that formed the basis for the company's future transformations.

The next transformation phase, the *eighth*, is comparatively short at around eight years, from 2008/09 to 2017. After the breathtaking upheaval of the previous years, the development came to a halt for the time being or at least lost significant pace. This is also reflected in the structure of the company's revenue, which stabilized at the 2008 ratio of 60 percent automotive and 40 percent rubber in the subsequent years. On closer inspection, however, many transformation processes that were almost perceptible to the outside world took place during this period. Among the changes that were outwardly noticeable were the new appointments to the Executive Board and Supervisory Board. With Elmar Degenhart as chairman of the Executive Board, which was significantly younger and expanded, and Wolfgang Reitzle as chairman of the Supervisory Board, the company quickly succeeded in calming the waves of unrest caused by the large fluctuations in management in the preceding weeks and months and headed into calmer waters. The uncertainty that the takeover battle had triggered was overcome, and Continental gained a new sense of self-awareness and self-confidence. By 2010, the company was already "back on the road to success" after a jump in sales and profits, something the media also acknowledged. After the hard months of acute crisis management, corporate policy once again shifted to pursuing the long-term strategy. The company continued to push its automotive business, but its tire and rubber businesses also moved back into focus and would soon prove to be the strongest and most reliable sources of earnings during these years. The company experienced a phase of extensive expansion and growth, which this time resulted from its own strengths to a much greater degree than ever before, without major acquisitions. It transformed into a company with great inner strength. For many years, it had been structurally weak, and after the exhausting acquisition phases in 1990/91 and 2007/08, its weaknesses became apparent and made it vulnerable to attack. Now it became more robust. In fiscal 2013, the company returned the highest profits in its history—almost 2 billion euros, which enabled it to quickly reduce its crushing mountain of debt. "At Continental, a new era of crisis resilience and future viability has begun," announced Degenhart, with market observers declaring Continental to be "potentially the fastest-growing automotive supplier in the world." It even succeeded in overtaking its main competitor Bosch—not in revenue, but in terms of returns in the automotive business.

Organizational measures had also contributed to these successes. Collaboration between key corporate functions, regions and countries, as well as operative organizational units in the decentralized divisions and business units, was adapted, and cross-divisional functions and tasks in particular were strengthened. To manage the complex corporate structure, which by now had spread out across 46 countries with almost 300 branches and production locations, as well as almost 150,000 employees worldwide, network structures and network thinking were introduced. In 2013, a new Tires division was created within the Rubber sector, thereby rectifying the decades-long separation of the passenger car tire and truck tire businesses, which had inhibited synergy and used to be even more problematic when the tire business for North America had also been separate. Another key impetus for the transformation was the realignment of the corporate culture, which was to act as superstructure for the three de facto companies Tires, ContiTech and Automotive—each of which was by now the size of an independent corporation. The aim was to forge a new Continental corporation from the many purchased conglomerates and business areas, and to replace the previous culture of control with a network culture that emphasized independence and entrepreneurial skills among employees. Since 1998, no fewer than 100 different corporate cultures had come together under the Continental umbrella as a result of acquisitions and integrations. As well as organizational integration, therefore, a process of cultural amalgamation had to be promoted, not least as a means of steering the corporation under a common set of values.

Fig. 15: The 300 top executives at the Senior Executive Convention in Hanover in mid-February 2011.

However, this time powerful transformation stimuli also primarily came from the outside: the company's development was boosted by a long and rapid economic upturn, accompanied by virtually unabated dynamism in the capital market, which pushed Continental from one sales and profit record to the next and drove the company's share price to previously unknown heights, making it a darling of the stock market. The boom was driven primarily by the development of demand in Asia, in particular the Chinese market, which now also became a focus of the company's strategy. Continental built new plants for all three divisions in China and opened new sales offices, in order to have a local presence along the entire value chain, from research and development to purchasing, production and sales.

Fig. 16: Opening of the new ContiTech plant in Hangzhou, China (2014).

A milestone in ContiTech's history was also the acquisition of US company Veyance Technologies Inc., the former Goodyear Engineered Products division, a rubber and plastics technology company with 9,000 employees worldwide and sales equivalent to 1.5 billion euros, a purchase which significantly strengthened ContiTech's market position in the fields of hose and conveyor belt production. The acquisition of long-established surface specialists such as Konrad Hornschuch AG also played a role. Above all, however, fundamental changes in mobility were a massive impetus that forced the company to transform. Not only the quantitative scope of global motorization changed with great dynamism, but even more so the demands on means of transport for individual mobility, above all due to the transition to electric mobility and autonomous driving pursued and funded by the government. As a result, the automotive industry faced the biggest upheaval in its history, while the relationship between suppliers and original equipment manufacturers was placed on a completely new footing in favor of the former. At the same time, the pressure on Continental to change increased massively in the form of legal requirements for radically stricter emissions standards and the general public's demands on companies—accelerated by climate change—to not only formulate environmental protection and sustainability as goals in their corporate strategies, but also to actually integrate these issues into their corporate policies. Faced with the combination of government-regulated economics and society's moral demands, all of Continental's business units were forced to make substantial efforts to cater to these new requirements in addition to those of the markets. The company found itself in a position where it had to examine both its self-image as part of the capitalist economy and its position within society as a whole. Technological developments also resulted in completely new challenges, with the focus now being on software, artificial intelligence, cloud computing, hybrid and electric drives and high-speed trains, as well as the new levels of performance required from communication technology for Internet and data transmission.

Following Continental's launch into the knowledge-based industry of the 19th century in 1890 and having gone through several transformation processes in its R&D, the company had now arrived in the "new knowledge economy of the 21st century." Continental faced and is continuing to face a classic problem in the history of business and technology: the transition from a technology that is aging or aged, yet which can still be sold widely and profitably as a mature product, to a new future technology, often beset by losses and teething problems in its early years. The transition from the combustion engine to electric mobility is likely to only start gaining momentum between 2025 and 2030, meaning a cautious strategy made sense. "If you invest too early, you end up throwing away billions. But if you invest too late, you will lose out on the market," wrote Degenhart in his letter to shareholders in 2016.

In many cases, the "new Continental" also found itself confronted with a "new world." Balancing shareholders' profit expectations with obligations for corporate social responsibility, sustainability and environmental awareness increasingly demanded by stakeholders became more and more difficult. In this context, the company launched another transformation process that will fundamentally change the organization in the long term: to become a green and sustainable company with product and process innovations that promote sustainability and the goal of achieving strict environmental standards and climate protection at all locations throughout the corporation. Many companies have taken up this goal and presented it to the public in colorfully illustrated sustainability reports. But hardly any of the global groups on Continental's scale can match the company's efforts to consistently implement this objective into its operations and make it a reality. Sales figures and workforce headcount in these eight years of the first phase of the Degenhart era are therefore only one side of the actual transformation process that Continental underwent: the 2009 revenue of 20 billion euros increased to 44 billion euros in 2017, i.e. more than doubled despite the already high level, while the number of employees grew from 133,400 to 230,700 in the same period. And the company behind it really was a "new Continental."

However, the corporation's steep success curve flattened and came to an end, once again due to the cumulative effects of different external and internal factors and the ways in which they mutually amplify each other's negative impact. The *ninth* transformation phase—the one that Continental is currently undergoing— started around 2018 and is still in its infancy. The end of the company's self-imposed and explicitly announced transformation program is targeted for 2029, but the transition to a "new Continental" may take longer and occur outside of a targeted corporate strategy. The latest crisis in which the company finds itself is the result of an escalation in the secular and historic upheaval in the automotive industry, with the associated sales declines in the global automotive business accelerated by catalysts such as the diesel scandal on the one hand and the meteoric rise of the politically enforced electric drive on the other. In the face of year-on-year declines in production and sales figures in the global automotive industry, Continental's sales have stagnated since 2017, but at the same time the share of the automotive business has increased significantly to 71 percent of total sales. This means that Continental's dependency on the fate of the automotive industry has increased during the very phase where stronger decoupling would have alleviated the crisis. More than ever, however, the traditional Tire sector has been the cash cow, as has ContiTech, whereas the highly competitive and research-intensive Automotive sector has continually required high investments and was deep in the red in 2019. Continental tried to counteract this downward trend in the industry earlier than other automotive suppliers. Two profit warnings within a few weeks of each other caused a considerable stir in 2018, along with a letter from the chairman of the Executive Board to executives written in September of the same year, which criticized negative developments and management errors in "half a dozen business units." "Continental's reputation and shares tarnished—but financial strength high" was the headline in the Handelsblatt business newspaper in its balance sheet check in April 2019. The following year, 2020, subsequently turned into one of those years in the company's history when it had to fight problems on all fronts simultaneously: dramatically decreased global vehicle production, the technological and structural crisis in the automotive industry and upheaval in the sector, warranty claims from the 1990s, the confrontation with problem business areas such as Powertrain, and last but not least, the coronavirus pandemic, with the resulting dramatic stock market crash and deep economic crisis, the duration of which is still unknown. After many years of investing in the modernization and construction of new production facilities, a third phase of plant closures and reduction or relocation of production capacity is now currently underway. The focus of these measures is on the company's remaining plants in Germany, in particular its long-standing location in Aachen.

The core focus of the "Transformation 2019–2029" structural program announced by the Executive Board in 2019 is, firstly, to increase efficiency and productivity by means of adjustments to the portfolio and organization—with the Powertrain business area spun off as a first step. However, this was not the "biggest organizational upheaval in the company's history." This would only come with the spin-off of the Rubber sector, as repeatedly demanded by investors, be it the Tires division or ContiTech or both together, in order to finance a possible expansion of the automotive business and the countless modular system options it would offer for cars and the "mobility of tomorrow." The second part of the structural program concentrates on promising growth areas, a goal which, by only being vaguely formulated for the time being, keeps all options open. From within the scope of a rehabilitation and restructuring phase, a new change dynamic is to be unfurled for the next major transformation step toward a "new Continental." The aim is to make a switch to other technologies and to expand the company's competences and self-image both as a mobility supplier and a mobility service provider. "We are undergoing a profound transformation. It affects everything that makes up our business, from products and processes to business models and structures," stated Degenhart while presenting the annual report for 2019. "While it poses major challenges, it above all presents major opportunities." On this road, the company has certainly caused quite a stir, for example with headlines about rear-view mirrors being replaced by integrated vehicle cameras in the future, deliberations on manufacturing its own battery cells, as well as the development and testing of CUbE (Continental Urban Mobility Experience), a driverless minibus taxi with an electric drive. In addition, attempts were made to diversify into the fields of agricultural machinery and the agricultural sector, which Continental intended to supply with state-of-the-art technology and tires from its reactivated Agricultural Tires business unit, thereby reducing dependency on the automotive sector. However, the 2020 economic and industry crisis, dramatically exacerbated by the coronavirus pandemic, halted almost all activities, tore a large new hole in the company's sales and earnings, and forced it to embark on a strict policy of fiscal austerity. As early as June 2020, Degenhart predicted billions in losses for both the supplier and automotive industries, as well as the most difficult quarter in Continental's history since the end of the war. Come the end of the fiscal year, the figures were quite dire. Sales fell to 37.7 billion euros (- 15 percent). After all, the loss was slightly reduced from 1.2 billion euros (2019) to 0.96 billion euros. In the fall, the chairman of the Executive Board also unexpectedly resigned.

Continental is in the midst of an era of digitalization and post-industrial late modernism, and the current transformation phase may prove to be the biggest test in the company's history. Above all, there is no certainty that these many individual phases of transformation will ultimately lead to a large-scale transformation of Continental, as described by CEO Elmar Degenhart in 2019, and this remains at present more of a vision than a factual development. "In the past we grew with horsepower and hoof buffers," explained Degenhart. "Nowadays, our growth is driven by billions of bits and bytes. It is a process of transition. Continental the tire manufacturer, automotive supplier and industrial partner has become Continental the manufacturer of leading technologies and services." But will this course beyond rubber, which Continental embarked upon almost 30 years ago as the only global tire company to do so, and which aims at an unprecedentedly "new Continental," be successful in the long term? Perhaps, by the time of the 175th anniversary in 2046, the answer will be known. Whatever the case, the connecting core and the supporting pillar for all these transformation phases is ultimately the history and historical development of Continental. Since its inception, Continental has undergone a process of metamorphosis, constantly maneuvering through a mix of autonomy, compulsion and constraints. Even as the various transformation phases change its perspective, this history is and always will be a genuine part of the company, eluding any transformation processes yet at the same time constantly being fueled by the company's present and future. The certainty that it has successfully mastered many large and small phases of change throughout its time, as well as a range of regulatory economic polities by governments and economic orders, two world wars, hyperinflation, four currency reforms, various stock market crashes and at least five global economic crises, emboldens its strength of character, confidence, motivation and obligation to keep tackling new challenges and thereby continue the Continental success story.

This book is far from a classic corporate history of Continental with the overall events divided up chronologically and by subject, since this has already been done many times before. Instead, it will take the form of eight chapters, the topic of each of which is briefly described below, that are more like historical essays looking at individual key fields of inquiry across Continental's overall history. Deconstructing this company history to a certain degree into carefully reconstructed individual topics is an attempt to create a new kind of corporate historiography rather than a traditional narrative based on examining problems, yet which still ultimately follows the overall timeline of events. Neither approach is superior to the other, but to some degree, the approach selected here makes it possible to circumvent some precarious and traumatic events and developments in the company's history whose ramifications are in some cases felt to this day and that still evade an in-depth, source-based historical analysis. Regardless of their storytelling character, all chapters are critically compiled, source-based and supplemented with information from a series of eyewitness interviews. For the sake of simplicity, however, the printed version does not contain individual remarks or references. In case of doubt, these can be looked up in the manuscript version in the Continental archive. Chapters 1 to 6, and Chapter 9 were written by Paul Erker. Chapters 7 and 8 by Nils Fehlhaber.

The *first* chapter describes the lines along which corporate governance developed and the people who shaped it, starting with the 50-year Siegmund Seligmann era from 1876 to 1925 and continuing with the highly influential managing directors Willy Tischbein and then—albeit closely linked to the Nazi period—Fritz Könecke and the Opel family, who as a major shareholder helped determine Continental's destiny for a period of close to 50 years, from the end of the 1920s to the beginning of the 1970s. It also analyzes the influences of Alfred Herrhausen, the long-standing chairman of the Supervisory Board and executive board member of Deutsche Bank, and Carl H. Hahn, who successfully led the company out of the long crisis of the late 1970s. Subsequent developments in corporate governance and the turbulent establishment of the Schaeffler family as new key shareholders are also touched on in passing.

However, the identity of a company is not just determined by the leaders who shape it, but primarily by the people employed there. Therefore, in the *second* chapter, the Continental workforce is examined throughout the course of history, with a detailed look at their diversity and the context of change within the manufacturing organization, upheavals in the working world and the fate of individual plants. The *third* chapter deals with rubber and provides a short history of its transformation as a key raw material, but also looks at the topic of resource management in the light of environmental awareness and demands for sustainability. The *fourth* chapter takes a closer look at the company's defining product, the Continental tire—virtually the last visible product of the company. It not only deals with the innovation cycles of a high-tech product that is more than 130 years old, but also with its status in Continental's product portfolio, which has undergone numerous changes over the course of its history.

The *fifth* chapter investigates the eventful history of Continental shares, an aspect that is in general rarely included in the histories of companies and frequently neglected, despite being extremely interesting and—with spectacular highs and crushing lows—providing a seismograph of a company's development. Marketing, advertising and the history of the Continental brand are the subject of the *sixth* chapter. This perspective—a company's history examined through the life cycle of its brand history—has also rarely been used or included in historical analysis to date. The *seventh* chapter focuses on Continental's early phases of internationalization and globalization, which were initially somewhat tentative and belated, sometimes affected by war, and later characterized by the competitive pressures and merger activities of the industrial sector. The *eighth* and final chapter, entitled "Between Vision and Speculation," concerns the future of Continental. On the one hand, it traces the company's prevailing plans for the future through the different eras, while on the other, it depicts potential scenarios—some admittedly highly subjective—for how the "new Continental" of the year 2046, the company's 175 anniversary, might look.

The argumentation in the chapters is not interdependent, meaning they can be read in any order. Only after reading the book as a whole, however, does a differentiated overall picture of Continental's equally complex and exciting history over the past 150 years emerge, knowledge which can be used as orientation and as a basis when considering the years to come. Corporate history as contemporary history is not a linear narrative of progress and success, but rather a "history of problem generation" (Hockerts), i.e. it analyzes how the problems of the present have arisen and can thus raise awareness for where problems might occur in the future. This thus avoids it being instrumentalized for unacademic, ideologically motivated needs, yet at the same time, as an "interpretative science of the present" (Wirsching) so to speak, it also creates a prerequisite for reflected, critically distanced identification with the company and appropriate corporate self-understanding. Like democracies, companies are reliant on "continuously recalling their history" (Schlotheuber/Conze) in order to, in the future, continue to exist as capitalist organizations committed to the values and norms of "social responsibility." Anniversaries of the company's founding are simply special focal points of what is in principle an ongoing examination "since yesteryear" of developments inside and outside the company.

2 Founder Consortia, Major Investors and Key Shareholders
Corporate Governance and Prominent Figures in Continental's History

No detailed account has been written to date about the eventful history of Continental's corporate governance—i.e. the structures and procedures used to manage and monitor the company—and the prominent persons behind it. This is particularly true for the present and for living persons, whose place in history is difficult to assess in part because of problems arising due to critical analysis of sources. In addition, space constraints dictate that only a few of the company's leaders can be examined closely. Persons who had to be excluded from the present text include previous general directors Georg Heise and Wilhelm Siercke, who significantly shaped Excelsior AG (which later merged with Continental), as well as industrial pioneers such as Louis Peters, Alfred Teves and Adolf Schindling, who left their mark on the companies that were later taken over by Continental and thus were also part of its rich history.

Siegmund Seligmann:
The Rise to Become a Large Modern Enterprise

The illustrious group of founding shareholders and key shareholders who acted as members of Continental's Supervisory Board consisted mainly of private bankers from Hanover. Their Jewish religious background was only to become common knowledge decades later when it was assigned political relevance by external parties for ideological reasons. Their names were Ferdinand Meyer, Moritz Magnus, Bernhard Caspar, Theodor Rosenthal, Hermann Peretz, Julius Mendel and Jakob Goldschmidt. They acted as members or chairmen of the Supervisory Board for many years—Caspar for no less than 21 years—and exerted significant influence in their roles. Compared to these bankers, the four manufacturers and merchants in the syndicate of founders had little say, especially after banking house Magnus became the main shareholder in 1874 with just under 30 percent of the shares, partly through an equity contribution but largely as a result of unsecured receivables amounting to 300,000 marks that were soon to become due. Moritz Magnus can be considered the most important of the nine founders, since he not only owned the plots of land on Vahrenwalder Straße but also took the initiative to perform required restructuring measures at Continental between 1874 and 1876. In the years to come, Magnus further increased his share and, together with banking house Peretz, held more than 57 percent of Continental shares by 1879. In 1888, Magnus then also became chairman of the Supervisory Board, a position he held for nine years until his death in 1897. It was during these years that the share ratios shifted too, however. Banking house Caspar had already become a shareholder in 1880. Bernhard Caspar, another Jewish private banker, had founded his own banking company in 1874. He became rich by successfully investing equity in up-and-coming trade and industrial companies of the time, quickly becoming aware of Continental as an emerging company as a result. At the Annual Shareholders' Meeting in 1882, he already accounted for 500 shares and thus held over 35.7 percent of the shareholder votes in attendance. In 1897, Caspar took over as chairman of the Supervisory Board, a position he held until 1918. He was one of the key figures among the industrial and financial middle classes in Hanover, had a wide network of contacts throughout the local and regional clubs and foundations, was member of the boards of various other companies and banking houses, and also enjoyed high standing as the consul general of the kingdom of Sweden.

Fig. 17: Bernhard Caspar (1844 to 1918).

In the following years, there were virtually no changes in the shareholder structure—and thus also not in the governance structure—in spite of several capital increases performed in quick succession from 1897 onward, which also led to Continental shares becoming available on the stock market for the first time. The new shares were regularly acquired by a consortium of four banking houses—Magnus, Mendel/Rosenthal, Caspar and Peretz—who effectively divided them up among one another. After the turn of the century, incorporated banks increasingly became involved as shareholders, for example the Hanover branch of Dresdner Bank from 1902 onward, but without owning a significant number of shares. Darmstädter Bank was another shareholder at the time, as it had taken over several Hanover private banks that had owned Continental shares, and in 1907, banking house Magnus was purchased by Commerz- und Discontobank. However, overall, the shares were relatively evenly distributed. At the Annual Shareholders' Meeting in April 1907, the private bank Mendel & Rosenthal accounted for the largest share of Continental at 18.4 percent, while the other banking houses, i.e. Commerz- und Discontobank, Dresdner Bank, Bernhard Caspar and Emil Arnstädt, each owned between 10 and 11 percent. Relationships between Continental's core shareholders were not without conflict, particularly in May 1907 when there was a dispute about the sale of shares with a nominal value of 180,000 marks, which represented 3 percent of the company's 6 million marks of share capital at the time. Eduard Magnus, who had taken over his father's banking business and seat on Continental's Supervisory Board, was commissioned with handling the sale on behalf of the syndicate, with the explicit condition that the small circle of owners that had hitherto constituted the majority share of the company should not be disrupted by new shareholder groups. When Bernhard Caspar then found out that Magnus had already granted a significant percentage of the available shares to Hannoversche Bank and Commerz- und Discontobank, he was most aggrieved. This was made worse by the fact that Caspar already bore a grudge against Magnus from a few years earlier, when the Continental shares were initially floated on the Dresden stock exchange, believing that Magnus and Peretz had "contacted Dresdner Bank behind [his] back." By 1913, a group consisting of three of the banking shareholders had formed. These were B. Caspar (11.7 percent of the voting rights), Rosenthal & Mendel (15 percent), as well as the Hanover branch of Commerzbank (18.8 percent), which had ultimately managed to penetrate the earlier circle of core shareholders.

The era of local private bankers as major shareholders at Continental lasted until the end of World War I. By now, the previous prevalence of private bankers in the financial world had been replaced by the fast-dominating incorporated banks. This, combined with the period of hyperinflation, also led to significant changes at Continental. The initial stability in the shareholder structure had given the Executive Board the necessary security to also think of the long term in their policy decisions. Since January 1878, Siegmund Seligmann, who was only 25 years old at the time, had been the main decision-maker, even though he was just an authorized officer and would not be voted onto the Executive Board until September 1879. Seligmann had initially been employed by banking house Magnus in 1876, where he drew up the reorganization report for the struggling Continental company. In April 1876, he then joined Continental, where, backed by then major shareholder Magnus, his career quickly advanced. This was the beginning of the Seligmann era in Continental's history, which lasted until his death in 1925. Seligmann shared corporate policy-making with chemist Heinrich Prinzhorn, who had been working at Continental since 1874 and was appointed a member of the Executive Board in 1876. Prinzhorn was responsible for technical management and production, while Seligmann, as commercial director, handled sales and all financial matters. The two also shared an office in the first few years. "Early in the morning, the management read all the incoming mail together," a contemporary witness recalled.

> When they were done, Mr. Prinzhorn went to the factory, while Mr. Seligmann handed out the mail and dictated important letters to Bühren, the authorized officer. The apprentice responsible for completing incoming orders on time also received the incoming complaints from Mr. Seligmann, with relevant criticisms, and later had to inform Mr. Seligmann when the goods for which complaints were received would leave the factory. [...] Mr. Seligmann also made sure that the company rules were strictly adhered to; for example, he stood by the window of his office at the main entrance to Vahrenwalder Straße many a morning, pocket watch in hand, to check up on who was arriving late for work. [...] Mr. Seligmann turned the Christmas bonus into a festive event by personally handing out the annual payment to a significant number of employees just before Christmas, in gold coins, something his former employees still remembered with pride and joy decades later.

Soon, many anecdotes and legends abounded about Seligmann, who became something of a cult figure. This was due in no small part to the fact that, in a few short years, the young member of the Executive Board had turned the formerly struggling company into an unprecedented profit machine, with Continental's dividend payments breaking record after record. The shareholders were the main beneficiaries, but the workers also profited. What is more, he managed this feat before the company even entered into the tire business, which only attained

Fig. 18: Siegmund Seligmann (1853 to 1925).

Fig. 19: The shared Executive Board room (director's office) of Prinzhorn and Seligmann in 1890.

a noteworthy size in the 1890s and whose future prospects were initially by no means as certain as they might appear in retrospect. At the time, bicycles and— even more so—cars were still expensive, often tailor-made luxury goods that, at least until the turn of the century, were far from being mainstream consumer items and mass-produced means of mobility or transport. During Seligmann's first 10 years on the Executive Board, Continental's main line of business was technical rubber products and toys, especially rubber balls, which were very profitable. The latter business area was organized by a rubber ball convention that included all manufacturers and had cartel-like structures. The company also manufactured balloon fabric for the up-and-coming aviation industry and other products that resulted from the almost endless areas of application of the raw material rubber, as scientific and application-based research became all the more intensive.

Seligmann soon developed a whole range of measures on corporate strategy and policy. First, he came to an understanding with the neighboring potential competitor Hannoversche Gummi-Kamm-Comp., which later became Excelsior, regarding demarcation between production and sales areas, although this was soon annulled when Continental's activities increased. He also pushed the export business from early on, acquiring strategic and financially lucrative stakes in the leading Belgian rubber company Manufacture Liégoise des Caoutchouc O. Englebert, Fils & Co. and the Vienna-based Österreichische Amerikanische Gummifabriken, which later became Semperit. The chance to take over Englebert completely and become an international enterprise was tempting but, after thorough consideration, this route was not taken, as there was a risk of management's energy being spread too thinly and the purchasing price was also deemed too high. In 1903, there were then more concrete plans to acquire the German branch of Dunlop in Hanau and simultaneously found a Continental factory in England. This would have led to a cross-holding between Continental and the British Dunlop Company, which was also undergoing dynamic development as a rubber corporation at the time. In fact, in 1904, 20,000 Dunlop shares were bought at a rate of 600 percent, calculated as a percentage of the nominal value of the share. The purchase of Dunlop and foundation of a company abroad failed to materialize, however. The export strategy was supplemented by a twofold innovation strategy. The R&D activities of the central laboratory, which had been set up at an early stage, were expanded, and, parallel to this, a patent policy was pursued through the timely acquisition of valuable tire patents. Additionally, despite the soon-to-be-booming tire business, Seligmann did not neglect the company's other lines of business and continued to drive forward the diversification of the product portfolio. "The new 'waterproof clothing' range has already developed to our satisfaction in its first year," stated Seligmann in the 1912 annual report. In this respect, Continental differed from other major European rubber companies such as Michelin and Dunlop, which during this time had developed almost exclusively into tire corporations. Finally, Seligmann also pursued a shrewd strategy of raising capital by issuing new shares in line with capital increases, as well as issuing corporate bonds and home loans. This strategy became the backbone for the high investments required to ensure that the rapid yet costly expansion would not lose momentum. Continental's share capital rose at a breathtaking pace, from 900,000 marks formerly to 15 million marks in 1913.

Seligmann's corporate policy was modern in many respects and received all the greater recognition—including from his contemporaries—because of the highly adverse economic and political conditions business leaders were confronted with during this period. The bicycle industry, which had initially grown very quickly and was one of Continental's main customers, went through several cyclical economic and sales crises around the turn of the century. The severe crisis in 1898, for example, prompted Seligmann to set aside 300,000 marks as a precautionary measure. The bicycle industry was in the midst of a transformation process in many regards, particularly with several companies developing into automobile manufacturers. As a result, Continental's original equipment business was also repeatedly exposed to considerable fluctuations. However, the young automotive industry was still at a stage of development where tailormade sedans for rich gentlemen and different power transmission technologies were the main focal points. For example, in early July 1907, the Austria-based Société Mercedes Electrique, which was affiliated with Daimler-Motoren-Gesellschaft, wrote to Seligmann, apparently in response to an inquiry on his part. This letter referred to the lucrative business with purely electrical cars and mentioned the manufacturing of electrical test buses for the Berliner Omnibus-Gesellschaft, thus painting a picture of bright prospects for a potential equity investment. This was compounded by a number of events in international politics which had a lasting effect on export sales and often also led to unexpected rises in the prices of rubber as a raw material, or at least to highly speculative transactions. In April 1894, for example, Seligmann lamented to the Supervisory Board that the business was suffering "as a result of the revolution in Brazil, the financial crisis in the United States and the unfavorable price of silver." A tariff war was also raging between the German Reich and Russia, although Continental was relatively relaxed about this as the company was not yet particularly active in the latter region. Just a few years later, a war in South Africa and the Boxer Rebellion in China had political ramifications around the world, but the main threat to Continental's business was the trade and tariff war waged between Germany and France, which was initiated by the government of the German Reich in 1901. For years, Continental and Michelin had been engaged in a fierce price dispute in their home and export markets, which was often accompanied by harsh, nationalist overtones. This feud got particularly heated when Continental attempted to set up its own tire factory in Clichy, near Paris, shortly after the turn of the century, which resulted in a legal dispute before French courts in 1904, as Michelin wanted to prohibit Continental from entering the market. Regardless of these confrontations, Seligmann, who was by now also president of the Zentralverein der deutschen Kautschukindustrie, the central association of the German rubber industry, attempted to exert political influence on the government in Berlin, with the goal of achieving a turnaround in its protectionist tariff policy, which he deemed highly damaging, and concluding new export-friendly trade agreements with other countries. A short time later, in 1908, business was hit again by a new global financial crisis "that could not pass without having some effect on our company, with its business relations all over the world," as Seligmann reported at the Annual Shareholders' Meeting in 1909. Management in those days, at the mercy of the uncertainties of the time, was no less challenging than today, more than 100 years later.

Siegmund Seligmann's aura as the grand old man of the German rubber industry and, above all, as the guiding figure pulling the threads behind Continental's unprecedented rise, had already grown so large by the turn of the century that his anniversary celebrating 25 years of service as "director of the global corporation Continental" in April 1901 not only received a full-page article in the Gummi-Zeitung newspaper but was also considered quite a societal event both within the company and in Hanover itself. To show their appreciation and memorialize the proceedings, the Supervisory Board presented Seligmann with a silver replica of a rubber tree. Factory officials also gave him a photo album with pictures of the factory, all the branches and the commercial staff, and the youngest Continental apprentice performed a quartet on the keyed trumpet entitled "The development of all means of transport, from the stagecoach to today's automobiles." Thereafter, the entire staff of 1,200 marched en masse to the event hall of Hanover's workers' association, where a deputation of workers presented Seligmann with another photo album. This was followed by a festival and a tableau vivant ("living picture") performed by the workers' association, which told the history of rubber and the company. The event concluded with a specially written "rubber song" and a tattoo ceremony devoted to raw rubber, before the celebrations ended with men and women, workers, technical officers, directors, authorized officers, factory supervisors and members of the board all dancing together. The respect Seligmann enjoyed among the workforce was undoubtedly great, in part thanks to a corporate social policy that set Continental apart from other companies and corporations both in Hanover and beyond, and which was pursued intensively and deliberately to cultivate loyalty. Benefits included corporate health insurance, company housing, payments to compensate loss of wages during the summer vacation, and last but not least, individual life insurance of more than 5,000 marks for salaried employees and 1,500 marks for waged workers after 10 years of employment, which were placed at the disposal of the insured persons after their 65th birthday. It was therefore no wonder that Continental was spared strikes and labor conflicts prior to World War I. Even the socialist press of the time called Seligmann the "highest wage earner at Continental," more as a compliment than a criticism.

This was simultaneously an apt description yet quite incorrect. Seligmann was employed as a manager with employment contracts that expired after 10 years respectively. At these intervals, the contracts were extended by the Supervisory Board for another ten years, and the salary and bonuses were renegotiated. However, Seligmann also held a considerable number of Continental shares, making him an owner-manager, which was also how he regarded himself. At the Annual Shareholders' Meeting in 1905, Continental's Executive Board accounted for a total of 533 votes, representing 15 percent of the capital present, and most of were held by Seligmann, with 349. Seligmann and Prinzhorn in particular were highly confident in their dealings with the Supervisory Board, especially regarding the company's distribution of profits and bonus policy. In 1907, this resulted in a fierce dispute, which Prinzhorn was largely responsible for initiating by demanding that the Executive Board receive greater consideration at the expense of the payouts to the Supervisory Board and his resistance to equal bonuses for the Executive Board and Supervisory Board, though he was also supported by Seligmann here. The dispute remained unresolved and was postponed when Prinzhorn announced his withdrawal from the Executive Board in 1908 and became a member of the Supervisory Board instead, a step that was very unusual at the time. Nevertheless, the topic resurfaced in the spring of 1916, with Seligmann himself locking horns with Caspar, the chairman of the Supervisory Board. This time, the issue was the hidden reserves that had by now grown to millions of marks but were not being taken into account for the calculation of bonuses. Seligmann objected to this and called for an immediate recalculation of the bonus payments. In his view, the ratio of the three elements into which net profit was divided—dividends, bonuses and profit brought forward, which accumulated as hidden reserves—should be redefined. In particular, the amount spent on bonuses should be allocated in a certain ratio to the amount of dividends. The purpose of his suggestion was to value the services of the members of the Executive Board, who generated the profits, appropriately in relation to the shareholders.

Just as Seligmann saw himself as an owner-manager, some members of the Supervisory Board also viewed themselves as more than just a controlling and monitoring body and believed they were entitled to be involved in operative business. Especially when it came to foreign business, a number of the board members were "active in the interests of our company," as Bernhard Caspar stated in a note in 1903. "Mr. Coppel, the councilor of commerce, visited Paris several times, I myself was involved in matters in France and England, a large commission in Germany cooperated with the Executive Board, conducting long negotiations on an important topic, and whenever circumstances dictate it, the Supervisory Board its members are in constant contact with management." Yet claims in later years that, during his time on the Executive Board, Seligmann also actively influenced the composition of the Supervisory Board, aiming to loosen the company's close ties to the banking industry and thus reduce its influence, are unfounded. Noteworthy new appointments to Continental's Supervisory Board from outside the banking sector, for example in 1889 or 1891, were the result of family-related developments. In 1883, Seligmann married Johanna Coppel, the daughter of the Solingen-based producer of steel goods Gustav Coppel, who was also active in the wheel rim business and therefore, like Seligmann, was an automotive supplier. Coppel acquired Continental shares and owned 17 percent at one time, holding a position on the Supervisory Board until his death in 1914, a position later taken over by his son. In another case, in 1880, the marriage between Adolf Prinzhorn and Marie Günzler, daughter of court chamber director Ernst von Günzler, indirectly led to Ernst von Günzler briefly joining Continental's Supervisory Board. However, the appointment of Heinrich Tramm, the city director (first mayor) of Hanover to Continental's Supervisory Board in April 1903 may well have been the result of Seligmann's influence. Directly integrating the highest and most influential municipal official into the company certainly amounted to cunning political strategy, although even at that time there was a public outcry regarding the foreseeable conflict between corporate and municipal interests.

In the following years, celebrations for Seligmann's birthday and years of service were at least as extravagant as those for the company's anniversaries. When the outbreak of World War I interrupted Continental's ascent, Seligmann reduced the scale of his management work and increasingly allowed his Executive Board colleagues to take the reins in this area. Even before Prinzhorn left the company, Albert Gerlach was appointed to the Executive Board in 1905 and Willy Tischbein in 1907. Gerlach was responsible for technical management, Tischbein for sales and above all the tire business, while Seligmann focused on the finances and business with technical products. Although he was officially entitled to the title of general director, Seligmann explicitly waived this right and preferred to act as an equal alongside his colleagues on the Executive Board. Before the end of the war, his only son Edgar Seligmann also joined Continental after completing his law degree and was appointed to the Executive Board as soon as 1921. While Seligmann may have intended for his heir to complete his life's work, Willy Tischbein was in fact already pulling the strings in company management. When it came to public matters, however, Seligmann was still Continental's first point of contact, just as he was in 1914, immediately after the start of the war.

Seligmann remained loyal to the German Emperor but did not become involved in party politics, meaning his reputation remained intact even after German Revolution of 1918. In 1921, on the occasion of Continental's 50th anniversary, Seligmann was awarded an honorary doctorate from the Hanover Institute of Technology in recognition of his outstanding achievements in promoting scientific research in the rubber industry. In 1923, he was then named an honorary citizen of the city of Hanover. Later claims that he had "bought" this honorary citizenship appear doubtful. On October 12, 1925, Seligmann died of pneumonia at the age of 72. Shortly afterward, a large funeral service was held in Continental's administration building, at which numerous dignitaries from politics and industry gave eulogies honoring his accomplishments. Having passed away on a Tuesday, the company shut down all its operations for 24 hours from Wednesday to Thursday. When Seligmann took over as head of Continental, the workforce numbered just 261 workers. Ten years later it had almost doubled to around 500, and in 1913 it amounted to nearly 7,700. By the time of his death in 1925, there were around 14,500 people working for the company. Meanwhile, the disclosed net profit climbed from just under 100,000 marks (1880) to approximately 400,000 marks in 1891, still prior to the tire era, before rising to 8.7 million marks in 1913—the company's best result to date. It was often said at the time that "the man and the plant are one," meaning that Seligmann was, essentially, the face of the modern Continental and the personification of the corporate culture of the day—a status that none of his many successors would ever come close to achieving in the decades that followed. Rarely has a company benefited so much from a manager who initially stepped in merely to restructure it.

Willy Tischbein and the Americanization of Continental in the 1920s

Besides Siegmund Seligmann, another member of Continental's Executive Board was regarded by his contemporaries as key to Continental's success: Willy Tischbein, who had a decisive influence on the company in the 1920s as chairman of the Executive Board and Seligmann's successor. Born in 1871, the year Continental was founded, Tischbein joined the company in 1894 after completing a commercial apprenticeship and quickly made a name for himself. His status as a highly successful international racing cyclist also made him very valuable to Continental. With his dual expertise, he was given the task of establishing and expanding the fledgling tire business, which he quickly turned into the company's main sales driver. In December 1906, Tischbein was appointed to the Executive Board. Like Prinzhorn and Seligmann before him, he had to deposit a security with the Supervisory Board as a safeguard against possible damage or loss during his term of office—in this case, Continental shares with a nominal value of 5,400 marks. This corresponded to roughly twice his annual income as a new member of the Executive Board and thus a substantial amount. Very quickly, Tischbein began to put his own stamp on the company. In 1910, the first factory technician was hired, followed by the first tire engineer with an academic degree in 1911, which raised the bar for company expertise in development and tire manufacturing technology to a new level. With company cars not yet common practice, Tischbein himself is also said to have repeatedly carried out test and trial runs with Continental tires in his own private vehicle. At the same time, he engaged in systematic networking within the plethora of emerging societies and industrial associations that subscribed to the propaganda about automobiles. For example, he sat on the executive board of the Verein Deutscher Motorfahrzeug-Industrieller (German Automobile Industry Association), one goal of which was, in 1908, to finance an automobile traffic and training road in the Taunus mountain range. Later, he also became a member of the executive board of the Reichsverband der Deutschen Industrie, chairman of the Reichsverband der Automobilindustrie and president of the Verein Deutscher Gummireifen-Fabriken (the associations of German industry, automobile industry and German rubber manufacturers respectively). For a long time, Tischbein was overshadowed at Continental by the popularity surrounding Siegmund Seligmann, but as the tire business for which he was responsible grew, so did his internal standing and importance. With Seligmann's blessing, he increasingly took over the reins of the company toward the end of World War I.

Fig. 20: Willy Tischbein (1871–1946).

Huge challenges lay ahead for Tischbein: first and foremost the period of hyperinflation, then the growing emancipation of the labor movement, characterized for example by legislation in favor of works councils and worker participation that resulted from the Weimar Republic's development into a welfare state. At the same time, a modern, mobile society was forming in the (ostensibly) "golden 1920s," with the bicycle making a breakthrough as a mass means of transport and motoring becoming increasingly widespread at the same time. This led to the formation of an industrial combination between the (tire) supply industry and the large automotive companies as original equipment customers. Additional difficulties were presented by frequent changes among the main shareholders and shareholder groups of Continental, resulting from the specific conditions of financial market capitalism in the Weimar Republic, and last but not least, by the economic upswings and downturns that culminated in the global financial crisis at the beginning of the 1930s. Successfully steering Continental through all these challenges and adapting to the circumstances was a Herculean task.

Due to the changed political conditions after the war, Tischbein and the company management were also confronted with different sociopolitical conditions within the company. The introduction of the eight-hour working day, wage policy demands and a growing willingness to strike led to conflicts between management and the workforce. And unlike Seligmann, whose charisma led him to be viewed as the benevolent company patriarch of the large "Continental family," Tischbein quickly acquired the reputation of a stubbornly elitist magnate of capitalist industry and a hardliner in matters of working hours and wages. For the trade unions, Tischbein was much better suited to the role of antagonist than Seligmann, particularly since the former was also on the executive boards of the Arbeitgeberverband der Chemischen Industrie (employers' association of the chemical industry) and the Vereinigung der deutschen Arbeitsgeberverbände (union of German employers' associations). In the spring of 1924, conflicts between Willy Tischbein and the Works Council that had meanwhile been formed reached their first peak with strikes and lockouts, with the Executive Board and employee representatives engaging in a full-scale communication war of appeals and declarations. No doubt the prospect of a communist majority winning the upcoming Works Council election, the first to be held at the company, caused some sleepless nights for Tischbein. But even back then, the rubber workers, who belonged to the union of chemical workers, proved to be far less radical than their colleagues in the iron and metal industries.

The next cause of bad blood and serious conflict at Continental was the wave of rationalization that Tischbein initiated in the second half of the 1920s, which fundamentally altered the wage and working time structures used hitherto through the introduction of work assessment procedures and performance-oriented remuneration on the basis of the American Bedaux system. These rationalization measures were highly controversial within the company since the unions considered the Bedaux system to be ruthless and exploitative, whereas Tischbein praised it as a successful means of increasing productivity and simultaneously reducing costs. The fact that he was also chairman of the new Deutsche Bedaux-Gesellschaft, a company founded to promote the use of this rationalization system in German industry, did not help matters. In hindsight, however,

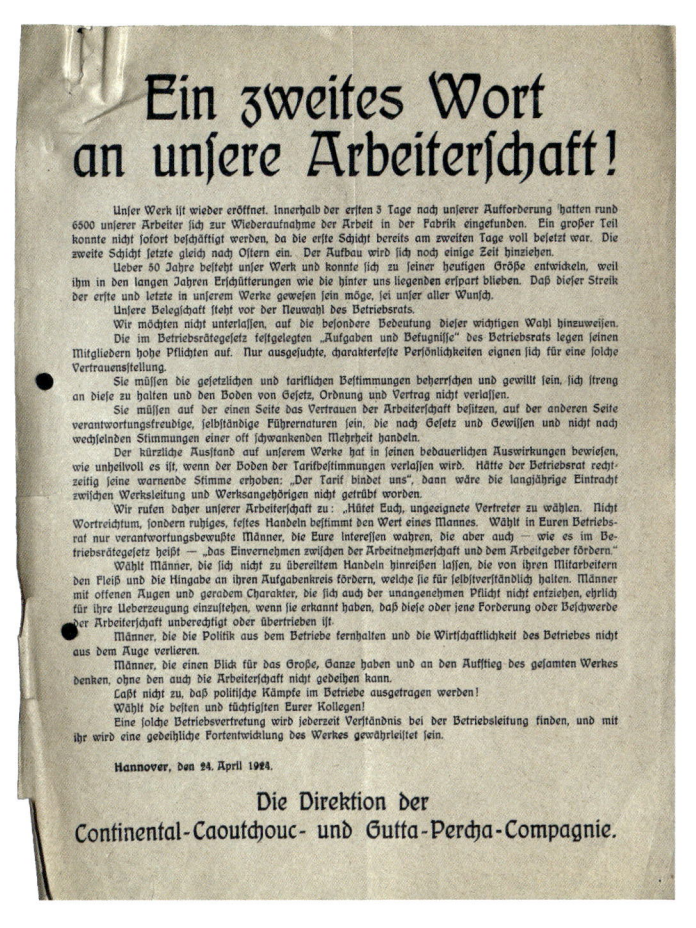

Fig. 21: Notice posted by Continental management on April 24, 1924, to the workforce explaining its view of the strike action.

the measures proved to be one of the decisive factors that enabled Continental—unlike almost all its competitors—to come through the global economic crisis relatively unscathed. Forewarned by the short but sharp economic and stock market slump in 1926, Tischbein had developed some intuition about the crisis years that lay ahead and therefore began to take precautionary cost-cutting measures early on. "The fiscal year of 1926 was one of the most difficult in the history of our company," reported Tischbein at the Annual Shareholders' Meeting in April 1927. Price declines, sales slumps and an "excessive tax and social cost burden" placed on companies by both the Reich and state governments—a burden that Tischbein repeatedly criticized—had caused a significant drop in sales and profit. From the perspective of the Executive Board, this meant that mass layoffs were unavoidable at Continental in the crisis years between 1929 and 1932.

At the same time, Tischbein's attention was also focused on modernizing the way in which the company was organized, using American systems as a role model for steering Continental toward a divisional structure with a more pronounced separation of tires and technical products. The sales organization was also streamlined and adjusted accordingly: the bicycle and passenger tire business was assigned to dedicated branches, many of which were also equipped with their own workshops and further services, while technical and surgical products were handled by a separate sales force and field staff. Tischbein also proved to be a highly innovative marketing genius—before such a concept existed. He realized the value of sponsoring motor sports events and was the first to not only let famous athletes appear with Continental products but also adorn their shirts with the company name. With this combination of sports and advertising pursued under his leadership, Continental became a pioneer of early sports marketing in Germany. For Continental, the constant association and equation of high-performance tires with top performance in racing created a brand image that the company benefited from and took advantage of for decades. This was further strengthened by the introduction of the latest American tire technology on the German market as early as 1921. Continental was the first company to offer new balloon tires, which constituted a revolution in tire engineering.

Under Tischbein, Continental also launched a communications strategy aimed at widely stratified groups of customers and buyers. The customer magazine "Echo Continental," first published in 1913, reached a circulation in the tens of thousands in the 1920s and presented the company as a key manufacturer of countless products indispensable for the rapidly growing leisure, sports and consumer society of the Weimar Republic. Such image campaigns were in fact much needed, at least among the population of Hanover in 1926 and 1927, when the city's magistrate had to deal with a number of complaints from various groups about "fly ash and odors originating from Continental's factories." These complaints about smoke and soot only came to an end after new boiler systems and ventilators were installed in Vahrenwald. Unlike in later years, when the car's rise to a mass means of transport meant the replacement business moved into focus, the original equipment business, with the automotive companies as customers, was key at the time, and Tischbein had a clever strategy for this. At Opel, Germany's largest automotive manufacturer, Continental held a virtual monopoly as a supplier of tires and hoses, partly due to the close personal relationship between Tischbein and Fritz Opel, who had a shared past as successful racing cyclists. By March 1925, Opel was ordering approximately 300 sets of tires and hoses per day from Hanover; together with other orders from Opel dealers and private customers, weekly demand totaled around 4,000 tires and hoses. In a separate secret agreement, Tischbein guaranteed Opel a volume discount of 3 percent in return. This discount went to a separate special premium account, where five to six-figure amounts of reichsmarks quickly accumulated. With this money, Continental shares were then purchased in Opel's name and placed in a special stock portfolio registered to "Adam Opel" at the Hanover branch of Commerzbank, thereby automatically increasing Opel's shareholding. Between the fall of 1924 and June 1926 alone, bonuses and share purchases amounting to 780,000 reichsmarks were accumulated. The underlying agreement was regularly expanded as needed to include further tire sizes and types, and the required tire prices were renegotiated and fixed. Although the difference between the price of 256 reichsmarks that Continental originally charged for each tire set and the 245 reichsmarks actually paid by Opel amounted to almost 5%, the system worked to the advantage of both parties. Tischbein secured a key customer in the long term and, at the same time, helped to build up a potential major shareholder as a counterweight to the banks.

Tischbein, with his myriad of memberships in boards and steering committees of associations, bodies and institutions, had long become the grand seigneur of the automotive and supplier industry in Germany. At the end of the 1920s, he personally instigated an attempt by accessory manufacturers to force automotive companies into finally introducing set standards and types with the aim of surviving on the increasingly competitive international market. To this end, an agreement was concluded between Continental, Bosch, Sachs (i.e. the ball bearing industry) and the wheel factories such as Kronprinz. The attempt failed, however, and the majority of automotive manufacturers at the time did not survive the economic crisis that followed. In addition to his influential position as chairman of the Reichsverband der Automobilindustrie (Reich Association of the Automotive Industry), Tischbein was also on the advisory committee for automotive engineering of the Reich Ministry of Transport, a member of the governing body of the stock exchange in Hanover, and a member of the supervisory board of the Darmstädter- und Nationalbank. In 1929, the list of his countless offices, functions, decorations and awards in the Reichshandbuch der Deutschen Gesellschaft—the who's who of German society at the time—took up dozens of closely spaced lines.

As an industrialist, Tischbein had arguably the best and widest network of contacts in the Weimar Republic.

Although the size of Continental's Executive Board was significantly increased after Seligmann's death, first to four and then even for a while to ten members, corporate management was almost entirely in Tischbein's hands. In 1926, he not only had himself appointed as Seligmann's successor as chairman, but also was the first to claim and use the title of general director. There was considerable turnover within the Executive Board, and it is quite possible that Tischbein encouraged this by repeatedly restructuring management. He was probably also responsible for Seligmann's son Edgar leaving the Executive Board rather surprisingly in 1929 and joining the Supervisory Board instead.

However, Tischbein's attempts to return to the global market were met with much less success, not least because he went about this somewhat half-heartedly and hesitantly. Between 1920 and 1922, he also tried to reclaim the expropriated factory in Clichy near Paris, with the assistance of the American rubber company Goodrich, and to secure a major share in a French rubber company. Yet these attempts failed, probably in part because the Americans had just set up a subsidiary factory in Colombes near Paris themselves and had little interest in having a new competitor on the French tire market. Tischbein was unable to carry on Seligmann's pre-WWI success in founding factories abroad and subsequently expanding Continental to become a multinational corporation, in part because he was averse to the risk this entailed due to changes in global economic circumstances. As a result, Continental fell far behind large European competitors such as Michelin and Dunlop, not to mention the US tire companies that were aggressively pushing into the global market and building numerous factories abroad during this period. Ultimately, this made Continental more dependent than ever on the foreign trade and currency policies of the Reich government, whose fixation on tariffs made it even more difficult for the company to return to the world stage. "You have probably read," wrote Willy Tischbein in an August 1925 letter to Fritz Opel, with whom he was on first name terms, "that we are the only industry in Germany that was sacrificed for the tariff negotiations. I fear that, due to the associated 10 percent ad valorem duty, only a few rubber factories in Germany will be able to compete in the long term."

After Bernhard Caspar stepped down as chairman of the Supervisory Board in May 1918, Julius Mendel, who had been a member of this shareholder representation and monitoring body since the mid-1880s, became the new chairman and thus Tischbein's counterpart. The tenures of Mendel, who stayed in office until

April 1926, and his successor Julius B. Caspar (the son of his predecessor), who in turn filled the position until 1935, signaled continuity and stability in Continental's shareholder structure, yet this was far from the case. Although the remaining members of the Supervisory Board, Hermann Hecht and Heinrich Tramm, continued to serve as long-standing shareholder representatives and three shareholders—Julius B. Caspar, Ernst Magnus and Alexander Coppel—had taken over the board positions of their fathers (Seligmann's son Edgar was to join this list in 1929, when he switched from the Executive Board to the Supervisory Board), Continental's Supervisory Board was in fact subject to many coming and goings when viewed over the course of the years. The first of these new additions, which included some illustrious yet also dubious or shadowy personalities, was the American Bertram G. Work, whose appointment was in fact a strategic coup on the part of Tischbein. Faced with the emerging decline of the mark as a currency, Tischbein protected Continental against hostile takeovers by foreign companies by convincing the American rubber and tire company B.F. Goodrich to take on around 25 percent of the share capital and thereby become a key shareholder, but without getting involved in the company's dealings. This not only brought the company fresh capital in a stable currency but also access to the latest tire technology. The participation entitled Goodrich's chairman, Bertram G. Work, to a seat on the Supervisory Board, something which remained a mere formality. In actual fact, Work transferred his mandate and the representation of his voting shares at the Annual Shareholders' Meetings to Tischbein.

The second new face on the Supervisory Board was Ernst Rosskopf, a dazzling yet dubious figure who emerged as if from nowhere at Continental's Annual Shareholders' Meeting in April 1922 with a voting share of 20.9 million marks, or 34,952 votes, which amounted to 41.6 percent of the represented capital. Rosskopf was co-owner of the Bank für Niedersachsen AG, which was founded in 1921 by land owners and bankers in Lower Saxony but which was short-lived and went into liquidation in 1926. As suddenly as Rosskopf appeared as an apparent major shareholder, he vanished again. At the Annual Shareholders' Meeting in April 1923, at the peak of inflation, he registered 107,133 votes or 26.4 percent of the capital present. Thereafter, he no longer shows up in the attendance lists of the company's Annual Shareholders' Meetings. By now, however, Commerzbank in particular had taken on the role of major shareholder at Continental, as it at times owned up to 30 percent of the declared capital, particularly after it took over banking house Mendel & Rosenthal in 1918. For the first time in Continental's history, after laws on codetermination came into force in August 1922, two representatives of the Continental staff also attended the Supervisory Board meetings as new members.

The third notable figure among the board members and shareholders was banker Jakob Goldschmidt, personally liable partner of the Darmstädter- und Nationalbank (Danat-Bank), which took over the Caspar banking house in 1920 shortly after it had gone through a merger itself. Goldschmidt first acted as a shareholder of Continental in 1920. By 1922, he had already managed to obtain a seat on the Supervisory Board as part of the expansion of the controlling body from seven to nine members. Even during the years of inflation, Goldschmidt and his bank had increased their share to just under 30 percent and, on April 28, 1924, at the first Annual Shareholders' Meeting after the currency reform, they presented themselves as Continental's new major shareholder with 71.5 percent of the voting shares. In the subsequent years, this stake dropped back to around 50 percent, yet the Danat-Bank remained the main shareholder ahead of Commerzbank, the second-largest, which held a little over 10 percent. By now, other large banks such as Deutsche Bank, which took over Hannoversche Bank in 1920, and Dresdner Bank had also acquired significant shares and attended Continental's Annual Shareholders' Meetings. The upheaval that occurred in the banking landscape after 1918 was reflected almost identically in Continental's Supervisory Board and its shareholder structures. The fourth illustrious major shareholder, who initially stayed in the background and did not serve on the Supervisory Board, was finally Fritz Opel and the Opel family. Fritz Opel had been buying Continental shares since 1922 and had successively increased his stake to just under 20 percent of the share capital by 1928. After successfully selling his automotive company to General Motors in 1929, he significantly increased his purchases of Continental shares. At the Annual Shareholders' Meeting on June 1, 1932, Opel held a majority share of 50.04 percent of the represented capital. The Danat-Bank never appeared as a shareholder again. It went bankrupt in July 1931 in the wake of a balance sheet fraud scandal, becoming the main victim of the major banking crisis in the Weimar Republic.

Willy Tischbein, who had purchased a large number of Continental shares himself and held up to 5 percent of the share capital at times, was confronted with convoluted shareholder structures for many years and it was only in the 1930s that a new setup was formed, with the Danat-Bank and Opel as major shareholders. For a long time, banks held the reins on Continental's Supervisory Board. With Coppel, Opel and the ball bearing industrialist Ernst Sachs, who joined the Supervisory Board in 1926, Tischbein was also able to recruit key representatives from the automotive and supplier industries to Continental's Supervisory Board. In operative matters, the Supervisory Board granted Tischbein free rein. Although the Supervisory Board set up a financial committee in November 1922 to act as a steering and control body for the Executive Board, its powers did not extend very far and ultimately it only served to mobilize the financial expertise of the members of the Supervisory Board, who helped to steer the company through the turmoil of the hyperinflation period. Two other Supervisory Board committees were formed at the same time, one for labor welfare and the other for general social affairs. Throughout the numerous capital measures that were to follow, the conversion of the share capital from mark to the new Reichsmark currency, the issuing of preference shares and the measures to adapt the capital resources to the economic crisis, it was Tischbein who was in charge and not the respective major shareholders. Two adept capital market transactions in particular were not only the result of his initiative but were also successfully implemented by him. They showed how Tischbein had mastered the art of maneuvering the financial markets of the time.

Tischbein's first masterstroke was the successful handling of Goodrich's exit and the buyback of the American company's shares in Continental in December 1928. After long negotiations, for which Tischbein flew dozens of times to Akron in Ohio—then the rubber capital of the world—he succeeded in reaching an agreement whereby not only Goodrich but also the banking syndicate that took over the shares were satisfied with the financial transactions and all parties involved were able to save face. Originally, Tischbein's vision was to establish a "close cooperation" with Goodrich in the long term, to conquer the European tire market together with the Americans and to push competitors Michelin and Dunlop out of the field. However, after Goodrich president Bertram G. Work suddenly died in August 1927, there was no longer support for this vision among the Goodrich management, and the Americans wanted to get rid of their equity interest. The second feat was his consolidation of the rubber industry, which Tischbein pursued with endurance and strategic foresight and which resulted in the gradual acquisition of a number of competitors, in particular the takeover of Excelsior AG and its eventual merger in 1929. Continental emerged as the dominant corporate trust in the German rubber industry, even though not all Tischbein's plans worked out. For a long time, negotiations were conducted for a takeover of and merger with Hamburger Gummiwerke Phoenix, with the press already reporting in July 1928 that its finalization was imminent. In the end, however, the move did not take place. A capital increase to finance the merger would not have been necessary.

On the one hand, Continental still had more than 6 million treasury shares that could be used as purchase currency. On the other, the stock package of around 7.5 million reichsmarks bought back from Goodrich by the banking syndicate, under the lead of the Danat-Bank, was almost enough by itself to exchange the 9 million Peters Union shares and the 2.1 million Polack-Titan shares when taking into account the respective exchange rate of 3:4. In his long-term strategy to consolidate the industry through mergers and acquisitions, as well as push the competition out of the market and reduce existing overcapacity, Tischbein time and again managed to skillfully play off the interests and vanities of the bankers against one another to his own advantage. This applied in particular to the representatives of Deutsche Bank or Diskontogesellschaft, who were pushing for greater influence and who, in November 1925 for example, were concerned that they were being excluded from lucrative credit and stock transactions "as a result of the close personal relationship between director Tischbein and Mr. Jakob Goldschmidt." Rumors and speculation soon abounded in public about Tischbein's takeover activities. These ranged from suspected additional orchestration of mergers by Continental, including with non-tire rubber companies, to the suggestion that Continental itself had now become dependent on a domestic or foreign automotive corporation, accusations to which Tischbein responded with fierce denials.

After the formal acquisition of the four rubber companies, Tischbein immediately started merging the individual parts and shaping a new corporation. He was not shy in his approach either, with some of the acquired factories and locations closing and the acquired company Titan-Polack liquidated completely. However, the other plant locations were initially allowed to keep their identity and manufacturing autonomy, while at the same time emphasizing common corporate cultural values. As early as 1928, Tischbein sent a 12-point missive to all senior staff that he recommended be "taken to heart."

In his numerous public comments and interviews, Tischbein radiated confidence and trust in Continental's position, which also had a positive effect on staff. In December 1931, he told the Berliner Börsen-Courier, a German daily newspaper: "We are staying calm about the difficulties of the current situation, since we have been following a very cautious policy on dividends, depreciation and provisions for many years now. We have taken the expected shrink in the economy and deterioration into account by putting in place corresponding savings measures, which are already starting to bear fruit in the current year." In fact, Tischbein had not only taken his consistent cost-cutting measures out on the backs of Continental's workers, but had equally subjected administrative staff to Bedaux rational-

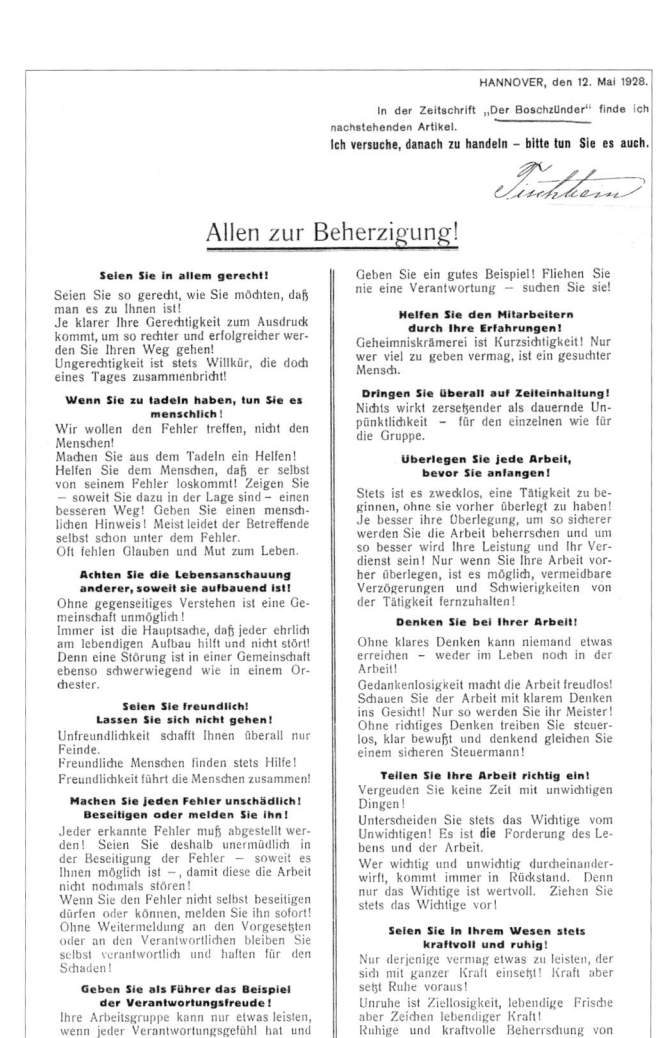

Fig. 22: Tischbein's circular from May 12th 1928 about the code of conduct.

ization and personnel adjustment and, above all, had demanded significant cutbacks from the shareholders through reduced dividends. In doing so, he risked breaking with the tradition of high double-digit dividend rates, which the shareholders had been spoiled with up to now and had cemented Continental's image as a generous distribution machine. In the hyperinflation year of 1923, there was no dividend payment for the first time in the company's history. Although the payouts resumed in the first post-inflation years of 1924 and 1925, the dividend only amounted to 10 percent in each case. In the crisis year of 1926, the dividend payment was canceled again, before resuming between 1927 and 1932 at rates of between 6 and 9 percent. This did not sit well with the shareholders but was well received by the workforce. Tischbein now regularly addressed the latter, on the one hand to demand discipline to cope with the problems at hand and on the other to increase motivation and solidarity. In September 1929, for example, in an appeal to the corporation's factories in view of envisaged further shocks on the money market, he urged that obligations to customers be monitored closely and that all receivables be consolidated (at this time, they already amounted to close to 4.5 million reichsmarks). In his report on the business situation in 1931— in the middle of the crisis—he used the occasion of the company's anniversary to predict that this sixth decade in Continental's history would in the future be considered "a milestone for forward-looking, harmonious cooperation between shareholders, management and staff." A speech Tischbein gave to his senior executives on January 8, 1932, which was later printed in a twelve-page brochure, also became famous among the workforce and infamous among competitors. In it, he attempted to mobilize the "dynamic forces" inherent in the company to overcome the crisis, the end of which was not yet in sight, while his description of the desolate position of competitors compared to the "extraordinarily favorable position of our own company" had the desired motivational effect.

On balance, Tischbein's corporate policy could be labeled an "Americanization," but ultimately he swung back to the national path. He is rightfully regarded as the second father figure behind Continental's long years of success. However, he also implemented his corporate policy with much tougher tactics than Seligmann. What is more, he organized Continental's smooth transition into the era of National Socialism. In a series of communications, Tischbein expressly welcomed the new regime and its propagandist goals of economic and national greatness for Germany. The apex of Tischbein's adaptation to the Nazi regime was arguably Hitler visiting the Continental booth at the International Motor Show (IAA) in Berlin in May 1934. He also forced his Executive Board colleagues and senior executives to join the NSDAP. The latter included his protégé, Fritz Könecke, whom he had undoubtedly intended as his successor but who, due to his being only 34 years old in 1934, initially only became a regular member of Continental's Executive Board before being appointed chairman in 1938. Against this background, any assessment of Tischbein's corporate policies is therefore ambivalent. He also fell out with Fritz Opel, with whom he had already clashed in 1932 over a planned cut in dividends before having to back down. In December 1934, Tischbein left Continental's Executive Board ahead of schedule, partly due to health problems, and moved back to his Rixförde country estate near Celle, where he died in 1946.

The Major Shareholder between the Weimar Republic and the Era of the Economic Miracle: Continental and the Opel Family

As a major shareholder of Continental, the Opel family of entrepreneurs shaped the company's fate for almost 40 years, starting with Friedrich (Fritz) von Opel and followed by Wilhelm von Opel and Georg von Opel. The paths of the two companies had already crossed at an early stage. Friedrich Opel, son of company founder Adam Opel, was a successful (high-wheeler) cyclist just like Willy Tischbein, and became friends with him. In addition, Continental became one of the most important bicycle and automotive tire suppliers for the Opel corporation. Fritz Opel competed in soon-to-be-commonplace automobile races as what was known as a gentlemen driver (participants who raced in their own cars instead of being employed by an automotive company to drive the company's cars) and achieved numerous victories with Continental tires, including Germany's first automobile race, the 1904 Gordon Bennett Race through the Taunus mountain range. In the early 1920s, Opel also acquired a stake in Continental through the purchase of shares, albeit initially as a purely financial investment. At the Annual Shareholders' Meeting on April 12, 1922, Fritz von Opel made his first public appearance as a shareholder when he proposed tripling the company's capital and offering the new shares to the existing shareholders at a price of 150 percent. However, all other votes cast rejected the motion. At that time, Fritz von Opel held 3.17 percent of the shares together with his brother Carl von Opel. By April 1925, he had increased this share to 4.9 percent, before quickly amassing more Continental shares as a result of the special bonus account, reaching 20.5 percent by May 1928. Opel remained in the background following his 1922 appearance, but in May 1932, the "Opel group" publicly appeared at the Annual Shareholders' Meeting again, having successively sold off its automotive business to General Motors between 1929 and 1931 and subsequently acquiring a total of 43.8 percent of Continental's capital in its search for lucrative investment opportunities. As an ultimatum, Opel demanded that Tischbein rescind the planned dividend cut from 8 to 6 percent and that the Executive Board, Supervisory Board and senior executives forfeit the corresponding percentages of their bonuses. This was a source of fierce conflict between Tischbein and Opel, since the money for the dividend increase was not covered by profit but instead had to be financed by dissolving hidden reserves. Ultimately, Tischbein was forced to bend to the will of the majority shareholder. "Is Conti to be gutted? What are the Opel family's plans?" was the headline in a Hanover newspaper. However, while Fritz von Opel, who had been elected as vice chairman of the Supervisory Board in May 1932 and was thus also formally a member of this body for the first time, subsequently proved to be critical of the Executive Board as a majority shareholder, he was also interested in continuing Continental's success and further expanding the rubber company, in addition to protecting his investment. Nevertheless, Tischbein had to vacate his Executive Board position in the course of 1934. His successors, especially Fritz Könecke, who was appointed in 1938, then gained considerable influence and importance within Continental's corporate governance structure. For the spreading of the National Socialist economic system changed the position of shareholders immensely—in particular that of major shareholders.

Fig. 23 and 24: Fritz Opel (left) und Wilhelm von Opel (right).

By April 1937, Opel had once again increased its stake in Continental slightly to just under 50 percent, but the new German Stock Corporation Act of January 1937 not only gave the Executive Board, as the managing body, greater power than the Supervisory Board, but, through legislation on dividend taxes, also curtailed shareholders' ability to withdraw company profits. Between 1935 and 1939, Continental again distributed dividends of up to 14 percent, in part at Opel's insistence, but in the meantime 6 percent of this had to be transferred to trust funds of the Deutsche Golddiskontbank. During the war, the dividend rate fell to 5.5 percent, and from 1944, no dividends were paid. Fritz von Opel initially spoke out against the ever higher and ever more risky armaments investments that the National Socialist regime demanded from companies such as Continental as part of its policy of self-sufficiency and armament. Although he joined the NSDAP in 1933, he was largely reserved toward the National Socialists and handed over the chairmanship of Continental's Supervisory Board to his confidant Joseph C. Uebel, the young head of Opel's asset management, in April 1936. Conflicts with the Executive Board now became increasingly frequent, whether over staff increases (Opel advocated a cautious policy), investments (in 1935, Opel called for massive cost-saving measures and, in 1936, for a "year of standstill" in the financial program), the calculation and distribution of gratuities and bonuses (Opel was strictly against any increase), appointments to the Supervisory Board (Opel added two long-serving companions from the automotive industry to the Executive Board in April 1937), and last but not least the "self-alignment" of the company (Opel advocated stalling tactics in the face of growing political pressure to dismiss the Jewish chairman of the Supervisory Board, Julius B. Caspar, while Könecke wanted a quick removal from office). All of this ran counter to Könecke's corporate policy, which was increasingly aligned with the goals of the National Socialist regime. At the end of August 1938, Fritz von Opel died unexpectedly and, early in 1939, his brother Dr. Wilhelm von Opel and his nephew Georg von Opel, who was only 27 years old at that time, joined the Supervisory Board in his stead.

Although Uebel, as chairman of the Supervisory Board, continued to actively represent the interests of the Opel family as a major shareholder, he largely acted as a sort of accountant and did not have anywhere near the same assertiveness or business acumen as Fritz von Opel. In addition, the two direct representatives of the Opel family largely saw themselves as passive financial investors and refrained from interfering with the corporate policy of the Executive Board. In spite of the Opel family intervening frequently as the main shareholder, the triangle of power between the Executive Board, the Supervisory Board and the

Consultative Council shifted in favor of the former, where it was centered around Fritz Könecke, who followed in the footsteps of his mentor and role model Willy Tischbein by having the title of general director granted to him in November 1942. Continental was one of those companies that celebrated the new National Socialist principle of the "collective" both internally and externally and very quickly transformed into a model National Socialist company, with a strong focus not only on company culture but also on corporate policy, which closely followed the Nazi regime's ideologically political goals—however, without neglecting the interests of the corporation. With the Supervisory Board now weaker, running the operative business became easier for Continental's Executive Board, although the constraints and room for maneuver of corporate policy, the negotiation of decisions and the assertion of company interests largely no longer fell within the remit of internal corporate governance. In principle, nothing changed in the stake of the Opel family, as it still amounted to 30.6 percent of the share capital in April 1940. Significant changes only occurred thereafter. In July and October 1941, even before adjustment of capital, the share of the major shareholder dropped to just 17.2 percent, whereafter Georg von Opel increased the stake again slightly to 17.9 percent and 18.1 percent of the share capital in 1942 and 1943 respectively. Nevertheless, the Opel family's share had been almost been halved. Although this did not change anything about Opel's principal influence, the shrinking share did signal a decline in the interest of the main shareholder.

The majority share of the Opel family also survived the end of the war. However, the interests of the individual family members soon diverged. Wilhelm von Opel died in early May 1946, causing the share distribution within the family to shift so that Martha von Opel, Wilhelm's widow, held the second largest share and Margit von Opel, Wilhelm's niece, increasingly asserted her claim to a seat on Continental's Supervisory Board. Georg von Opel then took over as chairman of the Supervisory Board and, as main shareholder, once again pursued a more active role in policymaking at Continental. Initially, however, he had to deal primarily with the turbulent conditions, both politically and in-house, of the immediate post-war years, a period which was characterized by black market trade, the food crisis and the currency reform. In particular, together with the new Executive Board, he found himself confronted with trade unions and works councils confidently pushing for increased influence on company policy. Between 1946 and 1948, Continental was hit by hunger strikes and mass protests against the prospect of Fritz Könecke returning to the Executive Board and the reelection of Joseph Uebel to the Supervisory Board. The Works Council and the workforce demanded direct involvement in the Executive Board and the Supervisory Board and, in the fall of 1946, Opel gave in and signed a works agreement, according to which a worker representative could attend Executive Board meetings in the future and also take part in meetings of the Supervisory Board. Additionally, in early 1949, Georg von Opel supported the Works Council's rejection of Könecke's reappointment, which failed to materialize as a result. Even in the following years, when many companies were again caught in the conflict-ridden climate of a class struggle between corporate management, major shareholders and trade unions or works councils, von Opel continued to favor moderate diplomacy and adopt a wait-and-see attitude, in particular in view of the fact that the sociopolitical legislation on codetermination and employee rights had not yet been passed. He did briefly panic, however, after he read a small notice in the Frankfurter Abendpost newspaper in April 1949 with the headline "What is happening at Conti in Hanover?" It was a report on the results of the Works Council election, in which a twelve-strong majority of members of the KPD, the Communist Party of Germany, was elected together with only five Works Council members that belonged to the SPD, the Social Democratic Party. However, as Ernst Fellinger, then chairman of the Executive Board, quickly reported to Frankfurt, this was only the case at the Hanover plant. SPD members still dominated the works councils in Stöcken and Limmer by large numbers, which led to an overall power ratio of 13 KPD members to 35 SPD members within the overall body of workers' representatives. Georg von Opel in principle considered the direct participation of workers in the company through shares to be a solution to the old conflict between capital and labor and, in February 1951, was therefore already heavily advocating the creation of micro shares with the purpose of establishing a class of employee shareholders. In this respect, von Opel was far ahead of his time, particularly compared to the attitude of Continental's Executive Board to handing out employee shares, which it saw as a gateway to a company takeover by "Marxist trade union secretaries."

 Georg von Opel was also very America-oriented and wanted this to play a larger role in company policy in the future. He was probably also the driving force that led to the Continental Executive Board's investigative visits to the USA and its contact first with the US corporation General Tire in 1949 and then later with Goodyear. A contract for the manufacturing of "asbestos tiles" as a floor covering was also concluded with the US corporation Johns-Manville. The members of Continental's Executive Board were also regularly sent specific information or newspaper articles with relevant suggestions on how Continental's corporate policy could benefit from using America as a role model. Some of these suggestions look strange seen from today's perspective but they always contained a serious message at their core. In mid-March, for example, Ernst Fellinger received a letter from von Opel in which the latter noted that American tire companies had placed advertising on two bridges in Frankfurt, where it was seen by the drivers of the thousands of vehicles that passed by daily. "I therefore suggest you issue instructions for Continental to lease around 50 bridges in the western zone for advertising purposes as well, before it is too late." However, Continental's Executive Board had other concerns around this time such as their inability to provide sufficient supplies, which would have rendered an advertising campaign on this scale somewhat absurd. Nevertheless, von Opel's advice, which looked beyond the current problems of the day, was certainly far-sighted. Another area in which he looked to American models was the obligation to publish financial statements and the way figures were presented in annual reports. Von Opel welcomed the presentation of the annual profit-and-loss statement as a percentage-based income statement, which was unusual in Germany at the time but "commonplace in the USA." Continental was undoubtedly breaking new ground here compared to other German companies.

Fig. 25: Georg von Opel, around 1966.

Georg von Opel also did not shy away from sharply criticizing not only individual measures but also general corporate policies of the Executive Board. "It is to my regret that Dunlop seems to have succeeded in securing a larger market share of the flooring business, even though we were the first to be active in this area," he wrote in a letter to the Executive Board in April 1953. "In my opinion, the sales business is not being run aggressively or intensively enough. To be honest, I was surprised you did not share my view." In mid-January 1954, Opel wrote another strongly-worded letter to the Executive Board. "We have exchanged many letters since I began as chairman of the Supervisory Board, yet today's should be regarded as the one most worth taking note of," it said, and went on to express his utmost concern about the downward trend in Continental's overall earnings and performance since 1949. "I am writing this letter with the intention that you consider my ideas straight away and think about how the current development can be halted." Long before the Executive Board, which was often blinded by the rising sales figures of the "economic miracle years," even took notice of the company's actual problems, von Opel attempted to take countermeasures.

However, at this point in time, Georg von Opel had to deal with a completely different problem: an "Annual Shareholders' Meeting and shareholder opposition" initiated by his cousin Margit's husband on the basis of their shares, which made accusations against Continental's Executive Board and previous Supervisory Board regarding improper reimbursement of Continental's foreign assets in Spain and Switzerland, as well as various allegations of embezzlement. The matter caused a stir at the time and took until the middle of 1956 to resolve. There were several points of contention. One regarded accusations of influence on the agenda of the Annual Shareholders' Meeting in July 1954 and the calling of an extraordinary Shareholders' Meeting in June 1955, at which it was decided to increase the number of members of the Supervisory Board from six to nine. Another was the constant public speculation regarding the alleged sale of the "Leimer package" of Continental shares to interested foreigners, in particular to the Firestone corporation, which already owned a significant share of Gummiwerke Phoenix at this time. The dispute among the major shareholders involved dubious bankers and intermediaries, opportunistic groups of small shareholders and competitors acting for their own benefit, such as the German company Dunlop, which joined the opposition at the Annual Shareholders' Meeting while its own Continental shares were worth 400,000 German marks. In a series of discussions with his cousin, Georg von Opel tried to mediate and in particular to liberate her from what he considered to be the damaging influence of her husband. The matter was eventually settled by the sale of the shares to various investors, including Deutsche Bank.

Thereafter, the 1960s were very much about the looming crisis and the discussion about excessively high wage and personnel costs, as well as the cost-saving measures this necessitated at Continental. By this time, the company was once again paying out lavish dividends of between 12 and 18 percent. In fiscal 1961, the divided had been 16 percent although this could have been set even higher, as the Executive Board and the Supervisory Board explained in a joint statement in May 1962. However, having called for unions to forgo wage and salary demands at this time, dividend payments were kept lower in the spirit of moderation. Regardless of this, the Executive Board had set a gigantic program of expansion and modernization in motion, at a cost of 500 million German marks, which von Opel was quite skeptical about even though in principal he reminded the board to step up attempts to rationalize manufacturing processes at Continental. In September 1964, he also questioned Continental's involvement in plastics at all. Von Opel advised the Executive Board to divest this segment and urged it to concentrate on the core business, namely tires. In view of the red figures generated in the non-tire sector, he questioned "whether, in view of the major problems to be overcome in the rubber sector, it is appropriate to invest so much time, work and money into plastics. For years, the Executive Board has been agonizing over these questions, without making any noteworthy progress," von Opel said, according to the minutes of a Supervisory Board meeting. He saw developments at competitor Metzeler as a warning sign about the risks of a diversification strategy which was too expansive and imitated the American model too closely. Since 1957, Metzeler had been managed by the autocrat Willy Kraus, who was both the main shareholder and executive board chairman and had purchased a conglomerate comprising stakes in 33 companies in the chemical, plastics and construction materials sectors in the 1950s and 1960s, with the result that the old tire business now only played a marginal role in terms of sales and workforce.

Von Opel was also dissatisfied with the decision-making processes of Continental's Executive Board, which now comprised nine persons and was holding on firmly to the principle of collective management with no designated chairman, even though Opel had long insisted that Continental's size now necessitated such an appointment. At von Opel's request, Dr. Georg Göbel was then at least appointed spokesperson of the Executive Board on January 1, 1964, though this had little effect on the cumbersome decision-making processes. Von Opel was also skeptical about the importance the Executive Board placed on entry into the plastics market. Sufficient profits in this sector were only possible with concerns of a certain size, which Continental was still far from reaching, he commented at a Supervisory Board meeting in January 1964. Additionally, the Executive Board faced harsh criticism for its handling of the tire business. In view of the enormous growth figures in the automotive industry, von Opel considered Continental's growth rates "very modest." Once again, he penned one of his peculiarly worded letters to Continental's Executive Board. In September 1964, in light of the labor shortage that even migrant workers from other European countries were unable to fill, he suggested hiring Chinese workers. In America, this had worked just fine, he opined. Two years later, he went to considerable lengths to convince the Executive Board, in its search for new and lucrative business areas, to start producing plastic ski runs, as they were the latest trend in the USA and should also be of interest to Continental due to the global popularity of skiing as a leisure activity. Continental, he suggested, was presumably unaware of this because "contact with the USA no longer exists," and such ski runs would of course only become popular if a cheap surface material were developed, but "development is not Continental's thing."

These lines clearly expressed the gap that had grown between von Opel and the company by this time, as well as his disappointment with its development up to this point. In May 1966, when Georg von Opel held the 100th Supervisory Board meeting at Continental, the share price was a source of displeasure as it had slumped significantly and been in decline for many years. The two capital increases in 1965 and 1966, from 140 million German marks to 266 million German marks in total, in which Georg von Opel had been involved, also considerably burdened him as a major shareholder, having torn large holes in his finances and even forcing him to take out extensive loans. He saw that Continental was heading for a crisis long before the Executive Board, yet his warnings were ignored and action was even taken to ensure they did not reach the public. In July 1967, von Opel wrote to Göbel complaining vehemently that his statements about the increasingly strong invasion of the Americans, including in the tire industry, had not been published in the media. "I suspect that here, once again, some overanxious person—of which there are many at Continental—stopped this going to the press. One thing is certain: if we try to fight a battle the way the Americans did in South Vietnam, then Continental is lost." Von Opel was also displeased with the excessive use of external consultants that had now become commonplace in the company and their lack of transparency, which he viewed as a symptom of the Executive Board's long-running insecurity and indecisiveness. Additionally, he saw that the Executive Board was pretending problems did not exist. The Supervisory Board was regularly provided with extensive reports, peppered with lots of figures and above all forecasting a highly optimistic, rosy future but, as von Opel warned in March 1967, "too little attention is paid to the company's current problems." At the Supervisory Board meeting in September 1967, von Opel emphasized the particular importance of the meeting, "as the situation at Continental is more serious than ever before. Decisions vital to the future of Continental need to be made. It is imperative Continental avoids the fate of Borgward or Glas, for example." One solution about which speculation was already rife at the time, concerning possible restructuring mergers between struggling German rubber and tire companies such as Metzeler, was dismissed by von Opel. "One day, the expansion policy pursued by Mr. Kaus will end badly, and overnight Metzeler will find itself in a very difficult situation," he accurately predicted in March 1966. He also held a critical view of the talks that occurred a little later between Continental's Executive Board and Pirelli, Dunlop and Michelin concerning the creation of a European tire group as a counterweight to the seemingly all-powerful Americans, although he did not oppose further negotiations.

In the fall of 1969, the von Opel family sold its remaining Continental shares of around 20 percent, half of which belonged to Georg von Opel himself, to Deutsche Bank. The transaction was completed relatively quietly and protected the company's interests, unlike a sale to an external foreign party, from whom von Opel certainly could have demanded a better price but which would have brought incalculable interests into play. He did in fact receive a lucrative offer from Dunlop, which was interested in purchasing the Continental shares and integrating the German Dunlop subsidiary into the new company. However, von Opel preferred a national solution to the problems facing the German tire industry. On October 23, 1969, "in the hope that better developments are in store for Continental in the near future," Georg von Opel handed over his chairmanship of the Supervisory Board to Dr. Karl Klasen, executive board member of Deutsche Bank, but remained a member of the Supervisory Board. At the beginning of July 1971, he spoke up again at the Annual Shareholders' Meeting, this time strongly criticizing the merger between Continental and Phoenix, by now a much talked about topic. "In my opinion, Phoenix is currently on two crutches while Continental is on one. I therefore do not expect much from this triple jump of a merger, or rather the high jump that Continental and the young people running it will be forced to make. To negotiate correctly, it is in the best interests of all that Continental appoints a general director as quickly as possible!" However, it took until April 1973 before such a position was created, albeit under another title, and assigned to Dr. Carl H. Hahn. Georg von Opel did not live to see this chapter in Continental's history, however. A few weeks after his speech at the Annual Shareholders' Meeting on August 14, 1971, he passed away suddenly. For decades, the von Opel family had been a reliable key shareholder of Continental. Ultimately, however, they were unable to counter the Executive Board and Supervisory Board's differing perceptions of the economic realities and corporate development of Continental, which had been drifting apart since the early 1960s. The courage to make drastic changes to the Executive Board in due time was lacking, and there was probably little support for such measures among the other major shareholders such as Deutsche and Dresdner Bank. But even for a company like Phoenix, which had caught up with Continental in the post-war years and enjoyed a great rise thanks to its charismatic chief executive Otto A. Friedrich and a long-term participation by Firestone, the future looked bleak by the end of the 1960s, with the existential crisis that was to hit the German tire industry also affecting the company.

Alfred Herrhausen and Carl H. Hahn: Steering Continental through the Major Crisis

In the years that followed, two personalities shaped Continental's development, each in his own way, with different roles and personalities and for different durations, yet they were in many respects closely interwoven: Alfred Herrhausen, executive board member of Deutsche Bank and chairman of the Supervisory Board at Continental from October 1970 to November 1989, and Carl H. Hahn, chairman of Continental's Executive Board from April 1973 to December 1981. Both led the company through the biggest and longest crisis it had experienced to date with a mix of persistently pursued plans about industrial policy, various restructuring attempts (some of which desperate), a bold forward-looking strategy and a tough rehabilitation policy. The phase in which they were active also represented the start and end of "Deutschland AG"—a term used to describe the period of close involvement of major banks and insurance companies as key shareholders in German industrial companies. When Alfred Herrhausen was appointed to the Supervisory Board on October 16, 1970, and became its new chairman just a month later, on November 19, Continental was already in free fall. Unusually, Herrhausen was not elected by an Annual Shareholders' Meeting but instead was appointed by the court in accordance with Section 104 of the German Stock Corporation Act (*Aktiengesetz*). After von Opel stepped down as chairman of the Supervisory Board, the position was initially filled by Karl Klasen. Klasen was an executive board member of Deutsche Bank and had sat on Continental's Supervisory Board since July 1953, with Deutsche Bank having already reentered

Continental and acquiring shares since the early 1950s. However, shortly after, Klasen was elected as president of the Deutsche Bundesbank (the central bank of the Federal Republic of Germany) and handed over his office as chairman of Continental's Supervisory Board to Hans Janberg, another executive board member of Deutsche Bank. Janberg unexpectedly died only two and a half months later, however, and Herrhausen had to step in at only 40 years of age. Within a year, Continental's Supervisory Board had had four chairmen, which may be one of the reasons why it almost completely failed to provide the consulting and overseeing functions that were urgently needed by the increasingly insecure Executive Board in these turbulent times.

Herrhausen not only came from a different generation than the Executive Board but also from a different industrial era, and had a much clearer perception of the dramatic situation facing Continental from the outset. In the cross-ply tire business, low-cost imports—which became even more affordable as a result of the revaluation of the German mark—combined with increasing wage costs at Continental itself were putting the company under pressure; at the same time, Continental was fighting a losing battle when it came to manufacturing and sales of radial ply tires. In the early 1970s, Continental was in the midst of a restructuring process when a macroeconomic downturn began. Its workforce was too large—by a rough estimate, it had 2,000 to 2,500 too many waged and salaried employees in 1971. However, the actual number of layoffs were to be much higher in the end. The first task for Herrhausen in office, however, was to celebrate Continental's 100th anniversary. At the celebrations on October 8, 1971, he gave a memorable speech on the "risks and opportunities of democracy" and the reasons why large sections of the general population were dissatisfied with the social market economy system and its perceived shortcomings—a speech worth rereading today more than ever. Against the backdrop of the 1968 movement, the reverberations of which were still being felt, and the acute debate on co-determination, Herrhausen saw companies confronted with a social transformation for which they were insufficiently prepared. Although the next generation was only slightly younger than Herrhausen, he was unable to understand their rebellion, as well as the radicalized dissatisfaction with the status quo, such as in the rise of the Red Army Faction (RAF), a West German far-left militant group. But the changing social climate gave him great concern, and he tried to find explanations to counter the discontent. "For him, it was clear that the Federal Republic's economic and social model had to be defended against its critics" (Sattler). Never before had there been a German manager who contemplated fundamental sociopolitical questions such as "What is our current reality, what is it concerned with, what are we concerned with?" with similar analytical depth, nor has there been since.

At this time, Herrhausen was already intensively involved in the industrial policy efforts of Deutsche Bank to rehabilitate the German rubber and tire industry, the focus of which was a merger between Phoenix and Continental. Deutsche Bank held a majority of shares in Hamburg-based rubber company Phoenix, and the CEO of Deutsche Bank, Hermann Josef Abs, was also the chairman of Phoenix's Supervisory Board. Nothing therefore appeared to stand in the way of a rapid merger of the two companies, particularly as the logic behind the attempts appeared sound in terms of industrial policy. However, Deutsche Bank and above all Herrhausen himself had not reckoned with the stubborn resistance and active policies of obstruction on the part of the executive boards, in particular on the Phoenix side. Nor had he taken into account the disagreements between the other major shareholders at Continental: the chemical group Bayer, Dresdner Bank, and the two insurance groups Allianz and Münchner Rück. All major shareholders had pooled their shares in a holding company named "Corona"—a move that further fueled sociopolitical criticism of the domination of financial capital over private property and the working class—but coordinating their different interests and the varying industrial policies and strategies proved to be far more complex than Herrhausen expected. Dozens of attempts at a merger of Continental and Phoenix failed between 1970 in 1973, some of which were very advanced. All of this diverted attention away from the necessary restructuring effects and caused insecurity and paralysis among the respective management and workforce. As early as March 1972, Herrhausen asked himself why he, as chairman of the Supervisory Board, had not intervened earlier in the half-hearted and ineffective restructuring efforts of the Executive Board, before coming to the conclusion that he had clearly been blinded by the Executive Board's overly optimistic forecasts, figures and information, which were far removed from reality. In the spring of 1973, he finally brought in Carl H. Hahn as the new chairman of the Executive Board—the first in Continental's post-war history, with the board having merely consisted of members that co-ruled as colleagues since 1951—to at last press on with Continental's internal restructuring.

Carl H. Hahn came from an industrial family that had been closely connected to the automotive industry in Germany right from its start. His father was one of the co-founders of Auto Union in 1932. After studying economics and political science, Hahn joined Volkswagen in Wolfsburg in December 1954, where he first worked as an assistant to the legendary VW head Heinrich Nordhoff. From

Fig. 26: Carl H. Hahn as Executive Board chairman in 1974.

1959 to 1964, he headed Volkswagen of America and conquered the USA with the VW Beetle. During this time, Hahn significantly contributed to the Volkswagen corporation's extraordinary export success in North America, which resulted in his appointment to the executive board of VW in 1964, at the age of 38. There, however, Hahn was confronted with growing differences and conflicts regarding the strategic orientation and corporate policy of the automotive group, with the result that nothing stood in the way of Herrhausen tempting him away to be appointed as chairman of Continental's Executive Board. In the following years, he implemented a hard restructuring program that left no stone unturned. Within two years, 4,500 employees were laid off, the convoluted and unprofitable investment business was restructured, and production processes were modernized, which significantly improved profitability. Hahn also had no qualms about disposing of Continental symbols. In November 1973, he sold the Continental high-rise building, the landmark of the corporation, and then leased it under a sale-leaseback arrangement. Not least, Hahn broke with the old Continental habit of producing thick situational reviews and operational reports filled with dressed-up, obfuscating figures that were anything but transparent. Instead, the Executive Board's situational reports, whether written or spoken, now contained unvarnished, self-critical and plain statements. Mere weeks after taking office, at the Supervisory Board meeting in May 1973, Hahn indicated the new tone that was to become commonplace at Continental and in communication with the public for the first time. There was a debate about whether or not the company's real loss should also be publicly reported, i.e. whether, in its communication with the workforce and shareholders, cosmetic balance sheets or true balance sheets should be used. At this point in time, the total assets corresponded to the sales figures, which implied a loss of 41 million and meant that Continental would, in everyone's eyes, appear to have fared the worst of all its competitors in the German rubber industry, as Herrhausen admitted with frustration. The Supervisory Board followed Hahn's suggestion and resolved to issue a corresponding press release. For the first time in Continental's history, its balance sheet showed a loss.

Hahn also largely disempowered the remaining aging members of the Executive Board by assigning general power of representation to a group of young executives, who then moved up as new members of the Executive Board shortly afterwards, thus completing the long overdue generational change in company management. In the years that followed, Hahn set out to eliminate Continental's biggest problem areas: outdated technology, archaic research and development structures, run-down factories with low productivity and high personnel costs, inefficient sales channels, and poor working conditions for the workforce, which had led to severe quality problems. This cleanup had to be done under enormous time pressure, as sales continued to fall, the company continued to incur rising losses, and its debt increased rapidly. With a policy of "management by walking around," which at first glance seemed quaint but in fact had considerable value, not least because of its symbolic effect, he promoted solidarity and created a sense of a new beginning among Continental employees. Hahn was a regular guest at the works meetings in the plants, both to make the gravity of the situation clear to the staff and impress upon them that the road back to being in the black was still filled with thorns, but also to describe the measures initiated by the Executive Board to find a way out of the crisis as quickly as possible. As early as March 1974, Hahn also adopted a policy of cooperation with strong international partners, in this case the US tire group United States Rubber Co. (Uniroyal), which had taken over the long-standing Belgian company Englebert as part of its expansion policy in Europe and whose plant in Aachen was also Uniroyal's European headquarters. In May 1975, Hahn presented a "long-term plan for Continental: 1975 to 1979" to the Supervisory Board for the first time. It consisted of "minimum goals for Continental's survival," and the short time span of just four years clearly shows the extent to which the company could only be steered by sight or, in some cases, through thick fog.

Despite all the radical measures, success was slow and frequently interrupted by new setbacks. In the fall of 1976, three and a half years after Hahn took office, the figures were still in the red, not only in the tire sector but also for technical products. From an employee perspective, Continental had now been fighting for survival for five years. Almost 10,000 employees had had to leave Continental since 1970, but the layoffs had not brought about a turnaround. However, without the reduction in wage and salary costs that resulted from the redundancies, the company would probably have incurred a loss of 145 million German marks by 1972, i.e. more than half of the share capital, and would not have survived into 1974. In view of this, Herrhausen increasingly believed that the unprofitable tire business should be sold, which would mean Continental departing from its traditional area of business, but his suggestion met with strong resistance from Hahn. At the Supervisory Board meeting in December 1976, he pointed out that losses were also accumulating in the technical products business, and at this point in time, no one would want tire plants if they were given them for free, let alone pay money for them. "The question arises as to whether Continental should withdraw from the tire business. Since this decision would mean liquidation of the company, Continental must pursue a tire policy offensive," he pleaded. Although Continental had now "reached the limit of creditworthiness" and had no more room for financial maneuver, Hahn chose to forge ahead. At first, this took the shape of considering new cooperations and mergers, potentially with Munich-based tire company Metzeler, which had the financial strength of its major shareholder Bayer behind it, and another with Phoenix, where renewed attempts were made to convince its executive board to approve the merger. However, by the end of 1977 at the latest, Herrhausen and Hahn had to admit that these efforts had failed again. Continental was still caught up in the vicious circle of structural problems across the entire industry, shrinking markets with overcapacity, falling sales as a result of increasingly fierce price disputes and in-house problems. Continental's brand was also rapidly losing its shine and was in urgent need of a repolish. "We have a good reputation," Hahn said openly in a discussion with shareholder representatives in May 1977, "but this is rooted in the subconscious. We all remember the 1960s, but today's 20-year-olds have grown up in the Michelin world." One ray of light on the horizon was that the business with conveyor belts, foam materials and tubes, with its broad range of products, was now back in the black to offset the unprofitable tire sector. And in the course of 1977, the passenger and light truck tire business, which had been incurring losses for many years, was no longer in the red. For the first time, a double-digit net income could be reported again, with 20.2 million German marks, though the next crash was to follow soon after in 1978. For shareholders, this was the seventh year without dividends. The major shareholders, especially Herrhausen, felt increasingly resigned and were becoming convinced that Continental would "ultimately bleed to death from the tire sector." The difficulties of the industry at large caused all visible successes and improvements to shrink to comparatively marginal sizes. At the same time, however, he still felt an obligation to continue. At the Annual Shareholders' Meeting in June 1978, he commented: "It is a Herculean task to put a large company, in which nothing was the way it should be, back in order—but this is what we will continue to do."

In December 1978, however, it became clear that Continental was still fighting for survival. Its operating result was minus 30 million German marks, and once again, the tire business played a major role in the loss, with a dramatic decline to minus 45.2 million German marks. At the Supervisory Board meeting on December 15, 1978, the nerves of the members of the Executive Board and the Supervisory Board were therefore on edge. For the first time there was also an open dispute between Herrhausen and Hahn, which ranged from the exact causes of the worsening operating costs to the general policy of the major shareholders, whom Hahn admonished. "Continental has not only received no support from shareholders, but the shareholders have fought each other like the worst of enemies in a wartime scenario." Hahn was quite justified in his criticism. Herrhausen's problem was that, for shareholder Münchner Rück, the stake in Continental had long become a troublesome, low-yield investment, while Bayer, with its stake in Metzeler, was pursuing its own policy of streamlining the industry structure, with a focus on selling its own synthetic rubber raw materials. It is indeed legitimate to ask whether Herrhausen's search for a purely German solution to the rubber industry's problems might have been, to a certain extent, pressured and dictated by the specific interests of major Deutsche Bank customer Bayer, whose sole focus during merger talks was on securing sales for the synthetic rubber of its subsidiary Chemische Werke Hüls AG (CWH). "There is an agreement between Deutsche Bank and Bayer," states an internal memo dated April 1971, "according to which DB will provide cover for the Conti and Phoenix package only if the raw material interests of Bayer and Hüls are safeguarded." In the meantime, however, Deutsche Bank found itself increasingly alone with its far-reaching industrial policy plans, meaning that, at the end of the day, Continental's seemingly stable large shareholder structure on the outside did not actually provide stability and support, but rather the exact opposite. By now, even Herrhausen had to admit this. In the end, a feeling of helplessness had spread. Under the "prevailing conditions," there was no recipe for "guaranteeing the survival chances of Continental," said Herrhausen at the Supervisory Board meeting. He remarked that he had "for years been fighting for Continental's survival with all his available energy," but he was now bereft of ideas and no longer knew what else to do. Such open, honest and undoctored statements from a chairman of the Supervisory Board are probably unique in Germany's corporate and industrial history, especially since they have been documented and handed down for posterity. Today this would no longer be possible, particularly due to changes in how the minutes of Supervisory Board meetings are recorded. Meanwhile, at the same Supervisory Board meeting, Hahn strongly advocated the continuation of the tire strategy offensive. While Continental's earlier German competitors, such as Phoenix and Metzeler, were closing their tire factories one by one, Continental had no other strategy or alternative but to continue on its chosen path. Hahn was aware that Continental could not expect any support from the German automotive industry, which at the time was suffering due to extreme cost pressure from Japanese competitors.

The breakthrough came in July 1979 with the purchase of Uniroyal's European business, as part of which Continental acquired four tire plants in Belgium, Germany, France and Scotland, finally attaining the critical size needed to be a player on the international tire market again. In the European tire industry, this shifted Continental from seventh to third place. The financing of this coup, which Herrhausen himself described as a risky "ride over Lake Constance," was cleverly devised by CFO Horst W. Urban and Herrhausen's staff. With Continental's precarious situation preventing either a capital increase or the issue of a bond on the capital market, they came up with the idea of taking out unsecured loans from a number of major investors, which could then be exchanged later for marketable convertible bonds or shares. At the same time, Hahn was also negotiating another coup that would have significantly increased Continental's European focus: the acquisition of French tire company Kléber. Despite intensive negotiations with Michelin, however, this project fell through in the summer of 1980. In fall 1981, Hahn therefore initiated new merger and cooperation talks, this time with Pirelli, for Continental to acquire Pirelli's tire division and, in turn, hand over its technical products business to the Italians. However, negotiations were still in progress when Hahn returned to VW to take over as chief executive in 1982.

Alfred Herrhausen and Carl H. Hahn: Steering Continental through the Major Crisis — 91

Fig. 27: Annual Shareholders' Meeting on September 7, 1979 (from left: Alfred Herrhausen, Albert Englebert (member of the Supervisory Board), Helmut Werner (member of the Executive Board) and Carl H. Hahn.

Over the years, Herrhausen and Hahn, four years his junior, became congenial partners who shared the unconditional will to rehabilitate Continental, even if they often had different opinions about the means and methods, and, above all, the speed with which the changes were to be implemented. Without Herrhausen's support and his calming influence on Deutsche Bank and other major shareholders, Hahn's rehabilitation policy is unlikely to have succeeded. The willingness to go the distance would have been lacking on the part of the company. And without Hahn's boldness, determination and hands-on attitude, with which he also occasionally disregarded the opinion of the chairman of the Supervisory Board, Herrhausen's mission to create an internationally competitive German rubber and tire industry would also have failed. He himself often had great doubts whether it would succeed. Hahn had led Continental to a successful turnaround, set the company onto a new course and laid the groundwork for its future corporate policy. However, when he left the company in December 1981 and returned to VW to become the new chief executive, the transition that had been initiated was by no means complete and the existential problems had not yet been conclusively averted. As recently as March 1980, Hahn had announced that there had been "a significant upturn after difficult years," and thus proclaimed the end of the long crisis. A net income of 12.7 million German marks had been achieved that year, but another massive slump followed the year after, in part due to the economic circumstances, and Continental was once again forced to declare a loss of 17.8 million German marks.

It was not until 1983 that Continental could be considered to have achieved a lasting recovery, accompanied by steady growth in sales and profit. For almost 12 years, Continental had struggled to survive. This had been the longest crisis phase in the company's history and more than once, its fate had hung in the balance. In the fall of 1982, however, Herrhausen and Deutsche Bank were once again the focus of public attention, as rumors of a possible sale of their Continental shares to Goodyear arose—rumors that persisted in the following years. Despite Herrhausen vehemently denying such intentions, there was considerable mistrust among both the Continental Executive Board and the Works Councils at the time. This was just one sign that the relationship between the Supervisory Board and the Executive Board had changed since the acquisition of Uniroyal. Since the coup, which he had engineered largely on his own initiative, Hahn had become much more confident in his dealings with Herrhausen and provided him with only scant information about the operative business. When details of the negotiations with Michelin and Kléber appeared in the press before the Supervisory Board was officially informed, Herrhausen erupted in a fit of anger. Moreover, Herrhausen did not learn until afterward, in the autumn of 1980, of Continental's risky foreign exchange dealings, which it had undertaken on its own initiative without consulting Deutsche Bank and which had resulted in losses of 5.5 million German marks. This attitude continued under the leadership of Helmut Werner, who succeeded Hahn as chairman of the Executive Board in 1982. In effect, this meant Herrhausen was faced with a proper "partial loss of control" (Sattler). In 1983, Deutsche Bank eventually sold the majority of its Continental shares, but it was done quietly on the regular stock exchange, a move that apparently surprised Herrhausen himself.

Herrhausen remained as chairman of the Supervisory Board but no longer pursued any major projects during these years, which were now not necessary considering Continental's newfound growth trajectory. Under Werner, who came from Uniroyal, Continental once again underwent a certain amount of Americanization. With a sophisticated multi-brand strategy and intensified innovation management, as well as strategic alliances with American and Japanese tire companies, Werner further promoted Europeanization and internationalization at Continental. Just shy of six years later, in November 1987, Werner then handed over management of the company to Horst W. Urban, who had been the CFO up to that point, and moved to Daimler Benz. A consolidated net income of 77.2 million German marks was reported in 1985, which climbed to 200 million German marks by 1988. On November 30, 1989, shortly before Continental announced new record sales and profit figures, Herrhausen was murdered in an attack by the left-wing militant Red Army Faction (RAF). Nevertheless, his death and Deutsche Bank's widespread withdrawal by no means put an end to the long-term industrial participation at Continental. Even after 1983, Deutsche Bank still retained about 5 percent of the shares, and in 1990/91, in connection with the attempted takeover by Pirelli, it was to increase its share again and become a major player, albeit only behind the scenes, in the ensuing struggle. A complete exit only followed in November 2002, when Deutsche Bank informed the administration in Hanover that it had sold its Continental shares of 7.65 percent to a large number of institutional investors.

Two Takeover Attempts and the Search for a Key Shareholder: Turbulent Corporate Governance Structures Between 1990 and 2010

Corporate governance structures at Continental went through many turbulent changes from the 1990s to the present, with two acquisitions in particular, both deemed hostile by the members of the Executive Board at the time, playing a major role—a failed attempt by Pirelli in 1990/91 and another by Schaeffler in 2008, which ultimately succeeded. The incidents considerably strained the relationship between the Executive Board and the Supervisory Board, due more to publicly anticipated perceptions of differences in interests to the other relevant managing body rather than to these actually having existed, but which nonetheless led to grave mistrust. However, the period was also characterized by a great deal of fluctuation on the Executive Board and by a further generational change at management level. In April 1997, the first woman was appointed to an executive position at Continental, albeit only as general authorized representative for purchasing and strategic tire technology, with a position on the Executive Board itself still being out of her reach. Continental's Executive Board remained a traditional gentlemen's affair until 2012. The Supervisory Board also had a dynamic turnover. In the context of the two hostile takeover attempts and thereafter, fluctuation among the members of the Executive and Supervisory Boards increased. After "Deutschland AG" was broken up and with it the era of large shareholders from banking and insurance, broadening shareholder capitalism saw Continental enter an era of free flotation, with rapidly growing investments by institutional and in particular foreign investors. With private equity companies, entirely new players and stakeholders entered the field.

Even after Hahn left Continental, Pirelli continued the negotiations on cooperation and agreement he himself had initiated—first with Herrhausen, then with his successor, Ulrich Weiss, who was both chairman of the Supervisory Board at Continental and an executive board member at Deutsche Bank. Continental's Executive Board was unaware of these negotiations and therefore surprised when, in mid-September 1990, Pirelli publicly submitted its offer of a merger, coupled with the information that, together with partner companies such as Mediobanca and Fiat, it held significant shares in Continental and would make their weight felt accordingly at future Annual Shareholders' Meetings. The lack of protection from a large key shareholder had long since turned Continental into a publicly discussed takeover candidate, with speculation about possible new major shareholders ranging from VW and the Flick corporation to Goodyear and speculative investors—feared at the time as dreaded raiders who were redefining the financial scene in Europe. Yet Pirelli was as interested as ever in acquiring Continental. Under the telling code name "Varus," Continental's Executive Board then developed a defensive strategy to foil the Italian takeover, with armies of external consultants and business attorneys playing a key role. At an extraordinary Shareholders' Meeting on March 13, 1991, the first battle was won when the majority of shareholders rejected the merger, but the confrontation dragged on, mainly due to internal differences between Weiss and Urban as chairs of the Supervisory and Executive Boards respectively. This went so far that the Executive Board, suspicious of the position of the Supervisory Board and the potential strategic considerations and interests of Deutsche Bank, prepared its own versions of board meeting minutes and internal consultations for the Supervisory Board. It was not until April 1993, when Pirelli finally ended its involvement in Continental shares and options, that the chapter was considered closed. Yet it had led to high costs—in terms of energy, money and reputation—and caused the heads of the chairmen of the respective executive boards to roll.

Fig. 28: Extraordinary Shareholders' Meeting on March 13, 1991.
At the podium: Ulrich Weiss, chairman of the Supervisory Board.

The case caused a sensation, not least because it ventured into new territory in many areas of stock corporation law and corporate governance—though the term itself was not yet in use. Dozens of specialist lawyers subsequently dealt with the question of the admissibility of restrictions on voting rights, limits of executive board and company management conduct in case of shareholder changes, and the obligation to maintain strict neutrality i.e. the right to exercise influence on shareholder groups. The Continental Executive Board's decidedly defensive conduct certainly went against the prevailing opinion at the time that the hands of the board were tied and that it was forced to bend to the will of the potential majority shareholder. One of the conclusions was that the topics of shareholder structure and conduct were not seen as taboo for the Executive Board and Supervisory Board but rather as a constant challenge that, in the company's interest, also implied continuous monitoring of the capital market and sufficient acceptance of the company among shareholders, in particular in the form of as high a share price as possible. In May 2002, as part of the legalization (and complexification) of the corporate governance constitution, Continental also formulated and officially established corresponding principles for the first time, taking into account the provisions of the German Stock Corporation Act that had since been further developed. "Good corporate governance" was taken to mean responsible and transparent corporate leadership and oversight aimed at creating value and through which the trust of shareholders, customers, employees and the public was won and strengthened. Six years later, these rules were put to the test and, as developments at the time showed, failed to pass muster.

The starting point for the second takeover event in summer 2008 was completely different than that in 2001, but was ultimately a consequence of the first. By now, Hubertus von Grünberg had taken over as chairman of the Executive Board, but the shareholder structure of Continental had not changed much in the meantime. In 1994, Deutsche Bank, Nord/LB, Dresdner Bank and Allianz, which held between 5 and 17 percent of the shares, were only major shareholders in a restricted sense, while what was referred to as the free float amounted to 60 percent. This had changed somewhat by 2005, to the extent that there were only two major shareholders, the insurance corporations AXA and Allianz, with 10 percent each, while the free float amounted to 80 percent. This once again made Continental a potential takeover candidate, despite the now significantly increased share price, but the Executive Board and the Supervisory Board—which both found a takeover equally undesirable—thought any pursuing party would come from China. At companies such as VW, BMW, Bosch and ZF, the Chinese, who were forcefully pushing into the German automotive and supplier industry, were facing insurmountable obstacles due to foundation structures, state participation, familial anchor shareholders and other regulations regarding shareholder structures. Only at Continental were they met with virtually open doors. "We do not want to end up as the subsidiary of a Chinese corporation," announced Manfred Wennemer, Continental's Executive Board chairman at the time, in the spring of 2005. In summer 2006, however, the Executive Board was suddenly confronted with a takeover attempt by private equity company Bain Capital, which though rejected, raised initial doubts as to whether the Executive Board and Supervisory Board were still pulling in the same direction. In 2007, Wennemer and von Grünberg contacted Maria-Elisabeth Schaeffler who, together with her son, owned the automotive supplier of the same name based in Herzogenaurach. They presented the idea of her taking on the role of a "Johanna Quandt of Continental" in the future (the "grande dame" of the German automotive industry) and acting as a key shareholder with a blocking minority of approximately 15 percent. Schaeffler signaled her willingness to do so, but in spring 2008, Continental was suddenly confronted by the Schaeffler corporate group's demand for a 30% share. This was followed by dozens of formal and informal talks between the responsible parties at both companies, concluding in July 2008 with the announcement of a very large participation and the revelation that Schaeffler already directly and indirectly held 36 percent of Continental's shares. The relationship between the two companies was further burdened by the fact that confidential information from the meetings was regularly leaked to the media.

Fig. 29: Annual Shareholders' Meeting in March 2008.

A real battle between the two companies ensued, which to a large extent was also fought publicly, involving numerous parties, armies of external consultants and the media. The latter also played a significant role in the dispute, as the mix of speculation, leaked confidential information and official statements distributed by the respective press departments contributed to the confusion of the situation and the rapid souring of relations between Continental and Schaeffler. The large number of different interests of those involved and the impending stock market crisis led to the situation spiraling completely out of hand and personal relationships of trust being destroyed. For a time, Continental turned into a plaything of the seemingly new rules and mechanisms of financial market capitalism. Most importantly though, assessments of the situation and options of the Supervisory Board and Executive Board were once again controversial, just as in 2001 in Hanover. Under the code name "Project Comet," Wennemer developed a defensive strategy against Schaeffler's takeover attempt, which by this time was long deemed hostile and in his eyes was aimed solely at breaking Continental apart. This focused on getting the BaFin (Germany's Federal Financial Supervisory Authority) to classify the "Schaeffler swap"—the possibly fraudulent method by which the 36 percent share of Continental had been acquired—as unlawful. His attempt failed. In August, an extensive investor agreement was concluded with Schaeffler, detailing its future role as major shareholder with a maximum investment limit of 49.9 percent of the share capital until 2012 and including commitments regarding the preservation of the sites and corporate structure, i.e. no break-up of the corporation. Wennemer stepped down from his position after the Supervisory Board gave the green light for this negotiated investor agreement. At the beginning of January 2009, Schaeffler's takeover bid was finalized and the investor agreement came into force. However, in the interim, the severe capital market crisis and the stock market crash that followed the Lehman insolvency in September 2008 had resulted in massive turbulence that threatened to sink Schaeffler, and Continental with it. In addition, further negotiations between Continental and Schaeffler regarding the various possible future scenarios for the two automotive suppliers revealed persistent differences. "Highly confidential information" circulated through the press, with the claim that von Grünberg was thinking about spinning off Continental's rubber business—as part of a management buyout and with the help of major investment companies such as KKR and Goldman Sachs—and then merging it with Goodyear. In the spring of 2009, this caused a rift between Schaeffler and von Grünberg, who resigned as chairman of the Supervisory Board in March.

It took months to steer developments back to calmer waters; in August 2009, Elmar Degenhart was appointed new chairman of the Executive Board and, in October 2009, Wolfgang Reitzle took over as chairman of the Supervisory Board. From January 2009 onward, the Schaeffler Group's stake in Continental consistently amounted to 49.9%. A capital increase at the beginning of 2010 lowered this percentage to 42.17%; in 2012, acquisition of shares held and sold by banks brought the figure back to 49.9% before finally, in 2013, it was reduced to 46.0% as the result of a sell-off. This caused the free float to increase to 54 percent again, but also brought new blood into the circle of Continental shareholders, such as the wealth manager and major investor Black Rock, with 4.49 percent of the shares. Since then, the shareholder structure has remained relatively stable. The original objective of the search for a key shareholder at Continental was thus achieved after all.

3 The People of Continental Identities and Interests in Times of Upheaval in the Working World

"Homo Continentalis" probably never existed, even if he is a consistent presence in various sources. It would actually be more accurate to refer to the "people of Continental," since the proportion of women in the Continental workforce, both on the factory floor and in the offices, has always been significant. Capturing the respective identities and interests of employees in a historical review, even a cursory outline, is a complex task. When and how did a Continental employee become a "person of Continental"? It could be based on the historical process of creating class consciousness in the workforce. Accordingly, a process of identity building and self-understanding could be established for all Continental staff, for the entire workforce as a collective, in which they were, on the one hand, an object of company social and wage policy, and on the other, developing a growing self-confidence as "people of Continental" and therefore active subjects in their own right with their own interests and a willingness to fight for them. The development from being a "Continental employee per se," i.e. as an object, to a "Continental employee for themselves," i.e. as a subject, was not a linear process from the 19th century to the present, but was more ambivalent and uneven. In most cases there was a level of congruence between company and employee interests, but time and again throughout the company's history, class struggles and conflicts of interest erupted, which—albeit rarely—led to public protests, work stoppages and strikes. The process of promoting identification and creating an identity among employees was often controlled "from above" through corporate policy, through operational social policy, corporate-ideological objectives, and identification- and loyalty-promoting measures, the aim of which was primarily to boost quality and productivity, but mostly it was effected by conveying corporate culture values, a process which became all the more important as the workforce became more heterogeneous, larger and more complex. However, the process also took on an uncontrolled momentum of its own.

 The employees developed multiple identities and self-images in this process—as blue-collar or white-collar workers, a status awareness that ultimately dissolved into a general concept of employee status, or as employees with a strong location identity, i.e. as "Limmeraners," "Stöckeners," "Uniroyalists," or "Korbachers," "Tevesians" or "Ate-Isten," or VDOer at the existing traditional locations. These were joined by the employees from the dozens of small and medium-sized companies who together shaped the heterogeneous and "multicultural" ContiTech over the decades. In the meantime, the overarching corporate identity immediately came into play in the newly established greenfield operations. However, the identities and self-image of the "people of Continental" were also heavily influenced by the products they manufactured (and their pride in them) and their often interconnected hierarchies in the working world. For decades, tire builders were the elite of the employees, not just compared to those who had to do the dirtier work in the compound units, i.e. mixing facilities and calendar halls, but also compared to the "non-tire people" who produced the technical or surgical rubber items, as well as the countless consumer goods formerly made from rubber such as balls and dolls. However, further differentiations were made here with the "automotive people" and their visible and increasingly invisible products. Over the years, individual elements of these multi-layered identities faded away (among other things, when locations were closed, but also because the people concerned later identified themselves as simply being Continental employees), some were also suppressed by ideologies imposed on them (particularly during the Nazi era), while others strengthened over time.

 Diversity has always been an issue for corporate management, even though it has had different names in the past: after the merger in 1929 and the arrival of employees from four other companies, after 1939/40 with the deployment of foreign forced laborers, in the 1960s during the recruitment of "guest workers," and finally since 1979, and especially in the 1990s and afterward, when the internationalization and globalization of corporate activities meant new production sites initially in Europe, then in the USA, and finally worldwide with workers from a wide variety of cultures, countries and ethnicities. Even the terms themselves and with them the various different ideological bases have changed: at times, there was talk of a works community, of the workforce, the employees, the staff, of plant and company employees or members of the "great Continental family," of (regular) personnel or plant staff, or of human resources. However, the focus was never just on identification and self-confidence, but also on the power processes within the company, the distribution of influence on decision-making processes and the distribution of money, whether in the form of investments, dividends or wages/salaries. It was also always about experiential processes in which the company was perceived as a place of transformation, as a political space of social partnership and co-determination in practice, as a place of solidarity and collegiality as well as a cultural space in which there was a certain pride—sometimes more, sometimes less—in being part of the company. Outside their working day, Continental also became an essential part of the Continental employees' living environment.

The Development of the Continental Workforce Through the Lens of Corporate Social and Welfare Policy (1871 to 1918)

At the beginning of this period, the company had a dozen employees; at the end, that number was approximately 4,500, almost 3,000 of whom were blue-collar workers. It was only in September 1873 that the Vahrenwald plant started production, mainly of rubber balls, hoof buffers and solid rubber tires for carriages and the first automobiles. With the start of tire production, the number of blue- and white-collar workers increased rapidly: while Continental had just under 600 employees at the beginning of the 1890s, their number rose to over 1,500 at the turn of the century, peaking at 11,590 in 1913.

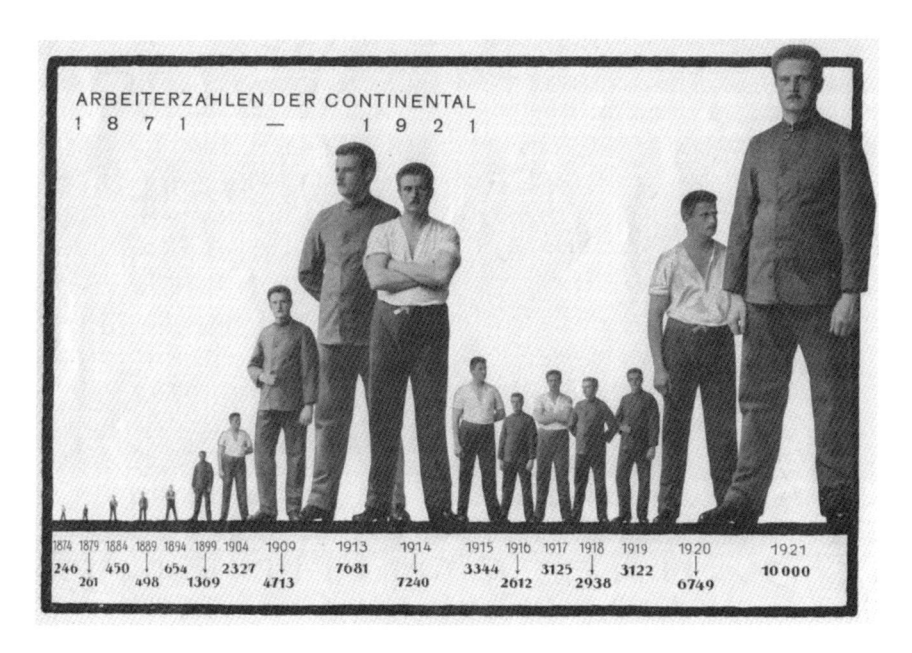

Fig. 30: Chart depicting the development of Continental workers from 1871 to 1921.

The majority of Continental's workforce came from the rural/agricultural hinterland of Hanover and were unskilled; staff turnover was very high due to the initially unfamiliar, tough and dangerous working conditions. From the 1880s and increasingly in the 1890s, corporate welfare policy measures were implemented at Continental in order to "permanently bind a cohort of capable workers to us," as described in the 1882 annual report. As early as 1872, a health benefit fund had been set up. It became a mandatory fund in 1875 and a regular company health insurance fund in 1884. In 1882, work began on the creation of a pension and disability fund "for workers and foremen who have served the establishment well." In 1892, plant associations such as the "Club of Older Workers" and the "Paraclub" were founded and construction of company dwellings began. As a result, in 1905, a company residence was built on Spittastrasse in what was then still largely the rural outskirts of Hanover. The 100 apartments there were made available primarily to white-collar workers and plant officers and soon received the nickname "the rubber village." Continental played a pioneering role, even at times beyond the rubber industry, not only because of when its corporate welfare policy was introduced but also because of its sheer scope.

One special feature was, for example, that from 1885 the company management took out life insurance for all employees with more than 10 years of service to the company, which paid out over 1,500 marks (workers) or 5,000 marks (plant officers) when they turned 65 years of age. The premiums for this were paid by the company for the duration of that employee's service and the benefit remained the property of the beneficiary even in the event of premature departure from the company. In 1911, as many as 510 employees already had one of these life insurance policies. In addition, there was a workers' fund and a "fund for the support of widows and orphans," bonuses were paid to the workforce, and all supervisors, foremen and workers who were employed at Continental for at least 10 years also enjoyed an eight- to fourteen-day vacation with full pay. In 1907, 608 employees—14 percent of the workforce (male and female)—benefited from this regulation. From 1907, there was also an annual bonus, the amount of which also depended on length of service to the company. Men who had been with Continental for at least one year received 40 marks, while their female colleagues received 20 marks. However, as in the tire industry as a whole, Continental's workforce was very young. From the age of 30, the increased migration of employees to easier and safer work in related industries became generally evident. At the turn of the century, only around 10 percent of the Continental workforce had five or more years of service. This and the corporate welfare policy of company management led to the rubber workers being relatively immune to unionization, especially since it was not until 1890 that an organizational entry point was offered in the form of the recently established "Verband der Fabrik-, Land- und gewerblichen Hilfsarbeiter Deutschlands" (Factory, Agricultural and Commercial Workers' Trade Union of Germany), or FAV for short.

Women represented a growing proportion of the workforce at Continental. Not only did they come to the company as a result of the trend toward increased bureaucratization of the industry and the resultant increase in office personnel, they also made up significant proportions of the staff of entire production departments. According to a summary of the factory organization from 1899, out of a total of 1,537 employees at Continental, 590 were women, i.e. 38.4 percent. Just under 100 of them were employed in the ball maker and ball painter hall, but 419 were also in the tire halls, where they accounted for more than half of the workers deployed there. Bicycle tire manufacturing was almost exclusively a female domain.

After the turn of the century, automation and rationalization processes found their way into the company's systems, especially in mixed rolling mills, washing rollers and vacuum driers as well as in the production of tubing and tire winding, making work easier and ensuring greater productivity. At that time, a crew of fifteen to eighteen workers was required for the production of a 40-meter-long rubber hose, twelve to fourteen of whom had the sole task of moving the hose on the table forward; after the introduction of winding machines, this same task could be performed by just one worker. In 1910, the injection molding machines developed in the USA made their way into Continental's production halls. Simple machines used in tire manufacturing now allowed a tire worker to manufacture four to five times as many tire cores in the same time, thereby significantly reducing the cost of production. In the beginning (1893), Continental produced only 10 car tires a day, but by 1912/13 output had increased to 3,000 per day. Many work processes such as rubberizing the fabric layers in the coating hall—one of the production processes with the worst working conditions due to the high risk of fire and toxic vapors—but also significant parts of the tire building process still managed to avoid the push toward mechanization. As before, the job of a rubber worker required a great deal of skill, strength and increasingly machine knowledge. In the early years, production disruptions caused by workers' lack of knowledge and inefficient use of machines were commonplace, particularly in the complicated production of car tires. A rapid response to the increased qualification requirements, such as for tire builders, by intensifying and extending the

Fig. 31: Tire production around the turn of the century (above bicycle tires, below automotive tires).

approximately six-week induction period, as was the case at Continental, quickly paid off. Shortly after the turn of the century, there was high demand for well-trained "professional rubber workers" and academically qualified rubber technicians.

Continental's company management and that of its neighbor Gummi-Kamm-Compagnie also implemented measures to make working hours more flexible, which were based on efforts to reduce working hours if possible by doing away with or shortening breaks. For example, the start of the work day at Continental was shifted from 7:00 a.m. to 7:30 a.m. and the breakfast break was omitted. As a result, the company's management had an uninterrupted period of work in the morning and, no less importantly, a rested workforce. Compared with their colleagues at other industrial plants in Hanover, rubber and tire workers' earnings were not bad, but, from today's perspective, wage rates are hard to believe. The average hourly rate was around 33 pfennigs (1892), rising to 47 pfennigs by 1913. In December 1902, a tire builder in Continental's engine hall I therefore earned between 35 and 37 marks, which amounted to a monthly wage of 130 to 145 marks, with women receiving just over half the amount of their male counterparts. However, the income and wage differences between the workers employed were considerable depending on their activity. In 1907, only 22 percent of workers received the aforementioned monthly wage, which corresponded to annual earnings of between 1,500 and 2,000 marks, 35 percent achieved average monthly salaries of just over 100 marks, and the largest share of 43 percent, including all women, only achieved average monthly wages of 80 marks, i.e. less than 1,000 marks for the whole year.

Conspicuously, Continental was almost completely spared any work stoppages. The exceptions to this were a one-day strike of 120 workers from the automotive tire department in December 1905 and brief work stoppages by machinists and heaters in February/March 1906. Having a wage level that was above the industrial average and the extensive measures introduced early on by paternalistic corporate social policy clearly had an effect. The address made to Continental workers on April 20, 1906, by director Adolf Prinzhorn was indicative of this. At the request of the Executive Board, Prinzhorn said, the previous day's Annual Shareholders' Meeting had earmarked very large sums of money "for the good of the workers." Large amounts would go, for example, to the pension fund, the widow's and orphan's fund, a workers' support fund, as a profit participation directly to the workforce members and not least in the form of voluntary benefits to the health and disability fund. "By informing you of these figures," Prinzhorn went on to say, "it is to show you that we are going far beyond our legal obligations to look after you. For us, you are not just a number that will receive a pay packet on Saturday. No, we take a very human interest in you, in your well-being and in that of your family."

At the same time, Prinzhorn also linked these words to "some serious exhortations." First:

> Every wage increase request submitted appropriately to us will be reviewed sympathetically. Never, however, will we be pressured by force or threats to give consent to something that we previously rejected following mature consideration [...] Second: we will never conduct negotiations with our workers through intermediaries who come from outside our plant. I love negotiating eye-to-eye, and I am convinced that every reasonable man and every decent woman will agree with me; and third, I wanted to say that over the course of the year, green and yellow notes have been distributed several times around 6 a.m. here at the gate. They called workers to a meeting to discuss the operating conditions at Continental and to make clear the grievances here. My colleagues and I have already told you on a number of occasions that we strongly object to our workers running off to these meeting organizers and newspaper editors to speak to them before coming to their foremen or to management here. We know very well that there are sometimes grievances within our plants. With such huge operations as ours that have grown massively in a very short space of time and now have almost 4,000 workers, it is not possible to avoid things going wrong from time to time, and we—my colleagues and I—are grateful to everyone who comes to us and says that something is not ok. And while we firmly intend to remedy such situations, sometimes things do not move as quickly as we ourselves would like. But it is our constant concern that everything be in perfect order and that our company is a model business and we make every effort to ensure that.

Prinzhorn concluded with words that, in principle, could still be found in Continental's corporate culture today:

> Only through harmonious collaboration and mutual trust can we achieve the results that we have achieved, and only then can we look after you in a manner that goes far beyond our legal obligations, as we have been doing for decades. Worker and capitalist should not fight one another. They are dependent on one another and should work together with a third factor—intelligence; without this, all will fail. If these three work together, then our factory will flourish, industry and trade will flourish, and then something extraordinary can happen for you.

Just a few months after Prinzhorn made these statements, however, the Continental Executive Board made efforts to participate in the establishment of an employer association of German rubber factories. As the Executive Board explained to the Supervisory Board, a merger of employers was as necessary as it was desirable,

> all the more so because the workers are, almost without exception, members of formal organizations or have been forced into them in the event of wage wars. [...] Unfortunately, employees in our industry too have been organized for a long time, and the strength of that organization was demonstrated during the major strike at the Gummi-Kamm-Compagnie in fall 1906. I believe that close cooperation between factories, carefully avoiding any provocation and recognizing equal rights for the employees, is the best way to prevent disputes.

However, the chairman of the Supervisory Board Bernhard Caspar expressed concerns about individual provisions of the new employers' association, particularly with regard to the conditions under which lockouts could be instigated, so that Prinzhorn resigned as association chairman in June 1907 and Continental left the association again in order to "be and remain completely independent, a gentlemen in his own house," as Caspar noted.

The workers in the Gummi-Kamm-Compagnie in neighboring Limmer proved themselves to be far better organized than the Continental workers and also far more self-assured in terms of representing their own interests. Jakob Lewin, head of the Hanover administrative department of the Factory Workers' Association, sent regular, extensive reports to the company management of the Gummi-Kamm-Comp., which was renamed Excelsior AG shortly afterward, in which he denounced numerous abuses in the company and called for immediate remedy, detailing specific names and incidents. "In a departmental meeting of the workers in the box adhesive hall on the 9th of the month," it was said, for example, in a letter dated August 10, 1912, "the workers complained strongly about the disgraceful treatment accorded to them by supervisor Mr. Wossitzki, and the undersigned organization was tasked with conveying the complaints to you." The Continental workforce was far from taking similar measures. Departmental meetings or complaints about foremen and supervisors seemed unthinkable, even though workers at Continental also had cause for complaints about the numerous problems in their day-to-day work. However, these only found their way into the public sphere anonymously via a detour through various articles in Hanover's socialist daily newspaper, *Der Volkswille*. In December 1902, it published reports on the "monstrous Continental dividends" and denounced the expensive privileges of management, such as trips in company cars with company chauffeurs to vacation locations in Bavaria. In February 1903, a report on the poor working conditions at the Vahrenwald plant caused a stir. "For a large number of workers, the 10-hour working day is merely something written in the factory regulations," it was said. "Overtime is the order of the day. There are probably only a handful of colleagues who do not have to work for up to 12, 13 or even 14 hours [...]. Workers feel that it is almost spiteful when they are told only in the final few hours of their shift that they must work overtime [...] We cannot check the maxims by which workers' sweat is turned into money here," but the descriptions showed the fate of the workers, "from whose bones such enormous dividends are made." In the eyes of Continental's management, these public accusations were completely unjustified, but were evidently seen as being so serious that they were forced to take a countermeasure. In a handwritten declaration signed by 48 workers, the workers gave assurances that, due to the tire season, the overtime worked was "performed voluntarily and without coercion" and also that they had "not performed long hours of overtime continuously."

Continental's management maintained what was from its perspective—all things considered—a successful course of paternalistic welfare and social policy within the company, which it had developed itself and also operated for its own account, even in subsequent years. In 1912, an in-house brochure was printed about the "welfare institutions of the Continental-Caoutchouc- und Gutta-Percha Compagnie," in which the extensive voluntary social benefits were listed in detail, from the aforementioned bonuses and life insurance policies through the construction of company housing to the paid half-hour nursing breaks and nursing bonuses for female employees and the "special monetary gifts" at Christmas for sick workers. In 1912, a "pamphlet for workers" strictly banned workers from bringing spirits on to or consuming them on the company premises. However, as early as 1910, 1,110,500 liters of coffee with milk and sugar was distributed free of charge to the plant employees, and "so that workers could freshen up while working at the factory," they ensured "that every worker can take a shower bath within the factory during working hours without wage deduction and provided soap and towels for this purpose." Continental was able to afford this generous workforce policy thanks to its rapidly growing profits. Even if only a fraction of these measures were actually implemented, the workers at the other Hanover plants could only dream of them. This mixture of discipline and social care afforded to the Continental staff evidently succeeded in its aim to build a sense of loyalty and created an environment in which industrial unrest did not flourish, particularly while Siegmund Seligmann was at the helm of the company. Seligmann was a father figure and man of unwavering authority who enjoyed the respect of all his employees—as evidenced by the huge celebrations marking his 25-year anniversary with the company in April 1901. The Continental workers were as good as immune to the radicalization efforts of the emerging trade unions and their calls to workers to involve themselves in the class struggle and fight for their own interests. This was to change quickly after 1918 in a much frostier working atmosphere against the backdrop of the changed political setting of the Weimar Republic.

But first, with the outbreak of World War I, the corporate social policy was actually expanded further at Continental under the flag of war welfare. Of the almost 12,000 employees at that time, 5,200 blue- and white-collar workers, or "plant officials" as they were called then, were drafted into the army within the briefest space of time; in the end, 6,234 Continental employees were called up, i.e. more than half of the total workforce, 776 of whom would not return from the war. To replace the men, more women were hired, who then often took on the heavy manual work at the plant.

Fig. 32: Wartime deployment of women, November 1917.

A support fund with a total of one-and-a-half million marks was set up for the surviving dependents of the fallen Continental workers. To bridge the cash shortage, particularly in the first few months of the war, Continental printed its own war vouchers as a stable-value replacement. The company also made a one-hundred-thousand-mark donation for childcare in Hanover and Linden, and a separate *Con-*

tinental War Echo was printed for "the employees of our company in the field," in which not only the decorated "heroes" were named but also the fallen. All in all, by the end of the war, the company had spent more than 10 million marks on war-related social assistance purposes, according to the Executive Board. Continental's "unique social actions" were also reported in detail in the newspapers at the time, including the *Hannoversche Courier*. For a long time, Continental was widely regarded as an exemplary pioneer of company social measures, from which the workers also benefited. Anyone employed at Continental now thoroughly enjoyed the recognition and reputation that went along with that name, and it was a source of considerable pride, especially if they had experienced and participated in the company's meteoric rise to the level of renowned global company.

Self-confident Continental Employees and an Instrumentalized Company Community. Working Worlds, Conflicts and Identity (1918 to 1945)

In the following years, the structure of the Continental workforce underwent numerous and extensive upheavals. Both sets of annual figures for the period under analysis mark the end of a World War, while economic crises also caused high fluctuations in purely numerical terms. In 1918, there were approximately 8,000 employees on the company's payroll, 2,900 of whom were blue-collar workers. At the end of 1945, the number was almost the same, although the composition by age and gender had changed massively. In addition, the figures hid some dramatic developments: by 1929, the Continental workforce had initially grown rapidly, to 14,125 employees in 1922 and to 16,765 in 1929 as a result of acquisitions, before declining by more than 40 percent to 9,800 as a result of job redundancies. This was followed by another expansion phase up to 1938, during which the number of Continental employees climbed back to 16,478. It remained at this level until 1943, before falling by more than 10,000 to 6,739 at the end of the war. Two processes accompanied these dramatic fluctuations: first, the addition of new Continental employees, initially as a result of acquisitions, when, among other things, around 7,000 "Limmeraners" from Excelsior AG and several thousand blue and white-collar workers of the Peters Union in Korbach, Hesse, joined the workforce. Then, after the start of the war, there was an unprecedented heterogeneity and turnover of employees, with foreign forced laborers, German drafted laborers (primarily women) and also other new Continental employees at the two newly established plants in what was formerly Poznan in Poland and Krainburg in Slovenia, where almost 2,500 blue- and white-collar workers made tires and tubing for the German military as part of the Continental corporation. On the other hand, these years saw a massive politicization of Continental workers, who for the first time developed a new sense of self-confidence and a strong willingness to become involved in conflict due to the new co-determination legislation of the Weimar Republic and the breakthrough made by the trade unions and works council movements dominated by the SPD (Social Democratic Party) and KPD (Communist Party of Germany). This was followed, however, by subordination and integration into the National Socialist works community ideology, flanked and promoted by specific measures of corporate social policy, which aimed to form a new company community from the heterogeneous workforce in order to mobilize work performance and productivity in the Nazi war economy.

The new era after the demise of the German Reich and the lost war made itself felt at Continental with a significant change in the working environment and permanent changes in the working world. Shortly after the end of the war, production was switched to "modern working methods" (based on American examples) with the introduction of the transport chain, which, as an endless belt, continuously connected all workplaces and transported the product being created from one worker to the other, in some cases over several floors. This quickly developed into modern assembly line work in accordance with the American system.

Fig. 33: Assembly line production at Continental in the late 1920s.

The modernization of working methods also had a major impact on administration, and thus in the areas of activity of the white-collar workers. Posting machines and parlographs, i.e. writing and dictation devices, revolutionized accounting and correspondence.

Fig. 34: A view of Continental's administration. Above: the parlograph department, below: the bookkeeping department ("accounting").

The eight-hour day, fought for and introduced by the trade unions in 1918 and made generally binding, as well as the Works Council Act of 1920 and the Co-determination Act of 1922, which for the first time provided for the assignment of employee representatives to the Supervisory Board, lent a massive boost to the representation of interests of both blue- and white-collar employees without and outside companies. However, the first employee committee formed at Continental, which was later followed by a workers' council, was faced with severe opposition from the Executive Board and Willy Tischbein in particular, who fought against it hard from the outset. An initial test of in-house power came in March 1919, when the employee committee demanded that management withdraw plans for a series of layoffs. In addition, two petitions formulated by typists and factory foremen were handed over in which they called for "a revision of their wages," higher bonuses, cost of living bonuses, and general equality with white-collar employees. Tischbein, however, was not prepared to make concessions, arguing that the overstaffing of administration as a result of the war, coupled with the uncertain economic prospects of the post-war era and the large number of Continental workers returning from combat, meant that larger-scale redundancies were essential. As a result, considerable disquiet spread among the workforce. During these months, meetings and formal petitions, submissions and demands to corporate management were the order of the day in Vahrenwald, and at the end of March 1920, this discontent was unleashed in a four-day general strike proclaimed across the country. Continental employees also took part in the strike, to which Tischbein responded with clear sanctions in line with the employers' associations. If the factory employees were not prepared to offset their lost working hours with overtime or collectively agreed vacation days, stated Tischbein in a circular dated April 27, 1920, the time would be deducted from their pay. An exception was made only for those who would sign a preprinted declaration affirming "that I was willing to work during the general strike. The failure to fulfill my work obligations is due to reasons beyond my control."

Karl Brinkmann (and later Hugo Schlesinger) for the white-collar employees and mechanical technician Fritz Leyfeld (replaced from October 1924 by Albert Kammann) for the blue-collar workers joined the Supervisory Board as representatives of the workforce. But as early as March 1924, there was a new test of power and another strike. The reason for this was the attempt by the employers' associations to overturn the eight-hour day and to return to the old 10-hour day via the back door. The state arbitration ruling in the conflict between employers and trade unions provided for a nine-hour working day, but the blue- and white-collar workers at Continental also firmly rejected this "compromise" and the KPD works councils in particular, who by now were strongly represented in the company, finally instigated a wild strike—to which Tischbein responded with a radical and uncompromising lockout of all 11,000 Continental employees. The strike lasted three weeks, although some groups of strikers started crumbling after just a few days following an appeal from Continental management and increasingly workers returned to the factory. This was a clear indication that the conflict had caused a division within the workforce, with radicalized workers on the one hand and those who were more willing to agree to union compromises on the other. On April 25, 1924, Tischbein was pleased to report to the Supervisory Board that "the strike that had broken out at our company has completely collapsed. Most of the workforce has resumed work under the old conditions."

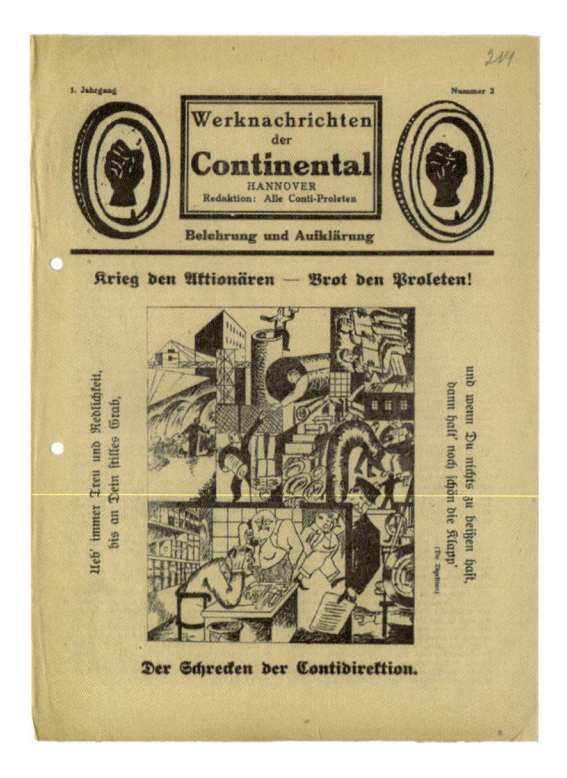

Fig. 35: One of the first artfully designed trade union factory newsletters for the workforce in 1925.

Tischbein adopted a hard-edged tone not just with blue-collar workers but also with white-collar employees and management personnel. From 1925, he pursued stringent cost-saving measures that not only affected blue-collar workers but also involved extensive white-collar redundancies, and "[demanded] increased efforts from those who remained." In a strongly worded appeal to his executives dated November 12, 1925, Tischbein lamented "that many of our staff have not yet understood the gravity of the situation [...] and if we do not succeed in bringing the percentage of costs to a correct level in relation to sales, we will all pay for this in a very short time." The Continental general director went on to demand that each department head immediately deliver a list of further employees to be laid off.

However, the main point of dispute between the company's management and the workforce was the Bedaux system. Introduced gradually by Continental from 1927 (as one of the first companies in Germany to do so), this was as a comprehensive and, at the time, highly modern rationalization system that closely interlinked and enhanced work performance, wages and work processes. From a business perspective, the Bedaux system was an entirely modern-looking operating management and accounting system, as the Bedaux analysis sheets provided a clear picture—compiled in weekly and monthly overviews—of the cost factors and the relevant degree of profitability, i.e. the performance factors of the respective workshop and operating department. At a glance, it was possible to determine productivity losses, idle time, waste, etc. and thus also whether the department manager had properly managed the work or not. The figures on the Bedaux analysis sheet gave immediate grounds to investigate the causes of performance impairments and cost increases. Once established and integrated, this resulted in a permanent compulsion, so to speak, to systematically identify and combat sources of operational losses as well as ongoing operational improvements of a technical and organizational nature. It also allowed the effects and effectiveness of new working procedures to be checked and compared. In February 1928, 60 percent of the total workforce, i.e. 5,500 employees, worked in Hanover using the Bedaux system. The average increases in performance were between 40 and 50 percent with earnings increases for workers of 18 percent and total wage cost savings of 25 to 30 percent. "The system," Willy Tischbein told a business friend, "is increasingly gaining the trust of our workforce. The workers see that company management have been made aware of existing mistakes, consider themselves fairly rewarded and, above all, see their pay as guaranteed, so that the feared 'piece work rate debacle' is completely eliminated."

Employees, however, often regarded the new work assessment and wage incentive system as a driver system, but at the same time they were also thoroughly aware of the positive effects of making work processes more flexible and of the positive performance incentives, which also resulted in noticeably higher wages. Once again, there was a division in the workforce, but this time less between blue-collar and white-collar workers, because these latter were also subject to the strict rationalization system and also felt, fueled by new agitation from works councils who were closely associated with the KPD, that they were "Bedaux slaves" and victims of the "Bedaux hell" at Continental. Instead, there was a rift between the "old Continental employees" at the Vahrenwald plant, where the Bedaux system was instigated comparatively quickly, and the "new Continental employees" from Excelsior AG at the Limmer plant, who merged with Continental in 1929, some of whom were hugely resistant to the new system. Moreover, three weeks after the system was introduced, the results achieved there were downright destructive and performances decreased instead of increasing. "This is due," said the responsible Bedaux engineer in his weekly report dated July 5, 1928, "to the fact that the series leads and clampers are withholding their services and providing passive resistance [...] They claim that the performance required of them according to Bedaux is not possible." When the situation was unchanged at the beginning of August—instead of the hoped-for cost savings, costs actually increased, and poor machine utilization was identified as being due to poor work organization—the company's management stepped in. All "unusable" clampers who had come to management's attention as a result of their refusal to perform were laid off, and the vacant positions filled by women who, in management's experience, quickly rendered above-average performances—not least because the Bedaux premium was non-gender-specific and therefore brought about a wage alignment for them with the higher male salaries. But the supervisory staff also came under attack. A number of foremen and supervisors were downgraded or transferred to worker level. From mid-August, significant improvements in performance were evident.

All in all, the "Limmeraners" felt the takeover by Continental in December 1928 was extremely hostile. "The horse is eating the clover," it was said, alluding to the respective trademarks and brand emblems of the two Hanover companies. In addition, there was a mourning song doing the rounds about the end of Excelsior with the refrain: "Cover your head with a black veil, start to weep and lament: dear old Excelsior is being carried to the grave today." Initially, the Peters Union people or "Korbachers," who were also integrated into the corporation as part of the large merger, had not yet or if so, only to a limited extent, become the object of Tischbein's cost-saving and rationalization program, evidently due to the geographical distance from Hanover. They would retain their independent self-image into the future, particularly as they and their plant, which was located far from any large city, were spared the air raids and destruction of World War II and would become the main beneficiaries in the war-determined relocation of production within the Continental corporation.

The implementation of the Bedaux system was expected to take until the early 1930s, but the effects of cost reductions, savings and increases in productivity proved to be very quick. This was also helped by the introduction of improvement suggestion systems in September 1930. The first suggestion submitted dealt with improvements to the blow-out device for the hose machine and was awarded 10 francs. In the fourteen-strong Employee Council, the social-democratic Allgemeine freie Angestelltenbund (General Free Employees' Association) now dominated with eight representatives. However, since 1931, these were opposed by two representatives of the National Socialists, with whom the two representatives of the right-wing German National Association of Commercial Employees made common cause during votes. Shortly afterward, when the National Socialist German Workers' Party (NSDAP) took power, trade unions and works councils were banned and replaced by the new National Socialist collective system with the German Labor Front, consultative council and operations manager ideology. The Continental plants soon had a new production regime with initially highly uncertain working conditions due to significant fluctuations in raw materials, then massive labor mobilization, increasing working hours, the wage ban regulation and, above all, deteriorating working conditions, which resulted in the switchover from natural rubber to artificial Buna rubber. In contrast to the widely lauded "beauty of work," a concept also presented in the Continental company magazine *Die Werks-Gemeinschaft* with images of bright and clean work spaces—the administration building in Limmer, newly constructed in 1937, was considered a model example of this—many workplaces were still poorly lit and full of noise, dirt and toxic vapors. And in many areas of the manufacturing process, women were employed more than ever before; initially they were recruited to step in as replacements due to labor shortages, and then for the men who were drafted into the military.

However, the Nazi collective ideology also eroded the still-existing self-image of the blue- and white-collar employees who joined Continental as part of the merger and promoted an overarching corporate identity as a new, large community of Continental employees. The incentives to create this identification and loyalty, partly controlled from above by the Nazi regime, partly organized and driven forward by the new corporate management at company level, were numerous and diverse, including skills competitions, presentations of plant awards, performance certificates, DAF flags, being named as "Nazi model plants," and works meetings and company roll-calls. And they did not fail to make an impact. At the same time, a culture of denunciation against political dissidents and employees who were critical of the Nazi regime began to take hold in Hanover. And then the increasing use of foreign forced labor led to additional changes in the working climate and in the working world of staff. In 1944, the typical Continental employee had only a few years of company service, was female and skilled or male and a prisoner of war or a Frenchman who had been brought in as forced labor. Both groups found common ground in the forced nature of their employment relationship and, above all, in the constant fear and shared experience of the air raids; but they were also separated by antipathy, when the use of forced labor increasingly led to the release of fathers, sons or spouses formerly employed at Continental for deployment on the Eastern Front. In addition, many experienced plant supervisors, foremen and management staff had in the interim worked in Continental's corporate network, which was spread across the whole of Europe, in the countless leasehold, support, participation and consulting firms, as well as at the two new "domestic" plants in Posen and Krainburg, where they monitored the introduction of the new Buna technology, set up new production branches and trained the local workforce in the use of "Continental methods." However, some of them were also involved in the use of concentration camp prisoners at the largely unfinished new plant in Nordhafen and in the preparation of underground production facilities, and were complicit in abuses. With the corporation's implosion in the last few days of war, there was many a hasty return to Hanover, where the Continental engineers and foremen found only rubble.

Cold War and Class Struggles at Continental. Collective Bargaining Conflicts, disputes about production sites and Solidarity (1945/48 to 1990/91)

The post-war era brought a new upturn in employment figures, but also fluctuations due to crises and a wave of mass redundancies. From 1979, supported by the addition of Continental employees, this time from across Europe as part of the company's expansion policy, there was a departure on a whole new scale in terms of the number and structure of employees. At the time of the currency reform in 1948, workforce numbers at Continental had increased back up to 11,332, a number that would more than double to 27,447 by 1965. Never before had so many people worked at Continental; the previous record high of employees from 1938 had already been exceeded in 1954. But then came a major crisis, during which the number of employees initially declined to 18,100 by 1977 and then even to 15,400 by 1984. But these figures related to the "old Continental." By contrast, the workforce in the newly formed corporation rose first to 31,100 in 1979, reached 45,907 in 1988 amid fluctuations and interrupted by temporary staff reductions, and finally jumped above the 50,000 threshold in 1990 (51,064 to be precise). These were eventful years: the economic "miracle years" brought a new diversity to the workforce in the form of "guest workers"; there was a modernization of HR management, accompanied however by a hardening of the line between the company's management and employees, which at times had all the hallmarks of an overt class war; there was short-time working, wage conflicts and a new strike; initial disputes about the future of the traditional plant locations and long-term upheavals in the working world; but there was also a slow introduction of co-determination in practice and of corporate social partnership, which, at the end of 1990/91, resulted in a common solidarity against the perceived threat of an attempted takeover by Italian tire company Pirelli.

In the early post-war years up to around the mid-1950s, at first glance at least, the power structure within the company initially shifted considerably in favor of the works councils and organized representation of employee interests. Immediately after the end of the war, the newly elected Works Council went on the offensive against the likewise new company management with a whole series of demands for personnel changes, wage supplements and co-determination regulations, while the company management, also as a means of counteracting the growing power of the reinvigorated KPD groups somewhat, set about creating "plant and company harmony," entirely in the Continental tradition of the turn of the century. In fact, a KPD works group was very active at Continental. It regularly published its own employee magazine, the *Roter Reifen* (Red Tire), and also arranged a highly publicized visit in 1946 by a delegation from the Socialist Unity Party of Germany (SED; Sozialistische Einheitspartei Deutschland) from the Soviet occupied zone, headed by Walter Pieck, to the Vahrenwald plant. However, they were unable to draw any benefit from the general unrest among employees in connection with the food crisis, which resulted in temporary "hunger strikes" even at Continental. "As before, we have made every effort to promote the justified interests of our workforce," noted the chairman of the Executive Board in his report on the 1949 fiscal year.

"For years, the chairman of the Central Works Council has been a member of our Supervisory Board; another member of the Works Council also attends Supervisory Board meetings. Through an extensive exchange of views with the Central Works Council and individual members of the Works Council, we have made it possible for the workforce to participate effectively in the life of our company. We are gratified to see that our workplace peace has remained undisturbed, and that employees are also actively looking to work for our company."

In the same breath, reference was also made to the considerable wage increases and income improvements that had occurred in the interim. Compared to the indicative reference of 1938, the Executive Board maintained that in May 1953 a Continental employee was able to earn more than twice the gross hourly income.

Fig. 36: Works meeting in Vahrenwald, 1950.

However, the main problem for Continental in these miracle years of the postwar boom was to find sufficient numbers of new staff. In terms of remedying the labor shortages that were tangible as early as 1946, the political sensibility of the British military government was, from today's perspective, as curious as it was lacking, and was solely interested in taking measures to rapidly increase production. "There has been a change [in the labor problem] since mid-August 1946," said a report from the Executive Board to the Supervisory Board,

> as, by order of the military government, Eastern workers from the Baltic region and Ukraine are to be deployed in our company; specifically, up to 100 men are to be hired weekly until further notice. After the committee representing the workforce had the opportunity to present its considerable concerns to the representatives of the military government, it was agreed that this deployment of Eastern workers should not be made in the scope described, where it is possible to obtain German workers for this purpose. Up to now, however, there has not been any significant allocation of foreign workers.

In fact, through, inter alia, extensive measures in corporate social policy, in particular an intensification of residential construction for 450 staff members and their families in 1948, it was possible to recruit new Continental employees.

However, reading through the HR reports from the 1950s and 1960s, which were declared strictly confidential at the time, makes it clear that the labor problem remained a dominant issue. The aim was not only to recruit new employees, but also to retain the old ones and often those who had just been hired. Right from the outset, attempts were also made to overcome the still problematic issue of the substantial aging of the workforce through the targeted recruitment of young staff, particularly in the area of qualified employees. The report on the HR situation in 1950 tellingly highlights the situation at that time: "The shortage of suitable stenotypists persists," it said. By contrast, the hiring of engineers, designers and chemists, which were also required, "ensured that existing requirements were optimally satisfied." This was also helped by the training school, which had been set up by then, where young engineers received practical training in the most important factory departments for about a year. The program was based on the tradition of the "Continental plant school," which had been in place since 1913. This was part of the dual vocational training system that was emerging in Germany and in which more than 300 young unskilled male and female workers received additional general school education. In contrast to previous decades, the proportion of women in the Continental workforce was rather low at around 20 percent, and despite the hesitant efforts since the mid-1950s to include a general trend in the wage agreements to bring women's salaries closer to men's, the pay differences were still huge. A male commercial employee received 384 marks a month at Continental in 1950, while his female colleague received only 248 marks, a discrepancy of over 35 percent. Initial attempts at modernizing human relations at Continental did not get off the ground until 1958.

The heterogeneous Continental workforce was then "discovered" as an object of systematic personnel organization, staff appointment schemes, personnel training and HR management within the concept of a deliberate HR policy. "The more our operations are rationalized from an economic and technical point of view," a corresponding concept stated, "the more the people in them become our most important resources." From today's perspective, and even when compared to the many modern-looking measures of the Continental Executive Board's workforce policy from the 19th century and thereafter, HR management at Continental in these years was, however, more akin to something from the Stone Age. It relied wholly on the efficacy of a series of booklets with the title "Richtig führen" (Good Leadership) aimed at their department heads and, above all, was concerned with the right "personnel selection." The style of the relevant documents was an eloquent expression of the perspectives at that time and of practiced HR policy.

From the second half of the 1950s, the focus shifted to the battle against the rapid increase in staff turnover. In 1960 alone, 32 percent of female white-collar workers, 9 percent of male white-collar workers and 29 percent of blue-collar workers changed at Continental. An industrial psychologist was hired specifically to investigate the causes of the labor turnover in the plants and departments, ranging from macroeconomic causes and causes not influenced by the company, such as the general labor shortage—interestingly still in the area of stenotypists and typists even in 1960—to personal circumstances and the numerous working conditions mentioned by the outgoing employees as being insufficient. However, the result of the labor turnover study that was submitted surprised those responsible on the Executive Board. This was because, compared with other large companies, the labor turnover rate at Continental was relatively low, for which three reasons were put forward: first, "our location in Hanover away from the industrial conurbations; second, [the large] proportion of a long-standing employee base, some of whom have grown with us for generations; and third, the predominant position that we have in Hanover due to the company's reputation on the labor market." However, the study also concluded with the forecast that it was to be expected "that these advantages will decrease over the years due to the overall trend." And in fact, the turnover rate among blue-collar workers did climb temporarily to over 35 percent. With the strong expansion of its workforce and the construction or acquisition of no less than three new plants, Continental had made a significant contribution to the labor shortage.

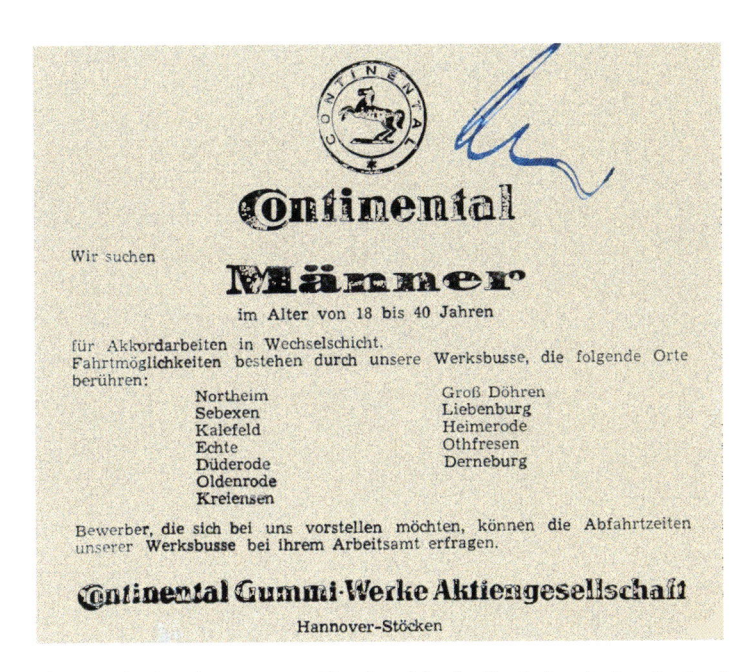

Fig. 37: Job advertisement recruiting (men) for the Northeim plant on September 28, 1963.

At that time, more than 1,000 guest workers were already working at Continental. The first foreign workers, initially from Greece, Italy and Spain, came to Hanover in 1962. Around a third of them were women. "For the additional 600 to 1,000 guest workers who absolutely need to be procured, there are approximately 600 beds available in company-owned and rented homes," as stated in the January 1963 report to the Supervisory Board under the heading "personnel situation." "In addition to the difficulties in attracting suitable guest workers, the particular efforts and costs required to classify appropriately and train the various foreign-language workers must not be overlooked. Our supervisory and management personnel are put under a considerable additional burden as a result of the guest worker situation." Here, too, the cadences of the report spoke volumes about the perception of this deployment of labor; at any rate, there was no mention of new "Continental employees." By 1973, the number of foreign employees, who now came from 29 countries, had risen to over 4,000, or 23 percent of the workers employed; as early as 1965, some smaller departments had more than 50 percent guest workers. In subsequent years, the proportion then shrank—in some cases considerably—and only in 1980, at 3,175, did it reach the level of 1970 again. However, the share of the German workforce, which had shrunk sharply in the interim, was now almost 17 percent. By then, the majority share with almost half was made up of workers from Turkey. The recruitment of foreign labor did solve the "people problem" at Continental, but at the same time, since these were usually initially unskilled, the accident figures increased significantly as did the labor turnover rates. For a wide variety of reasons, the turnover among male guest workers was more than twice as high as for German employees. By contrast, job changes were much lower for foreign women and only about a third higher than that of the female German Continental employees. However, this was also due to the overall employee status of the guest workers, who usually received temporary employment contracts only for a few years, with just a minority of "guest contract workers" receiving longer-term or permanent employment. This gave the company management the opportunity to practice a flexible HR policy with recruitment and redundancies or early termination of employment contracts depending on the economic situation.

Fig. 38: Tire production in 1958.

In view of high turnover rates and a growing percentage of foreign workers, the major challenge was to create an overall workforce that was characterized by a shared Continental identity, without this being explicitly formulated as a goal. In the meantime, the works councils and union workplace representatives had played their part in promoting the fact that there were common interests and creating an awareness of the need to establish common working conditions for all. This was also increasingly tangible in everyday operations. After six years of negotiations, the old work rules, which originated in the Nazi era, were replaced, and the new ones included, among other things, the stipulation of a legal entitlement to a loyalty bonus. And in 1956, bonus payments were re-regulated. From then on, in the event of a distribution of dividends to the shareholders, all employees received, on a sliding scale, 10 additional hourly salaries per percent of dividend. The old work performance bonus was built into the bonus guidelines at a fixed rate of 12.5 pfennigs per working hour. In addition, termination was on an annual basis instead of monthly. In 1957, the working hours were shortened to 45 hours for the first time. These were reduced further in subsequent years until the introduction of the 40-hour week in 1967. Moreover, a majority of the blue and white-collar workers at the three Continental plants also voted in favor of a community ballot for the works council elections, thereby rejecting the anonymous list system.

Fig. 39: Shift change at the Stöcken plant in 1965.

In the 1960s, the political and social landscape which was changing against the backdrop of the Cold War and class struggle also impacted on Continental's work climate. In November 1963, the human resources department fired three workers without notice after they were arrested as part of an investigation into members of the illegal Communist party, carried out by the Office for the Protection of the Constitution; tellingly, the investigation was codenamed "Reifenpanne" (puncture). They were accused of forming a prohibited Communist party works group and of producing and distributing the company newspaper "Conti Worker." The affected persons fought back and the whole matter finally ended up before the Hanover Labor Court. The case was quickly made public, which caused those in human resources to fear reputational damage to the company. "Continental is a protected company. In such a company, it is particularly difficult to judge communist activities that are punishable by law," was the reason given for the radical course of action. However, the matter was by no means as clear as the HR department claimed, as one of the accused was an elected member of the Works Council and therefore had special protection against dismissal. In the case of two of the accused, the terminations had to be overturned; by contrast, the labor court considered the termination to be justified in the case of the Communist Party Works Council representative and of another colleague. However, "communist activities" in the Continental plants did not decline, but instead increased. As early as March 1964, Continental hit the headlines again, this time in both the East and the West. "The Red sabotage ring intended to destroy the plant facilities," reported the *Hannoversche Rundschau*, while at the same time the *Neue Deutschland* paper in East Berlin announced: "At Conti, anyone who rejects the war policy is being laid off. There are lockouts and black lists against progressive worker officials." The Cold War had thus reached the company, and the case even led to a special broadcast on RIAS Berlin, in which the "misleading and distorting propaganda of the SED regime" was lambasted.

In 1967, the domestically controversial emergency legislation led to another spectacular incident that pushed Continental back into the public limelight. An article appeared in the June issue of the satirical magazine *Pardon*, according to which, as a way of anticipating the emergency legislation so to speak, armed factory security guards were to be deployed in numerous large companies. The article was written by the investigative journalist Günter Wallraff, who, during his "research," presented himself as a representative of a fictitious Civil Defense Committee at the Federal Ministry of the Interior and had also contacted the Continental plants using the alias Kröver. There, he was put in touch with a senior executive, from whom he elicited a series of statements that helped to easily create the impression that an armed factory militia was being set up at Continental as well, which would be deployed to protect the company in the event of wild strikes and workers' protests. The incident had far-reaching implications, because it created real unrest amongst the Continental employees, coming as it did against the backdrop of a heated domestic political climate in what was then the Federal Republic of Germany. IG Chemie (German Chemical Workers' Union) also took up the case in a flyer that was critical of the emergency legislation and made it the subject of two works meetings in Vahrenwald and Korbach. In their own circulars to the staff, the respective plant management teams were even forced to comment on the groundlessness of the allegations, and the Continental Executive Board also denied them in the strongest terms.

It was no wonder that, in this climate, Gerhard Lohauß, who had been head of the Continental HR department since the mid-1960s and a member of the Executive Board since October 1970, evolved into an adversary of the "left-wing" activities of the various works groups and the Works Council. "One lesson from this year's collective bargaining meeting seems particularly important," he noted in 1968.

> The trade unions and the Works Council—which, contrary to the expectations of the creators of the Works Constitution Act increasingly appears to be an extension of the trade unions— exert an influence on the workforce, which we currently cannot counter. This lesson may be painful, especially when you consider that the general situation of employees in the workforce currently gives much less cause for this than it did 70 years ago. In the longer term, we will only change this if we provide not only management personnel but also the workforce in general with more information about our viewpoint and the factual circumstances.

With a mixture of diplomacy and tough intervention measures, he wanted more than anything to end communist activities at Continental and was particularly concerned about the timely political immunization of management personnel. In 1969/70, Lohauß organized a series of presentations and information events "for senior executives," which were held under the main theme "Society today. Analyses and forecasts for partial civil unrest in our industrial society and prosperous democracy." The following year, the title of the series of presentations was "The new Left. Threat to the social market economy?" in which the speakers, including Lohauß himself, spoke about the challenges of the coming years.

In the meantime, the various Communist party groups in the company had intensified their—primarily journalistic—activities. The *Roter Reifen*, which had competition from a cell of the Communist Federation of West Germany and its newspaper *Arbeitersache*, was regularly distributed at the plant gates. And then there was also a Conti works group from the KPD/Marxist-Leninist, which published the company magazine *Roter Conti-Arbeiter* (Red Conti Worker). To finally provide a counterbalance with statements and reports from the perspective of the company's management, Lohauß ultimately launched his own plant magazine, *conti intern*, in April 1971. Almost 30 years after the last publication of the National Socialist workforce magazine, *Die Betriebs-Gemeinschaft* there was once again a newspaper, initially referred to as an "employee letter," for all Continental employees. In the years that followed, both newspapers often found themselves engaged in a war of words.

Fig. 40: Cover page of the *Roter Reifen* company newspaper of the Communist party's Conti works group from January 1977.

All in all, Continental's workforce policy was very successful, especially its focus on the rejuvenation of the workforce as a whole. The workforce report, which was first prepared in 1965, said of the workforce structure: "Miss Conti was born in 1930, so the average age of our female employees is 35, and this Miss Conti has already worked with us for almost five years, that is the average length of service to the company." The average age for men was 38 by that time, and they had almost 10 years of service at Continental. After this, however, growing wage conflicts and, above all, the end of the miracle years and the long decade of crises at Continental, with short-time working and redundancies, caused the workforce to be shaken up once again. The relationship between the company's management and the Works Council became noticeably abrasive. This became clear for the first time in the crisis year of 1966/67, when the Executive Board reacted to the production and sales declines with 25-day short-time work in the affected production departments and a withdrawal of voluntary social benefits, and then also by cutting jobs. Between 1965 and 1967, almost 3,000 Continental employees left the corporation, corresponding to 10 percent of the total workforce. The then chairman of the Works Council, Benno Adams, signaled to the Supervisory Board a thorough understanding of the adjustment measures and explicitly held back on making demands for wage increases. At the same time, however, he pointed out the growing predicament in which the trade unions and works councils found themselves, in that they were at risk of losing their hold on the workers in the face of a growing willingness on the latter's part to embark on "wild strikes." The disquiet in the workforce was actually considerable due to the ending of current bonuses—a topic that had always been very emotionally charged at Continental—the correction of piece rates and cutbacks in social benefits. In addition to this, 1960 saw the start of an extensive relocation process, whereby a whole range of production departments and manufacturing groups were moved from the Hanover plants in Vahrenwald, Stöcken and Limmer to the more cost-effective, cheaper locations in Northeim, Dannenberg, Korbach, and to the tire plant in Sarreguemines, France, that was newly built in 1964. This began the decades-long process of relocating production branches from Hanover's long-established plants to more cost-effective production locations; first in line were the state-subsidized "zonal border areas" of the Federal Republic. "In the long term, the company will have to forgo wage-intensive production at its main plants in Hanover," was the oft reiterated guiding principle of the Executive Board.

One reason for the relocations was, however, that the Hanover factories were now completely outdated, and covered in such grime from soot and chemicals that one critic at the Annual Shareholders' Meeting was moved to say "that working at Continental is absolutely no longer enjoyable," particularly since there was no longer an active cleaning service there for cost-saving reasons. The winner of these measures was the Korbach plant, which was on its way to becoming the corporation's most important tire plant, taking the traditional top spot from the original headquarters in Vahrenwald. "If we had Korbach's salary levels throughout the corporation, the operating result would be many millions better," was a reproach leveled at the Hanover works councils many times by the Executive Board in the following years. And when the social-liberal coalition took power in 1969, combined with the new German Works Constitution Act that was enacted shortly afterward, this led to an additional political charging of the working climate. Nobody knew exactly how the "new basic rules" for businesses created by the law would affect them, but the fears on the one hand and expectations on the other were high. The only thing that was clear was that this would directly or indirectly affect entrepreneurial decision-making and planning expertise in a wide range of areas, particularly in corporate HR policy, but also in economic and corporate strategy matters. "It also complicates and slows down the operational and corporate decision-making processes," as Lohauß noted in information provided to the Supervisory Board. The new law required some rethinking from a human resources department, which viewed employees—until well into the 1980s—almost solely from the perspective of "personnel expenses per employee," "proportion of absences in gross working hours," and "personnel expenses per hour worked."

The huge crisis in the years between 1970 and 1982 brought about the first test for the new relationship between the workforce representatives and the Executive Board, and saw fierce fighting over labor costs, months of short-time working and massive redundancies. Declared by the Executive Board as "new forms of remuneration" and "flexible HR policy," employees were left with the distinct impression that they were the sole victims of the stringent restructuring and reorganization policy that had now been adopted. At the Supervisory Board meeting on March 1, 1972, the Works Council therefore issued a long statement on behalf of the workforce, expressing on the one hand the continuing concerns of employees for their jobs, and secondly the "incomprehensible failure" and the negligence of the Executive Board, which also appeared to have allowed itself to be "completely steamrolled by Phoenix" in the ongoing merger negotiations, opening up the threat of further job losses. Finally, a list of detailed questions was submitted so that the workers could finally get information on the company's future policy to resolve the crisis. No answer was received, even though Alfred Herrhausen, chairman of the Supervisory Board, expressed his understanding for the statement and had also, behind the scenes, sought consultation with IG Chemie. At this time, many Continental people had lost trust in "their Conti" and, above all, in their Executive Board; their identification with the company was crumbling.

Fig. 41: The Continental Works Council in the mid-1970s; from left to right: Bartilla (chairman), Berkemeier, Lehnhoff, Riemer, Gall, Bernd, Schubert, Appel, Holzhausen, Gussner, Bergmann, Sammann, Muß, Ziulkowski, Graser, Gonschiar.

In addition to the opinions expressed by the works councils to the Supervisory Board, the union representatives as well as individual Continental employees and the representatives of the workforce shareholders took advantage of the Annual Shareholders' Meeting as a platform to air "a taste of the mood among the workforce" during this time. "When you listen to the staff and attend works meetings, you hear time and time again that Continental has probably missed its shot and that, despite excellent research, it has probably never really succeeded in bringing products to the market that have real sales opportunities and are also of good quality," was the message of the Hanover-based general manager of IG Chemie at the Annual Shareholders' Meeting in July 1973. In the following year too, in an effort to get Continental back on track, the workforce representatives presented a comprehensive situation analysis with suggestions for remedying the identified weaknesses, but received only a reserved response from the Executive Board. At the end of January 1976, the heated atmosphere culminated in the "wild strike" that the trade unions and works councils had long feared. Counting only the genuine Continental-specific conflicts, after the walkout of 1924, which had also been a "wild strike," this was only the second major work stoppage in the company's history. It was caused by the revised version of a works agreement that the Executive Board and the Works Council had negotiated. It involved the re-regulation of working hours and work on national holidays, but this simultaneously incurred wage losses for the affected employees of between 30 and 120 marks per month. When the Works Council announced the results of the negotiations to the workforce, the backlash was instant and decisive. Most of the workers in the Vahrenwald tire factory walked off the job; there were intense discussions about the new agreement, and vitriolic attacks against the Works Council. The calls from management and the Works Council to resume work immediately were ignored, and in the following days, further sections of the workforce—including at the Stöcken plant—joined the work stoppage. While the Works Council desperately pleaded with workers to return to their jobs, the Executive Board introduced layoff measures against "some of the ring leaders," which added further fuel to the fire. At the same time, however, there were increasingly controversial statements made regarding further action within the workforce, particularly as the whole matter had caused a huge stir in the media, especially in the Hanover issue of the *BILD* newspaper. In addition, Continental plants were inundated with a flood of leaflets during the strike from left-wing political groups attempting to take advantage of the situation. The strike was not broken until five days later, on February 4, 1976. Almost 1,300 employees had taken part, and even weeks later, there was still no peace in the factories. "The measures that triggered the strike were the subject of discussion at all Hanover works meetings, and resolutions were adopted to withdraw the dismissals [of the strike leaders that had since been announced]," reported Herrhausen at the Supervisory Board meeting on April 12. He then read a motion of no-confidence from two union workplace representatives from the Vahrenwald plant, which was directed against the Executive Board.

> Due to the ruthless personnel and wage measures imposed by the Executive Board, which have destroyed the formerly good working environment and trusting cooperation, our colleagues in Automotive Tire Heating, department 15407, and many colleagues from other departments in the Vahrenwald automotive tire factory believe that they can no longer work with the Executive Board and hereby express their distrust. They request a hearing before the Supervisory Board. Perhaps this will help us to find a rational solution for both sides in order to secure the well-being of the company and the maintenance of jobs for the future,

it said.

In June 1976, the situation was exacerbated further by the equally intense and just as controversial discussions around enhanced co-determination. Executive Board member for Human Relations Gerhard Lohauß and then chairman of the Central Works Council Benno Adams traded barbs, documented and distributed in the company magazine *conti intern*, over the advantages and disadvantages of the new provisions. And from the perspective of the Continental employees, there was a whole host of other controversial points that urgently needed to be clarified, which, if left unresolved, would sow the seeds of new dissent. This involved the regulation of company pension provisions, new forms of wages such as a "buffer wage," "selection guidelines" for appointments, secondments, redeployments and layoffs, as well as an end to staff cutbacks and the assurance of job security. Production data acquisition and the use of new IT technologies were also controversial and often unresolved. However, the Works Council and the Executive Board finally put their heads together on all issues and, in July 1978, concluded the first "job security agreement" in Continental's history; the negotiations were led by the Hanover district manager of IG Chemie and the Arbeitgeberverband der Deutschen Kautschukindustrie (Employer's Association of the German Rubber Industry). All in all, the number of employees fell between 1970 and 1984 from 27,880 to 15,400 in the core company, i.e. the old Continental AG. 12,500 workers at Continental were laid off or, frustrated and disappointed, left voluntarily, amounting to 45 percent of the total workforce. In addition, there were significant wage cuts for the remaining employees. Without these sacrifices and the associated drastic reduction in personnel costs, however, Continental would not have survived. In particular, the tough restructuring program of Executive Board chairman Carl. H. Hahn demanded considerable concessions from employees and employee representatives on, among other things, the merely moderate wage increases. At the same time, Hahn also continuously attended works meetings at the plants and meetings with the 136-member Works Council, 44 of whom were released from their duties, in order to draw attention to the gravity of the situation with his unvarnished assessment ("Conti has become too expensive") and thus also to create a new sense of solidarity in a crisis between the company management and the workforce based on trust and determination. And, truth be told, an ever-increasing spirit of optimism started to spread throughout the company as a whole.

 At the same time, Continental employees were also confronted with considerable upheavals in the world of work, which, through further automation, often reduced the physical strain at the workplace but also required different qualifications. In the factory halls, the tire builders had highly specialized individual work stations, which were subject to multiple inspections, including by department managers and shift supervisors. In mid-1982, the Korbach plant began experimenting with the new concept of group work. Tire builders, working as part of a team, assembled, checked, supplied and managed the tires and had to think about the production context together with their colleagues. Given that they had to monitor their own quality performance and bear responsibility for that, it was in their own interest to produce quality from the outset. However, it would take years before the general introduction of group work at the other plants. Nonetheless, the latest Japanese production methods and new forms of work organization had by then found their way into the plants everywhere. Under buzzwords like TQM (total quality management), lean management, Kanban and just-in-time production, work processes and shop floor organization were being constantly restructured. Some of this resulted in separate programs designed for and geared toward Continental-specific processes, which were announced and introduced under further abbreviations such as AMF (Arbeitszufriedenheit verbessern, Motivation verbessern und Fehlzeiten normalisieren; improving job satisfaction, improving motivation and normalizing absenteeism), flanked by new "quantum leaps in tire production," such as the soon to be legendary one-step building machine ESA, a fully automatic tire wrapping machine from the company's own mold and machine factory.

With two measures, Continental made headlines far beyond Hanover and presented itself as a pioneer of modern workforce policy. First, a research project was launched as early as 1975 into the "humanization of the working world," a hugely popular concept at the time, which focused primarily on optimizing working conditions for older employees, i.e. "age-appropriate jobs for tire builders." Second, in 1978, a pilot project was launched, in which for the first time women were trained in occupations previously reserved solely for men such as shop fitters, milling cutters, production technicians, lathe operators and chemical specialists. The long tradition of women's work at Continental thus took on a new dimension, even if implementation in the workplace and, above all, promotion to management positions were still a long way off. Just the fact that Continental publicly advocated for the innovative measure using the regressive headline formulation of "girls for men's jobs" spoke volumes.

From 1986, due to a shortage of qualified university graduates in the technical and scientific fields, the company also adopted new approaches to personnel acquisition and the promotion of young talent. Booths were set up at trade fairs, and contact made with universities. "Personnel marketing" was the term that defined the hunt for skilled workers. From 1980, recruits were also offered a new form of training as "rubber and plastic molders." Male tire builders were still the elite among Continental workers despite women advancing into this field as well. Employee hierarchies also shifted in the administrative sector, while occupational fields became more academic.

Eine von 14 952
Heute Michaela Kaefer

Eine Frau muß besser sein, um von Männern akzeptiert zu werden

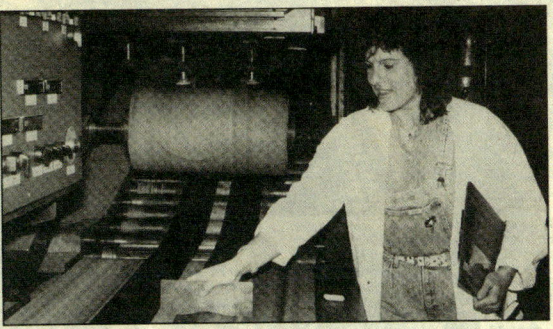

Einzige Frau unter vielen Männern zu sein — daran ist Michaela Kaefer gewöhnt. Als Diplom-Ingenieurin für technische Chemie hat sie diese Erfahrung bereits im Studium gemacht.

Auch bei Continental, als Mitarbeiterin des Technical Service LKW-Reifen in Stöcken, bewegt sie sich in einer reinen Männerwelt. Probleme bereitet hat ihr das nie, räumt allerdings ein, daß man als Frau fachlich sehr fit sein muß, vielleicht sogar besser als die männlichen Konkurrenz, um akzeptiert zu werden. Natürliches, unkompliziertes Verhalten, so ihre Einschätzung, erleichtert dabei den Umgang mit neuen Kollegen.

Michaela Kaefers beruflicher Erfolg scheint ihr Recht zu geben, denn sie gehört als Gruppenleiterin mittlerweile zum kleinen Kreis weiblicher Führungskräfte im Unternehmen.

Erste Kontakte zur Conti knüpfte sie mit der Diplomarbeit im Bereich Forschung und Entwicklung Reifen. Sehr gute Betreuung von Seiten der Conti-Mitarbeiter und ein angenehmes Arbeitsklima sorgten für einen nachhaltig positiven Eindruck, so daß Michaela Kaefer 1984 auch beruflich in diesen Bereich einstieg.

Materialentwicklung und Produktionsbetreuung der Werke Herstal und Stöcken sind ihre bisherigen Stationen bei Continental. Seit Anfang 1988 setzt sie jetzt im Technical Service die F+E-Vorgaben für den „optimalen Reifen" in maschinenmachbare Anweisungen um und begleitet die Produktion von der Fertigmischung bis zum Endprodukt. Dabei heißt es, die Eigenschaften von Material und Maschinen gut zu kennen, um so schnell und so schonend wie möglich zu produzieren. 60 Prozent ihrer Arbeitszeit verbringt Michaela Kaefer dann auch vor Ort, in der Fabrik.

Eine berufliche Endstation ist für sie noch nicht in Sicht. Karriere versteht sie als einen durchaus positiven Begriff, der das Kennenlernen neuer Bereiche ebenso beinhaltet wie ein Weiterkommen in der Hierarchie. Basiswissen, Engagement und Flexibilität natürlich immer vorausgesetzt, so Michaela Kaefer.

Ersteres hat sie bei Conti bereits unter Beweis gestellt, letzteres als Tochter eines Fußball-Trainers (für Insider: Hans Merkle) mit Wohnorten von Bern bis Malente bereits als Kind gelernt. Bestimmte Erfahrungen schon mal gemacht zu haben, hält die gebürtige Schwäbin deshalb auch für einen ganz wichtigen Faktor, wenn's darum geht, sich auf neue und ungewohnte Dinge einzulassen, risikobereit zu sein.

Michaela Kaefer setzt das auch in ihrer Freizeit um, die sie gern mit Motocross und Motorradrennen verbringt. Geschwindigkeit muß sein, kommentiert sie ihr Hobby, mit dem sie sich mal wieder in einer Männerdomäne bewegt.

Fig. 42: Report from the employee newsletter *conti intern* from December 1988.

Structural shifts in Continental's workforce were also the result of another development: the takeover of the Uniroyal-Englebert Group in 1979 added almost 8,000 new Continental employees to the company. There was, however, little common ground within the corporation because the two companies had a completely different corporate culture. In particular, the 2,044 employees at the traditional Aachen location still saw themselves as Englebert people or "Uniroyalists." There were also between 1,000 and 1,700 employees each at the plants in Belgium, France, Great Britain and Luxembourg. The Continental workforce was becoming international. Strictly speaking, this was already the case from the late 1960s, as the corporation owned a holding company in South Africa as part of a participation strategy. The name of this company was Conti-Calan Ltd. It had around 1,300 employees in five factories that produced technical rubber articles such as battery boxes or rubber work shoes. Since 1970, a similar form of participation had also existed in Brazil. From the Executive Board's point of view, the participation was economically successful. Hanover knew little (or did not want to know) about the situation of "non-whites" under the then apartheid regime. The same was true for the Brazilian workforce who were suffering under a military dictatorship. In 1978, awareness of apartheid was increasing among the German public. A trade union magazine published an article titled "Blacks oppressed. How Conti supports racist policies in South Africa." The Executive Board immediately denied the veracity of the article. In the employee newsletter *conti intern*, the manager in charge of the participation stated that the accusations had no basis in fact. Nonetheless, in 1987, the typical Continental employee was a German worker in tire production. He had been at the company for 17 years and was 42 years old. This statistic changed dramatically that year with the acquisition of General Tire and the addition of almost 13,000 new employees, with four tire plants in the USA, one each in Canada and Morocco, and two in Mexico. The 17,700 German Continental employees were now in the minority, as the corporation employed 24,500 workers abroad.

The new production sites abroad quickly reignited the debate about the costs and focus of production at the traditional locations in Germany. In January 1980, Hans Kauth was appointed labor director in accordance with the new co-determination regulations. Two years previously, Hans-Joachim Nöthel had replaced Günter Bartilla as chairman of the Central Works Council. Two new representatives of the company's social partnership thus faced each other. Initially they were still wrestling with the aftermath of Continental's long struggle for survival and had to make an effort to build mutual trust. In June 1981, "Principles of Occupational Safety" were first formulated in the company. These principles were given equal importance as corporate objectives to the quality of the products and economic success. In case of doubt, the principles would always take priority. These were expanded in May 1984 by a "Company Quality Guideline" in three languages. In February 1982, a program to restructure and modernize the Hanover plants, involving an investment of 80 million marks in total, brought at least a temporary end to the long period of uncertainty among the Hanover employees. The most modern mixing plant in Europe was built in Limmer at a cost of 7 million marks, while a considerable portion of tire production was transferred from Vahrenwald to Stöcken, strengthening the production site there. The future of the Vahrenwald plant was uncertain, however, and remained so until well into the second half of the 1980s. In 1988, there were increasing signs that the plant had no future as a production site in the medium term. The competitive cost structures propagated by the new Executive Board chairman, Horst W. Urban, certainly seemed to indicate this. "Hanover makes a loss, Korbach a slight profit, and Sarreguemines a better profit," stated former CEO Carl H. Hahn in 1977, and nothing had since changed regarding this cost and profitability situation. Urban's criticism of the Vahrenwald location caused a lot of controversy at works meetings, in particular because he simultaneously presented a 15-point cost saving program. The new savings program created considerable conflict between the Executive Board and Works Council, but in the end, consensus was reached. "Competitive again with new wages," the Executive Board member for Human Relations, Kauth, enthused about the agreement. The new Central Works Council chairman, Rudi Alt, formulated the view of the employee representatives in a more sober tone. "We only agreed in order to avoid a worse situation."

For the employees at Vahrenwald, it must have been even more painful given that it coincided with the celebrations for the 50th anniversary of the Stöcken plant. "Stöcken should become a model plant," was the message coming down from the Executive Board. In 1984, the production of the 50 millionth steel belted tire was celebrated at Korbach, which had not been hit by the restructuring measures. As a result of a surge in demand through economic growth, in 1989 all of Continental's plants were operating at full capacity. A six-day week was introduced at the Stöcken plant because of this. In Aachen there were similar efforts to introduce a continuous working time model, i.e. a seven-day week with five shifts. These efforts failed, not because of resistance from the workers, but rather from the North Rhine-Westphalia state government. The plant at Korbach also increased its capacity by introducing a 16th shift. Furthermore, the restructuring and extension of the Irish plant in Dublin commenced.

Fig. 43: Automated tire production at the start of the 1990s.

The new international production sites presented Continental's HR management with entirely new tasks and challenges. The same was true for the works councils. In most countries there were trade unions, but the German system of co-determination was unfamiliar. In many cases, other forms of representation of employees' interests prevailed, or if not, had to be established. And when it came to dealing with work conflicts, other traditions existed. Hanover found this out on September 20, 1989, when a strike was called by the United Rubber Workers (URW) at the US General Tire plant in Charlotte. The strike was caused by a conflict over pay at the plant where 1,850 workers made 25,000 tires every day. After a bitter dispute lasting 67 days, the strike finally ended in late November.

Shortly beforehand, a comprehensive rationalization and cost analysis program was announced. This had caused more uncertainty among the Continental staff. The management consulting company, Roland Berger, was commissioned to perform a cost value analysis on the entire corporation in Germany and abroad under the keyword OIS (optimal infrastructure). It was the largest rationalization program since the Bedaux system was introduced in the late 1920s. It also linked performance, cost and productivity analyses, which were broken down as far as the individual departments. For Urban, this program was "necessary to secure the future existence of the entire company." Nonetheless, unlike with Bedaux, it had little lasting effect. It was not long before Continental employees were confronted with the next restructuring and rationalization program. As the corporation slowly became an international entity, management was also fine-tuning the principles for the company's new orientation. The aim was to create an awareness among employees of being part of a globally operating corporation. Seven basic principles of a new corporate culture were devised that would overcome cultural and linguistic differences, different ways of thinking and long-standing corporate traditions. This also entailed a radical rethinking of the personnel and workforce policy enacted just a few years earlier. Improvement of professional skills, self-management, participation, interdisciplinarity and internationality, as well as synergies from culture-specific decentralization—these were the catchwords and concepts formulated at the start of 1989. Never before in Continental's history were the effects of the corporation's internationality so palpable. At the same time, however, it was soon clear that the corporation's geographical advance was far ahead of its employees when it came to "international behavior" and self-image.

Continental employees did not believe the next years would be trouble-free, even after the major crisis of 1983 was overcome. More turbulence was indeed caused by the hostile takeover bid by Pirelli in 1990/91. This time, however, the attacks came from the outside. A new Executive Board and Works Council chairman meant a departure from the conflict-ridden years, and this relationship was now characterized by constructive cooperation. From the start, Urban and the new Corporate Works Council chairman, Richard Köhler, were united in their rejection of the takeover bid. At the extraordinary Shareholders' Meeting in March 1991, this consensus was made public in a resolution signed by all 200 Continental works councils in Germany. The works councils and the union representatives on Continental's Supervisory Board supported the Executive Board in its rejection of the takeover by Pirelli. They drew attention to the absolute importance of the principles of co-determination and issued a clear refusal to all financial speculators. In the end, this show of unity was one of the main reasons why the takeover bid failed. 20 years later, the tables were turned.

The Globalization of Continental in the Context of Production Relocations and Transformations in the World of Working (1990s to the Present)

In this phase, the corporation's workforce was greatly expanded. At the same time, employee diversity also gained a new quality as a result of Continental's expansion and acquisition strategy. These 30 years were hallmarked by four main problems: the long departure from the traditional locations in Germany, transformations in the production system and the world of work, the development of a modern human relations management, and lastly, the experience of co-determination, including protests and labor disputes, in the context of Continental's globalization.

Drastic measures were taken to reduce personnel, both at the start and end of this period. As part of the restructuring program and the "streamlining of resources," the number of employees sank by more than 10,000 (20 percent) to just over 40,000 between 1991 and 1993. In 1993 alone, 5,041 employees were let go worldwide. This reduction in personnel continued until 1997, albeit it at a more moderate pace. The structure of the workforce was still entirely shaped by the old business model, and oriented toward tires and technical products. 36.3 percent of employees worked in the car tires area; 10.2 percent produced commercial vehicle tires; 10.5 percent were involved in trade; 14.9 percent belonged to the American tire sector, i.e. the General Tire division; 26.3 percent worked in the ContiTech area; and 0.3 percent managed the corporation as part of the holding company. Added to this were apprentices, who made up 1.3 percent. The picture was dominated by the "tire people" in Germany, Europe and the USA, who made up over 60 percent of employees. Only around 40 percent were still employed at the German locations, with 20,522 working in other European countries and 7,131 in North America. Continental was therefore still a European company despite its global sales activities. Between 1997 and 2008, major acquisitions such as Teves, Temic, the automotive area of Motorola, Phoenix and Siemens VDO saw a rapid increase in employees. Within a decade, the number tripled from 44,800 to 148,400. At the start, the majority of the new Continental employees did not actually see themselves as such. In particular, the newcomers from Teves, Phoenix and VDO had their own self-image and corporate culture. Furthermore, their manufacturing tradition was very different to rubber and tires. They were coming from a working environment characterized by metal processing, the handling of electronics and sensor technology, as well as software competencies. In addition, they were represented by a far more radical and conflict-oriented metal union, and not the moderate chemical union. The structure of the workforce changed dramatically both in the corporate areas and in the regions: by 2009, the "tire people" made up only 25.4 percent of the workforce, with 16.4 percent working in ContiTech. A good 58.1 percent now belonged to the Automotive Group. Only a third of Continental employees were now working in Germany. Another third were based in other European countries. 14 percent were in North America, 14 percent in Asia, and a further 6 percent in various other countries. By 2019, the structural shifts became even more pronounced. Above all, the proportion working in Germany sank further (to 25 percent), while the number of employees working in Asia rose (to 20 percent). Continental was no longer just a globally operating company, rather a worldwide producing corporation.

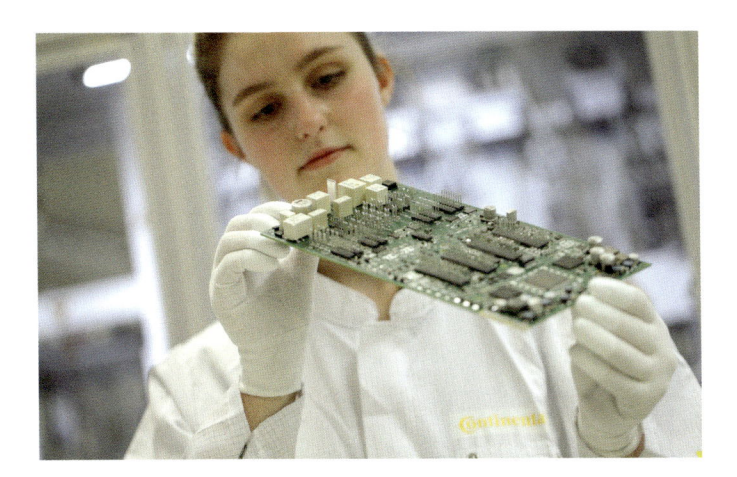

Fig. 44: A Continental employee carries out a visual inspection of a bodywork control unit.

Before this multicultural Continental could gradually turn into a new Continental with new employees and a cross-cultural, comprehensive corporate identity, the global economic crises of 2001 and 2009 created turbulence and temporary reductions in staff. Afterward, a new phase of growth commenced with the number of employees rising to 244,100 by 2019. Within just a decade, 100,000 new employees from 70 acquired companies had joined Continental. In February 2015, for the first time ever, the company boasted more than 200,000 employees worldwide at over 400 locations in 53 countries. The typical Continental employee was now an "automotive man" working in Europe (outside Germany) or Asia. His average age was 38.5, and he could look back at 10 years working for the corporation.

Fig. 45: The employees at the Brandýs Continental plant (Czech Republic) proudly present the millionth "OVIP silverbox" infotainment unit on January 11, 2018.

In contrast, women were in the minority at just under 22 percent (2009), although their proportion rose to over 27 percent in subsequent years. Then, however, the supplier sector was hit by a structural crisis. This was exacerbated by the collapse in growth during the worldwide coronavirus pandemic. Drastic personnel measures resulted, culminating in the loss of 30,000 jobs globally, a third of which were in Germany.

These numbers are not just job losses due to crises, acquisitions, or the purchase of new factories and companies. They also include the change in production locations that has been accelerating since 1992. On the one hand, plants seen as too expensive have been closed, while, on the other hand, new less expensive greenfield plants have been built. At corporate level and to the public, these personnel adjustments seemed moderate. But the changes were huge for the affected employees. Some workers were confronted with site closures. Others took up employment opportunities at new flagship sites, and had to get to know new colleagues and learn the Continental way of doing things. The previous Executive Board under Horst W. Urban made the start by closing tire production at the traditional Vahrenwald plant. Here, on April 28, 1989, the last tire left the vulcanizing mold.

Fig. 46: The last tire that was manufactured at the Vahrenwald plant on April 28, 1989.

The outdated tire factory was torn down in 1990/91, and a new administration building went up in its place. The new Executive Board chairman, Hubertus von Grünberg, then got serious with the reorganization of production sites and introduced a radical restructuring program. He introduced measures to close plants throughout the whole corporation. One of the first places to close was the Canadian General Tire plant. He also initiated the relocation to cheaper production locations, mainly in Eastern Europe. In late 1993, as employees in Korbach celebrated the production of their 100 millionth tire, their colleagues in Aachen and Traiskirchen (Austria) feared for their jobs. The future of the traditional Limmer and Stöcken in Hanover locations, in particular, was under discussion. The Nordhafen plant was secure for now at least. There, the Executive Board reduced tire production by 1,500 employees, but invested 100 million marks in a new technology center. This focused on tire R&D activities for the entire corporation and created 450 highly qualified workplaces. In spring 1995, it was the turn of the employees at the traditional Limmer location. At a company meeting on May 9, the 1,500 remaining employees were informed of the plant's closure. By 2000, all production and administration areas, including the mold and machine factory (for decades at the heart of Continental's production modernization) were to be moved to Stöcken. After 50 years, destiny had caught up with the Limmer plant. The location had not been destroyed during World War II and so was able to contribute significantly to Continental's resurgence. Now though, the plant structures were way too big and mostly outdated. Part of Limmer's production had already been relocated to a new ContiTech plant in Slovakia.

Further relocations took place within the corporation. Truck tire production moved from Sarreguemines in Alsace-Lorraine (France) to Barum in the Czech Republic. Agricultural tire production was transferred via an external contract to Poland. Bicycle tire manufacture now took place in part in Thailand, while the tire plant in Dublin (Ireland) was closed. Production capacity in Traiskirchen (Austria) was also shut down. "Traiskirchen stays—but 1,000 jobs gone by end of 1997," wrote the employee newsletter *conti intern* in November 1996. This location also ceased tire production in July 2002 and was finally closed in 2009, after cessation of the remaining pre-production of rubber mixtures. The General Tire location in the one-time world tire capital of Akron/Ohio also had a long history. In 1982, tire production ceased here with only the administration headquarters remaining. Now this was closed and moved to the plant in Charlotte, North Carolina. The winners of these relocations were the sites in the Czech Republic, Portugal and Slovakia, which were then still viewed as European low-cost sites. It was argued that "the costs for low-tech products such as car tires for low speeds and certain agricultural, industrial and bicycle tires could no longer be covered in Germany." The same was true for labor-intensive products and production processes by ContiTech. At the same time, new Continental flagship plants were constructed at Mt. Vernon (a General Tire production site in the USA), in Otrokovice in the Czech Republic and in Lousado (Mabor) in Portugal. The new plant at Púchov (Matador) in Slovakia became the largest and most modern truck tire plant in Europe. "Will Conti tires soon be made in Belarus?" asked Continental's employee magazine in June 1998. On the same page could be read, "Next year, tires will already be made in Brazil." In 2000, the corporation's most modern tire factory was built on a greenfield site in Timișoara in Romania. This project was part of the recently developed car tire production strategy "Vision 2003 Continental Greenfield." At first, 218 workers were employed in production. In July 2003, the 10 millionth car radial tire left the factory. By 2019, over 2,500 new Continental employees worked there.

Several of the relocation projects did not work out, however. One example is the participation in the new construction of a "Moscow Tyre Plant." This started in 2001 but was given up after several loss-making years.

Fig. 47: The 10 millionth tire that was produced at the Timișoara Continental plant.

It was not long before new discussions started about the tire production location in Stöcken. In 2000/01, millions were invested in a car steel cord center, which was meant to secure the location. A high-end tandem mixer supplied the rest of Continental's "tire production world" with preliminary products. A new working time model was then introduced in 2003 in order to react flexibly to cyclical fluctuations in demand. The work shifts, which could range between 12 and 32 shifts, were recorded in time accounts and balanced at the end of the year. Temporary workers would also be used for future peaks in production. This move created a new type of Continental employee. The "Stöcken model" reduced labor costs by up to 25 percent. It was combined with further investment in the automation of tire production and modern process technologies. Even so, the 1,000 workers in car and truck tire production were only helped for a short time. Under the new Executive Board chairman, Manfred Wennemer, another round of production relocations to low-wage countries commenced. A bombshell was dropped in

December 2005 with the announcement that car tire production in Stöcken would cease a year later. Despite all the measures, Stöcken had become the smallest and most expensive car tire production plant in the corporation, which produced in total over 105 million tires annually. The average profitable plant capacities were at least 8 million tires. In Stöcken, only around 1.3 million tires were manufactured. To compensate for this, around 20 million euros were invested in the modernization of the remaining truck tire production. But by the end of 2009, this area closed too, and the remaining 780 employees were let go. Plants were also closed at other European production locations such as Herstal (Belgium), Newbridge (Scotland), Gislaved (Sweden) and Clairoix (France).

Fig. 48: Opening of Continental's first Chinese tire plant in Hefei on May 18, 2011.

By contrast, just a few months before in December 2007, work commenced on the first Continental tire plant in China. 150 million euros were invested in the production facility in Hefei, in which from 2010, 4 million car tires would be manufactured. There was also the option to ramp up production capacities to 16 million tires a year.

Continental was also building new tire plants at other locations around the world, or obtaining production facilities through acquisitions. This happened in Malaysia in July 2003 and in Brazil in 2006. The latter plant had a capacity of almost 7 million car and truck tires and was built to supply the NAFTA region.

2011 saw a plant constructed in India, and October 2013 it was Kaluga in Russia's turn. In 2014, a new tire plant was opened in Sumter in the USA, where just a few years earlier the plants in Mayfield and Charlotte experienced a considerable reduction in tire production capacities during restructuring. In 2019, Continental finally opened its first tire plant in Thailand to produce premium tires for the Asia Pacific region. The last two remaining German tire factories in Aachen and Korbach remained unaffected at first due to booming tire sales worldwide. Korbach produced its 150 millionth car radial tire in 2003, and in 2007, its 3,200 employees celebrated the site's 100th anniversary. The plant was even strengthened in 2016 by the millions of euros invested in a high-performance technology center. The tire production plant, which creates 350,000 high-performance tires annually, is the most modern of its kind worldwide. By interconnecting all machines with one another, it marks the start of tire production 4.0. This also makes it a blueprint for all the other plants. In contrast, during fall 2020, the decision was made to close the tire plant in Aachen at the end of 2022 after 91 years in operation. In 1989, Vahrenwald was closed; in 2000, the plant at Limmer; in 2009, Stöcken; and in 2021, Aachen. Only Korbach has been able to survive the production relocations from the high-wage German locations. By now, all the traditional plants of the "old" Continental have fallen victim to globalization, high-cost competition from large competitors, and the geographic shift in supply and demand. This development was announced in the late 1980s. Now 30 years on, after several relocation waves, it has (almost) been completed. The ContiTech and Automotive Systems areas were not left unscathed either by the long-term production relocations, with old plants being closed and new production facilities constructed. A new plant for vehicle electronics was set up in Romania in 2003. Shortly beforehand, ContiTech had opened a new production location nearby.

This was by no means an inevitable development, however. The fact that the process dragged on so long had to do with the ultra-modern and innovative production concepts that kept being developed and implemented. This also meant that tire production was able to continue in Germany for business reasons. As in the past, this involved concepts that closely interwove the production system and the world of work, i.e. manufacturing output, production costs and remuneration. These concepts were in part modern and revolutionary, while some were merely borrowed from Japanese industrial methods and given a new guise and abbreviations that were both confusing and meaningless. Examples of this are QFD (Quality Function Deployment for holistic quality improvement processes), MMP (Modular Manufacturing Process), TPM (Total Preventive Maintenance),

CTMS (Conti Tire Manufacturing System), CPS (Conti Production System) and CBS (Conti Business System). In the course of this, a new remuneration system was introduced in 1994 that replaced the previous piecework wages with a system of fixed wages and performance targets. Since the mid-1990s, production engineers at Continental and other companies had visualized a "highly flexible factory." In 1997, this resulted in the concept of a modular production technology that aimed to build many different tire models on standardized production platforms. In some MMP factories, tire dimensions with strong fluctuations in demand would be produced flexibly and economically in small quantities. MMP promised entry into new or developing markets. "Globalization is becoming affordable," a Supervisory Board presentation reported in June 1997. The concept was based on "minimill projects" that were also being pushed by others like Continental's competitor, Michelin. The costs incurred by type and brand variety were reduced through the pre-production of a standard green tire at a low-cost location. Shortly before delivery, the desired tread and side wall were then provided. Continental even registered its innovative production concept as a patent. "Continental revolutionizes tire production," were the media headlines back then. Three MMP locations in Europe were planned and driven forward, from where the markets were to be supplied. In 1999, two "MMP lines" for tire production were set up at a cost of 5 million euros at the Traiskirchen plant. A third line was meant to follow soon afterward. However, after many years of testing, the concept of a "green basis tire" that would be given the requested profiles ultimately failed.

Many of the production concepts were especially aimed at improving manufacturing quality. The abbreviation TPM was a management program from 1997 that was launched first in Stöcken and then at other tire plants. The aim was to increase equipment efficiency. TPM teams were installed with the aim of reducing scrap and improving quality and the overall utilization of production facilities. Machine failures, waste, speed losses and defective products were no longer to be taken for granted and included in calculations. Instead, preventive maintenance of the machines and other measures would rule these issues out from the outset. Basically, TPM was a variant of the quality circles and group work that have been in place for some time. Three years after its introduction, feedback from the responsible managers was mostly positive, but included some criticism too: "TPM is good and is worthwhile, but it requires a lot of discipline and commitment. Without this, it cannot be successful." The concept was transferred to the foreign plants in Lousado and Otrokovice, and above all, to the new plant in Timişoara, where it proved very successful. The acceptance there was higher than in the German plants. All things considered, the program was the first big step toward a common Continental standard at the worldwide production locations.

Maintaining a high level of manufacturing quality to thus guarantee product quality was an ongoing problem, however. In the period that followed, quality offensives and strategies with different concepts were repeatedly implemented throughout the corporation. In 2008, for example, the Continental Tire Manufacturing System was introduced in the commercial vehicle tires area. It combined standards for controlling and organizing plants with lean manufacturing tools and aimed at continuously improving standardized processes. Under the slogan "Quality First," a new strategy for quality improvement was advanced in 2010. By 2015 at the latest, this was declared the corporation's main challenge and a top priority. "A third of our automotive business units are not delivering the quality that our customers expect," the Executive Board chairman, Elmar Degenhart, commented on the situation in large parts of the company. The leading Japanese production concepts were the inspiration when it came to solving the problem. The Jidoka principle, for instance, is a quality and efficiency enhancement program, while Kaizen is the permanent improvement of activities, workflows, processes or products by all company employees. Yokoten is defined by best-practice sharing and daily efforts at improvement, as well as the instilling of a quality-oriented way of thinking. Then there is the "Gemba walk," a regular tour of the production area by managers, so that problems can be looked at on site. The 5S method includes the five steps sort, set in order, shine, standardize and sustain. Lastly there is the idea of the "lean factory" or "learning factory," which can be seen in many cases as merely a rehash of the "lean management" concept marketed by consulting groups. "Toyota-ism" continued to shape the rationalization concepts of Continental and the rest of German industry well after the turn of the millennium. Two concepts universally propagated since 2007 and especially since 2011, the Continental Production System (CPS) and Continental Business System (CBS), were variations of this, tailor-made for the needs of Continental. The tried-and-tested improvement suggestion system was also rediscovered by the industrial engineering experts. An attempt was made to give it new life as in-house innovation management and knowledge-transfer. It was known by the abbreviation CIM (Continental Idea Management) or just as "Contivation."

The goal of the many measures was to optimize manufacturing processes; and they can be judged differently depending on one's perspective. From the viewpoint of Continental employees, the continuous new mobilization concepts, quality offensives and productivity measures meant being confronted with unreasonable demands. This was especially true when the concepts originated from expensive external consultant firms, and the measures that read nicely on paper had little to do with the realities of implementation—even after countless workshops, training sessions, discussions and conventions. In the eyes of company management, however, these measures were essential. On the one hand, they broke up routines and drudgery in everyday work and installed permanent quality management. On the other hand, they were vital in establishing uniform Continental principles for production standards and conditions at all plants and locations worldwide. Recently, a fundamental transformation in production systems and thus in working environments has also begun. The ensuing change in employees' working situation is a challenge that has demanded enormous adjustments. Up to now, the changes can only be defined using buzzwords such as "Industry 4.0" or "smart factory." These stand for digitalization, and production networked via sensor systems and software, as well as for the completely new orientation of the entire manufacturing processes toward resource conservation and sustainability. Another element of this new world of work is the use of robots, even directly with individual employees to help with manufacturing activities that require difficult physical movements or heavy loads. These cobots (collaborative robots) and human-machine collaborations were already introduced at Continental in the automotive area in 2015.

The challenges posed to Continental's HR and human relations policy by such changes were significant. The many changes in the working and social environment had a considerable impact on employees' working lives too. Globalization, technological transformation and competition between locations demand maximum flexibility and adaptability, especially in terms of qualifications and professional skills. Work processes are becoming increasingly complex, and tasks that require specialization more frequent. Instead of tire builders, software engineers are now forming the new elite of the workforce. Personnel development and in-service training have become a key strategic task in the face of a workforce numbering over 200,000 and that is characterized by cultural and national diversity. At the same time, demographic changes mean that working lives are getting longer. Continental employees are becoming older due to the increase in the number of years that people work. As well as qualifications, more attention is now paid to workplaces and work processes when it comes to helping people to stay working for a longer time. The focus is on reducing and eliminating accidents, with comprehensive health management also implied.

The 1990s saw a new push toward modernization in Continental's personnel development. The focus was primarily on managers, however. They were given trainee programs to ensure their international management potential. These courses were usually 12 months long. There was also the already long-established Junior Management Training Program for the managers of tomorrow. The medium-term corporate strategy from 1995 contained a long list of company guidelines for "employees." It formulated general principles of human resources policy. These included: equal advancement opportunities for all employees, performance-related pay, improvement of the working environment and safety, cooperative leadership and delegation of responsibility, trusting cooperation with elected employee representatives, and the development of awareness of belonging to a globally operating company. It also aimed to build up management resources for future corporate growth. The guiding principle was clear: "Continental expects and encourages the commitment, qualification, training and further education, performance, mobility and loyalty of its employees as the most important prerequisite for the success of the company." Nevertheless, after the turn of the millennium, personnel development in the corporation was still primarily a management policy and a "personnel policy from the top down." In May 2002, the Supervisory Board discussed and adopted yet another new personnel development concept. The main points were the need to increase the internationality of managers, the recruiting of junior managers from outside the company, and the "still unsatisfactory proportion of women at senior management levels." The concept did little to address the discrepancy between the claims made by theoretically convincing and well-formulated "HR concepts" and the "employee reality" in all corporate divisions. Even so, it was at least mentioned.

Numerous concrete topics were awaiting practical implementation and solutions. In April 2000, for example, the issue of a new company pension scheme was at the top of the agenda. The resulting pension model "ContiPlus" was a contribution pension plan that was praised by the general public as a "clever alternative to the insecure state pension." The topic was very complicated, even in relation to just Germany. In the course of the company's international acquisitions, it became even more complex, with many different pension obligation plans for the USA, Canada and Great Britain. The second major problem area was the concern for clean and safe factories, a classic area of personnel and social policy. In April 2004, the "Health Protection, Occupational Safety and Company Protection" (HISS) unit was especially created to deal with this. HISS took on the task of reducing the number of accidents in the corporation. Within five years, the rate in relation to 1 million working hours was more than halved from 11.2 (2004) to 5.0 (2009). In 2006, it was confronted with a completely new challenge, i.e. organizing precautionary measures against pandemics for the global workforce. At the time, bird flu was spreading. Tamiflu tablet supplies for 30 percent of the workforce were purchased and stored locally. Around 15 million protective masks were also acquired for respiratory protection. At the locations that were especially at risk, crisis teams were created and emergency plans put into place. The measures were renamed ESH policy (Environment, Safety, Security and Health). In 2008, they were rewritten, and in 2012 they were revised again to include environmental protection management. Already in 2009, managers were faced with a new test in the form of another large-scale pandemic. This time it was "swine flu" or "H1N1 virus infection." From May 2009, a detailed pandemic plan was drawn up for all locations worldwide. This ensured that the number of infected Continental employees was relatively low (with the exception of Malaysia).

In 2010, Continental signed the Luxembourg Declaration (which had already existed since 1997). A commitment was now made to the principles of occupational safety and health prevention at all its production sites worldwide. A health and demography project launched the year before focused on ergonomically designed workplaces for all employees. By examining the suitability of workplaces for older employees, the company took on a pioneering role internationally. The number of Continental employees between 55 and 65 years of age in the production facilities was predicted to triple from 2005 to 2015. This made the "demography program" even more pressing. Since 2005, Continental had also been using the "Stress Documentation System," a labor management instrument to measure work-related stress and strain, and to make the Continental working systems more employee-friendly across the corporation. It is impossible to ignore the historic continuity to the Bedaux system and the "humanization of the world of work" projects. The company's global expansion also created new challenges in another classic area of company social policy, i.e. strategic personnel planning as anticipatively organized vocational training. This was used to find answers to the following question: "Which employees with which skills will the company need in the future in order to continue to develop successfully?" The question was relevant to further training programs in Serbia for young Continental employees, to competency tests for especially talented production employees in Turkey, to apprenticeship initiatives for woman as machinists in Mexico, and to AIDS prevention and literacy programs in South Africa. Through this, Hanover learned in 2003 that 35 percent of Continental employees in South Africa could not read or write. Training simulators were also developed for tire builders and other machine operators, while at the same time "cross-move" programs were launched to encourage transfers between departments and functions, between the company divisions, and ultimately between countries. Furthermore, systematic recruiting offensives were developed with close relationships to universities and technical colleges in the different countries, so that the company could keep up in the emerging "war for the best talent."

With its personnel policy, HR management was thus already pursuing a holistic perspective on all employees in the various areas or work and responsibility. This change of perspective became externally visible in 2014 when the term human resources was more or less officially changed by the corporation to human relations. This new orientation of workforce policy was also reflected in the fact that "diversity management" was now explicitly promoted. Already in December 2008, Continental signed the "Diversity Charter." The company was thus making an outward commitment to fairness and appreciation of all employees and, above all, to the further promotion of gender equality. The target given at that time was to double the number of women in management positions from approx. 8 to 16 percent by 2015. The percentage actually achieved was 10.5 percent, so the target was clearly missed. Nonetheless, the number of female managers at Continental was and is rising in an industry (tires) that has traditionally been dominated by men. The Continental Executive Board committed to the aim of diversity management much earlier than other large companies. Its aim was to use the socio-cultural diversity of employees in such a way that the company's performance as an organization would improve. This was also true for the more flexible working conditions, which were now being discussed under the slogan "work-life balance."

By means of regular employee surveys, the Executive Board tried, at least in part, to listen to the concerns and mood of the workforce. The gap between well-formulated programs, declarations of commitment, sophisticated HR concepts and high-profile pledges on the one hand, and their implementation in Continental employees' work on the other, has gotten smaller. It still exists, all the same, and must always be looked at critically. These commitments apply to the observation of basic socio-political principles of human rights and fair working conditions. As part of its company culture, Continental's management committed to making an active contribution to implementing human rights. This caused the company some dilemmas, as it had production facilities around the world and in countries such as China, Turkey and Russia. This commitment was and is particularly true when conflicts arise between the workforce and its representatives and management. Such conflicts repeatedly put the social partnership to the test.

The number of conflicts and disputes between staff and company management at Continental from the early 1990s until the presents is not high. Nonetheless, compared with the early periods of company history, these conflicts have been marked by a particular intensity. With Hubertus von Grünberg and the new Central Works Council chairman, Richard Köhler, two new players in Continental's social partnership faced one another. Other parties were Wolfgang Schultze, vice chairman of the Chemical, Paper and Ceramic Union, Adolf Bartels, head of the Hanover District Trade Union, and Wilfried Hilverkus, of the Stöcken works council, as employee representative on the Supervisory Board. There were already arguments with management in 1990/91 over the restructuring of the traditional Vahrenwald location. Further conflicts were caused by the wave of layoffs under von Grünberg and the accelerated relocation of production locations. In fall 1995, when the future of Stöcken was at stake, the local works council created a list of demands and points that would prevent the worst-case scenario. The paper was presented at the Supervisory Board meeting by the Supervisory Board representatives, without however changing Stöcken's fate. In September 1995, in advance of the Supervisory Board meeting, direct and frank discussions took place between von Grünberg and Schultze. The unions were told that the plant had a staff surplus of 1,300. When normal fluctuation was taken into account, this still left around 1,000. This was a scale that "we have managed in the past without any major problems." However, the financial situation at Continental was such that the company could not afford any expensive severance schemes. It was seen as best for management and employee representatives to negotiate with the employment office for help with early retirements. This is then what happened for the most part. The discussion about the three traditional Hanover plants, Vahrenwald, Stöcken and Limmer, even saw a revival of the Communist Party's Conti work group. The group started selling a new edition of the *Roter Reifen* magazine at factory gates in order to spur the employees into protest. "Are you just a yes-man?" This was the question that *conti intern* put to works council head Köhler. He then had to defend his recent cooperative and non-confrontational approach to management's plans.

At the time, the Executive Board was facing much more difficult conflicts at Austrian subsidiary Semperit. Here, the announcement of staff and production reductions had led to considerable disquiet and protest actions. Then came the radical strike behavior of the workforce at the General Tire plant in Charlotte (USA) in June 1999. This was started by the US trade union and was a completely new departure in the history of labor disputes at Continental. The US trade union even submitted a countermotion to the planned measures at the Continental Annual Shareholders' Meeting, and thus brought the conflict to the German public too. In April 2002, a workforce delegation from Traiskirchen and Gislaved (Sweden) demonstrated in front of the head office against the closure of their plants. The works councils at Hanover supported their protest openly. In 2005, employee representatives engaged in a conflict similar in its intensity to the June 1999 dispute, when the tire factory in Guadalajara, Mexico, was closed. As with the previous protest, the trade unions sent a delegation to Hanover so that their demands could be submitted at the Annual Shareholders' Meeting.

The German employee representatives were again raising some contentious issues too. These mostly related to the introduction of the 39-hour week or its withdrawal, cuts in bonuses, and further personnel reduction measures. As before, Richard Köhler, the Corporate Works Council chairman, still relied on constructive dialog, but his stance was severely tested by new Executive Board chairman Manfred Wennemer, who took up the reins after von Grünberg. At the Annual Shareholders' Meeting in May 2005, Wennemer defended the reintroduction of the 40-hour week without extra pay. It was, he admitted, an unpopular and frequently criticized measure, but it was necessary if jobs in Western Europe were to be secured. The competition was tough and there was no room for special treatment. By now, Köhler had joined Continental's Supervisory Board as vice chairman. He left in May 2004, and after 33 years representing employees, he retired in June 2005. With his retirement, Continental lost a personality that could bring people together. "Conti was what always drove you," Wennemer said, honoring his counterpart's work.

Köhler could not prevent the working atmosphere and the relationship between management and Works Council from becoming much frostier in the period that followed. Sitting on the committee now were Peter Hüttenberger, North Regional Director of the Mining, Chemical and Energy Workers' Union, as it was now known. Next to him was Heidemarie Aschermann, from the Northeim plant works council, Dieter Weniger, trade union secretary of the Mining, Chemical and Energy Workers' Union, Hartmut Meine, District Manager of the Industrial Union of Metalworkers for Lower Saxony and Saxony-Anhalt, Gerhard Knuth, chairman of the works council at Continental Teves plant in Gifhorn. Three further works council representatives from Korbach, Northeim and Vahrenwald were also on the committee. The representatives from the more moderate Mining, Chemical and Energy Workers' Union still held the majority on the Supervisory Board and works councils compared to the Industrial Union of Metalworkers. This would soon change in the course of further acquisitions. Conflicts were sparked by the planned closure of the Stöcken tire plant, in particular. Following the previous closures or partial closures of the traditional Vahrenwald and Limmer sites, Stöcken was "the heart of the works councils from Continental's rubber world." Closure would mean far more than just a sacrifice for those affected in the struggle to keep the company competitive. The employee representatives also accused Wennemer of breach of contract and betraying trust, as the measure would violate an earlier company agreement. The CEO replied with the terse remark: "A principle stating that jobs are safe as long as certain company targets are met is unacceptable. There can be no job guarantees because there are no order and turnover guarantees." On December 6, 2005, in protest against the plant closure, a meeting of all employees at Germany's 26 locations was held. This was the first time this had happened in Continental's history. During this meeting, it was demanded that the Executive Board resolutions be withdrawn. Further protests took place on January 23, including a demonstration of around 2,000 employees in front of company headquarters in Hanover-Vahrenwald. Negotiations were held between the Executive Board, Works Council and trade unions, during which the union openly threatened to strike if the talks failed. A compromise was found, whereby the closure would be postponed to late 2007, as would the associated loss of 400 jobs.

The main problem during this phase was that there was no list of actions requiring approval in the Supervisory Board by-laws. This meant that Wennemer did not even have to put the plant closures to a vote in the Supervisory Board, but only had to give notice of them. As a result, not only the works councils but also the employee representatives on the Supervisory Board were ultimately powerless in the face of Executive Board decisions. The employee representatives knew this just as well as the Executive Board.

Calm was restored in the relationship between Works Council and Executive Board, but only for a short time. Then as a result of the economic and financial crisis, and exacerbated by the Schaeffler takeover, the social partnership at Continental was subjected to a new test. Already in 2008, management was forced to let go 8,000 employees worldwide in the face of drastically sinking turnovers and growing overcapacity. At the end of March 2009, a restructuring program was announced, during which a further 6,000 jobs would be lost, 2,600 of which in Germany. Particularly affected this time was the automotive area at the Regensburg location. In April, Continental employees came to Hanover to demonstrate against this. Employees from France were also present, as plant closures had been announced there as well. Company management announced in June 2009 that it wanted to avoid compulsory redundancies and plant closures. But just a few weeks later, the further economic developments forced it to tighten its restructuring policy considerably. It was announced that up to 20,000 jobs could be affected by the adjustment measures deemed necessary within the next few years. This included around 7,000 jobs in Germany. Compulsory redundancies were not ruled out either. On top of that, two locations, one in the USA and the other in Malaysia, were closed.

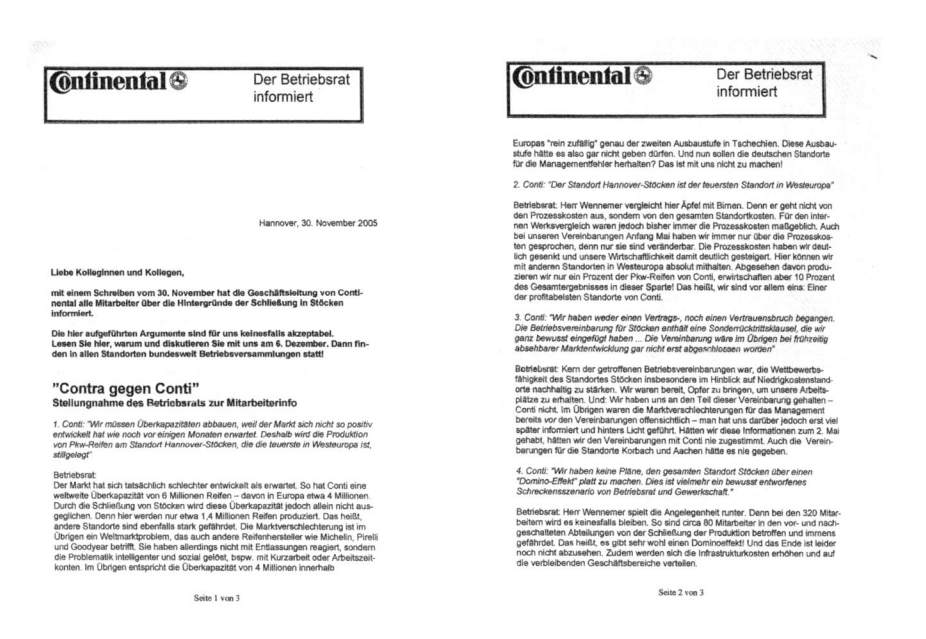

Fig. 49: Statement by the Works Council on November 30, 2005, on the proposed cessation of car tire production at Stöcken, and a call for company meetings.

The real test, however, was the takeover by Schaeffler. Not only did the Executive Board and employee representatives close ranks again, but a situation also briefly occurred that turned the possibilities for influence and distribution of power between the two social partners on its head. Even under Wennemer, the Executive Board had plans for an investor agreement with Schaeffler, which also included a number of fundamental demands from the trade unions and works councils. These were, above all, the demand that production sites and co-determination on a parity basis were preserved. A commitment was also made to the validity of the current pay agreements. These points were then actually included in the investor agreement concluded after Wennemer's resignation on August 21, 2008. The next day also saw a joint declaration from Schaeffler and Continental's employee representatives. It was signed by the then Executive Board chairman, Schaeffler's Central Works Council chairman, and for Continental by Hartmut Meine (Industrial Union of Metalworkers), Werner Bischoff (Mining, Chemical and Energy Workers' Union), and the acting Corporate Works Council chairman, Bruno Hickert. Among other things, it stated that: "The entry of Schaeffler KG shall not endanger any jobs at Continental AG, and Schaeffler shall not work toward abolishing parity co-determination without the consent of the Executive Board and the Supervisory Board [...] The same applies to the sale of divisions of Continental AG or the closure of locations. The corporate headquarters shall remain in Hanover, and the existing tariff agreements shall not be called into question." In return, the Mining, Chemical and Energy Workers' Union, the Industrial Union of Metalworkers, Continental AG's Works Council, and the employee representatives on the Supervisory Board would support the entry of Schaeffler AG on the Supervisory Board and in public.

The Continental employees were made to feel a little more secure because of this. As far as the Continental Executive Board was concerned at the time, however, there could be no talk of security. The new CEO, Karl-Thomas Neumann, had quickly lost the trust of the Schaeffler side and in spring 2009 was acting practically without a power base. The newly appointed chairman of the Supervisory Board, Rolf Koerfer, was not without controversy either. Continental's employee representatives took advantage of the opportunity that arose from this power vacuum, both for their own interests and in the interests of the company. First, they achieved the inclusion of restructuring measures on the list of actions requiring approval, and this became part of the Supervisory Board's by-laws. In the event of future site closures, the employee representatives thus had additional opportunities to resist. Second, a meeting was convened by Commerzbank in Frankfurt on August 11, 2009. Commerzbank had put up substantial loans for the takeover, and so had a strong interest in ensuring that both companies did not go under in the worsening situation on the capital market. Present were Maria-Elisabeth and Georg F. W. Schaeffler, the chairman of the Supervisory Board, Koerfer, as well as Werner Bischoff and Hartmut Meine, the two leading trade unionists on the Continental Supervisory Board. Nobody was invited from the Continental Executive Board. The aim was to find ways out of the ongoing crisis, which in many ways had become an impasse. The employee representatives gave their agreement to Executive Board chairman Neumann being replaced by Elmar Degenhart. At the same time, the resignation of Koerfer was discussed, with Wolfgang Reitzle earmarked as the new chairman of the Supervisory Board. In return, the employee representatives were given guarantees that on the new Continental Executive Board, both the chief financial officer and the three members for the divisions would not come from Schaeffler.

That it could even come to this was also down to structures specific to Continental on both social partner sides. Against the backdrop of this turbulent phase, these structures were not exactly advantageous for the company. After the resignation of the popular Central Works Council chairman, Richard Köhler, the power and influence structure within Continental's employee representation was rebalanced. This was between the representatives of the Central Works Council, the Mining, Chemical and Energy Workers' Union and the Industrial Union of Metalworkers. On the one hand, this led to an unspoken mutual acceptance and an unwritten non-interference pact between the moderate Mining, Chemical and Energy Workers' Union works councils and the Industrial Union of Metalworkers people, who in many cases advocated a more offensive protection of interests. Another consequence was that the Corporate Works Council chairman was in a weaker position now compared to that once enjoyed by Köhler. Bruno Hickert was from Aachen too, and so was not present during the many turbulent times at Hanover. In contrast to Köhler, Hickert also did not sit on the Continental Supervisory Board as an employee representative. There were also precarious structures in the directorship of human resources. In the 22 years between 1991 and 2014, eight labor directors and human resources directors had passed through the doors of Continental. On average, they had lasted less than three years. Each of them tried to reinvent the wheel, and also had to work at establishing a relationship of trust with the works councils and trade unions. In no other Executive Board positions were the fluctuations so high. Only in 2014, with Ariane Reinhart, did continuity prevail in this area of responsibility.

In fall 2009, calm finally returned to Continental's industrial relations after 10 years. It was flanked and fueled by a prolonged economic upswing and an unprecedented period of success for the company. Plant closures and conflicts over wages were now pushed so far into the background that they were no longer an issue. The Executive Board chairman Elmar Degenhart advanced the company's culture and implemented the "Continental value system." Employees were again able to identify confidently with Continental, and to look back with pride on the successful corporate development of those years. At the latest in summer 2018, this came to an end. After two profit warnings in quick succession, it became increasingly clear that a new crisis was on the horizon. Short-time work, layoffs, wage cuts and site closures threatened once again. In spring 2020, the first contours of a restructuring program became clear. 30,000 jobs were called into question, including several thousand in Germany. In 2019 and 2020, Executive Board announcements of staff restructuring measures caused the fronts to harden. In particular, the planned closures of Babenhausen and the traditional Aachen location caused a lot of anger, combined with fears and insecurity at other production sites as well. After intensive negotiations, a compromise was reached, and closures postponed at least for several years. As so often in Continental's history, this situation was again hallmarked by the ritual of protest, trade union criticism, and works council demands for the social hardship to be cushioned, while, at the same time, management insisted that the measures were necessary in order to save the remaining the jobs. In the end, both sides were united by the joys and sorrows of the company and the desire to overcome the crisis as quickly as possible. The social partnership at Continental would survive this crisis too, with staff and management finding new common ground.

Fig. 50: Protests at the Aachen location in September 2020.

The dirty, foul-smelling and exhausting work processes and workshops of the last 150 years, where, until well into the 1950s, Continental employees molded rubber by hand, are now a thing of the past. But, despite all the changes, the challenges of organizing manufacturing processes to produce quality products have remained. One of the greatest challenges always faced by Continental management has been to form a workforce from the heterogeneous worker and employee communities that identify with Continental and its products and feel part of the company. Even so, the development of Continental is often seen and experienced differently by employees than by management. Huge corporate entities such as Continental, with almost 250,000 employees at hundreds of locations worldwide, can therefore really only be managed by communicating corporate culture values. The development of Continental employees who identify with the company thus remains a permanent task in the future. The times when the workforce led the Executive Board chairman through the city in triumph on his service anniversary, and then showered him with gifts and expressions of loyalty, as happened to Siegmund Seligmann in 1901, are long over. Nonetheless, everyone profits when managers, workers and employees understand their common history, and proudly see themselves as people of Continental and as part of its long, illustrious history.

4 Rubber—Resource Management, Sustainability and Environment, or: the Metamorphosis of a Key Raw Material

The raw material rubber forms part of the company's original name: Continental Caoutchouc & Gutta-Percha-Compagnie (caoutchouc is a synonym for rubber). Only rubber was processed, however, and not gutta-percha, which is a rubber-like milk extracted from a tree in Malaysia. For decades, rubber as a raw material defined the company's identity, as it did for the entire rubber industry. Right up to the present day, the at times wildly fluctuating prices for natural and synthetic rubber have illustrated the industry's health and acted as a seismograph for political and economic developments. Continental's fixation with this raw material and the struggle to technically process it and understand its chemical and physical properties have been a common thread running through the company's history. Not only have the processing and knowledge of the raw material undergone a transformation within the organization, but also the way in which it is viewed and valued. Rubber also repeatedly proved to be a highly politicized raw material with strategic significance until well into the 20th century, whether this was played out in the trade conflicts of the 1920s between the USA and Britain, in the Nazi era with the ideologically charged propaganda of "German rubber" as one of the pillars of National Socialist self-sufficiency in raw materials, or in the years of the Cold War and the oil price crises. Today, society's views of rubber range from it being vilified in contemporary media as "blood rubber" in reference to the industry's colonial history and the exploitation of indigenous populations as rubber collectors in the rain forests of the Amazon and the Congo, to modern-day resource management based on the guiding principles of sustainability, prudence and environmental protection.

Global Conflicts over Natural Rubber and a Sunken Rubber Steamer Named "Continental" in Brazil (1870s to 1920s)

In November 1907, Adolf Prinzhorn, member of the Continental Executive Board responsible for research, development and processing of raw materials at the time, gave a long presentation on the company and its development to date to members of Germany's Vereinigung für staatswissenschaftliche Fortbildung

(Association for State Scientific Education). The focus was on rubber, which back then was still often seen as exotic and comprised almost exclusively wild rubber from Brazil. One part of the presentation dealt with trade, which was already taking on global dimensions and meant that managers at Continental needed to possess considerable logistical knowledge and precisely observe the supply chain from initial production to shipment and transport to the company's raw rubber warehouse in Hanover. In the 1850s, rubber was almost exclusively produced near the Brazilian city of Para, which lent its name to the best variety. With the rapid increase of worldwide rubber consumption, rubber collectors were forced to venture deeper and deeper into the rain forest. The result was that two new cities along the course of the Amazon became important export ports: Manaus, and Iquitos in Peru. Already in 1907, cargo steamers with rubber shipments were traveling from these two port cities directly to Liverpool and Hamburg. Rubber also arrived from the then colonies of the German Empire—Cameroon, Togo and German East Africa—but in smaller quantities and in poorer quality. The rubber trade differed markedly in the various European import centers: in Liverpool and London, the price was determined by auction, while in Amsterdam, Rotterdam and Antwerp, agents drew up lists of the type, quality and estimated price of the rubber, which were then followed by written bids. In Hamburg, dealers sent samples and written offers to interested parties in order to sell the product. At that time, the global trade market for raw rubber was dominated by a cartel of around 10 British trading companies, which attempted to manipulate prices via market interventions and artificial supply shortages. In 1906, Continental consumed over 1,500 metric tons of raw rubber, which represented 1/30 of the entire world market. The average price was 12 marks per kilogram, equivalent to a doubling of raw material prices in just a few years.

The second part of Prinzhorn's presentation therefore dealt with the massive price fluctuations in rubber. Supplying and processing the raw material was risky and associated with great uncertainty. And one of the basic experiences of Continental's management was that this risk had less to do with fluctuations in harvest yields and far more to do with global political developments and professional speculators. "The tire industry is one of the most high-risk industrial sectors because the raw materials for automobile tires, raw rubber and cotton, are subject to unusually high price fluctuations," wrote the Berliner Börsen-Courier newspaper after analyzing a Continental balance sheet. From the outset, the Executive Board's statements on the current fiscal year at Annual Shareholders' Meetings and in annual reports were dominated by the situation of raw materials and, above all, rubber prices. In March 1880, for example, the Continental Executive Board complained that raw rubber prices

> have increased so significantly in the past year that, we have been forced to raise the prices of our products on various occasions. Despite these higher quotations, which for some articles amounted to an increase of 40–50 percent, we were still unable to achieve the prices for our finished goods that we should have achieved given the raw rubber prices. This has led to a significant loss being incurred.

If prices collapsed, anyone who had stocked up too early or with excessive supplies of rubber could quickly find themselves at the limit of their competitiveness and liquidity. The same was true if rubber was purchased too late. At the end of the 1880s, after a short-lived calming of the markets, a new phase of the rubber boom began, culminating in a moderate price increase until the turn of the century and a rapid surge thereafter.

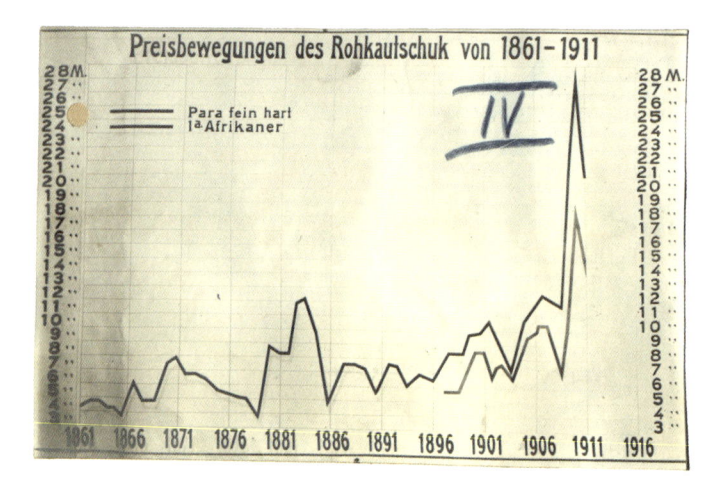

Fig. 51: Price movement of raw rubber from 1861 to 1911 in marks per kg.

"The price paid for raw rubber in 1899 has reached heights such as we have not seen for decades," the Executive Board reported at the Annual Shareholders' Meeting in March 1900.

> A more expensive price must be paid for even the lower and lowest grades than was previously paid for medium quality; and this price bears no relation to usability. In addition, the condition of the raw rubber is known to deteriorate upon arrival due to its careless extraction and rapid onward transportation. The percentage of impurities has increased

considerably, meaning manufacturers have to factor in far greater losses from washing than previously. And speculators play a role in this regard too, by exploiting the situation.

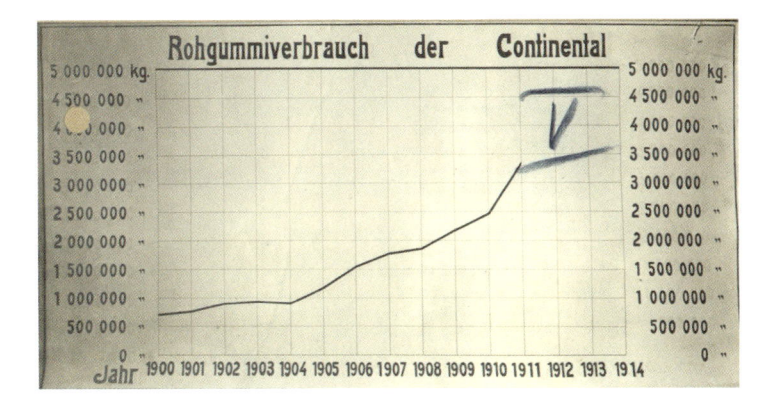

Fig. 52: Raw rubber consumption of Continental from 1900 to 1911 in kg.

In just four years, prices had almost doubled from 5.42 marks per kilo to almost 10 marks, but the real price explosion was yet to come. "The past year was one of the most difficult, if not the most difficult, that our company has had to contend with since its inception," the Executive Board claimed in 1905 when describing the situation to the Annual Shareholders' Meeting. "The reason is the extraordinarily high raw rubber prices, the likes of which we have not encountered before." In view of the further significant increase in raw rubber consumption by Continental by this point, additional expenses and cost burdens were already reaching the millions. In 1907, however, Prinzhorn took advantage of a short-term price slump to massively replenish Continental's rubber stocks. In 1903 too, favorable prices had meant the company was able to build up supplies. A considerable aspect of Continental's success was therefore without doubt its clever raw materials purchasing policy. In addition, rigid quality control had been put in place by then and proper monitoring and control bureaucracy also established in the purchasing department, not least because of the huge sums of money involved in the transactions. This involved multiple weight checks, invoice records, purchase ledgers and the monitoring of bookings made in the material account.

The Executive Board pursued several strategies simultaneously in the hope of making the company more independent of the strong price fluctuations and the resulting potential for supply bottlenecks. The first initiative was to found a raw rubber trading company in Iquitos, Peru, in 1895, together with the Austrian-US

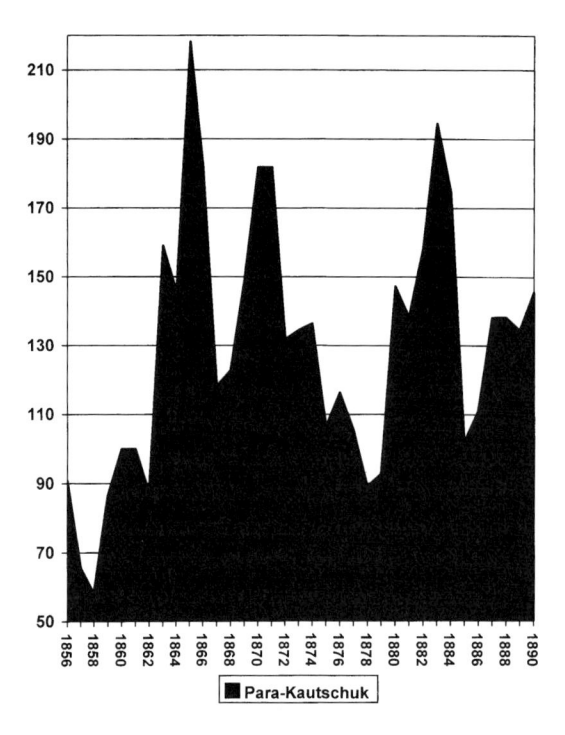

Fig. 53: Index of para rubber prices from 1856 to 1890 (annual average prices based on 1860 = 100).

company Gummifabrik AG, which was to be managed by two businessmen from Hamburg and Hanover respectively. Not only was a considerable sum of money made available for this venture, but a steamship was also purchased for 18,000 marks, which was to transport the raw rubber down the Amazon. Business had barely commenced, however, when the Executive Board reported the sinking of the "Continental" steamer along with its entire cargo on May 7, 1896. Further attempts at becoming self-sufficient in raw rubber were subsequently put on hold until, in April 1908, the Executive Board announced at the Annual Shareholders' Meeting that in view of tumultuous developments in the raw rubber business and the company's high reliance on European buyers and rubber traders, it had decided "to participate and invest capital in a rubber company located in the Brazilian rain forest, with which we have already had relations for some time." While initially successful, this venture into the raw rubber production industry as a means of backward integration was virtually wiped out by the turbulence in the raw rubber trade that followed shortly afterward, in addition to the rife speculation over shares in raw rubber production companies at the time. "Our participation

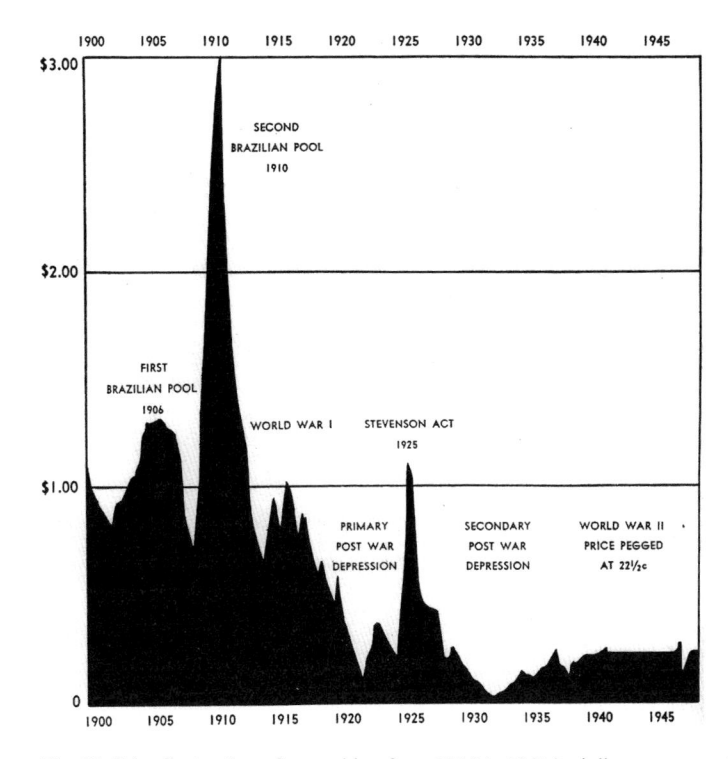

Fig. 54: Price fluctuation of raw rubber from 1900 to 1945 in dollars per pound.

in the raw rubber company in Brazil still exists," stated the annual report for 1913, "but we have decided to write it off in full in view of the unsatisfactory situation on the raw rubber market." Rubber from plantations in the British colonies, which was now increasingly pushing its way onto the market, played a decisive role in this, being much cheaper and quickly replacing Brazilian natural rubber.

A few years earlier, a completely different project had been launched for the supply of raw materials. Just a few kilometers away from Hanover, in Seelze, the company bought a factory building in 1903 complete with machines and steam plant and invested 350,000 marks in a facility for the recovery of regenerated rubber, i.e. the reconditioning and recycling of waste rubber. The Continental Executive Board presented its new factory proudly on elaborately designed official letterheads, and the plant gained in importance especially during World War I. After this, however, it ceased to play a major role in terms of raw materials and corporate strategy. While it remained the largest plant of its kind in Germany until

1929, with around 100 workers regenerating between 9 and 13 metric tons of waste rubber every day, no further investments were made in Seelze from 1926. A huge fire destroyed a large part of the factory, and it was thereafter only repaired in a makeshift fashion. "When people talk about Seelze, they mention it only as a ruin," an internal report stated. "Huge quantities of worn car covers, solid rubber tires, bicycle covers as well as countless sacks of rubber waste from the manufacturing process are piled up on the factory premises." The factory in Seelze was finally closed in 1929/1930 when a recycling plant started operations at the new company site in Hanover-Limmer. Nonetheless, the building in Seelze represented the first time the noteworthy idea of recycling rubber as a valuable raw material was put into practice.

A third measure taken by the Continental Executive Board to manage resources in the years preceding World War I was its involvement in research into the manufacture of artificial rubber. In 1906, at the instigation of general director Carl Duisberg, a research department for synthetic rubber was set up at Farbenfabriken Bayer in Elberfeld. At the same time, under the direction of Richard Weil, Continental founded its own laboratory to manufacture synthetic rubber itself. While Prinzhorn in particular harbored doubts regarding its prospects of success, the laboratory soon produced many other useful findings about rubber. Elberfeld was slightly ahead, and in August 1911, based on the compounds found there, it was able to produce a tire that was half natural rubber and half synthetic rubber. The practical results showed great potential, and Continental agreed to take on its first 1,000 kg of artificial rubber for 9 marks per kg—a deal with much promise given the price of 20.5 marks per kg for wild rubber at the time. However, in the course of 1912 and the following year it became increasingly clear that the ongoing skepticism of the Continental chemists was justified for, while processing the "methyl rubber" from Elberfeld, huge defects came to light and research was ultimately abandoned. The mystery of the composition and synthetic production of rubber thus remained unsolved for the time being, but the idea and the research goal themselves remained very much alive.

World War I brought upheaval to Continental's raw material situation on two fronts: the massive transition from wild to plantation rubber and its associated challenges in terms of quality and, above all, the cutting off of rubber supplies. Raw material management became as strict as it was bureaucratic because of the military administration that soon pervaded the entire economy. A rubber consortium comprised of the military and industrialists was formed, in which Siegmund Seligmann played a major role by coming up with particularly adventurous ideas and measures for organizing rubber deliveries from South America. A number of attempts to break through the wartime blockades using smuggler ships proved successful, most notably the famous voyage of the merchant submarine "Deutschland" in 1916 with almost 350 metric tons of raw rubber from the USA on board.

Fig. 55: An original piece of raw rubber from the blockade-breaking voyage of the submarine "Deutschland" in 1916, contained in the Continental corporate archive.

In April 1917, Seligmann pleaded for regular submarine trade to be established with Mexico in order to procure raw materials, but ultimately the only option left to Continental and other German rubber companies was the increased use of recycled rubber. Companies also had to open their books to close inspection due to wartime bureaucracy regarding raw materials and follow specifications on production. Compounds for car tires were only allowed to contain 10 percent raw rubber, with the rest being made of recycled material. On behalf of the War Ministry, the Deutsche Treuhand-Gesellschaft (German Trust Agency) regularly scrutinized Continental's calculations for the cost of raw rubber and the tire prices demanded by the war materials department and the military.

After the war ended, the raw material situation improved for Continental in that it quickly regained a presence in the world's most important rubber trading centers, especially the Dutch Indies and British India, and reentered international trade. However, acute shortages of other raw materials, especially coal, and rising inflation prevented production reaching peace-time levels. In light of this situation, the Executive Board enacted an ingenious strategic move by seeking a partnership with Goodrich, a US rubber company, in which it was to act as a capital provider and friendly cooperation partner. As well as foreign currency, this also brought American coal and rubber from US plantations to Hanover. Another advantage for Continental was the considerable overcapacity in world rubber production, which led to a dramatic collapse in rubber prices at the start of the 1920s. In particular, the recession in the USA had a global impact. Because of the lack of demand from the American rubber industry, raw rubber prices in East Asia slumped just when the plantations established in the pre-war era were yielding their first returns. By 1922, the rubber price (which was traditionally traded in British currency) had fallen by more than 80 percent compared to 1913—from 4.6 shillings (113 cents) per pound to less than 1 shilling (17.5 cents) per pound. This price collapse called the British government into action, whose Southeast Asian colonies were responsible for 85 percent of global rubber production. In order to prevent the ruination of their raw rubber plantations, the British came up with the Stevenson Plan. On November 1, 1922, a decree restricting production was enacted in an attempt to artificially regulate production and price, with exports of raw rubber limited to 60 percent of production from 1920. As a result of these restrictions and a parallel recovery in demand, prices did in fact start to climb steeply until 1925, when despite the regulations, they fell again considerably. On November 1, 1928, the British government saw itself forced to announce the end of the restriction measures. Not only had these caused wild price fluctuations on the raw rubber market, but they had also caused a boom for raw rubber producers in the Dutch colonies in the East Indies, thus ultimately failing in their rigidity. The most important long-term result was that, during the years when restrictions were in place, the British lost their supremacy in raw rubber production for good. This also permanently weakened the international competitiveness of the British rubber industry. US companies exploited this development to create and expand a dominant world market position, while Continental also used it to return to the international sales markets.

Apart from a sharp but brief rise in 1925 to an average price of 10.4 reichsmarks per kg of raw rubber, the cyclical nature of raw rubber prices diminished considerably in the second half of the 1920s, heralding a period of falling rubber prices. This suited Continental's cost structure, with the Executive Board having introduced rationalization and savings policies. In 1929, Continental consumed 13,000 metric tons of raw rubber—almost four times as much as in the last year before the war. In two months, the same amount of raw rubber was processed as was used during the whole of 1913. 144 railway carriages full of raw rubber were now arriving in the warehouses at Hanover each month, in addition to 35 carriages of cotton fabric, 600 carriages of coal and 17 carriages of gasoline. In order to produce 83,000 car tires, 44,000 metric tons of steam and 3,989 million kilowatts of electricity were also required. These were impressive figures for observers everywhere, but even more so for Continental's accountants and financial bookkeepers, since they concealed reductions in variable costs amounting to millions due to the onset of deflation in raw material prices. In the course of the global economic crisis, the average ex works purchasing price of raw rubber per kilogram fell to 0.42 reichsmarks by 1933—a tenth of the price that Continental paid for rubber in 1927 (4.6 reichsmarks). Instead of just under 60 million reichsmarks, only around 5.5 million reichsmarks now had to be paid for the same quantity. This factor also helped the company to weather the crisis.

Mobilization of Resources During the Nazi Era: German Rubber and the Radical Upheaval of Raw Materials

The period that followed, however, saw the return of rubber to the political maelstrom. And this time, Continental was no longer on the periphery but right at the center of events. Long before the outbreak of war, the Nazi regime had introduced a state regulation system for raw materials and set up a Reich rubber office, fronted by Hermann Goering as "Reich Commissioner for Raw Materials and Foreign Exchange Affairs." In order to implement the National Socialist policy of self-sufficiency and rearmament, a bureaucratic four-year plan was initiated, in the course of which the German economy was transformed into a "substitute materials economy." For Continental, this meant subjection to a new "raw materials regime." Continental needed cotton and carbon black from America, rubber from British India and Brazil, and cotton from Egypt. However, the notorious shortage of foreign currency in the German Reich and the breakdown in international trade during the global economic crisis meant that the company was suffering more and more supply bottlenecks. In June 1935, there was only enough raw rubber left in Hanover for eight to ten days, and so production was temporarily stopped. At Continental, a large proportion of management and the administration's time was now spent safeguarding the rubber supply and in permanent negotiations with the foreign exchange and economic authorities in Berlin. To temporarily ease the raw material crisis, manufacturing of recycled rubber was intensified again. A considerable sum was invested in expanding capacities for the reprocessing of waste rubber, which had now been transferred to the Limmer plant, from 7 to 16 metric tons a day. However, this was only a drop in the ocean. As before, the processing of natural rubber was dominant when it came to Continental's raw rubber consumption, which in 1937 stood at around 33,000 tons, with only 9,700 tons of recycled rubber used. For the first time, 574 tons of synthetic rubber were also utilized.

Under the new regime, research into synthetic rubber production and its development were quickly resumed at IG Farben and, spurred by the international race to artificially manufacture this strategic material, led to the first useful results. The Nazi regime and bureaucrats responsible for raw materials at the Reich Ministry of Economics placed all their hopes in the development and use of synthetic rubber manufactured in Germany (soon to be called Buna) as a long-term solution to the notorious shortages of foreign currency and precarious supply of raw rubber. At Continental, by contrast, the Executive and Supervisory Boards had been highly skeptical about this for a long time. "The articles appearing in the press about the possibility of adequate manufacture of synthetic rubber very much preempt actual developments," stated a memo from the director of the Deutsche Bank branch in Hanover in mid-February 1935 after a visit from Continental Executive Board member Carl Gehrke. The sole manufacturer of Buna was IG Farben, which at this time was only producing 30 metric tons a month. The rubber consumption of Continental alone was 75 to 80 metric tons per day. In addition, the price of synthetic rubber was around 10 reichsmarks per kilogram, and while Continental possibly thought a reduction to 6 reichsmarks per kilogram feasible in the case of large-scale production, a kilogram of natural rubber cost just 0.75 pfennigs by comparison. To make matters worse from Continental's perspective, the authorities implementing the four-year plan were trying to force it and the entire tire industry to make substantial investments in new Buna capacities while at the same time imposing high rubber import charges on the companies in order to finance the costs of Buna manufacture at IG Farben. Instead of 0.85 reichsmarks per kilogram of rubber, Continental was now paying 2.10 reichsmarks. The rubber policy was thus far removed from any business costing. Even so, Continental changed its course to follow the Buna ideology and the new raw materials policy of the Nazi regime. From 1938, all scientific research, development and testing resources were concentrated on this new Buna technology and its use in the manufacture of tires and technical products. After being one of its biggest skeptics only a short time before, the company now presented itself as a pioneer of this four-year technology plan.

Fig. 56: Buna propaganda at a Continental trade fair stand in 1937.

As with synthetic rubber, Continental was also subject to the Reich Ministry of Economics' plans for self-sufficiency when it came to the manufacture and processing of German carbon black, which culminated in direct financial participation in the construction of German carbon black plants. It was only when it came to the replacement of cotton by cellulose and artificial silk that the company was exempt. The massive use of "German raw materials" meant huge changes in production technology, however. The radical changeover of the raw material basis for tire production, as well as for the manufacture of technical, surgical and everyday rubber items, meant production processes had to be completely realigned. The processing of Buna was more complicated and labor-intensive, requiring new mixing machines and calenders, and it was also hazardous to health, especially with the increased use of chemical additives and plasticizers, which necessitated appropriate occupational safety measures. Ignoring the unsolved technical questions, the Nazi authorities put Continental under constant pressure to quickly increase the proportion of Buna in tires (which at the start was only a tiny amount compared to natural rubber) to 100 percent. This was to prove successful for car tires but not for the much more important truck tires used by the Wehrmacht due to their lifespan and performance capability. Nonetheless, during the war years, the use of natural rubber in Continental's raw material consumption rapidly declined to just 1,500 metric tons in 1943, while 7,800 tons of regenerated rubber and over 22,000 tons of Buna were used. By now, Buna technology was much more advanced and both IG Farben and Continental had mastered it despite all the drawbacks compared to natural rubber. It was no surprise then that Buna was used as a strategic weapon in the instrumentalization and subjugation of the rubber industry in both occupied areas and countries allied to Germany. Buna became a vehicle of the Nazi regime's plan to dominate the new German-led European economy. And Continental became a willing executor of these plans. Soon, an extensive network of participation, support, consulting and leasing factories spread across the whole of Europe, through which Continental attempted to control and coordinate its production and sales processes.

The subordination and alignment of Continental's own raw materials policy to and with the goals of the Nazi regime were demonstrated through its extensive involvement in the grand scheme by the authorities to extract natural rubber from Russian dandelions (kok-sadhyz). As of November 1940, rubber experts, process technicians and rubber chemists from Continental were part of a rapidly growing network made up of breeding researchers, the occupying authorities in Ukraine and other eastern territories, the Chief Representative for Motor Vehicles and, last but not least, the SS. In the autumn of 1942, despite the fact that neither the cultivation methods nor the extraction processes had yet been clarified, the first metric tons of "dandelion rubber" were processed in a specially constructed plant at the Limmer factory, from which attempts were made to produce a few test tires. The results, however, fell far short of the high expectations of all concerned. In spite of the failures in cultivating the plant and in extracting and processing "dandelion rubber," the Reichswehr and the Reich Ministry of Economics planned to create gigantic plant rubber plantations in the Ukraine, massively displacing the agricultural cultivation of food there. Due to the subsequent course of the war, these efforts were halted, however. Without the rubber tests and process developments by Continental, the Reich Ministry of Economics would not have been able to push forward with its grandiose plant rubber scheme in the East. With its commitment to plant rubber, Hanover was evidently pursuing a strategy of openness to a potentially promising process that would replace expensive natural rubber imports with huge plantations in the East. It was never considered that the Reich Ministry's vision of planting monocultures in the Ukraine not only entailed the destruction of vast agricultural areas, but also meant the intensive use of forced labor for sowing, growing and harvesting. Yet it was obvious that, due to the low level of rubber extraction and its inferior quality, the process was extremely uneconomical and could only function by exploiting the Ukrainian population and stealing their agricultural land.

After 1945, Germany lost its diverse raw material and rubber know-how to the Allied occupying authorities, especially to the USA, as German experts were lured away or appropriated in the course of "intellectual reparations." A few years later, this knowledge returned to Germany as American technology and know-how. The invention of synthetic rubber meant the rubber industry and the (rubber) chemicals industry were virtually united. Continental and IG Farben worked closely together, and the tire company's share in the development and technical application of artificial rubber was at least equal to that of the chemical company. As a result, there was at times great technological convergence in the raw materials sector, which was extremely dangerous for Continental because of IG Farben's possible entry into the tire business. This convergence resolved itself however after 1945, however, with the two sectors ultimately belonging to different worlds and going their separate ways after World War II at the latest.

Raw Material Management in the Context of the Korean War and Oil Price Crises (1950s to Early 1980s)

At the beginning and end of this period, two global political crises were to (again) massively influence Continental's raw material supplies and their costs, as well as those of other German companies. Raw material supplies in the first postwar years were initially precarious. Imports of natural rubber were extremely limited because of the difficult foreign exchange situation, and for its part, the German synthetic rubber industry was subjected to Allied control. Most of the Buna capacities were located at the Schkopau plant near Leipzig, which lay in the Soviet occupation zone, and were thus practically inaccessible for the supply of raw materials, while on the western side, the break-up of IG Farben by the Allies delayed the restart of synthetic rubber production at the Hüls plant. This factory itself was also under threat of being dismantled due to its classification as an armaments company. In addition, the British occupying powers enacted production bans for Buna and butadiene in June 1948 and April 1949, with the Allied demilitarization policy used to justify this. The real reason for the ban, however, was Britain's desire to prevent further advancements in synthetic rubber. Especially in these years, there was an extremely high surplus of Malaysian rubber, and Britain feared losing an important source of foreign currency. Germany was to partly compensate for the fall in demand for natural rubber caused by US rubber policy.

As early as 1949, in the face of rising demand on the global markets, Continental was confronted with a clear increase in prices for natural and synthetic rubber. The Korean War, which broke out in 1950 and was to last until 1953, then triggered a huge raw material boom and led to rubber becoming even more expensive. On January 1, 1950, a kilogram of natural rubber cost 1.80 marks, but by April 1951, the price had climbed four times higher. The price of a kilogram of natural rubber CIF Hamburg climbed at times to over 7 marks. "The risks resulting from the unusual price fluctuations on the raw material markets increased dramatically," stated the annual report for 1951. "As the transition to a buyer's market took place in all areas of our production, we were constantly faced with accounting difficulties of an unusual magnitude. At no time was it possible to set the sales prices according to the replacement price of the raw materials used." As many years earlier, Continental's managers again faced the problem of a risky rubber purchasing and storage policy, and in the annual reports from these years, the explanations for procurement measures soon took up more space than during the last major raw material price challenge at the turn of the century. Above all, the price increases caused problems for Continental with regard to the competitiveness that the company was trying so hard to regain in the post-war years. Its out-of-date tire technology in many cases meant that a considerably higher proportion of natural rubber had to be used in production and processing, while foreign competitors had recourse to a much great share of cheaper, synthetic rubber. Added to this were political measures concerning raw materials taken by the Federal Ministry of Economics that strongly reflected the state-regulating tradition of previous years and led to financial strains on the rubber processing industry. In May 1952, a price compensation fund was set up with the aim of subsidizing the newly resurrected German synthetic rubber industry, financed for the most part by the German rubber industry. The fund existed until April 1960, although price and production structures in the area of synthetic rubber had long since fundamentally changed.

Already during 1952, the global political situation had eased, leading to a considerable fall in prices on the world's raw material markets, which made both natural rubber and cotton vastly cheaper. In contrast to synthetic rubber, significant price fluctuations were also to dominate the natural rubber market in the mid-1950s. Political crises such as the Suez crisis in October 1956 no longer had such a huge effect on the natural rubber price, though by now Continental had clearly increased its share of synthetic rubber in its total rubber consumption— from 5 percent (1950) to 25.4 percent (1956). This finally brought the price and supply situation largely under control. However, a new and significant influencing factor had now emerged: currency relations, especially between the mark and the dollar which, as a result of devaluations or revaluations, could in turn trigger significant fluctuations for raw material prices. The revaluation of the mark in 1961, for example, was also expected to generate substantial savings for imported raw materials for Continental, which estimators in the purchasing department calculated at 5.184 million marks a year. "Experience shows that, just as quickly as we profit from the raw material situation, losses can occur," the annual report for 1962 stated a little later. "Our raw materials are still extraordinarily price-sensitive for political reasons." By now though, rubber had mostly lost its position as a strategic raw material, passing the baton on to crude oil, which was not only the basis for plastic production but also for the new varieties of American synthetic rubber. The health of the global economy and its development were now illustrated by oil price charts. Besides natural and synthetic rubber, the most important raw materials mentioned in Continental's annual reports were cotton cord, artificial silk cord, zinc white and brass. This mirrored changes in tire technology, which was oriented entirely to the USA, and included, for instance, whitewall tires. As a result, the share of synthetic rubber also continued to rise rapidly, reaching more than 50 percent of total rubber consumption for the first time in 1961. Price spikes for natural rubber that had been so feared for decades were finally a thing of the past, or at least this was what Continental's Executive Board thought at the beginning of the 1960s. But they were to be mistaken. Besides its function as an "excellent stabilizer for the price of natural rubber," the quality of synthetic rubber had also improved enough to displace natural rubber even further. Furthermore, the chemical industry had succeeded in developing artificial rubber varieties that mostly corresponded with the molecular structure of natural rubber. The major German chemical companies played a decisive role in this too, and Continental's research and development departments were also looking intensively at synthetic rubber once again, as well as at the new plastic technologies.

From the mid-1960s, however, it became clear that the era of politically influenced natural rubber prices was by no means over. In May 1964, a conflict that had broken out between Malaysia and Indonesia over North Borneo caused considerable concern for Continental's raw material purchasers. Taken together, both countries accounted for 65 percent of the world's natural rubber supply, and if an open military conflict were to break out, "the smooth supply of natural rubber would be jeopardized," as a report from the purchasing department stated in early March 1965. This was exacerbated by the conflict in Vietnam, one cause of which was the expropriation of Michelin's rubber plantations there. In Africa as well, Continental buyers noted the worrying rising tensions between Nigeria and Congo, with both countries also important for natural rubber extraction. The global raw material markets were threatening to sink into chaos and insecurity, at least when it came to natural rubber. At the same time, a different type of upheaval was affecting synthetic rubber too. By now, this type of rubber was marked by a massive oversupply, triggered above all by Russia as a new supplier entering the market on a large scale. This put severe pressure on prices, ultimately leading to international efforts to cartelize and reach agreements on production volumes and prices in part to end the "unnecessary competition between natural and synthetic rubber." Even so, the synthetic rubber market was fought for tooth and nail. The four largest European producers, for example, initiated anti-dumping proceedings against foreign manufacturers in order to prevent further penetration,

Fig. 57: Delivery of natural rubber bales in Hanover-Stöcken.

especially by the Americans. By the late 1960s, as the end to the "economic miracle years" loomed, a global economic downturn started, causing prices for natural rubber to plummet again. In 1967, the lowest quotations since 1950 were recorded, but these were followed by sharply rising prices the following year: a fluctuation that nobody had thought still possible. In addition to the Russians, the Chinese also came into focus as major buyers. The world of raw materials in the 1960s was hardly less turbulent than that of the late 1920s, even if the structures and, above all, the players had changed.

At this time, Continental was processing approximately 50,000 metric tons of natural rubber a year, with dozens of cargo trains rolling into Building 51 of the rubber warehouse in Stöcken every day. The era of secure and cheap rubber and raw material supplies came to a painful end, however, during the 1970s for several quite different reasons. First, an oil embargo was proclaimed by the Organization of Arab Petroleum Exporting Countries (OAPEC) as a result of an intensifying Middle East conflict in 1973, which resulted in an explosive increase in oil prices. This insecurity was to last until 1983. Not only did synthetic rubber rise considerably in price as a result, but natural rubber too: 75 percent between fall 1972 and March 1973. Only now did managers in Hanover realize that Continental was much more dependent on crude oil than had been suspected. "Naphtha: why Conti is so dependent on crude oil" was the title of the staff magazine "Conti intern" in June 1979, which tried to make clear to staff the seriousness of the situation. On average, Continental products were approximately 70 percent dependent on crude oil, and this dependence was also felt by the fact that the Bayer chemical group and its subsidiary CWH were virtually the sole suppliers of synthetic rubber and other raw materials. In 1972, Continental purchased from these companies 94.7 million marks worth of chemical agents, solvents, plasticizers, foam raw materials, synthetic fibers and plastics, as well as 50 million marks worth of synthetic rubber, which accounted for 70 percent of total requirements. When the chemical industry fell into a deep structural crisis in the wake of the oil price explosion, Continental also felt the effects. In 1974, purchasers in Hanover recorded a price increase in raw materials of approximately 30 percent, which meant added expenditure of 120 million marks—and this during a phase in which Continental was fighting for survival. In light of an increasingly unclear situation on the procurement markets, the purchasing department in Hanover was strengthened and further professionalized. In 1972, a separate department overseen by the Executive Board was set up entitled "Purchasing and Logistics," and the capital participations in the German carbon black plants and at Drahtcord Saar were expanded and secured with further investments, while modern IT systems were also installed in an attempt to gain a better overview of the network of suppliers, distributors, orders and invoices. As before, the motto "good purchasing is half the profit" still applied to Continental's procurement policy, but more than ever currency fluctuations and ongoing shifts between currency relations made life hard for purchasers. Natural rubber was still traditionally traded and invoiced in British pounds, while US dollars were used for crude oil and marks or French francs for steel. This was the birth of a foreign exchange management system that was as modern as it was complex, and for which Continental would become known in the 1980s.

The second reason for the end of the old synthetic rubber world was a revolution in tire technology triggered by Michelin. Steel cord radial tires required a raw material composition that deviated considerably from the previous tire structure. This was noticed in Hanover in 1969, even before the technology had been mastered and applied, because of a jump in demand for nylon cord and rayon, then afterwards for steel cord. With the potential to lead to a critical bottleneck at some stage, Continental tried to alleviate the problem through the early construction, together with Pirelli, of a steel cord factory in Merzig/Saar. When manufacturing the steel belted tire, it was the highest-quality rubber that was needed more than anything else, meaning in effect that use of natural rubber increased again. The forecast made by Continental's head chemist as recently as 1971, that in just two years only a third of the current natural rubber consumption would be needed, proved to be incorrect and also led R&D in Hanover down the wrong path. An inventory of the structure of the procurement market for 1975 makes clear the quantities of the materials used back then. As before, rubber dominated the landscape with 24 percent, followed by chemicals (23 percent), steel (13 percent), textiles (11 percent), auxiliary and operating materials (12 percent) and trading goods (17 percent). At 88 percent, Europe dominated when it came to the origin of the raw materials, with Germany alone accounting for 65 percent. 10 percent of raw materials came from Asia and Africa, and 2 percent from the USA. This was to change dramatically 40 years later.

The confusion and uncertainty on the procurement markets continued at the beginning of the 1980s, with renewed price jumps for natural rubber of up to 50 percent. In 1981, this led the Executive Board to seriously considering setting up or participating in its own rubber plantation in Indonesia—an opportunity that had arisen through its collaboration with the American tire company Uniroyal. The Indonesian government was interested in bringing foreign capital into the country and had opened up agricultural land ownership to external parties. In February 1981, the then general representative and later Continental Executive Board member Dr. Jens P Howaldt traveled to Jakarta to gain his own impression of the situation. Continental relied on partner Uniroyal's know-how since, in contrast to Continental, it had a wealth of experience in the management of rubber plantations, already operated one in the country (although it had been expropriated in the mid-1960s and since operated on a long-term lease) and had sufficient connections with the Indonesian authorities. The project seemed tempting, not least because the Americans tried to make the plantation business look highly profitable to Howaldt despite not having sufficient capital to start up a new project on their own. However, discussions with the Indonesians were "only partly successful," as the Continental manager soon stated soberly. Not only did the entire project require substantial capital (more than 35 million dollars), it was also impossible to rely on long-term investment security on the part of the Indonesian authorities. Instead of establishing a new plantation, the project subsequently shifted toward a partial purchase of the Uniroyal plantation by Continental for 14 million dollars. In October 1981, the project was put on hold owing to the ongoing high risks and was never revisited.

Sustainable Supply Chain Management, "Dandelion Rubber" and "Smart Rubber." Upheavals in the Raw Materials World from the Early 1980s to Today

In the 1970s, the relationship between economy and ecology was redefined, with limits to growth and the threat to nature becoming universal topics of discussion and chemical companies being widely criticized for processing toxic substances and disposing of them irresponsibly. Even so, the environmental implications of raw material extraction and processing had yet to make a real mark on Continental's company policy, with the same being true of sustainability in the face of the ecological consequences of the monocultural rubber plantations and the resulting destruction of rain forests. In 1977, a new cooling water circulation system was installed at the Vahrenwald plant, which enabled the previous use of drinking water for machine cooling to be dispensed with. Two years later, the Limmer plant was equipped with air filtration systems to neutralize the odor-laden exhaust air, especially during scrap tire recycling. Both the Vahrenwald and Limmer plants were located in residential areas, and the odor and noise pollution for local residents were a long-standing problem that was only really resolved with the closure of the recycled materials factory and the end of accumulator box production in the 1980s. Twice at the start of the 1980s, however, Continental was guilty of causing environmental harm: in 1983, a leaking oil boiler in Stöcken polluted the Leine river, and in June 1984, black clouds of soot could be seen over the same factory. These remained isolated cases, but coal and oil were still mainly used to generate steam in the vulcanization plants, and only gradually did the company switch to more environmentally friendly fuels such as gas. Ultimately, these were only individual environmental protection measures and were not integrated systematically into corporate policy. It is telling that, right up to the 1990s, the head of energy technology, a subordinate department, was also in charge of environmental protection.

Only in 1992 was a comprehensive plan for an environmentally friendly company strategy developed at Continental. "We understand environmental protection as the task of optimizing the relationship between the needs of civilization and the natural environment," it stated. A commitment was made to constantly review production in terms of its environmental compatibility and to find ways of saving resources through reorganization, while the manufacturing of products with "clear ecological benefits" such as low-noise, fuel-saving tires (thanks to their long mileage) was also promoted. Environmentally harmful raw materials such as chlorofluorocarbons (CFCs) or rubber chemicals containing nitrosamines were replaced and prohibited, while processes for optimizing the retreading of truck tires and recycling used tires were also emphasized. Last but not least, reference was made to the high proportion of natural rubber (around 30 percent in fact) as an environmentally friendly, renewable raw material in tire production. However, this positive view of a new, green Continental applied almost solely to Germany and was weakened considerably by extensive environmental problems at several factories that had been acquired in the USA, above all the former General Tire production site for synthetic rubber in Odessa/Texas. In the period after this, ecological efforts were intensified. In 1994, Continental founded an in-house recycling enterprise with its own tire disposal company, which tackled the growing mountains of rubber waste and organized the environmentally compatible reuse, disposal and recycling of old tires in accordance with international standards. On October 4, 1995, the Korbach plant was awarded European eco-certification for its efforts to reduce energy, heat and water consumption. This was the first time this certification was granted to a major German company and made

Continental a pioneer on the German industrial scene. In the subsequent years, all of its (German) plants were subjected to an ecological audit.

The actual supply of raw materials, especially of rubber, was dominated by international regulatory efforts. In 1980, for the first time since the 1930s, an "International Rubber Agreement" came back into force, which was initiated by the UN World Trade Organization (UNCTAD) and established rules between six rubber exporting countries and 26 importing countries to prop up the price of natural rubber within agreed fluctuation ranges. In 1987 and 1995, follow-up agreements were also signed. The raw material buyers at Continental realized that the purchasing of raw rubber had become more international and complicated, however. Already in the mid-1980s they were traveling to suppliers all over the world to gain an impression of their quality and reliability on site. The lion's share (76 percent) of processed raw materials still came from European countries, but the proportion from Asia and the former Eastern Bloc countries was rising noticeably. Despite all the international endeavors at regulation, in 1988 the Hanover company was confronted with prices for natural rubber that were steeper than they had been for a long time. Additional costs were also incurred for changes to raw materials that had been necessitated by stricter environmental protection and occupational safety regulations. The latter now developed into real cost drivers and made the supply of raw materials more expensive for Continental. Political events such as the Gulf War in 1990 also caused turbulence, albeit only for a short time. In April 1990, Continental opened its own purchasing office in Singapore "to improve the company's supply of qualitatively consistent, high-grade natural rubber." By now, Continental was using around 200,000 metric tons of natural rubber annually, and most of this came from Indonesia. Regular reports came into Hanover from Singapore on the supply and price situation on the natural rubber market. "The scarcity of natural rubber has continued through the year," stated one letter from October 1994. "China has been a very aggressive buyer and has spread out its purchasing activities across all Southeast Asian countries. [...] Only when the speculators withdraw from the market can we expect lower prices."

Indeed, Continental was confronted with drastic price increases in raw materials between 1993 and 1995. At the start of 1995, the price of natural rubber reached a historic high and carbon black was faced with an oligopoly that had been pushing through price rises of 20 percent. Overall, purchasing prices for that year were expected to worsen by almost 350 million marks compared to the company's original expectations. Against this backdrop, Continental also entered into negotiations with archrival Michelin, which resulted in a joint venture in 1996 to enable collaboration not only in recycling and retreading, but above all in the purchase of raw materials and semi-finished products. In contrast, the participation in a global electronic procurement market for the rubber and tire industry called RubberNetwork.com gained in importance in 2000. Especially after the turn of the millennium, the extent to which the world's procurement markets had changed in the course of globalization was clearly felt by Continental. The suppliers now had the say when it came to raw materials, as the markets had transformed from buyer to seller markets, the main reason being the rapid economic growth in China. This was strengthened by a long economic recovery in the USA and Japan with corresponding increases in demand. In 2004, a boom began in volatile, listed raw materials, above all natural rubber, which temporarily drove the price to over 1,200 dollars per metric ton—more than 30 percent higher than the previous year—before rising to a 10-year high in 2005. The crude oil price also rose to historic highs of over 55 dollars per barrel. All in all, in 2005, Hanover had to pay 100 million euros more than planned for raw materials, and the burden was only increasing. At this time, at a purchasing volume of over 8 billion euros, the exploding global cost of raw materials was the biggest cause of problems for Continental.

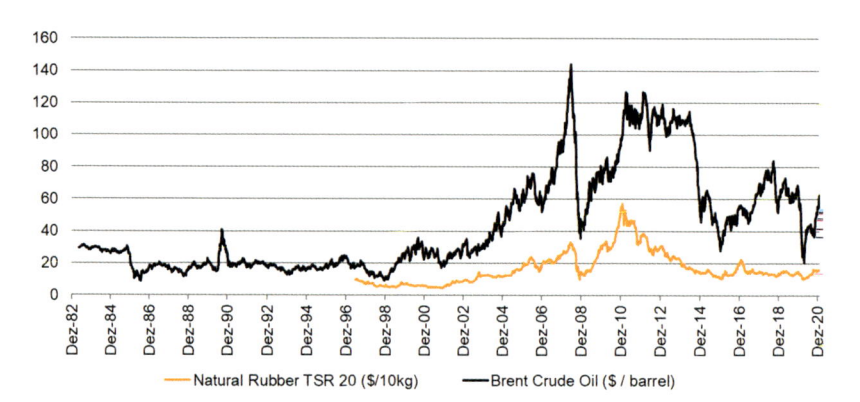

Fig. 58: Development of prices for natural rubber and crude oil from 1982 to 2020.

The raw material boom lasted until July 2008, when prices reached almost 3,800 dollars per metric ton of natural rubber and 145.7 dollars per barrel of crude oil. Following a sudden but short-lived collapse as a result of the financial and economic crisis, they resumed their ascent and had already increased significantly by 2010. In the meantime, Continental had further professionalized its procurement management and created a central corporate purchasing department in which its highly complex supply chain management and supplier policy were organized, with the focus increasingly on local quality assurance. For a long time now, life cycle assessments were being prepared at plants, showing the environmental impact over the entire life cycle of a product. However, a true merging of raw material management, environmental policy and sustainability objectives only really took place at Continental after 2006, in the wake of which a new way of looking at rubber purchasing and related supply chain management also became prevalent. After almost 15 years, the Continental environmental management system from 1992 was further developed and given a new focus. Only now was environmental protection explicitly understood as an integral part of operational management and embedded in a comprehensive management system. A separate "Quality and Environment" department monitored compliance with the principles of resource conservation and the commitment of employees to environmental protection, also ensuring that the ecological impact across the entire value chain and throughout the product life cycle was examined, as well as operational environmental relevance in production throughout the company. In 2018, the company also took the lead in an initiative of the world's largest tire manufacturers to investigate the connection between tire wear and particulate matter with the help of a scientific project by the World Business Council for Sustainable Development.

Consumption indices were now also recorded in production and the goal was to reduce these continuously. These covered energy consumption per metric ton of product, specific water consumption, waste generation and CO_2 emissions. After just a few years, significant reductions of between 30 and 40 percent were observed in all key figures. In addition, the various limit values for harmful substances, which had been made binding by European and national environmental directives, were also implemented in production early on. Tire manufacture at Continental had for a long time already meant working consistently on the environmental compatibility of the materials used. In addition, the company attracted public attention with a range of products designed to promote climate friendliness and energy conservation. These included energy-efficient conveyor belts and an ecological timing belt that broke new ground in drive technology by using a sheathing made of predominantly renewable raw materials and no carbon black. Added to this were carbon-neutral printing blankets, a fuel quality sensor to increase engine control efficiency and a piezo injection system that reduced diesel consumption. For the latter, Continental was awarded the German Business Innovation Award for Climate and Environment in 2010. Continental also caused a stir with a "hurricane machine" for recycling steel cord, which enabled the 2,500 metric tons of waste that the company produced yearly to be separated and recycled at the plant in Puchov (Slovakia). Previously, this waste had been disposed of at landfills in Eastern Europe or shipped to China as exported waste. Sustainability had thus moved from being a buzzword to become an integrated part of product and company policy.

"Continental goes green" was the motto which was announced to the public in 2011. Now the focus was on major environmental trends such as sustainable mobility. Ambitious targets were set for reducing emissions and waste, as well as for saving on raw and operating materials. Efforts were also stepped up to develop innovative resource-saving products. These activities then flowed into a new company-wide environmental strategy in 2014. The motto of this was now "creating sustainable solutions" and it continued the ambitious savings targets for another few years. Formulating a company-wide environmental strategy was one thing, but actually implementing it at company sites uniformly was another. As before, the environmental impact was greatest in the Rubber Group, with its large use of raw materials and chemicals and its energy-intensive mixing and vulcanization processes in production. In particular, the considerable need for renovation and retrofitting at "brownfield" locations, i.e. the plants around the world that had been acquired by Continental during takeovers, posed a permanent challenge and often lagged far behind the development of newly constructed production facilities, or "greenfield" sites. The Automotive Group too had to deal with a wide range of environmental issues, such as the problem of brake pad abrasion, which had remained unsolved for decades and was harmful to the environment and health.

Two developments illustrate how Continental's new approach to raw materials, especially its still dominant and main raw material rubber, translated into practice. One was a long-term research and development project on the industrial use of rubber from Russian dandelions. A prototype rubber (Taraxagum) extracted from dandelion roots had been developed since 2007 in close collaboration with the Fraunhofer Institute for Molecular Biology and Applied Ecology. In 2014, the first tires produced from Taraxagum were presented at the International Motor Show in Hanover, marking both a breakthrough and a milestone in the decades-long search for a sustainable tire raw material independent of traditional rubber. This would relieve the traditional rubber cultivation areas in Southeast Asia and also—in view of possible cultivation areas on the company's doorstep—shorten the long, environmentally damaging transport routes. The vision is that one day, instead of a Continental rubber steamer on the Amazon, a simple barge will suffice to transport the dandelion harvest along the Elbe and the Mittelland Canal to Hanover. There is, however, a long way to go before an efficient extraction process is developed or a tire prototype produced, not to mention industrial large-scale production of "Taraxagum tires." At the latest by 2025, if all goes to plan, another historical chapter will be written in the rubber revolution—from wild rubber through plantation rubber and synthetic rubber and finally to "dandelion rubber."

The second development was a fundamental reorganization of the company's raw material procurement, which in 2018 was reflected in a "Continental purchasing policy for sustainable natural rubber." The supply chains of the natural rubber industry were by now high complex, with some 6 million smallholders, 100,000 distributors and more than 500 processing plants. Already since 2011, the company had obligated its suppliers and service providers to comply with strict quality criteria. In addition, they had to recognize a code of conduct based on ethical, social and environmental aspects and adhere to this in their own supply chains. With the integration of sustainability into the procurement processes, these codes were then expanded and became subject to greater verifiability. In close collaboration with the Deutsche Gesellschaft für Internationale Zusammenarbeit (German Society for International Cooperation), a list of criteria was drawn up for Indonesia as an example to promote the sustainable production of natural rubber. This included, among other things, the training of local farmers in suitable cultivation methods and the tracking of extracted rubber from small farmers, through transportation, to its use in production at Continental. The broader goal was to focus more on protecting rubber plantation workers, local farming communities, forests and their biodiversity, and agricultural land, and to identify potential risks from undesirable developments such as deforestation of rain forests, corruption and land expropriation early on. Responsibilities and obligations were defined for all participants and stakeholders in the natural rubber supply chain, and mechanisms were designed to check these on location and to respond with sanctions in the case of non-compliance. In contrast to previous decades, Continental now felt a sense of responsibility as a customer and buyer with regard to the planting and cultivation of natural rubber and local working conditions. This was demonstrated by its involvement in Latin America, where Continental took over a rubber plantation in Ecuador in 2009 and set up a quality management system that included the planting and extraction of the rubber. Continental was also a founding member of the "Global Platform for Sustainable Natural Rubber," the objective of which is to make global supply chains more transparent in collaboration with other rubber processing companies. Together with Michelin, Continental additionally set up "Rubberway," a joint venture based in Singapore involving the use of a mobile application to map the natural rubber supply chain and evaluate supplier practices in different geographic areas.

The price development of raw materials and of natural rubber has also been characterized by turbulence and temporary shortages in the company's most recent phase since 2010. As before, the price fluctuations have still acted as indicators of health and seismographs for earnings development, particularly in the Rubber Group, and there has been a direct correlation between rubber prices and operating margins in this area of the company. First, in 2011, Continental was confronted with a jump in prices in all its raw materials. This amounted to 1 billion euros in extra costs. Butadiene, the most important basis for synthetic rubber, reached a new all-time high at double the price of previous years. In addition, specific raw materials processed in the Automotive Group, above all rare earths, now increasingly came into focus. This was followed, however, by a phase of significantly falling raw material prices, which lasted until 2015 and was mostly triggered by a dramatic fall in the price of crude oil. Synthetic rubber prices were noticeably affected first, but natural rubber prices were also under indirect pressure. Then, during 2016, the prices for natural rubber increased dramatically again. This time, the weather had created shortages, which resulted in a considerable rise in costs for Continental. The raw material markets remained highly volatile in the subsequent period, reflecting lower demand for tires from the USA and Europe—in contrast to the strong demand from China with its rapidly increasing tire production. In 2020, the coronavirus pandemic led to a virtual collapse of the raw material markets. In particular, the quoted price of crude oil was even negative for a short time, which was soon followed by a drop in the prices of synthetic and natural rubber. Already by fall 2020, however, futures on TSR20, the most heavily traded rubber variety on the Singapore Commodity Exchange, were quoted at new highs. As with all German industrial companies, Continental became painfully aware during the pandemic of its almost complete dependence on large-scale raw material supplies, especially in the case of synthetic rubber. China now accounts for almost 100 percent of synthetic rubber production, while 70 percent of tire cord fabric capacities are also located there. Rubber chemicals were once the domain of Germany's chemical industry, which monopolized its production at times. Now, there is not a single manufacturer left in Europe.

The crisis also acted as a catalyst for the implementation of Continental's new "sustainability strategy," which was formulated in 2019/20 and focuses on the four core topics of climate protection, clean mobility, circular economy and sustainable supply chains. The company is breaking new ground with newly integrated components in its drive and braking systems and environmentally friendly fabric technologies (which have also been made available to competitors), while also taking on a pioneering role in the industry. The implementation of this new direction is controlled by a set of sustainability key figures known as a "sustainability scorecard." This includes the proportion of company sales of products that demonstrably contribute to energy efficiency and the reduction of pollutants (40 percent in 2019), as well as CO_2 emissions, the waste recycling rate, the number of valid supplier self-declarations, certified labor protection measures in its factories, accident rates per million working hours and the rates of illness. The ambitious overall goal of the new strategy is to cut harmful CO_2 emissions to zero by 2040. Consequently, a permanent future challenge for company management will be to maintain the environmental key figures at all plants at a uniformly low level, and to facilitate production according to the same environmental standards at every Continental location around the world. Nevertheless, a big step has been taken toward achieving the company's vision whereby "Continental is recognized as a sustainable company."

Looking back through history, it is clear how strongly the upheavals in the rubber and raw materials sector have been felt by Continental; yet what is also clear is how many continuities there are, some of these surprising, such as its sensitivity to price fluctuations and political dependencies. Rubber and raw material purchasing has always been a difficult and very challenging job for Continental, something as true in 2020 as it was in 1880. But it is also evident how a holistic resource management structure based on complex sustainability has developed slowly over the decades out of a natural rubber procurement policy. The technical utilization of rubber has changed, as has the raw material's handling and the attitude and awareness toward it. Natural rubber has retained its importance: in 2019, it made up 37 percent of total rubber consumption at Continental, with synthetic rubber at 63 percent. Rubber has been joined by other important raw materials over the decades, including carbon black, nylon and other elastomers, cotton, plastics and later iron and steel, copper, aluminum, precious metals and rare earths. The 386 million euros spent on raw materials in 1979 have since grown into a purchasing volume of almost 30 billion. Today, rubber and its related raw materials such as carbon black and oil-based chemicals account for just 16 per cent. The company has also long since removed the reference to what was once the main raw material from its name. The composition and structure of Continental's raw material basis have changed fundamentally with the acquisition of large companies, above all in the automotive sector. At the same time, this has led to many new interdependencies between elastomers and plastics, electronics and software, from which products like "smart rubber" have been developed. Examples of this are conveyor belts combined with digitally networked monitoring systems, drive belts with data-collecting sensors, and tires that monitor themselves and adjust their properties depending on external conditions. Recently, the company has also increasingly shifted its focus to data as the main "raw material" of the future. While this will open up a completely new chapter in the history of Continental's resources, the fact remains that tires will only continue to roll in the future with the seemingly old-fashioned but indispensable raw material rubber.

5 A Brief History of the Continental Tire, or: the Metamorphoses of a High-tech Product and the Continental Product Portfolio

It was not rubber tires that Continental started with but hoof buffers, rubber balls and hard rubber combs. Soon, however, there was a wide diversity of rubber products at Continental with up to 60,000 items at times, offering something for buyers, users and consumers from the cradle to the grave. "A wise man once said that it's easier to live without love than without Conti," claimed a Continental advertising slogan philosophically in 1932. And indeed there was hardly any other company whose products were more closely intertwined with the world and lives of its customers due to its business model. At the focus of all this, however, was the Continental tire and the topics of motorization and mobility. In the years that followed, the Continental tire developed a veritable life of its own. Sometimes it was black (1920s), then whitewall (1950s), sometimes—figuratively speaking—brown (1980s) or green (1990s). It even changed gender, so to speak, and became female (in the 1920s, when women started driving); it improved its intellectual skills and became smart; if you know how to retrieve the data it stores, it might even be said to be capable of speaking. In any event, the Continental tire had a memory (in contrast to steel, rubber is always different, depending on what was done with it previously). It was and continues to be a high-tech product, but also another commodity. It became sustainable and environmentally friendly, but also an issue for recycling and disposal. By means of retreading, the Continental tire has not only had several life cycles, but also several "lives" thanks to the ContiLifeCycle. At the same time, it is part of a very large tire family and continues to live on in several generations. It features a wide range of properties that are still constantly being optimized: low-noise, non-slip, snow-resistant, high-performance and low-wear. The brand (image) of the Continental tire has evolved, but it has essentially always been very positive. It took obstacles in its stride, including nails and broken glass, and sometimes became deflated, only to pump itself up again into a donut or balloon (1920s). The Continental tire could sing (at times, young buyers of spare tires valued this conspicuous noise very highly) and even "shimmy"—a once popular American dance and a phenomenon which left the tire engineers of the 1920s puzzled—and it became the subject of countless poems, rhymes, songs and legends. At the same time, it was able to create a wide range of very different emotional experiences: it ensured ride comfort and was "a tire for well-being." However, it could also trigger trauma (1970s) and visions (1990s and present). Unlike some cars, however, it has never managed to become an icon.

Like the exterior, the inside of the Continental tire has also changed radically. At times it was made from cotton, then steel cord, at other times it had an air tube and then it was tubeless; at one time there were countless profile variants, at others hardly any; and once there were just a few compounds while today there are dozens that define the shapes and properties of the tire. The Continental tire has had unpleasant competitors and rivals who sought its demise, and it has also had to deal with fake imitations (counterfeit tires, predominantly from China in 2007); at other times, it has had brand friends. It has also changed nationality: initially, it clung to its roots (around 1900), then it was very American for a time (1920s). All at once it was very German (1930s) and later more European (1970s and 1980s), before becoming multinational with a strong Asian element. At any rate, the Continental tire was not the subject of a profound "tire philosophy," like its French counterpart, or the cause of a "tire war," which occasionally broke out among its Italian and Japanese competitors in Formula 1 racing, but came to be seen as representative of the "true history of German tire culture." The people developing Continental tires and the circumstances of that development have also changed many times: for decades, these tires were made by tire builders and vulcanized by hand, then they were wrapped by machine and created on conveyor belts with fully automatic systems. So it was no wonder that, in light of all this, the Continental tire actually entered the limelight itself.

Fig. 59: Continental promotional brochure from 1926.

Above all else, the Continental tire was one thing—the king of rubber products. Its innovation cycles over the past 130 years have featured revolutionary leaps, but it has mostly been a story of drawn out, R&D-intensive improvements to existing innovations. Time and again, the Continental engineers thought that they had reached the limits of what was technically possible, declaring that "the pneumatics question had finally been answered" (1907) or a tire type was "the last word in tire construction" (1930). The tires were praised as the "culmination of decades of work" (1921) and there were boasts that "the untiring progress made in our manufacturing methods has yet again led to the Continental tire being further refined" (1926); the tires were simply called "perfect" (1980s) and a fully matured product "whose scope for optimization was now thoroughly exhausted" (1996). Ultimately, however, the improvements continued, with new raw materials, new compound technologies, and adaptations to changed forms of mobility and changed areas of application. The principle that "with every new motor vehicle comes a new tire, and with every new tire comes new problems" was as true in the 1910s as it was in the 1920s, 1970s and 2010s. Every decade had its own "tire paradigms" as a function of the respective mobility paradigms. What is more, tires have always been accompanied by the need for specific "tire knowledge," whether for customers as a prerequisite for their use or, above all, their replacement and repair during the first few decades, or later on for replacement business customers, who, in the absence of product presentations, were entirely dependent on the recommendations of dealers.

Continental engineers have continually been looking to square the circle, i.e. to optimize the three most important product characteristics—rolling resistance, wet grip and low wear—where the improvement of one characteristic causes a deterioration in one of the others. Many tire engineers have dreamed of new tire paradigms for the 21st century, of making a revolutionary leap in technology and innovation, which, like Michelin's radial ply tires of the 1970s, would shake up the tire world and change everything. In this regard, Continental engineers can certainly look back on a proud list of fundamental innovations: the world's first pneumatic tire with tread in 1904, the first tubeless tire in 1943, the first special winter tire with studs in 1951, and the first self-supporting runflat tire in 1988/89. On closer consideration, this list can be extended even further: the first aircraft tire (1910), the first pneumatic tire for trucks (1924), the first agricultural pneumatic tire in Europe (1928), the first winter tire (1934) and the first purely synthetic rubber tire (1936). Added to this are the first "environmental tires" (1981 and 1987), the first runflat tire system (1987/89), the first "intelligent tire" with integrated sensor (2001), and the fastest tire approved for road use (2015). As part of its transformation from a pure tire company to an integrated technology corporation, however, Continental's product range has grown. Numerous products with long technological traditions and innovation cycles of their own have been added, such as speedometers and other measuring instruments as well as driver information systems, brakes and semiconductor electronics. The list of products installed in cars and that might be summarized using the key word "Conti inside" was already long in 1928 and has since become considerably longer; at the same time, it has become much more complex, supplemented by driver assistance systems, application software and data processing modules that are hidden from view. Continental products may be (almost) invisible but they can be experienced as an abstract feeling of safety, comfort and sustainability, and as a "user experience in the connected mobility of tomorrow."

The Eternal Search to Square a Circle, or: "A Tire for Well-being"

There are many myths surrounding the first Continental pneumatic tire for passenger cars. After starting with the production of bicycle tires in 1892, the Vahrenwald plant began manufacturing pneumatic tires for automobiles in 1898 in 41 different sizes, as the company's elaborately designed catalog shows.

"We believe that pneumatic tires are the right choice for all vehicles that aspire to high speeds and a comfortable driving experience and, without going too much into the question of whether the future belongs to pneumatic or solid tires, we believe it is right to recommend the use of pneumatic tires for all vehicles with loads of up to 500 kg per axle," the catalog states. Initially, however, it proved impossible to get the then leading motor vehicle manufacturer Carl Benz and his competitor Wilhelm Maybach to use the new tire technology, and it took a great deal of patience and persuasive power on the part of Siegmund Seligmann and Willy Tischbein to change this attitude. Continental was ultimately forced to purchase its own test vehicle in 1895 so that it could carry out the necessary tests itself. A pair of Continental tires was also expensive, costing between 143.75 and 537 marks, with a load capacity of up to 1,000 kilograms and a service life of 500 kilometers guaranteed. The Executive Board also personally vouched for the quality of the product. In addition to the Continental engineers, director Adolf Prinzhorn also took part in the first workshop trips to test the new tires, including to Bad Pyrmont, which was more than 70 kilometers away. Willy Tischbein, the tire manager at Continental at that time, is also said to have fitted Continental tires on his private car for testing purposes. The Continental tire's breakthr eventually came in 1901, not through private customer business, but instead through the emerging sport of automobile racing, when a new "Mercedes" car fitted with Continental tires won the Nice-Salon-Nice race. ough

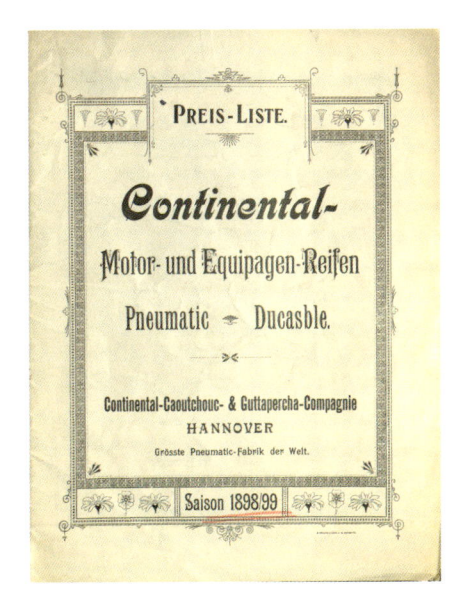

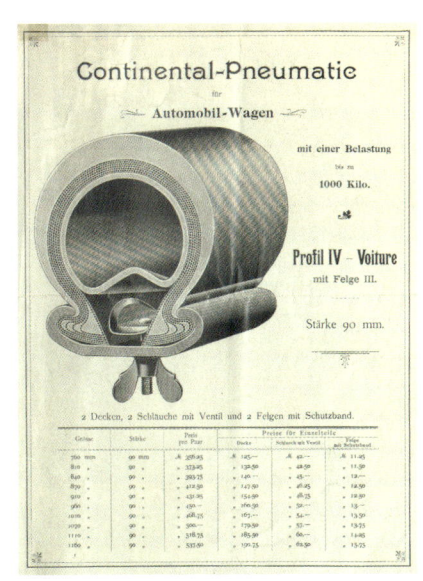

Fig. 60: Excerpt from the first tire price list from 1898/99.

At that time, however, the real "Continental tire" was still a bicycle tire. This offered a growing mass market beyond the automobile-owning elite, with the company's pneumatic tires attracting a great deal of attention at world exhibitions and trade fairs and receiving numerous awards and prizes. In terms of the still mass-produced solid rubber tire also, Continental continued to make significant gains for decades, despite the "old" tire technology, particularly thanks to their use in emerging heavy goods trucks. With guaranteed mileages of 15,000 kilometers and more, Continental's solid tires were recognized for their "excellent quality" until 1914. At the same time, however, the arrival of gasoline-powered motorcycles in 1894 also opened up a new sales market.

Fig. 61: 1904 advertisement for Continental rubber tires and photo of the Continental anti-slip "pneumatics".

In 1904, the first pneumatic tire for passenger cars with a ribbed tread was developed, followed the year afterward by Continental's "era-defining new product"— anti-slip pneumatic tires with replaceable steel cords. Due to their design, cars at that time tended to skid as they increased in speed, which was counteracted by heavily ribbed tires. At the same time, Continental engineers came up with detachable rims, which greatly simplified the hitherto laborious task of fitting a tire. Even many years later, various brochures and automobile magazines maintained that "the modern car is unthinkable without detachable Continental rims." Tire mounting demanded a lot of sweat and hassle, two full hours, and considerable technical knowledge of tires—something that well-heeled car owners left to their chauffeurs. It was for these but also for regular motorists in the years that followed that Continental published regular technical guides and repair and fitting instructions, creating additional revenue from the accessories these required, such as the Continental repair compound and the Continental universal combination lever. The Continental tire was a mobility technology that required explanation, and one of the sellers' main concerns was that it be handled with care to counteract any doubts about its quality. 58.3 percent of defects in tires and tubes, according to in-depth investigations in 1910, were "self-inflicted" and therefore not the fault of the tire manufacturer.

Fig. 62: Information brochure for tire customers, circa 1910.

From 1907 onward, Continental engineers also worked on applying the pneumatic principle to truck tires. Together with the manufacturer Büssing, they first developed air-filled hollow tires for high pressures, which were the first step on the road to replacing solid rubber tires. In 1911, the company presented the concept of twin pneumatic tires for fast trucks, in particular guest transport vehicles used by hotels and various delivery trucks. Improvements were also made to anti-slip tires. In 1913, the "new Continental snow slip protection" was presented in Hanover; this was a series of riveted leather belts that were strapped around the tires, thus preventing the damage frequently caused by the sliding protection chains that were in direct contact with the tread rubber. The year before, Continental had also unveiled another innovation—tires for the new and rapidly growing mobility sector that was aviation. "The most famous names in aviation mainly owe their great successes to our brand," proclaimed a self-published catalog for "airplane accessories and supplies." Willy Tischbein was also a founding member of the Deutsche Versuchsanstalt für Luftfahrt (German Research Institute for Aviation), which was established in April 1912, and this probably also factored into the development of the Continental airplane tire. World War I brought an abrupt end to all these dynamic developments. Continental tires were thrown back to the mobility technology of the Stone Age and were now made from wood, both for bicycles and trucks.

Shortly after the end of the war, the Continental tire not only reappeared in its old guise, but also in a completely new technological version: an American-style balloon and cord tire, which the company was the first to introduce

Fig. 63: Advertisement for tire innovations of 1921.

to Germany. The high-pressure principle that had prevailed for decades made way for low-pressure tires, while the rigid casing gave way to flexible cotton cord, which not only meant considerable ride comfort but also solved the old problem of pneumatic tires for trucks.

The technological improvements were also used for bicycle tires and the way tires were differentiated in 1921—in line with the various uses—is notable. It appears very modern, almost reminiscent of today and was especially far ahead of developments in the bicycle industry itself, anticipating many of these. There were tires for the "spoiled driver," simple everyday tires, robust touring tires, "Continental mountain tires" and own transport tires for business, courier and ambulance wheels.

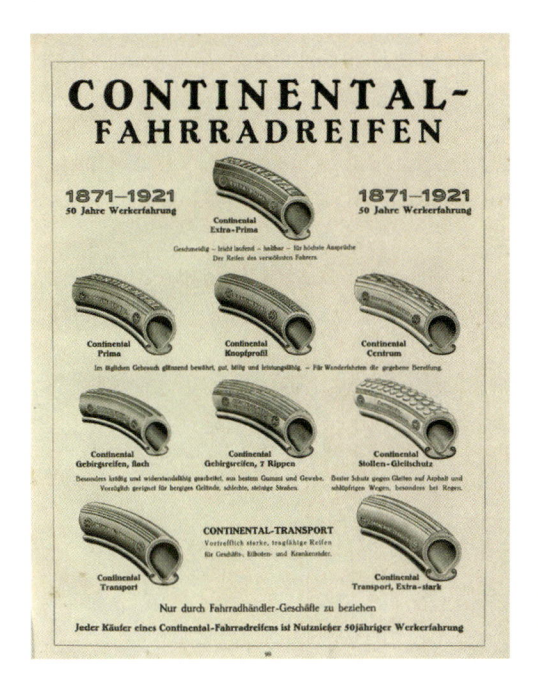

Fig. 64: Advertisement for the development of the bicycle tire range from 1871 to 1921.

In a world where at the time almost 90 percent of all cars were built by American manufacturers and also driven in the USA due to Ford's mass production, greater purchasing power and cheap fuel, individual mobility in Germany in the 1920s was still characterized by bicycles and motorcycles. And yet there were two significant developments that placed Continental automobile tires center stage during these years: the Continental tire became female, and it became a high-performance tire tried and tested in motor sport around which a group of elite and illustrious "Continental drivers" formed. These were subsequently courted by

Continental's ad men as "masters of the steering wheel." The company discovered the modern woman as a driver and car owner in her own right, and therefore also a tire customer. Successful female motorists such as Ada Otto now graced the cover pages of the customer magazine *Echo Continental* with cars fitted with Conti Cord tires. And after Clärenore Stinnes became the first woman to drive an Adler car around the world using Continental tires in 1927, and returned successfully two years later (almost) entirely without getting a flat tire, emancipated women drivers with the appropriate technical tire know-how became synonymous with modern Continental tires when it came to images and advertising. In addition, an appropriate Continental clothing range was launched, which perfectly combined elegance and function, with its chic Continental windcheaters for female motorcyclists and stylish Continental head coverings. Countless prominent actresses of the time such as Ossi Oswald were photographed out on excursions in their sedan cars with Continental tires or else posed in front of the latest cars with brand-new Continental balloon-type tires at the annual International Motor Show in Berlin.

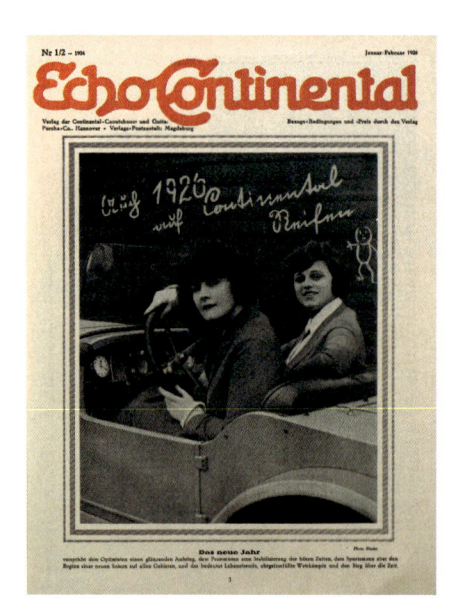

Fig. 65: Title pages of *Echo Continental* from 1926.

The "Continental 1927" and then the "Continental 1928" were launched onto the market like fine vintage wines, each the result of new intensive research and development efforts offering ever greater resistance, "unprecedented slowness to wear," and thus significantly increased mileage and fuel savings. Even then, Continental engineers were already confronted by the tire technology equivalent of having to square the circle. "The chemists and technicians at Continental," said an article in 1928, "have, over the past few years, vied to perfect each individual part of the tire on the basis of detailed studies in the laboratory and repeated practical tests on the road and race track [including on the newly opened Nürburgring], to the point that the final result embodies all progress achieved in tire technology and is no longer surpassed by any manufacturer in Germany or abroad."

Fig. 66: Tire advertising in 1921 and 1928.

Farmers also benefited from tire developments. From the late 1920s, anyone who could afford a tractor was able to till their fields using new Continental agricultural tires. Above all, however, Continental tires became synonymous with winning performances at high speeds. In countless national and international automobile races, the winners were fitted with Continental tires. Fritz von Opel chose Continental tires for his spectacular attempts to set a new world landspeed record with his rocket car in May 1928—the tires stood up to the challenge, the car did not. Initially, racing and commercial tires were developed distinctly apart from one another. For motor racing, tailor-made Continental tires of various types—"Avus," "Bergmeister," "Monza" and "Nürburg"—were developed, but the Continental engineers always understood how to leverage the experience gained in racing tires for normal tire assembly in relation to cross sections, rim type, tire dimensions, tread profiles and, above all, tensile members in the casing and tread. Prominent figures from motor sport, particularly Rudolf Caracciola and Hans Stuck, heaped praise on Continental tires, telling the growing numbers of Continental drivers they were using the "tires of champions."

Even Pope Pius XI placed his faith in Continental tires and had them fitted to his popemobile.

Fig. 67: Continental advertisement from 1932.

In aircraft tire construction, Continental also kept pace with the development toward ever heavier and faster aircraft and passenger planes. Lufthansa chose Continental airplane tires for its Junkers Ju aircraft. And in the field of truck tires, Continental presented the "Continental giant balloon tire" in 1930, another new addition that was also suitable for buses and thus public transport mobility and brought passengers in this segment considerable ride comfort. Long before BMW came up with the phrase, Continental was advertising its tires with the emotive promise of "driving pleasure."

Fig. 68: Advertisement from "The Continental Dealer" from 1932.

The Nazi era and World War II brought an incisive break to all this, a fact that was not initially evident. A series of new tire innovations was unveiled in 1934 with the "Continental Type Aero Gelände," a tire that was specially designed for rough terrain and heavy snow and might be regarded as the forefather of winter tires, two years before Austrian company Semperit claimed that it had launched the world's first winter tire in 1936. Continental never lost sight of bicycle, motorcycle and car drivers and continued to pay much attention to the spare tire business. Three new tires were launched in 1936, most notably the Continental FP 20, the first Continental all-weather tire with a fine tread profile and high skid resistance. There was also the robust Continental C 14, which in contrast to the traditional balloon tire featured a heat-resistant rubber layer between the protector and fabric to guard against destructive high temperatures—a reaction to the significantly increased average driving speeds and higher engine outputs of passenger cars. The third new tire was a giant truck tire, which was also a response to the higher demands being placed on pneumatic tires by automobile manufacturers. In addition, there were numerous special tires, from "T-tires" (taxi tires) to Zeppelin tires, to say nothing of bicycle and motorcycle tires in a huge range of sizes. In 1935, Continental also developed the "Volkswagen tire" in close collaboration with Ferdinand Porsche. There were also attempts to bring out a "Reichsautobahn" tire specially for the freeway. Ultimately, the old Continental "balloon" and "aero" type tires were gradually replaced by a plethora of tires with new designs and almost twice the lifetime.

Die drei modernen »Continental-Reifen« für den Personenwagen.

Fig. 69: The three main types of tires offered by Continental in 1930/31.

However, the four-year plan of the Nazi regime with its policy of using substitute raw materials and the state standardization stipulations that followed led to a radical decrease in the variety of types and the large number of tire dimensions available. In 1934, Continental had 114 different types of tire available in the passenger tire segment alone; in 1937, it was just 38. The situation in the bicycle tire business was similar, and the authorities had also ensured with their instructions that all special requests for red, yellow, brown or blue bicycle tires had to be abandoned. On the other hand, however, the very basis of tire technology also changed through the use of synthetic rubber instead of natural rubber as well as other "German materials" such as artificial silk rayon rather than cotton. Continental quickly became a pioneer of this new "German tire technology," and in 1936 manufactured the first tire made of 100 percent synthetic rubber. The Continental tire was now made of "Buna" or nitrile rubber, which had much poorer tire characteristics in terms of durability and performance than its predecessors. Though it may sound melodramatic to some, the Continental tire was robbed of its soul during the Nazi era. Downgraded to standardized tires, engineers focused in on the needs, specifications and goals of the Nazi regime and put a great deal of effort into optimization. This resulted in further innovations: as early as 1934, a patent had been submitted for a steel cord tire in which steel cords replaced the cotton fabric layer, while in 1943 the tubeless pneumatic tire was invented in Hanover, and a bullet-proof and thus puncture-proof air chamber tire was developed that was reminiscent of many of the efforts to develop puncture-proof, airless tires 80 years later. Rather than serving the leisuretime mobility of an emerging consumer society as they did earlier, the tires now ensured military personnel were transported to war zones and German fighter jets could safely take off and land. The Continental tire became the backbone of German wartime mobility.

The first Continental tire of the post-war era was made on July 10, 1945, at the still largely destroyed Vahrenwald plant. With the need for advertising greatly reduced—at a time when tire demand far exceeded supply— and the return to Formula 1 racing in 1954, earlier tire innovations such as tubeless tires and VW tires could now also be produced for the mass market. Not least the return to rubber as a raw material made it possible for the Continental tire to once again be manufactured to its customary quality, all of which helped Continental rebuild the close bond and sense of identification customers felt with its tires. Just as in the 1920s, new idols of the racing track such as Juan Manuel Fangio, Hans Hermann and Karl Kling drove their legendary Mercedes Silver Arrows to international victories using Continental tires, taking the world championship not once but twice. At the 1953 International Motor Show in Frankfurt, Continental caused a stir when tires were produced almost fully automatically in front of visitors' eyes for the first time. As early as 1950, Continental's Executive Board had announced new tire innovations at a major press conference: a steel cord tire that replaced the old textile fabric; an "SKS" tire with an original tread (S for Schnelligkeit (speed), K for Kilometerleistung (mileage) and S for Stehfestigkeit (stability)); a new "T4" tractor tire, a prerequisite for the revival of the agricultural sector, which was being increasingly motorized; and a siped tread tire for buses and trucks. In 1954, the first American-style "whitewall tires" to be manufactured in Germany were presented to the public, giving the tire a chic and modern look.

Continental was once again, and more than ever in fact, the most popular tire brand, as an Emnid survey confirmed in Hanover. The same survey also revealed that drivers had finally become more "tire-conscious." The *Small Continental Tire Glossary*, which had grown in the interim to around 40 pages in length, ensured that this attitude among its customers was supported with the required tire knowledge. When the "new Continental tire" was presented in 1960, it appeared (once again) as though the ultimate tire had been created. It was "a fundamentally new, optimal combination of all properties that a contemporary car tire must possess with regard to safety, ride comfort, speed, grip, low noise, cornering stability and service life," as the annual report proudly and confidently proclaimed.

However, this high-flying period in the history of Continental tires was short-lived. In the late 1950s, tragedies, scandals and fatal accidents involving competitors such as Firestone, Englebert, Pirelli and Dunlop caused Continental, although it was not directly involved, to withdraw from motor sports. With the development of the "steel stud tire" in 1963, Continental briefly dominated the winter tire business, before the legal ban on studded tires put an end to this type of tire. As early as 1962, the tire engineers at Continental had been researching the development of an emergency wheel too, which could be fitted without taking up too much space and be used to drive up to 150 kilometers per hour for 20 minutes. However, despite the tire making a great impression during a demonstration for the Teves company and being assured support, major automotive manufacturers such as VW and Daimler-Benz proved skeptical, so the idea was not followed up. Most notably, the company soon fell behind when it came to innovations in tire technology such as the search for a solution to the then new problem of aquaplaning experienced by mass produced vehicles, which the Uniroyal hydrodynamics researchers mastered with their "rain tires" in 1969. It also failed to preempt the most important tire revolution of the 1960s and 1970s: Michelin's steel belt radial ply tire technology. While there was universal acclamation in 1965 for the satisfying results in the tire sector—20 percent more mileage thanks to the use of new stereo-chemical treads and 7 percent shorter braking distances due to new grip-related additives, as well as 10 percent greater "deflection" and traction thanks to more flexible sidewalls—this was also the year that the fatal error was committed of pursuing development of the textile-cord belt tire instead of the steel belted tire. The initially hesitant original equipment manufacturers must also bear their fair share of the blame for this mistake, since radial ply tires also required numerous design changes to the automobile itself. It would take another 10 years for Continental to make up the lost ground.

Fig. 70: Advertisement for tubeless tires from 1955.

The first Continental steel radial ply tire with a modern design was the TS 771, which was manufactured in 1970, but a polyurethane tire that was molded not wrapped was almost launched, which would have spelled the end of the road for Continental. Since the end of the 1960s, American tire companies in particular had been researching plastic tires that would be simply molded from polyurethane, thus replacing rubber as an expensive raw material and the labor-intensive wrapping process. In the new "age of plastic," the idea of a "molded tire" appeared to be entirely feasible, particularly as the dream of such a tire had long been pursued by engineers. This was a scenario that made the Continental engineers feel uneasy and the Continental Executive Board even more so, forced to contemplate the horror of the company potentially missing out once again on a key technical innovation. When its competitor Phoenix presented a polyurethane tire to the public in 1978, backed by the expertise and financial strength of its major shareholder, the Firestone Group, the fears of all seemed to have materialized. Daimler-Benz angrily summoned the developers at Continental, its main supplier, to Stuttgart to explain their negligence, and within the Supervisory Board, Alfred Herrhausen expressed his fear that "we might suddenly find ourselves in a completely new reality thanks to the Phoenix tire." However, the assessment of the plastic tire by the R&D engineers at Continental was very soon unanimous and unambiguous: molded tires would have no bearing on the future, as they were not suitable for the passenger car and truck tire sectors, neither in terms of the costs of the raw materials nor their physical-chemical properties. Ultimately, they believed, it was all just clever PR from Phoenix. The Continental researchers were proved right as, by early 1979, these much vaunted tire prototypes had quietly disappeared into oblivion.

Fig. 71: Advertising brochure for the new "Continental R tires" from 1955.

The new Continental radial ply tire was not fully developed technically for a long time. The tire industry worldwide was beset by insufficient mastery of the complex production procedure and growing numbers of breakdowns and accidents. Even though Continental, unlike Firestone in the USA or Metzeler in Germany in the mid-1970s, was not involved in any fatal car accidents due to suddenly bursting or defective tires, it was also forced to recall tires for the first time in its history in March 1975. In the USA, recalls were already a matter of course at that time and apparently did little to damage the image of the tire brand, unlike in Germany—particularly since Continental had to start another recall campaign in fall 1976, which resulted in 17,000 tires being replaced by the end of the year. The height-to-width ratio of the tires had long since been permanently changed. The once narrow Continental tire with dimensions of 820 x 120, i.e. a height-to-width ratio of over 110 percent, had grown increasingly wider and, by 1978, had dimensions of 205/60-15, i.e. a ratio of only 60 percent. The range of Continental tires now once again encompassed more than 1,500 designs, with radial ply tires still making up only 60 to 80 percent of total production for passenger and truck tires. It was not until December 1979 that the last old diagonal VW tire was produced at the Stöcken plant, with precisely 37,522,751 units having been produced there over the previous 29 years.

Fig. 72: The last diagonal VW tire manufactured in December 1979.

All efforts were now put into restoring the reputation of the Continental brand, which had almost gone under in light of Michelin's market dominance, with the company's image having suffered greatly among car drivers. Gradually, these efforts proved successful. In early summer 1976, a new tire family known as the Conti Contact series was launched, which has since continued into its fifth and sixth generations. The successor generation of this series was presented back in 1983. The legendary ContiContact M+S TS 740 proved a sales hit as a winter tire, as did the fast ContiSuperContact CH 51 and CV 51 summer tires, in an automotive sector characterized by ever greater driving speeds. The slogan "Freie Fahrt für freie Bürger" ("Freedom to drive for free citizens"), which was familiar to all from the battle against speed limits on autobahns, also impacted tire development. Marketing gags such as "wicked weather tires from Continental" for the ContiContact TS

730 caused a stir back in November 1976, but it was not until the fall of 1981 that the company was the center of public attention when it presented its first energy-optimized "environmental tire" at the International Motor Show in Frankfurt. This Continental tire for trucks consumed less crude oil during production and saved energy. Instead of crude oil and carbon black, silica was rediscovered as a filler, resulting in the tire being a different brown color overall. "Save gasoline with Conti. Up to five percent less fuel thanks to reduced rolling resistance," proclaimed the Conti Energy Initiative, which was launched for passenger car tires simultaneously. The company also presented new products in the bicycle and motorcycle tires sector—a tubular tire with a zip opening, the endless bicycle inner tube, and above all the tubeless bicycle tire. Just as the racing tire had been used as an image for the automotive sector, this was now repeated in cycling. All of the famous professional cyclists of the time, from Dietrich Thurau and the German national cycling team, which won gold at several Olympic Games, to racing idols of the time such as Rolf Gölz, Jan Ullrich and Erik Zabel used the hand-sewn Continental super-bike tires from the plant in Korbach, including Richard Virenque—King of the Mountains at the Tour de France a record seven times—and all German postmen and women, after Continental received a corresponding equipment order from the German Postal Service in 1987.

However, Continental caused the greatest sensation in the mid-1980s, when it launched two revolutionary tire technologies within a short space of time. One was the continuation of the idea of an emergency tire, the new Continental Tire System (CTS), which for the first time conceived of the tire as a system in conjunction with other parts of the automobile and developed this technically. The other, this time continuing previous research into the brown environmental tire, was the Continental Energy Optimized Tire (EOT). The characteristic of what was initially called the CNR system (Conti-Notlauf-Reifensystem or Conti runflat system) was that the tire no longer rested on the rim's outer surfaces but instead gripped around the rim from the outside, with its bead seat on the rim's radial, internal surfaces. This suddenly opened up the potential to develop a range of performance features that could not be achieved with the tire previously. Lower system weight and larger installation space opened up conceptual advantages for the vehicle manufacturer; ride quality, power transmission on wet road surfaces, and protection against aquaplaning were significantly improved. Rolling resistance dropped noticeably, without any lasting impact on other tire properties. However, another property was remarkable: the CNR system maintained its ability to drive even in the event of a flat tire. The ability to run flat after a loss of pressure for several hundred kilometers meant that, in the future, there would be no need to carry a spare wheel. Behind the idea of tire and rim comprising a unit, the outlines of a completely new type of tire could be discerned, which then became part of a system concept. The press conference held by Continental's Executive Board in November 1983 heralded the start of a meticulously planned PR campaign, which caused something of a tumult in the world of tires. Continental proudly announced a world first that would literally turn conventional technology on its head and was convinced that the tire system, now known as CTS (Conti Tire System), would become established as standard equipment in just a few years. "Continental has reinvented the tire," the company confidently announced in its advertisements. In order to concentrate entirely on automotive tire production, the manufacturing of aircraft tires was discontinued in 1985—after almost 75 years.

But when it came to the technical development of the new tire system, it was not until 1987 that the goal was actually achieved. Technically, the CTS was highly developed and ready for volume production. For the Executive Board, this was reason enough to present these results to the public in a second major press campaign. "In 1988/89," they confidently declared, "the first car with the new CTS tire system will take to the road." However, only a small number of car models were actually equipped with the CTS. Ultimately, the once all-embracing new tire concept became just a special tire tailored to the specific runflat characteristic, and while it was produced en masse, it failed to become a mainstream technology because of the high production costs. The result, however, was an immense image boost, which caused not only the stock market price but also the sentiment barometer within the corporation to soar. The CTS project became something that people identified with Continental and finally enabled the firm to put the difficulty of its recent past and the ignominy of the radial ply tire defeat behind it. The fact that the technical innovation ultimately failed was due to the problems facing the company's external innovation management. Right from the start, it was clear that Continental could not establish the new tire concept on its own, due to the lack of financial strength and the mechanics of the competition on the OEM market. Continental needed two indispensable partners—the automotive industry and one or more competitors. However, their support was not forthcoming.

This failure was all the more painful for the tire engineers, since the second major innovation project that Continental launched in 1982 under the title EOT (Energy Optimized Tire), continuing the concept of a brown environmental tire, also failed to live up to its billing. By the time the tire was ready for production at the end of the 1980s, diesel fuel prices had already fallen significantly again, meaning that the cost saving that had been factored in was wiped out by the higher purchase price of EOT tires. Having only just been presented to the public, the new tires practically disappeared from the market a year later. The EOT tire had failed as a marketing project, but the topic of conserving energy remained high on the innovation agenda. As with the CTS experience, it was therefore filtered into subsequent tire developments along with all the other painful learning processes.

The following years focused entirely on the intensive search for "intelligent tires." Initially, a new generation of the ContiContact tire family was developed in the early 1990s, including spectacular items such as the ContiAquaContact from 1991/93, Continental's first and only genuine rain tire, which had a striking tread design, a new ContiWinterContact tire with honeycomb profile in 1994, and the ContiEcoContact, which, as a summer tire, offered good road holding even on wet bends with high mileage and above all lower fuel consumption, plus in 1996 the ContiSportContact with asymmetrical tread design for premium vehicles by Porsche, Audi, BMW and Mercedes. "Has the tire now reached full maturity?" This was the question posed by Hubertus von Grünberg, then chairman of the Executive Board, at the Annual Shareholders' Meeting in June 1999. In fact, he felt, it had reached a high level of maturity and there was only limited scope for further optimization. "We are approaching the optimum." The entire Executive Board was therefore behind the decision to think beyond the "mature tire," he explained. And this is what they did, together with the R&D engineers at the corporation's innovation center in Stöcken. "Coming soon: the 'intelligent' tire. Systems technologies for the car of tomorrow," was the name of a comprehensive brochure from as early as fall 1999. It presented a whole range of new systems, modules and functions, which significantly supplemented and expanded on the properties and tasks of tires within the concept of automotive mobility. The sidewall torsion sensor measured and regulated the forces during acceleration and braking of the car, the ContiSafetyRing functioned as a new runflat system, ABS and ESP ensured stabilization of vehicle handling, and the ContiWheelSystem presented a new tire/rim system that made spare tires obsolete. Finally, the Tire Pressure Monitoring System checked tire pressures continuously and automatically. The first version of the intelligent Continental tire went into production in summer 2002. A second version with sensors integrated in the tire, which not only monitored the tire itself with regard to tread depth and damage, but also provided information on its operating conditions such as tire pressure, temperature and road condition, was planned a few years later.

In its role of reliably transferring force and torque during contact with the road and thus guaranteeing driving stability and ride comfort, the tire is the system component that 'experiences' everything that happens between vehicle and the road. The development goal is a tire that, as an integrated component of the chassis, provides as much information as possible to driver and vehicle. This means that, in addition to its original function, it becomes a data carrier and provider,

stated the 2001 annual report. The concept of integrating the tires into the chassis control system had enormous potential for the future and, above all, the market. Intelligent Continental tires could supply a wealth of information—all the developers had to do was get them to "talk."

Implementation of this concept has shaped the work of tire engineers and experts in the automotive sector right up to the present day. At the same time, it was another vision that occupied the Continental Executive Board in the mid-1990s—a revolution in tire production technology based on a "green tire." Uniform non-cured blanks were to be manufactured for a wide range of tire types, with the blanks only having the relevant treads applied on site depending on demand and the order situation. This vision was part of the "lean tire concept" pursued by all tire companies, aimed at reducing the number of tire components and the number of sizes per plant, automating the still labor-intensive production process even further and ultimately improving their own competitiveness. Major competitor Michelin appeared to have gotten there first with its mysterious C3M concept, and Pirelli, too, had apparently introduced a similar concept known as MIRS for short (Modular Integrated Robotized System). Continental also developed its own MMP (modular manufacturing process) strategy, but the concept failed in Hanover just as it had in Clermont-Ferrand and Milan. Instead, there was at the same time a completely contradictory trend away from the concept of the modular "basic tire"—a massive increase in the volume of tailor-made tires for every new vehicle type and every new vehicle concept. The number of special tires with their own compounds and material technologies increased exponentially. In 2009, Continental developed the first SUV tire, the ContiCrossContact UHP, and simultaneously launched a product offensive with eight new premium commercial vehicle tires, followed in the subsequent year by a further 36 new commercial vehicle tires, including third-generation Continental bus tires. With this, Continental had the most state-of-the-art and widely diversified tire portfolio in this sector. At the time it was the largest product offensive the company had ever run in the commercial vehicle tires sector. Around 1,400 chemists and engineers now work at the main R&D location in Stöcken in Hanover, where they develop up to 9,000 different tires for a wide range of requirements. Some 12,000 formulas for different rubber compounds are processed and tested here before between 15 and 25 of them are incorporated into the respective car or truck tires. In addition to new high-speed tires, the new variety of drive systems in cars—from classic fuel combustion engines to liquid petroleum gas drives, hydrogen engines, hybrid drives and electric motors with batteries—required tires that are adapted accordingly such as the Conti.eContact, which was developed back in 2011. The new tires also had to be adapted to the specific operating principles of electronic advanced driver assistance systems, as well as countless new functional requirements for industrial tires, construction site vehicles, transport machines and forklift trucks. Continental's solid rubber tire, which is now almost 150 years old, lives on here in a modified form. The Conti Super Elastic tires (CSE) have been manufactured at the Korbach plant since 1966; back then some 4,000 units were made—a quantity which in 2015 was produced in less than three days to celebrate the production milestone of the 10 millionth CSE tire. In 2017, the production of agricultural tires, which had initially been discontinued in 2004, also resumed. By 2018, the corporation's special tire portfolio comprised a total of 981 different items. The specialization even went so far that tires were being developed and produced for special occasions and, above all, for marketing purposes despite small quantities, such as the ContiGoal tire, which was created in 2014 for the team buses used at the Soccer World Cup in Brazil.

Like never before, the tire portfolio was characterized by strong segmentation and a variety of tire types. The specialization and differentiation of synthetic rubber types and rubber chemicals made a major contribution to this, as did a technology that really revolutionized tires in the mid-1990s: the use of silica. Using silica in tire building made it possible to control the mixing process with extreme precision, thus taking the constant search to square the circle of tire properties forward in leaps and bounds. The "multi-component tread technology" (MCT) developed by Continental in this context in 2003 improved the handling characteristics of passenger tires in the long term and resulted in greater driving safety. This technology, which uses what are known as quadroplex extruders, allowed a total of four rubber compounds to be used in a tread. This in turn enabled the traditional conflicting objectives of tire production, such as dry and wet properties, to be resolved at a higher level. One key milestone in compound technology was the successful production of the BlackChili tire compound in 2007. The conflicting objectives that prevail in the bicycle tire sector, for example, with regard to the simultaneous optimization of grip, rolling resistance and service life performance, were practically eliminated by applying the latest findings from polymer and materials research. Highly sophisticated natural and synthetic rubbers were blended with nanometric carbon black particles and other fillers, enabling BlackChili tires to achieve performances that were previously unthinkable: 30 percent better grip, 26 percent less rolling resistance, and a 5 percent increase in service life. The best professional cyclists in the world were victorious at the Tour de France, among other races, using Continental's Competition Pro LTD tires, which were manufactured using this compound basis. In the context of sustainability strategy and public climate debate, the drive to optimize tire properties now focused on reducing rolling resistance, including by means of a new lightweight design, thereby significantly reducing CO_2 emissions. Thinking about Continental tires assumed a whole new quality against the backdrop of the environmental crisis and ecological goals, particularly with a view to their basic raw material. In 2013, a specially designed sound-absorbing tire was presented in the form of the ContiSilent tire, followed in 2014 by a prototype for a tire made from dandelion rubber. This may well lead once again to a change in the chief raw material basis of Continental tires in the foreseeable future. Further tire technology innovations followed too: in February 2019, Continental presented a new stud technology, ContiFlexStud, for the next generation of winter tires. In the long line of continuity of anti-slip protection, riveted belt and steel stud tire technology, stud bodies made of rubber were developed that are vulcanized into the tire and not only ensure greater driving safety on ice, but also quieter driving and reduced road wear.

 Finally, two new tire systems were presented at the International Motor Show in Frankfurt in 2017 that marked a new stage on the long road to intelligent tires while also looking to the future of Continental tire technology. Under the names ContiSense and ContiAdapt, two system technology concepts were presented that, on the one hand, enable ongoing monitoring of a tire's condition and, at the same time, the ability to adapt tire performance characteristics to the respective road conditions. ContiSense is based on the development of electrically conductive rubber mixtures through which electrical signals can be sent from a sensor in the tire to a receiver in the vehicle. ContiAdapt combines micro compressors integrated in the wheel to adjust tire pressure by means of a rim with an adjustable width. This allows the system to change the size of the contact surface. It is a crucial factor leading to safety and ride comfort in different road conditions. The tire's design comprises three different tread zones for driving on wet, slippery and dry roads. Different tread zones are activated depending on tire pressure and rim width, and this concept tire adjusts the required "footprint" in every case. This allows the tire characteristics to be adapted to the respective road conditions or the preferences of the driver. The independently thinking Continental tire, which will decisively shape the mobility of the future, was thus invented.

Fig. 73: Concept study for the new smart Continental tire of the future.

Nevertheless, Continental's automotive tires of the future will still face strong competition. In the R&D laboratories of major competitors, air-free tires are being looked at, as are sustainable tires that can be regenerated time and again by capsule, spherical tires (an idea that was pursued back in the 1920s), 3D printed tires and tires made from renewable raw materials such as straw. Smart car tires of the future will have integrated sensors, independent adjustment options and self-healing capabilities. For the time being, however, in terms of tires ready for practical deployment, the tire engineers in Hanover find themselves once again at the end of an innovation cycle, with the sixth generation of the summer tire, the PremiumContact. It is the perfect tire for "feel-good driving" and the result of ever shorter development times, which once lasted many years but have now been cut to an average of two. Looking back on the developments of the past 50 years alone, there have been some truly impressive achievements in innovation and improving the performance of the Continental tire: braking distances have been halved, mileage has been increased by 15,000 kilometers, i.e. doubled, and rolling resistance has been reduced by 30 percent and more. The Continental tire not only makes mobility considerably safer and more comfortable, but is also distinguished by its optimal environmental characteristics. Yet ultimately, it is still a metamorphosis that, driven by innovation, has evolved from the original 1898 tire. More than ever though, other Continental products are increasingly threatening to usurp the "king of rubber products."

Conti Inside. A Changing Product Portfolio, or: Aspects of a history of experience with Continental products

The list of lost Continental products is as long as it is spectacular, because it includes many of the items that shaped the image of the company as a manufacturer of products defining everyday life at all levels of society, which endured for several decades from the 1890s to the 1920s. It starts with soccer ball bladders and rubber balls, covers a wide range of surgical products such as rubber suction cups and rubber bed pads, and ends with rubber preserving rings, rubber gloves and the production of rubber dinghies, which was only discontinued at end of the 1990s. The Continental pool table cushion is also no longer available.

Fig. 74: Soccer ball bladder manufacturing around 1900.

Fig. 75: Continental raincoat adhesive and sewing room in 1913.

Two products stand out, the first being the famous Continental hot water bottle. This product, which had been manufactured since the early 1890s and soon became the most famous hot water bottle in the world, was still a common household item into the mid-1960s. Production was relocated from the Limmer and Vahrenwald plants to Northeim in 1966, but the product was taken out of the product range at the end of 1996.

Fig. 76: Advertisement for the Continental hot water bottle in 1928.

As recently as July 1982, a modernized and streamlined ContiMed program still existed with various medical rubber products including the hot water bottle. But then changes in social behavior regarding health and, above all, the fall in profitability forced the product out of the range. However, the hot water bottle had yielded profits for the entire hundred years of its existence. Second, Continental raincoats and its fashion range for drivers were once highly regarded products perceived as part of the company's standard range. Continental was indeed a producer of fashion items back then, from rubber perfume atomizers to sportswear such as swimming caps and ski suits, right through to the said raincoats.

Fig. 77: Article on contemporary Continental clothing for motorists in *Echo Continental* from 1922.

"I'm decked out from head to toe in Conti," proclaimed the advertising team in Hanover in 1931, presenting the modern woman as a fashion-conscious consumer of various Continental products from chic bathing caps to elegant Continental shoe heels.

Fig. 78: Continental products for the modern woman. Advertisement from *Echo Continental* from 1931.

Fig. 79: Advertisement for Continental ski suits from 1924.

These were all products that were as much a part of people's everyday lives as they were of their leisure time and sports. "Conti will be there for you throughout your life; with Conti heels, it'll be free from strife. All wisdom agrees, life with Conti's a breeze. By live a life content, it's Conti that's meant!" was the message in a 1932 ad. It was the ultimate expression of customer loyalty that appealed to the emotions and of the close relationship between the product portfolio and the lifecycle of the consumer.

Fig. 80: Advertisement for Continental swimming caps and beach balls from 1927.

The company's long goodbye to its role as a full-range supplier continued far into the 1960s. And this also began its departure from the world of the consumer's experience—with the exception of tires.

However, there is also an astoundingly long list of products that have persisted, some directly as a later-generation product, as with tires, and some that were reproduced or reinvented. These include shoe soles, which were manufactured at the Limmer plant until 1987, and then relocated before being finally discontinued in spring 1999, after 90 years. But barely 20 years later, the company proudly announced a new world record thanks to ContiGrip, after an extreme sports athlete wore adidas running shoes with Continental high-tech soles to run up the steep ski flying hill in Oberstdorf. The continuity of many ContiTech products is in fact uninterrupted: hoses that became "mobile fluid systems," conveyor belts and heavy-duty V-belts ("power transmission"), air springs and rubber/metal composites ("vibration control"), and last but not least Zeppelin balloon fabrics, airplane coverings and automotive soft top fabrics, which today are sold as "surface

Fig. 81: Continental items as lifestyle products. Advertising page from *Echo Continental* from 1932.

solutions." Count Ferdinand von Zeppelin was a frequent guest in Hanover, monitoring production of tailor-made external coverings for his airships, and Louis Blériot, who made the first airplane flight over the English Channel in 1909, also trusted the quality of Continental's airplane fabrics. The innovations and technical improvements by Continental engineers to the various items and product groups over the decades are impressive. The Continental V-belt, which was first developed in 1899, set new standards by providing three times more power for looms and other machines than the previous leather belts. Thanks to Continental engineers, V-belts have not appeared in ADAC breakdown statistics since the early 1990s, while the Conti V-Pioneer V-belt for industrial applications was the first "eco belt" to be awarded the German Future Prize in 2010. Since 1901, the conveyor belts used have made conveying easier in coal and ore mining and their ever-increasing performance—protected from imitators by the patented "Continental capped edge"—has also increased the productivity of mines, so much so that the longest coal conveying system with rolling conveyor belts was created by Continental in China in 2019. Since the 1920s, Continental developers had also been working on the problem of suitable suspension systems for rail vehicles, experimenting with pneumatic tires for railways and rubber bonded metal connections, but it was not until 1955 that the production of state-of-the-art air suspension systems for passenger cars, buses, trucks and later also subway trains was possible, and then it was only after the turn of the millennium that electronically controlled air suspension systems—the Continental Electronic Air Suspension System—were developed and became popular worldwide. Even Continental's original product, the hoof buffer, which had been manufactured into the 1920s, was resurrected in 2018 with the Continental turfcord, a rubber hoof protector that replaces the traditional horseshoe.

The longest list, however, is that of Continental products that are brand new and that were not part of the corporation's original production spectrum: these include advanced driver assistance systems, control modules, light systems, sensors, microchips, infrared receivers, electronic measuring devices, actuators, camera systems, and software and data processing systems for digital monitoring of the various drive and vehicle components. Looking at the car from that time to the present day and comparing the type and scope of the respective "Conti inside" programs, their unstoppable rise as essential components of the automotive technical system and "enablers" of the mobility of the future is evident—even if they have become increasingly hidden from view for Continental drivers. When, in 1928, Continental first drew up a list of its rubber parts used in automobiles, there were 24 structural accessories, from tires to rubber seals on windows, cooling water hoses and fan belts, as well as a further 21 equipment accessories such as windshield wipers, floor mats, rubber coating on the bumper and soft top fabric.

In 1937, when Continental presented a cross-section of a passenger car for the first time at the International Motor Show, the 45 accessory parts in total from nine years previously had grown to 157.

40 years later, in 1973, the picture had changed dramatically once more. Up to 300 Continental products made of rubber and plastic were in use in modern cars at that time, from leatherette roof fabric to upholstery foam, battery boxes, rubber joints and fuel tank lid seals to shock absorber protective tubing and fuel

pump diaphragms. The Continental accessory range for the automotive industry comprised exactly 6,136 items and components.

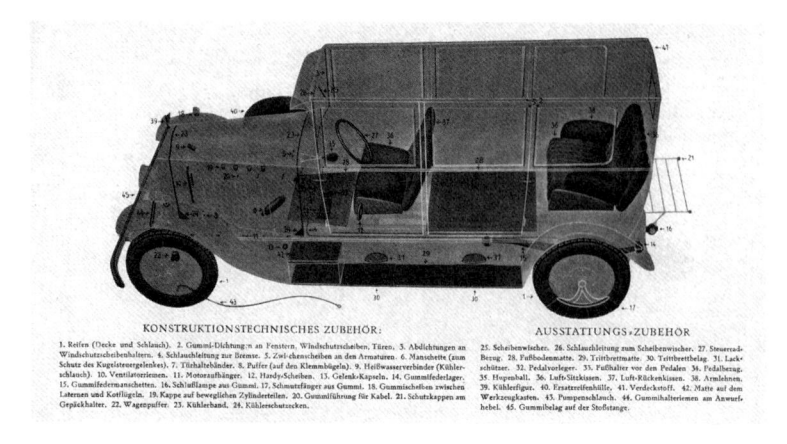

Fig. 82: Continental automotive products in 1928.

Wir befuchen unfere Ausftellungsräume
157 mal Continental=Zubehörteile am modernen Kraftwagen

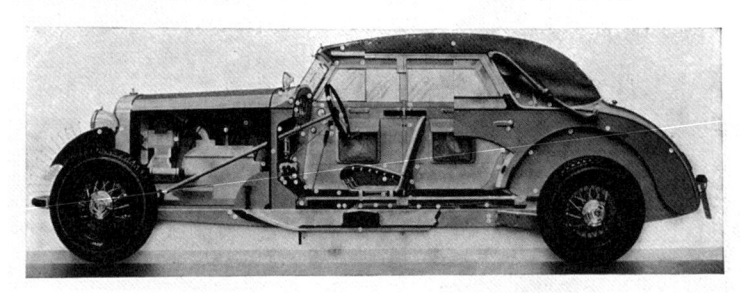

Fig. 83: Continental automobile products in 1937. Advertising model exhibited at the IAA in 1937.

Almost 30 years later, the picture had once again been completely overhauled. The number of Continental products in a car from the year 2000 had dropped significantly to around 30 to 40 parts, but complex systems and modules, semiconductor relays and control devices such as axle modules, anti-lock brake systems, electronic stability programs, sensors, electromechanical brakes and automatic distance control had now emerged.

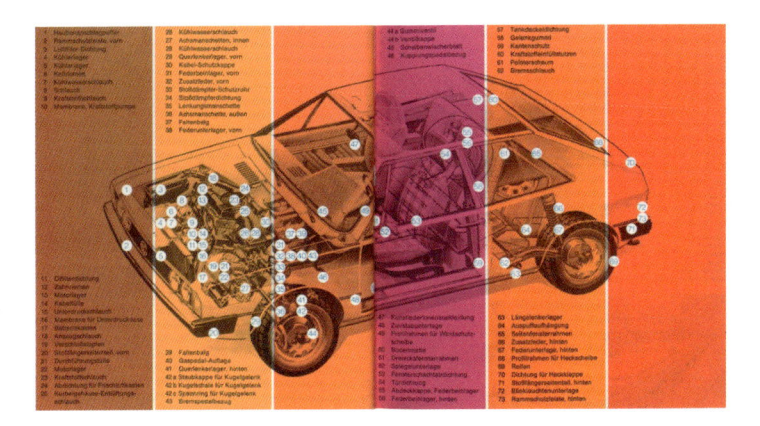

Fig. 84: Continental automotive products in 1973.

Again, almost 20 years later, the percentage of these assistance and control systems—and therefore the number of electronic, software-based components—has increased significantly. They now account for almost all Continental's supplier technologies, offering a high degree of safety, comfort and connectivity. From a purely mechanical product, the car has been transformed into a computer on wheels. More than 170 sensors, approximately 90 electronic control units and over 150 actuators are installed in modern vehicles, which, just a few years ago, still functioned largely distinctly from one another, but which now communicate via networks and form networks of their own. Today, the image of the automobile is one of an interconnected, data-gathering and data-processing item of mobility technology, and this also allows for completely new supplier services, especially digital mobility services. This development culminated in 2019 with the presentation of a brand new future mobility technology: the Continental In-Car Server CAS1, which put an end to the previous electronic clutter in cars. As a high-performance computer on wheels, it has become the heart of digital and connected mobility.

The innovative server solution has cut down on the 70 to 100 control units in cars and significantly simplifies the inner workings of the vehicle. The range of invisible Continental products is therefore increasing.

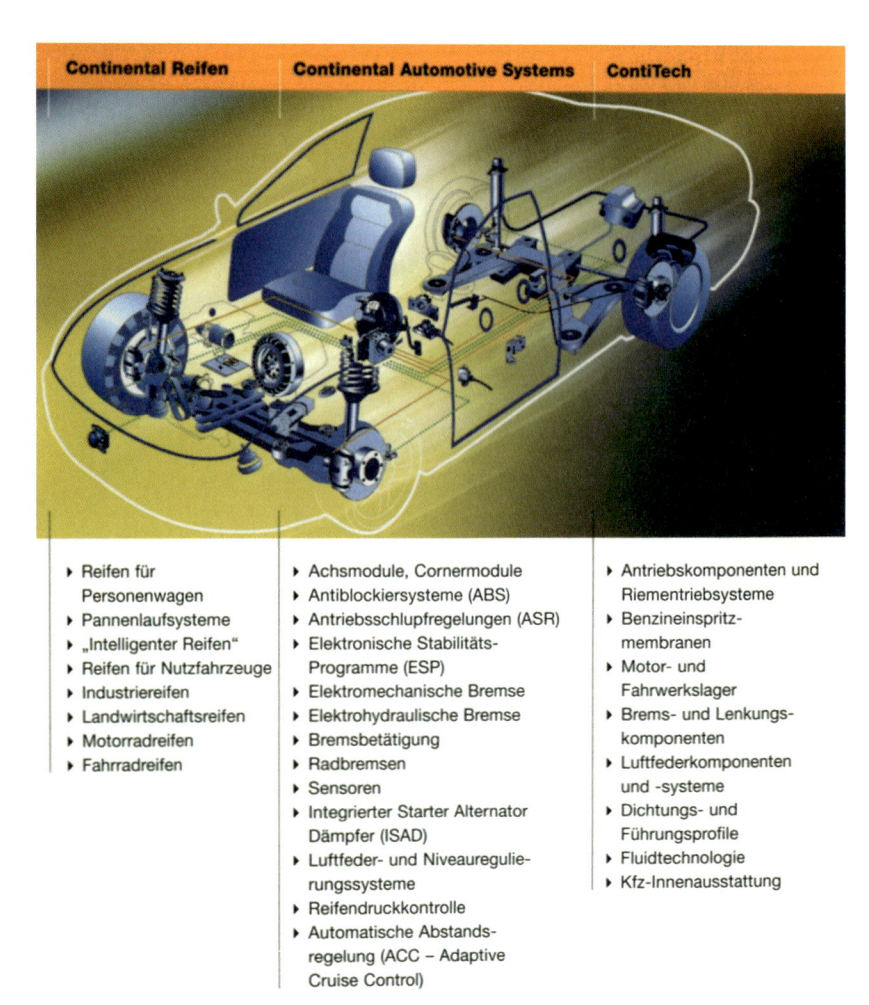

Continental Reifen	Continental Automotive Systems	ContiTech
▸ Reifen für Personenwagen ▸ Pannenlaufsysteme ▸ „Intelligenter Reifen" ▸ Reifen für Nutzfahrzeuge ▸ Industriereifen ▸ Landwirtschaftsreifen ▸ Motorradreifen ▸ Fahrradreifen	▸ Achsmodule, Cornermodule ▸ Antiblockiersysteme (ABS) ▸ Antriebsschlupfregelungen (ASR) ▸ Elektronische Stabilitäts-Programme (ESP) ▸ Elektromechanische Bremse ▸ Elektrohydraulische Bremse ▸ Bremsbetätigung ▸ Radbremsen ▸ Sensoren ▸ Integrierter Starter Alternator Dämpfer (ISAD) ▸ Luftfeder- und Niveauregulierungssysteme ▸ Reifendruckkontrolle ▸ Automatische Abstandsregelung (ACC – Adaptive Cruise Control)	▸ Antriebskomponenten und Riementriebsysteme ▸ Benzineinspritzmembranen ▸ Motor- und Fahrwerkslager ▸ Brems- und Lenkungskomponenten ▸ Luftfederkomponenten und -systeme ▸ Dichtungs- und Führungsprofile ▸ Fluidtechnologie ▸ Kfz-Innenausstattung

Fig. 85: Continental automotive products in 2000.

This new Continental product world went hand in hand with the corporation disappearing from other areas of people's lives. Continental products can now only be experienced in the highly specialized world of mobility. Back then, as now, the aim was to convey abstract feelings such as safety and environmental awareness. The Continental tire alone stands out here as the last visible product. Continental tire production records of bygone days have long since been forgotten, dwarfed

Fig. 86: Continental automotive products in 2020.

completely by new dimensions in manufacturing efficiency. At its largest tire plants in the Czech Republic, Portugal and China, the corporation now produces 16 to 25 million Continental tires per year, amounting to 150 million in total. This is but a fraction of the approximately 3 billion tires produced worldwide each year, however. Nevertheless, the Continental tire has again conquered the world, as it has done many times in its long history. Not only is it the company's last visible product but also virtually the last remaining direct link between the new Continental of 2021 and the old Continental of the 1890s. Its importance within the corporation has waned and, rather than being on a long road to intelligent tires, Continental is instead on the road to intelligent mobility. And yet the future of the tire is bright, as nothing exists far and wide that could ever replace it as a high-tech product. Continental tires continue to be an essential part of the "mobility of the future," unaffected by the technological convergence of automotive manufacturers and supplier companies occurring on account of software-based mobility and the reinvention of the car as a computer on wheels. The new world of mobility in the 21st century too cannot function without Continental tires, which essentially appears to make them immortal.

6 The Continental Shares
The Life Cycle of a Security in a Changing Capital Market

An even more important indicator of Continental's development than the rubber price is its share price, which acts as a seismograph of the shocks that hit the company either externally or internally. In their long life, Continental shares have experienced spectacular highs as well as huge collapses. They have survived two world wars, dramatic inflation and at least five stock market crashes, and also gone through extremely different stages of financial and capital market reality. These ranged from the mostly local stock exchange world during the industrialization phase of the German Empire (1871–1918) to today's global market capitalism. Over many decades, Continental shares have also made countless major and small shareholders wealthy as co-owners of the company and beneficiaries of company profits. At times of course, they also demanded considerable perseverance.

The Varied Career of Continental Shares, from a "Dividend Behemoth" to a "Widow-and-Orphan Stock" in Times of Crisis: 1879 to the Early 1930s

Continental shares were first traded on the Hanover stock exchange in 1897 and, until World War I, there was relatively little diversification of shareholders. This was due, on the one hand, to the consortium of company founders who, as "start-up entrepreneurs" of the time, had granted themselves far-reaching privileges when issuing new shares, combined with special voting rights for priority shares. The Executive Board eventually used high severance payments to persuade the founders to relinquish these claims. This paved the way for capital increases via the stock exchange, which in turn would lead to a potential broadening of the shareholder base. The low level of share diversification was also due to the high nominal value of a share that was customary at the time. This was 600 or 1,200 marks, or around twice the average yearly wage of a factory worker. In addition, the stock exchange was also restricted to a small group of the new economic middle class, making shares an exclusive type of asset. As a result of the capital increase in 1897, a total of 250 new Continental shares were offered on the stock exchange for a nominal price of 1,200 marks. The issue price was already

413 percent or 5,000 marks per share. Here, and in the numerous capital increases that followed in quick succession, the new shares were therefore generally underwritten by a syndicate of banks, behind which lay a core of Continental founders from Hanover's private banking scene. The shares were then offered to existing shareholders, who enjoyed pre-emptive rights. "The new shares were taken up by a bank syndicate at a rate of 248 percent and made available to the shareholders for subscription at a ratio of 2:1 to the price reference of 250 percent," the annual report stated in 1910. Only seldom was it possible for an outsider to penetrate this phalanx of Continental shareholders.

Indeed, Continental shares had already experienced a rapid rise in value. In particular, from 1892, the bicycle tire business was responsible for rising profits and optimal prices, a trend which continued for several years. At times, the price climbed to over 700 percent compared to the nominal value of the shares in relation to the then quoted price. From 1897/98 until 1914, it leveled off at a high level of between 500 and 600 percent, with some fluctuations. The start of automobile tire production in 1898 also created some short-lived euphoria, driving the share price to 880 percent by August 1899. At the end of that year, the price sank again to just above 500 percent. The graphic below does not show this price swing because the year-end exchange rates only have been used as a basis.

It was only after the turn of the century that the small and exclusive circle of Continental shareholders slowly grew as a result of new external shareholders. In 1900, 32 shareholders were represented at the Annual Shareholders' Meeting, while by 1903, this number had risen to 59—although almost all still came from Hanover's middle class. In 1905, the list of attendees at the Annual Shareholders' Meeting noted occupational titles for the first time, which showed a colorful mix of "small shareholders" with holdings of up to 10 shares. These were pharmacists, merchants, dentists, a timber wholesaler, a grain merchant, master bricklayers, senior teachers, architects and builders. The list also included lawyers, engineers, a few pensioners, commercial advisors and a large landowner from Silesia in present-day Poland. At 1910's Annual Shareholders' Meeting, this group made up almost half of the 86 shareholders in attendance. The low diversification of shares led to the share price fluctuating fiercely even in case of low demand or sales, as commented on in a note from 1903: "The shares are so expensive that one must be prepared for large price fluctuations at any time." Fluctuation margins with upward or downward price deviations of between 50 and 100 percent were therefore normal and an expression of a capital market that, during the period of the German Empire, was still underdeveloped in many ways. The Continental shares are also a good example of how, even back then, the prices were dependent on external economic and political events. Between September 20 and 27, 1911, Continental shares climbed from 585 to 628 percent of their nominal value without any obvious reason, before the price fell again on September 29 to 620 percent. This was triggered by the declaration of war between Italy and Turkey, with the fall in price continuing to 605 percent, i.e. a drop of 15 percentage points. This in turn was caused by "the known price reduction of a competing French producer for automobile tires."

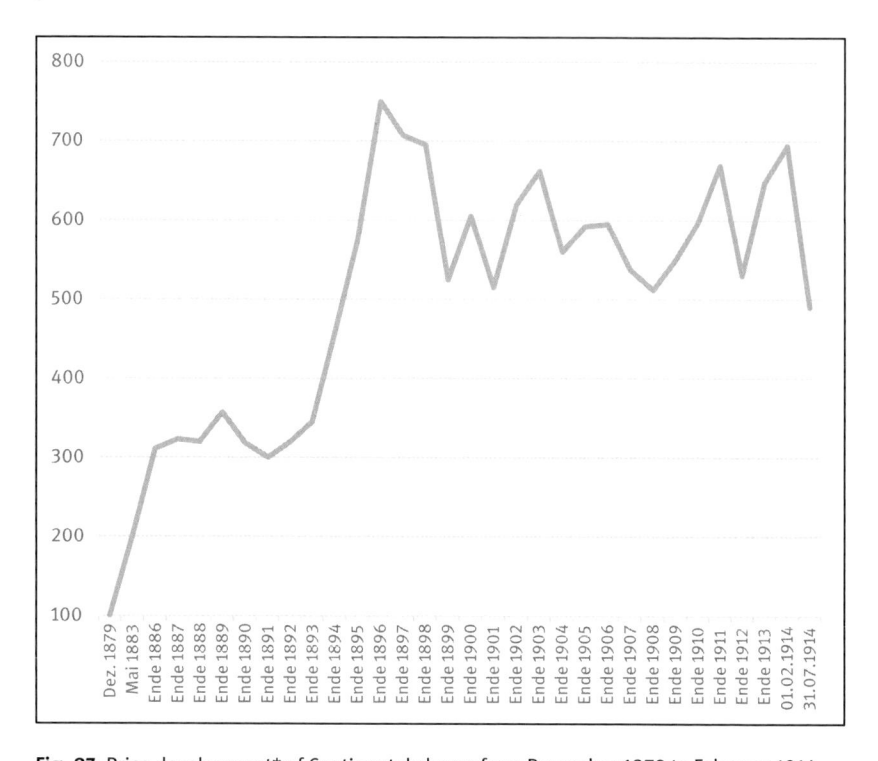

Fig. 87: Price development* of Continental shares from December 1879 to February 1914.
*In percentage of nominal value of 1,200 marks.

Interestingly, in spring 1911, a fierce and contentious debate took place in the specialist media over whether Continental shares should be introduced on Berlin's stock exchange. Rumors had been circulating to this effect since the start of the year. "Such a valuable share with 9 million marks of share capital should be traded in Berlin," it was said "and not on Hanover's provincial stock exchange.

This would be in the interest of both the shareholders and well-functioning trade." The Hannoversche Courier newspaper strongly contested this assertion, however. "The natural market for an industrial company's shares is first and foremost where most of the interested parties are located. This means in the narrower economic area of the company in question," it argued. "The introduction of Continental shares in Berlin will therefore not have any particular value for shareholders. Experience with other Hanover shares has also shown that being sold in Berlin does not offer any protection against large price falls, nor from a lack of business and becoming unsellable as a result."

Fig. 88: Invitation to shareholders to the extraordinary Shareholders' Meeting on June 27, 1905 (left). Entry and voting card of a Continental shareholder dated March 23, 1910 (right).

By now, there were new faces even among shareholders with larger holdings of Continental shares, mostly bankers from Berlin and Frankfurt. Since 1895, Continental had been distributing dividends of between 40 and 50 percent, so the shares were an interesting and lucrative investment. "In the 40 years of its existence, Continental's share capital has risen from 900,000 marks to 9 million marks through six capital increases," the Hannoversche Courier informed its readers in October 1911. "The value of the buying options is approximately 805 percent, meaning that a person owning shares since 1897 has benefited from buying options worth 805 percent. In addition, the market value after the last issue of April 19, 1910, is 500 percent. This price of 1,305 percent is thus the approximate real price on April 19, 1910, including the buying options." And then there were the lavish dividend payouts. In other words, anyone who had purchased three Continental shares with a nominal value of 3,600 marks in 1895 now owned 40 Continental shares and, if they exercised their subscription rights regularly, minus the necessary costs, could post a net profit of 271,496 marks at the end of 1912. "Allow me to conclude my statement," announced chairman of the Supervisory Board Bernhard Caspar proudly on behalf of the major shareholders at the Annual Shareholders' Meeting on March 21, 1912, "by expressing the hope that the excellent progress of our company, which is thanks to your outstanding leadership, may continue to develop on its current solid foundations despite all the difficulties a global business is presented with every day, thereby benefiting the company and our shareholders." Just two years later, however, all hopes were dashed in the ensuing swirl of political and military events.

With the outbreak of World War I, trade on the stock exchange came to a standstill. The last quoted price of Continental shares before the stock exchange closed on August 1 was 490 percent. When it opened again in 1918, Continental shares—like the rest of the capital market—were hit by the turmoil of inflation, which lasted until November 1923. These years were chaotic and, through annual capital increases of ever greater sums, Continental tried to keep up with the speed of currency devaluation. Its share capital rose from 15 million marks (1918) to 600 million marks (1923), while its share price likewise climbed to dizzying heights as an expression of inflation. Continental shares reached the 9,100 percent mark at the end of 1922 and a price of 6 trillion marks at the beginning of December 1923. Parallel to this, the company had introduced preferential shares with multiple voting rights. Stock market trading was extremely brisk, not least as a result of the general flight into tangible assets. The new stock exchange culture was the result of the growing interest in the share market, often born out of necessity. At the same time, however, it occurred against the backdrop of heavy political attacks against the "big capitalists." Calls were made for socialization, shareholders were defamed, and excessive dividends were harshly criticized. Already in 1918, Continental's Executive Board devoted half a page of its annual report to defend itself against such accusations, drawing attention to the "actually moderate interest" that its shareholders "received based on earnings from the company's operations." By 1922, Continental was in fact paying 30 percent dividends again. Then, in 1923, the Executive Board saw itself forced to suspend payments so that no dividends were paid for the first time in Continental's 48-year history.

Tab. 1: Price development* of Continental shares from December 1918 to December 1941.

Year	Highest	Lowest	Last trading day
1918	-	-	367
1919	-	-	570
1920	-	-	650
1921	-	-	1200
1922	-	-	9100
1923	-	-	6 trill.
1924	-	-	9,8
1925	-	-	85
1926	-	-	109,5
1927	150	100	120
1928	161,5	109	140,5
1929	175	132	144
1930	187	107	109
1931	124,7	90	101
1932	121	71	117,5
1933	123	116	120
1934	158	126	139
1935	160	140	159
1936	195	158	174
1937	-	-	190
1938	-	-	205
1939	-	-	208
1940	-	-	311,5
1941	-	-	362

*In percentage of nominal value of 1,200 marks. From 1924 in reichsmarks (RM). Price quoted on the Hanover stock exchange in Frankfurt am Main, and from May 1923 also in Berlin. The last official RM price and thus official stop price at the start of 1942 was 173.5 percent.

The rapid financial depreciation also brought with it the danger of foreign companies taking over German companies with hard currencies at ridiculously cheap prices. Continental set up to defend itself against this "foreign threat" early on by bringing on board Goodrich, a friendly US tire company, as a key shareholder. Goodrich then gradually took over around 25 percent of the share capital, with its participation in the capital increases bringing US dollars into Hanover's coffers. The robust dollar meant that valuable and stable investment capital was now available, which Continental's Executive Board used to buy up a lot of cheap shares from its competitor Excelsior, among other things. The clear objective here was a future takeover. At the same time, a new type of preferential share with up to 20 times the voting rights was created as a safeguard for the first time in June 1920, the nominal value of which was 9.6 million marks. Up until the fall of 1923, complicated and in many cases barely transparent share transactions took place: more and more new preferential shares were issued, voting rights were changed, preferential shares were converted into ordinary shares, and liquidation or reserve shares were created, i.e. large-scale de facto share buybacks as a means of payment for subsequent takeover actions. In the end, these measures ensured that Continental, unlike its competitor Phoenix in Hamburg, was not targeted by "inflation kings" or large-scale speculators such as Camillo Castiglioni or Hugo Stinnes.

Just as Continental's Executive Board knew how to skillfully navigate the complex capital market characterized by inflation—the rules of which remained unfathomable to many other companies—it was also able to act competently and with confidence during the Weimar Republic's brief phase of stability that followed (1924 to 1929/30). As a result, Continental shares soon returned to their earlier highs. The share capital had initially been converted to 40 million reichsmarks, supplemented by preferential shares amounting to 100,000 reichsmarks. The shares were now nominally divided into 40 and 80 reichsmarks and there soon followed a uniform conversion to a nominal value of 100 reichsmarks (200,000 ordinary shares) or 1,000 reichsmarks (20,000 ordinary shares). The conversion of the share capital took a long time. Even in November 1927, for example, new ordinary shares were introduced for 4 million reichsmarks (50,000 at 80 reichsmarks each). After the currency reform (1924), the shares (quoted on the Berlin stock exchange since May 1923) initially started the year at a significant discount of around 90 percent, reaching 144 percent by 1929. By now, Continental shares were now also within financial reach of the less well-off middle-class, which contributed to the boom. The main reason, however, was speculation that had repeatedly surfaced since 1926 that the von Opel family was about to become a major shareholder. There were also rumors that Continental's large-scale participation in mergers and takeovers would lead to a shake-up of the rubber and tire industry, which at the time was considered a modern high-tech sector. This did in fact occur, leading to the setting up of a large German rubber trust under Continental's leadership. Once again, complicated financial and share transactions took place—often in cooperation with the banks but in some cases against them—with the declared goal being the streamlining of the industry in Continental's

Fig. 89: Simple inflation-era Continental share in December 1922, and representative "normal share" from October 1923.

interests. One of the first challenges was to organize Goodrich's exit in a way that protected the share price as much as possible while also ensuring that nobody involved lost face. In the second half of the 1920s, whole armies of share specialists at large banks devoted their time to warily following any Continental share movements with the goal of getting involved in any pending transactions before it was too late. "We would like to inform you," read a note sent on April 8, 1929, from the Frankfurt branch of the Disconto-Gesellschaft bank to its headquarters in Berlin,

> that according to information from Rüsselsheim, the origin of the purchases of Continental-Caoutchouc shares over the last few days was Commerzbank rather than Darmstädter & Nationalbank. Apparently, Darmstädter Bank is pursuing the objective of a price reduction. Over the last few months, it has therefore been selling in order to create as favorable a price as possible for the Goodrich package. Commerzbank is said to have taken up all the shares sold. A similar battle of interests is thus taking place between the two institutions over these papers as was the case previously with the Pittler majority.

In February 1929, the Goodrich package, by now nominally worth 8 million reichsmarks, was eventually taken on by a German bank syndicate at a rate of 125 percent. The investment proved lucrative for the Americans, as they had initially only paid around 93 percent. It was Continental's general director Willy Tischbein who pulled off the real feat, however. At the time of the negotiations with Goodrich on releasing the Continental package, the share stood at 140 percent due to various speculation and the booming stock market in Germany. With a lot of effort and perseverance, he succeeded in convincing the Americans that the overvaluation of Continental's shares was completely unfounded and in pushing them down to the agreed price. At the same time, Continental itself intensified its activities on the stock market. In 1923, three-quarters of Excelsior's share capital was in Continental's hands and now, as a result of a capital increase, the company tried to take it over completely. But this hostile takeover ultimately failed due in part to resistance from the works council (similar to a trade union) and staff at Excelsior. In 1927, Continental tried to legally incorporate its competitor again. After a loss of 1 million reichsmarks in the previous year, Excelsior was financially weak. A restructuring program was necessary, which meant increasing capital and issuing new shares, after which Continental held 98 percent of the share capital. One of the main difficulties of the merger—compensating Excelsior shareholders—was thus cleared up.

With the advent of small shareholders, the 1920s saw a significant increase in stock market investors and also marked considerably reduced nominal share values. Continental also resumed its dividend payments, which further broadened its shareholder base. The company and its shares now became a major investment story attracting the attention of the general public. In the second half of the 1920s, Continental was a regular feature of stock market reporting in the financial press, with the renewed dividend shortfall for 1926 in particular being the subject of headlines and in-depth commentary in the spring of 1927. "American minority at Conti-Caout," was the later headline in the Berliner Börsen-Courier newspaper on December 7, 1927, which only then had learned of the Goodrich participation. In June 1928, the newspaper also led with big headlines on "the negotiations on concentration in the rubber industry," causing quite a stir in stock market circles at the time. "In recent days, shares in the company on the Berlin stock exchange have been remarkably strong," it was reported in December 1929, "with the final publication [of the merger] in particular generating much interest in the stock. There are now rumors that the Opel-General Motors group has acquired a considerable block of shares in Continental Gummiwerke AG in Hanover. [...] Over the last 10 days, Continental shares have strengthened by almost 30 percent to 180½ percent." As a result, more and more letters from individual shareholders, some of them lengthy and often expressing concern about the latest stock market rumors, now landed on the desk of Continental's Executive Board. Although the letters were answered by Tischbein in person, the replies were not exactly prime examples of modern investor communication. "In response to your letter of October 31, we hereby inform you that, as a matter of principle, we do not answer queries from our shareholders, as we consider ourselves neither entitled nor obliged to provide information about the circumstances of our company outside the Annual Shareholders' Meeting," read a letter to a state building officer in Kassel at the beginning of November 1926. "What would happen if the Executive Board of a company were to provide information on its relations to anyone who presented themselves as a shareholder? All we can say is that we have no knowledge of the loss-making processes we are supposed to be involved in, and of course we do not have or exercise any influence whatsoever on the price of our shares." Other shareholders were also troubled by rumors of considerable losses as a result of expensive purchases in raw rubber and cotton and the associated potential fall in share price. "In response to your letter," another reply from Tischbein stated on February 16, 1927, "it is nowadays well-known that price changes on the stock exchange are caused by speculation rather than a company's profitability. We regret that at present we are unable to provide you with an explanation for the lag in our prices."

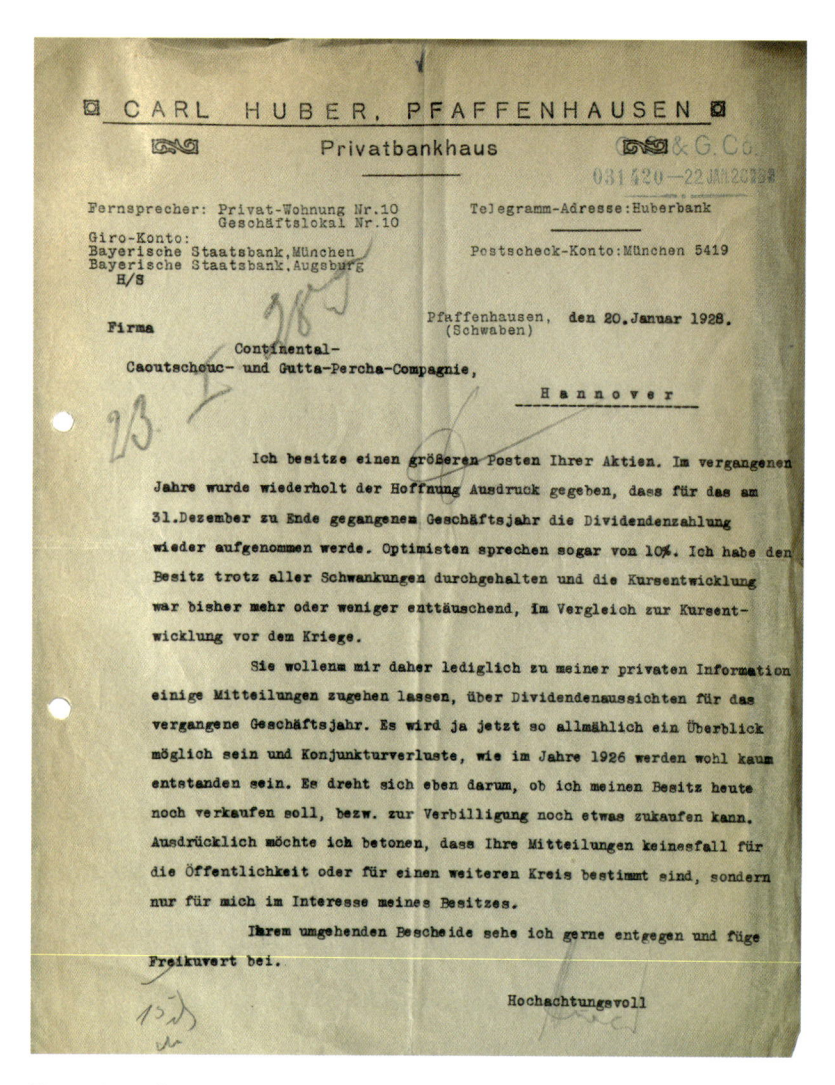

Fig. 90: Letter from a Continental shareholder to company headquarters dated January 1, 1928.

Stock market newsletters and offers of stock information services from a rapidly expanding group of self-proclaimed stock market analysts were now also being regularly delivered to Continental's Executive Board. These "experts" were contacting Hanover because of the rumors that Continental would again not be paying any dividends in the current year. Indeed, there had been a clear break from previous tradition in dividend payments. General director Tischbein's cost-cutting measures were responsible for the much lower level of share capital distributed in 1924 and 1925 (10 percent for each year). In the crisis year of 1926, the second dividend freeze in Continental's history occurred before, in 1927, 6 percent in dividends was paid out again. Continuous increases took place until 1929, when 9 percent was reached. Yet considerable disagreement arose with regard to the fixing of dividends during the years of the global economic crisis that followed, a quarrel which ultimately led Tischbein to resign in 1934. Tischbein had advocated reducing the dividend rates to 6 percent in order to retain the necessary capital in the company, while major shareholder von Opel stuck to the high rates of 8 percent. Continental was thus one of the few stand-out companies with unchanged dividend rates even during the crisis years of 1930 to 1933, yet this was at the cost of liquidity, for a considerable part of the dividend payments could not be financed by profits but had to be funded by the release of reserves. During the global economic crisis, Continental shares fell in value by approximately 40 percent. In 1930 and 1931, they were quoted at approximately 100 percent, which meant they were still at par. In the crisis year of 1932, they quickly climbed back to 120 percent. "Alongside a few other securities from the limited number of remaining over-par shares on the stock exchange list, Conti-Gummi rubber shares are particularly worthy of investment," wrote the Berliner Börsen-Courier in November 1932.

> This is down to the good earning power of the company, its more than sufficient internal funding and high degree of liquidity. Conti-Gummi covers the overwhelming share of Germany's rubber supply. The company also appears to have reasonable competitors since there seems to be little disagreement in the industry as to the adequacy of prices and terms of sale.

In the crisis year of 1932, shares were repurchased on a large scale for the first time. During a reduction of the share capital to 37 million reichsmarks, massive share buybacks of 3 million were undertaken at the favorable price level of 1931 and the start of 1932 before the shares were then canceled. In this context, preferential shares were also once again abolished. It was not until 1940, by then under completely altered conditions, that a significant increase in capital took place again, with this being more than doubled to 88.4 million reichsmarks.

The Nazi era was just a short episode in the history of Continental shares, but closer inspection reveals that far more (off-exchange) share trading and shareholder transactions took place than one might expect—even despite the restrictions on stock exchange trading, dividend tax regulations and stop prices introduced by the Nazi regime from the end of 1941. Since spring 1934, rumors were already circulating about Tischbein's pending resignation, and Continental share values were collapsing. This was in connection with speculation about a cut in dividends as well as apparently major losses as a result of a failed attempt to sell short in rubber. Having increased its dividend payments to 14 percent again, the company was then targeted by Nazi officials who railed against "the shareholders enriching themselves in a way that is damaging to the community." In 1938, a debate over the proportion of "non-Aryans" among the Continental shareholders broke out, and their "Jewish character" was condemned. Following relevant research, the Berlin headquarters of Deutsche Bank and Diskontogesellschaft then informed Continental that of the 13,016,700 reichsmarks in nominal company shares, 766,100, or just under six percent, was "recognizably" owned by Jews. Dresdner Bank reported that 13.2 percent of its shares were under Jewish ownership, while the percentage at Commerz- und Privatbank Hannover was as high as 21.6. All in all, the Continental administration was relieved since it was proven that 2.2 million reichsmarks, or six percent, of 37 million in shares belonged to Jews, while 34.7 million reichsmarks was in "Aryan" hands. In December 1938, there were also plans to list Continental shares on the Vienna stock exchange. Soon, however, regular price quotations were out of the question, especially in the face of increasing off-market share transactions. The last official price quotation of Continental shares was 362 percent, with the official stop price being 170 percent. In contrast, the unofficial black-market price in 1944 was approximately 4,000 percent.

From the Economic "Miracle Years" to a Long Period of Crisis: the Boom and Bust of Continental Shares from 1948 to the mid-1980s

After the currency reform in June 1948, Continental shares suffered a short collapse in price. This was similar to 1924, with all other shares at industrial companies being affected too. However, a long and steady upward trend was to follow. From an initial price of 56 marks per share of a nominal 100 marks, the price of Continental shares rose quickly to 112.2 marks. In 1951, they exceeded 150 marks and, by 1958, had doubled to over 300 marks. In the 1960s, the steep rise continued at first with the price breaking all records in 1960 at 1,150 marks. The shares then settled until the mid-1960s at a high level of between 500 and 600 marks. For a long time, the banks that had re-emerged everywhere fought bitterly over the conversion of Continental shares from the former reichsmark and their introduction on different stock exchanges. The leading role here was played by the Hanover branch of Deutsche Bank (in December 1951 still trading as Nordwest Bank). The private bank C.G. Trinkaus additionally held many shares, with a bank representative also sitting on Continental's Supervisory Board. The rehabilitation of stock exchange and share business from the Nazi era was complicated and lasted until the early 1960s. The first step was taken by the Securities Settlement Act of October 1949, followed by the Act Repealing the National Socialist Dividend Tax Ordinance, a law which did away with the Nazi-era restrictions and did not come into force until December 15, 1952. The final issue was the regulation of trust assets for shareholders, which had been created following the Dividend Tax Ordinance and the formation of a bond stock but were then only distributed to shareholders retrospectively in 1961. All these measures are evident from following the course of Continental shares. An analysis of the registered stockholders carried out in 1952 for the first time in years resulted in around 7,355 Continental shareholders being counted. The vast majority, 5,189, were small shareholders, who held Continental shares with a par value of between 100 and 4,000 marks (i.e. between one and 40 shares). Next came 1, 269 shareholders who owned between 40 and 100 shares each. 843 shareholders owned shares with a par value of between 10,000 and 100,000 marks, and finally 54 shareholders owned shares with a par value of more than 100,000 marks. This last group was led by the von Opel family, which remained the biggest shareholder. By summer 1957, the number of Continental shareholders slowly rose by approximately 13 percent to 8,206. Notably, the proportion of small shareholders increased from 70 to 80 percent. The Continental shares were now gradually reaching the prospering new middle class of the economic "miracle years." Capital increases did not yet play a role, as the capital market of the new Federal Republic was only slowly starting to function. Only in 1958 did Continental increase its share capital by 20 million marks, from 88.4 million to 110.5 million. By 1965, three further capital increases through the issuing of new shares had taken place, bringing the share capital to 210 million marks.

From the outset, Continental shares were always recommended by banks. For example, at the start of February 1952, the Bayerische Hypotheken- und Wechselbank recommended "Continental-Gummi," noting the gross profit and the high dividend payments of 6 and 9 percent achieved since 1951 and even predicting dividends would rise to 18 percent by 1963. In a short time, a significant number of shareholders had reappeared, who had high expectations regarding the company's future profits and demanded further dividend increases. At the Annual Shareholders' Meeting in fall 1965, the Executive Board had to deal with criticism that the 18 percent payout was not in line with the expansion of the business or the increase in profits. "I must protest against this unilateral subordination of the interests of the co-owners, i.e. shareholders, especially with the company talking of a falling dividend in view of the progressive devaluation of money" was one shareholder's comment. The representative of the Deutsche Schutzvereinigung für Wertpapierbesitz (German Protection Association for Share Ownership) took the same line. "Continental Gummi Werke is a company with a long tradition and has a great deal of symbolic value. This will have been clear to you again today when you received this horse at the entrance. The traditional Lower Saxony steed has jumped the billion-mark hurdle at a gallop. I think many shareholders regret that the Lower Saxony steed presented to us was not gilded with a billion-mark bonus." The fact was that, through its own information policy, the Executive Board had itself to blame when being confronted with spoiled and demanding shareholders. In response to a suggestion by Supervisory Board member Kurt Forberg, co-owner of the Düsseldorf banking house Trinkaus, to introduce modern quarterly reports, the Executive Board pointed out in July 1963, for example, that Continental traditionally "avoided giving figures," and if it did then only very carefully when sales were rising just slightly or even falling. "Shareholders in Germany are unfortunately not yet ready in terms of mentality to accept less positive developments without reacting with panic. For this reason, we weigh up very carefully the extent to which we should provide information on emerging downward trends when writing our shareholder reports. In general, only by making optimistic reports can we expect certain effects."

Continental was highly praised on a regular basis by the experts at Frankfurt's Institute for Balance Sheet Analysis. Its weekly report for July 1960 stated: "A shareholder would have to be a malcontent or short of reason to deny giving credit to the company's management." In 1961, shareholders also received additional payment from the trust assets which had finally been converted. Having originally contained 9,232 million reichsmarks, Continental's books now showed just under 1 million marks, from which successive payments were made. "Conti Gummi is again targeting 16 percent. Rumors about the sale of share packages are entirely unfounded," was the headline in the Handelsblatt trade newspaper in November 1962. This was prompted by dramatic price fluctuations, with highs of 695 marks and lows down to 355 marks, leading to a decline in Continental shares totaling 33 percent. The Executive Board then hurried to point out in an official statement that "the recent decline in Continental's share price is in no way due to poor earnings prospects." Furthermore, the board continued, rumors about a gradual exit of major shareholder von Opel were mere invention and had no basis. In the hope of dispelling further accusations of poor share price performance, the finance department went to the trouble of calculating the returns on Continental shares not just since 1949 but even as far back as 1872. The sums involved were considerable: anyone who had bought a total of 16 Continental shares worth a nominal 1,600 marks at the beginning of 1949 at the then price of 53 percent, i.e. for 848 marks, owned 25 shares at the end of 1963 at a price of 492 marks (taking into account participation in capital increases), i.e. 12,300 marks plus 3,645 marks in dividends. This meant an average annual profit of over 20 percent. The calculations used in going back to the founding of the company were fictitious and quite remarkable. According to the calculations of the financial experts in Hanover, three shares and 3,600 marks in 1872 were equal to shares worth 52,200 marks plus dividends of 39,494 marks, or 91,700 marks in total by the end of 1963—and this despite the wars, inflation and two currency reforms.

However, the present Continental Executive Board was no longer interested in using the capital market creatively or employing innovative methods to encourage a culture of buying and increasing the value of Continental shares. The previous style of Continental management under Seligmann and Tischbein had completely disappeared, making way for the mentality of a conservative accountant. The chairman of the Supervisory Board, Georg von Opel, was the only potential modernizer and was largely fighting a losing battle. In November 1958, for example, he had introduced the idea of having Continental shares listed on the stock exchange in the USA and instructed the Executive Board to carry out appropriate checks. In response, however, von Open soon received from the latter a long list of "negative points" and expressions of serious concern, causing the plan to fail. Attempts to launch the Continental shares on the Zurich stock exchange a year later proved equally unsuccessful. Georg von Opel was also the sole proponent of the idea in June 1957 to introduce employee shares and thus create small shareholders who could be recruited from Continental's workforce. For the time, and to the long-serving Executive Board members, this seemed revolutionary. In reality, the idea and the concept were nothing new. As early as the 1920s, there had been discussions about the concept of a "people's capitalism" pioneered in

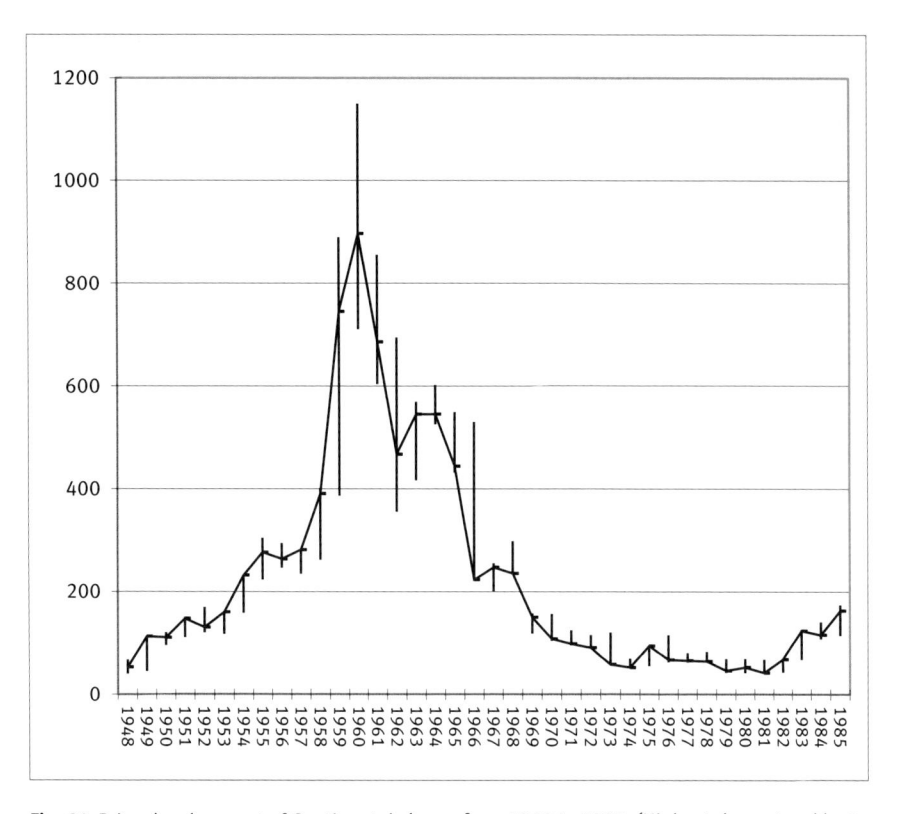

Fig. 91: Price development of Continental shares from 1948 to 1985. (Highest, lowest and last trading day prices in marks)*[1]

The following 15 years demanded a great deal of patience, perseverance and blind faith from Continental shareholders. And when this long, lean period ended, they were rewarded with an even longer recovery phase during which Continental shares reached new highs. Initially, however, share prices went downhill—albeit with heavy fluctuations. The sale of the Opel package to Deutsche Bank had no major repercussions on Continental's share price, despite its magnitude. The share price remained stable at 139 marks for a 50-mark share, which, with a dividend of 12 percent, amounted at first glance to an attractive dividend yield of

---

* Until end of 1968, quotation in marks for shares with nominal value of 100 marks; last price for nominal capital in January 1969 of 259 marks. From Feb. 14, 1969, unit quotation in marks for 50-mark shares.

4.4 percent. Even in 1971, Continental still paid a dividend of 6 percent. Payouts then stopped in 1972 for the fourth time in the company's history, after 1923, 1926 and 1944. At the Annual Shareholders' Meeting in July 1972, when initially only a significantly reduced dividend payment was discussed, Continental Executive Board member Adolf Niemeyer had almost desperately pointed out Continental's hitherto traditionally shareholder-friendly policy. A survey of the shareholder structure in April 1968 showed how much this had changed since the 1950s. Despite the still generally underdeveloped stock market culture in the Federal Republic of Germany, Continental shares were widely distributed and had indeed become "people's shares." More than 30,000 shareholders were identified, including 6,924 housewives and widows, 2,289 pensioners, 1,956 civil servants, 8,908 employees, 4,700 freelancers and 465 workers. The remainder (4,460) were entrepreneurs and institutional investors (1,785), such as banks or investment and insurance companies.

More than in any other period, Continental's share price between 1969 and 1983 reflected the capital market's perception and assessment of the company, with external factors such as a crisis in the automobile industry also playing a part. Changes in price were a key indicator of the extreme fluctuation in confidence and mistrust in Continental's company policy. To begin with, the share price declined rather gradually until 1972, when management changed hands from Göbel to Hahn. Thereafter the crisis really became apparent, and by 1974 the share price had plummeted to its nominal value. This was followed by a rapid recovery, not least due to various merger and cooperation negotiations, and another slump at the end of 1976 after the restructuring efforts apparently proved unsuccessful. By now, there had repeatedly been major price rises related to rumors of heavily funded foreign buyers. In mid-May 1973, for example, Continental shares shifted visibly on the stock exchange in connection with a rumored acquisition of a 15 to 25-percent stake by the US tire group Goodyear. The chairman of the Works Council at the time, Benno Adams, expressed his concern to Alfred Herrhausen, chairman of the Supervisory Board, who reassured him that Deutsche Bank was unaware of any purchases by specific parties. Shortly afterward, in late April 1974, around 7 percent of Continental's share capital quickly changed hands on the stock market and, in just a few days, its share price had shot up by 15 percent. This time, Royal Dutch was suspected to become Continental's new major shareholder. The Institute for Balance Sheet Analysis had already noted in November 1972 that "merger rumors, regardless of what type, are probably why the price of Conti stock has held up so well at around 93 marks per 50-mark share and the stock market still values the stock at 17 times its profit. Even so, we do not expect Conti to achieve a pronounced profit profile in 1972 either."

The mood of Continental's small shareholders also swung between hope and trepidation, with the increasing number of letters to the Executive Board providing a telling picture of this. The longer the crisis lasted, the more helplessly the Continental Executive Board reacted when communicating with shareholders. When the share price slumped in the fall of 1970, for example, the Executive Board's view was that this "without any justification." At the end of January 1971, it also responded as follows to a concerned letter from a small shareholder: "The sudden drop in Continental's share price within a few days has come as a great surprise not only to many shareholders, but also to us. [...] Nevertheless, the fall in price is in line with the general decline in share prices." Soon, however, many shareholders were no longer reassured by such appeasements. "There are already public rumors about the 'Conti situation'," a member of a stock promotion club wrote to the Executive Board in November 1970. Continental's share price had fallen almost as dramatically as IOS (Investors Overseas Services), he maintained. This was an allusion to the IOS stock market scandal, which was the largest case of investor fraud resulting from the collapse of a major investment company. Many letters expressed only growing despair. "Your company once boasted the impressive share price of 1,160 marks. In the meantime I have made a loss of around 500 marks on just three company shares," one of the letters stated. "Is there any chance of Conti paying a dividend this year, even if it is small?" a shareholder asked in March 1974. "I own 5,000 marks of stock and rely on the interest." Another letter commented: "I am a shareholder in Conti AG with shares based on a rate of 680 and 420 marks. At the time, I did not buy them as a speculator, but was of the naive belief that I had acquired a solid protected investment for my retirement. In the meantime, the share price has fallen in a way that is almost without parallel." The safe widow-and-orphan stock of past years had indeed become a speculative investment and a plaything of the capital market. There were also a few shareholders whose concerns extended beyond their own shares. "You are probably aware," wrote a shareholder in January 1975 to Carl H. Hahn, now Continental's chairman of the Executive Board,

> that the share capital situation at Continental is potentially endangered by the aggression of Iranian and Arab oil producers. These producers wish to invest their cheaply acquired billions of dollars in the industries of Western states. The purchase of shares on a large scale in the Federal Republic of Germany has already begun, raising the fear that Arab emirs and sheiks might also be thinking of buying Continental at a cut-rate price.

At this time, the daily rate for Continental shares was 52.50 marks. In the opinion of the letter writer this meant "that the great rubber company Continental could fall into the hands of the Bedouins for 283.5 million marks."

Fig. 92: Title page of *conti intern* employee newsletter, May 1978.

In 1980, a dividend of 2.50 marks per share, i.e. 5 percent, was paid out, triggering hopes that the downward slide was over and a brief rise in the share price. However, this only gave way to even greater disappointment when a stop to dividend payments was again announced for 1981. The employee newsletter *conti intern* among others had already raised hopes that the period of no dividends was ending back in May 1978, one reason being that since 1971 many shares were also owned by employees.

The plan to create shareholders from the workforce had indeed finally been implemented to honor the 100th anniversary of Continental's foundation. A broad advertising campaign had persuaded workers and employees to buy Continental shares at a reduced price. But the timing was even worse than in 1966. An employee who bought Continental shares from their wages in 1971 soon suffered bitter losses, though initially only on paper because of the six-year holding obligation. In this way, the idea of employee shares was done a disservice. The shock among the new shareholders from the workforce must have been all the greater as the campaign had originally met with great interest. In July 1972, after the completion of the two share acquisition campaigns, shares with a nominal value of approximately 4 million marks had been placed in the hands of workers and employees, amounting to approximately 1.5 percent of the share capital. Around 35 percent of Continental staff had taken part, with most employee members buying an average of four shares at 56 marks per share, compared with the official stock exchange price of approximately 90 marks. Nonetheless, the introduction of employee shareholders at Continental in 1971 was a milestone in the history of the company and Continental shares. At the Annual Shareholders' Meeting on July 26, 1972, employee shareholders spoke out directly for the first time and voiced clear criticism of the Executive and Supervisory Board for their "directionless business policy" and "public mismanagement." They also presented a long list of what they saw as managerial mistakes at Continental. The Schutzgemeinschaft der Kleinaktionäre (Small Shareholders' Protection Association) and the Deutsche Schutzvereinigung für Wertpapierbesitz (German Protection Association for Share Ownership) were regular attendees at the Annual Shareholders' Meeting in the guise of their relevant representatives. In July 1972, they launched an intense attack against the Executive Board. "Conti has long been asleep. There are other ways to say this but it unfortunately all amounts to the same thing: it has been business as usual for far too long […] This Annual Shareholders' Meeting is the most difficult one I have attended, quite simply because I do not see how or when Conti will emerge from its dire earnings situation," state the shorthand minutes of the Annual Shareholders' Meeting.

The German Protection Association for Share Ownership (DSW) played a very specific role during these years. In July 1976, a new co-determination act came into force, which introduced equal co-determination in all larger industrial companies. The representative of the DSW asked Continental's administration to comply with the statutory expansion of the Supervisory Board by appointing a small shareholder—which was in fact done, at least indirectly. On September 7, 1979, Wilhelm Helms, managing director of the DSW for Lower Saxony was appointed to the Continental Supervisory Board, a position he held for 14 years until July 2, 1993. Before this, however, in the summer of 1977, a complaint had been filed against Continental with the Hanover Regional Court that a reshuffle of the Supervisory Board according to the new law would infringe the ownership rights of the shareholders and was therefore unconstitutional. The proceedings only ended in 1979 with the ruling of the Federal Constitutional Court and the subsequent withdrawal of the lawsuit brought by the DSW against Continental. As a result, the company was one of the last in Germany to implement the new co-determination regulations, and in March 1979, the Supervisory Board was duly expanded.

Continental Shares in the Era of Financial Market Capitalism (1985 to 2020): From the Soaring Flight of a Stock Market Darling to the Stall in the Wake of the Corona Crisis

The fall in Continental share values came to an end around 1983. The shares entered a new life cycle, partly because the company was reinventing itself in a major way. There was also once again a new Continental Executive Board that quickly acquainted itself with the rules of the new investor capitalism. Based on the doctrine of shareholder value, it was able to sell Continental shares as a promising investment story to an increasingly international circle of investors. In 1983, Continental benefited from the tailwind of the recovering global economy and took its place among the dividend-paying German companies again. All three areas of the company—tires, technical products and participations—were making profits. In 1985, Continental acquired Semperit, which pointed to the further internationalization of the company, while the General Tire takeover in 1987 was a coup that catapulted the Continental shares to a price of 377 marks for the first time. From mid-1982, the share price was decoupled from the still moderate development of the FAZ share index. In 1983, it was quoted above 100 marks again after many years. This was despite the almost complete sell-off of their 30% stake by the three "anchor shareholders" Deutsche Bank, Bayer and

Munich Re in June. Suddenly, Continental was without the protection of a major investor and became an object of speculation and even takeover. Nonetheless, the situation had now changed for the better. The Continental Executive Board was actively trying to arouse the interest of foreign investors and open up Continental shares to new investor groups, both national and international. In 1983, Continental shares worth around 1 billion marks were sold on the stock exchange, equivalent to four times the total share capital. It was an indication that no new major shareholder seemed to be in sight and Continental had developed into a genuine public company. Nonetheless, the Executive Board and Supervisory Board feared that an oil power or a foreign competitor was behind the run on Continental shares, and that this investor may have been buying the Hanover company's innovation potential and success for a cheap price. Professional speculators were in fact behind the boom, as became clear at the end of June 1984 when Goodyear was offered a Continental share package. The US company rejected the offer, but for the Executive Board the development was reason enough to propose a limitation of voting rights to the Annual Shareholders' Meeting, which was agreed to in July 1984. Following in the footsteps of Deutsche Bank, Mannesmann, Daimler-Benz, Siemens and other major German corporations, some of which had already introduced such limits in the mid-1970s to deter undesirable package buyers, especially from the Middle East, Continental now also set a five percent maximum voting right. The introduction of the voting limit was fiercely disputed. Proponents saw this as the best way to ensure the independence of a publicly traded company, while opponents complained of an "arrogant partial expropriation" of independent shareholders. They also saw far better long-term prospects for the tire company with a major investor. Many experts also questioned the effectiveness of the 5-percent voting right, which, unlike the state monitoring and approval procedures in Switzerland, Japan, the USA or France, seemed easy enough to circumvent.

Spurred on by the expectation of future profits from the innovation activities, which were presented to investors as a "revolution on wheels" under the names Energy Optimized Tire (EOT) and Conti Tire System (CTS), and further fueled by corresponding announcements by the Executive Board, the share price of what had become the most sought-after stock on the German stock exchange climbed to a historic high of 377.50 marks by mid-1987. "Conti Gummi on the verge of a breakthrough," was the headline in a Swiss stock exchange magazine in December 1986. In September 1987, Continental ran an advertising campaign in the Neue Zürcher Zeitung newspaper with the slogan "We may not have invented the wheel, but we never stop making it better," portraying the company as a lucrative investment.

Fig. 93: Continental share with a nominal value of 50 marks in 1966.

The stock market crash of October 1987 led to temporary turbulence. Not only did the price of Continental shares almost halve within a short space of time, but the new market transactions to finance the General Tire purchase through the placement of a warrant bond and a multi-stage capital increase also threatened to come to nothing. The second part of the capital coincided with the stock exchange collapse, which meant that the shares offered for a price of 320 marks could not be sold and remained with the syndicate banks. However, as early as the beginning of 1988, the share price began a strong recovery, bringing Continental shares close to their former highs. The spread of share capital remained comparatively low. An internal analysis of the registered capital undertaken for the Annual Shareholders' Meeting in 1984 showed that Continental was now owned by approximately 45,000 shareholders. As before, Deutsche Bank, even after departing as a major shareholder, was responsible for the main share of the capital represented at 13.8 percent. The remaining banks represented a further 22.3 percent without any significant shareholdings of their own. Nevertheless, there had been significant shifts, as the holdings of small shareholders and the protective associations representing them had increased sevenfold and now represented 5.5 percent of the share capital. Since 1986, the dividend yields with a 12 percent payout ratio or 6 marks per share were attractive again and international investors were actively sought. In December, Continental shares were listed on the stock exchanges in Switzerland and Austria. In fall 1987, an internationally oriented campaign commenced in which the company was presented to potential investors by chief financial officer Horst W. Urban at roadshows in Zurich, Geneva, Tokyo, New York and London. A focal point of Urban's campaign was the company's price increase from 42.10 to 372.50 marks or 885 percent between January 1982 and August 1987, which was the best performance of all German blue-chip stocks at the time. Continental shares now really stood out compared with the prices of US, Japanese and Italian competitors. While Goodyear, Bridgestone and Pirelli were clearly overvalued, with a price-earnings ratio of between 22 and 29, Continental's ratio was just 16.5. Only Michelin's value was lower at 12.9, and such financial market terms and share key figures were eagerly communicated by Continental's Executive Board.

Looking after investors and observing shareholder values now became central elements of targeted financial marketing at Continental. This became clear when the Continental shares were given their own place in the 1988 annual report for the first time, after which developments during the previous fiscal year were then regularly reported on. The Continental share was now traded on all eight German stock exchanges of the day and on four of Europe's key foreign exchanges, and demonstrated a high liquidity. A long-term investor relations program was developed, and, in 1989, a sponsored ADR program (American depositary receipt), i.e. tradable depositary receipts of shares, paved the way to the New York stock exchange. After Volkswagen, Continental was only the second German company to do this. For 1986 and 1989, the Continental Executive Board carried out a comparative survey of its shareholder structure. This revealed that more than half of the shares (53 percent) were in foreign hands. The stock had by now attracted the attention of American investment companies and analyst firms such as Morgan Stanley, which in September 1987 produced its first comprehensive 14-page analyst report on Continental and its stock. The total number of shareholders had since risen to 57,650, and a third of the shares were in the hands of private owners. In 1986, Continental became the first German stock corporation to also create a stock option plan for senior executives based on the American model, which granted around 100 managers the right to purchase Continental shares at a more favorable price. In contrast, the promotion of employee shareholders was pushed into the background. The share of insurance companies and banks also shrank to a third between 1986 and 1989, primarily in favor of investment companies and commercial enterprises. All in all, this was by no means a worrying development in the shareholder structure and no domestic or foreign conglomerations of interest could be identified that lay behind this. "The price of shares," Urban wrote in the annual report for 1989, "corresponds to the general stock exchange trend and the valuation of other major tire manufacturers. No concrete evidence has been found for the rumors of a buyout that have been circulating." Only a short time later, it became clear how deceptive appearances could be.

By now, the "CTS euphoria" had largely faded and no longer had much influence on the company's stock market value. Even so, in June 1989, its price surpassed the 300 mark again, fueling new takeover rumors. At 2.5 billion marks for the complete share package, Continental was in fact comparatively cheap for a financially strong competitor. For this reason, in July 1989, the Executive Board submitted a stricter version of the maximum voting right for approval to the Annual Shareholders' Meeting. Whereas it had previously been possible to remove the voting right limit with a simple majority, in the future this was only to be possible with a majority of three-quarters of the votes. Although the corresponding amendment to the Articles of Incorporation was approved at the Annual Shareholders' Meeting, the speculation and rumors surrounding Continental did not die down, especially since a lawsuit filed by a private shareholder initially postponed the final introduction of the voting right regulation. 1990 then proved to be one of the most turbulent years for Continental shares. In summer, the Gulf crisis had already caused share prices to plummet worldwide. The price of Continental shares had remained relatively stable at around 300 marks, although a drastic cut in dividends from 8 to 4 marks per share had been announced for the fiscal year. With the announcement of the takeover proposal by Pirelli in September 1990, the share price then began a steep decline, reaching a low of 189.50 marks. Subsequently, until November 1991, it fluctuated depending on the actual or rumored state of merger activities and countermeasures taken. The main point of contention was not just between Continental and Pirelli but also the abolition or defense of the majority voting right and the applicable restrictions on voting rights for Continental shares between the Small Shareholders' Protection Association and other German shareholder groups that also became involved in the conflict.

In light of rumors that had persisted since 1989 about a new major shareholder, the Continental Executive Board again proposed at the Annual Shareholders' Meeting in June 1990 to tighten the voting right restriction as a protective measure. The decision taken on this had not come into effect a year earlier due to a lawsuit filed by a shareholder. With just 51.5 percent approval and a high abstention rate, the proposal was adopted by an extremely narrow margin. Various interest groups were now openly campaigning for the resolution to be reversed and for the voting right restrictions to be abolished again. "A blocking clause protects companies and small shareholders," argued Continental's Executive Board, but the regulation did not really offer protection against a takeover by Pirelli once the Italians succeeded in requesting an extraordinary Shareholders' Meeting and pushing through the abolition of the voting right limitation. In order to undermine the maximum voting right previously in force, Pirelli required approval for and voting options on eleven 5% voting packages. Under stock corporation law and the Articles of Incorporation, however, the purchase of these packages by the company itself and thus the formation of a controlling syndicate was prohibited. Pirelli claimed time and again that it held a majority of votes at Continental along with friendly shareholders, but stubbornly refused to disclose the true extent of its shareholding and to name these "friends." From the start, the Continental Executive Board was therefore convinced that the Italians were bluffing. Despite all the wild speculation in the press about the distribution of power and the affiliation of shareholders to the two hostile camps, and rumors about "bundling," there was no certainty about the actual composition of the shareholder group and their possible voting behavior. The extraordinary Shareholders' Meeting took place in March 1991, at which a merger with Pirelli was rejected by a clear majority but at the same time the maximum voting right was abolished. Due to repeated actions for annulment, however, the old regulation remained in force for the time being. In May 1992, Hubertus von Grünberg, the new chairman of the Executive Board, emphasized that the restriction of voting rights was not a philosophical question for Continental, but rather one of survival. In the meantime, legions of stock corporation and financial lawyers had been looking at the Continental shares, the wording of individual provisions of the company's Articles of Incorporation and amendments, shareholder relations, and their legality or illegality. The whole affair was a typical example of the complex legal developments and different interests at play in the new financial market capitalism of the Federal Republic, which was now replacing the old Deutschland AG era. The dispute over actions for annulment and the voting right regulation at Continental dragged on until May 1993, going all the way up to the Federal Court of Justice, before calm finally returned with the action's dismissal.

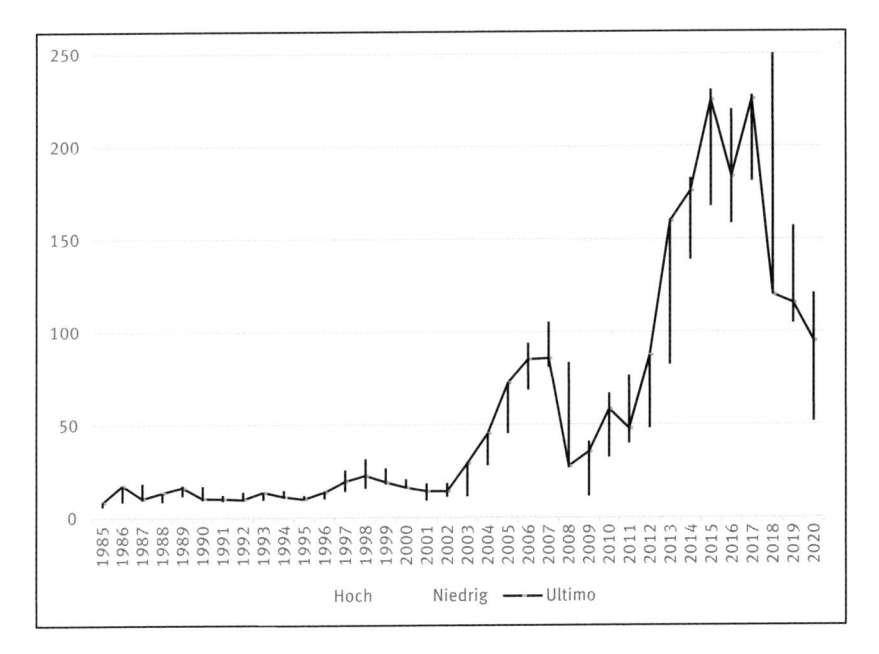

Fig. 94: Price development of Continental shares from 1985 to 2020 (recalculated in euros per unit). From August 1, 1994: conversion of 50-mark shares to shares with a nominal value of 5 marks.

Compared to the unprecedented boom in Continental shares between 2001/02 and 2007, and even more so, the highs between 2009 and 2017, the phase of growth of Continental shares slowed from 1983 to 1989 before seeming to stagnate. Nonetheless, the price swings were sharp and the gains substantial. Speculation over the attempted takeover by Pirelli was also reflected in the short-term share price development, which was followed by a decade-long phase between 1991 and 2000 in which Continental shares moved sideways, demanding patience again from shareholders. This began in 1991 and 1992, when no dividend was paid for the fifth time in the company's history. A turning point came in 1996 when Continental shares were removed from the index of the 30 most important German shares, the DAX, where they had been listed since its creation in 1988. This relegation to the MDAX stock market segment was due to insufficient market capitalization. The share price had been hit hard by the crisis in the automotive industry as well as the high restructuring costs incurred by Continental to make up for losses at General Tire and various plant closures. In contrast, the liquidation of Continental's 33.25 percent share package by Pirelli in April 1993 was not accompanied by any major price fluctuations, since the corresponding shares were placed directly with institutional investors with the help of Deutsche Bank and Norddeutsche Landesbank. Even so, at the Annual Shareholders' Meetings in June 1992 and 1993, the Continental Executive Board had to face some difficult and critical questions from the Deutsche Schutzgemeinschaft der Kleinaktionäre (German Association for the Protection of Small Shareholders).

After a break of 20 years, the topic of employee shares was also back on the agenda. In summer 1992, the Executive Board decided on an extensive program to revive the issue of employee shares and spent considerable time and effort promoting it. "For just under 500 marks, you can become a shareholder at Conti— with twice the asset value (at today's price)," the employee circular *conti intern* announced in September 1992. Once again, however, the timing of the issue in the fall of 1992 was inopportune. Of the 150,000 shares made available for Continental employees, only a fraction—18,930—were taken up. In the autumn of 1993, a second issue of employee shares took place, in which only 13,773 shares were purchased by employees. Assuming an average purchase of approximately three shares, less than 1 percent of the company's 50,000 employees (3,794) had shown interest in the employee shares. During the actions in the 1970s, around 40 percent of staff had taken part. Despite this, Continental created a new employee share model in 1995 with which, on top of traditional employee shares, an expanded concept of employee participation with share price hedging and external financing was offered. The model was called "Conti 100" and was the first of its kind to be offered by a German company. Employees could purchase up to 100 shares instead of the previous maximum of 40 shares. Rather than the purchase being subsidized compared to the stock market price, however, 80 percent of the price was granted as an interest-free employer loan. The holding period was reduced from six to two years, and any price losses during this period were excluded by guarantee. "We would welcome an increase in the participation of our company's employees to 5 percent and more in the medium and long term," the Executive Board stated. Nevertheless, the interest remained low here as well, and only approximately 16 percent of the eligible employees made use of the program. By now, the shareholder structure again showed a decline in the proportion of foreign investors to around 20 percent of the share capital (10.7 percent from the UK; 9.5 percent from the USA). At the same time, the proportion of major German institutional investors again grew strongly to 38.7 percent: 16.9 percent of the shares were held by Nord/LB, 10.25 percent by Deutsche Bank, 6.5 percent by Dresdner Bank, and 5.03 percent by Allianz. It was almost like a revival of the old Deutschland AG, except that behind the commitments of banks and insurance companies there were no longer any industrial policy interests but rather purely yield-oriented speculation and above all the maturity of earlier option bonds. In the meantime, Continental was paying out dividends again, which rose continuously from 20 cents (1993) to 51 cents per share (2000). However, as early as 1997, following the maturity of numerous option bonds, the proportion of Continental shares held by major German investors fell again significantly to under 10 or 5 percent. At the same time, because of the option rights being exercised, the share capital rose by over 20 percent to 572.5 million marks. The number of issued and outstanding Continental shares with dividend rights at the nominal value of 5 marks now totaled 114.5 million.

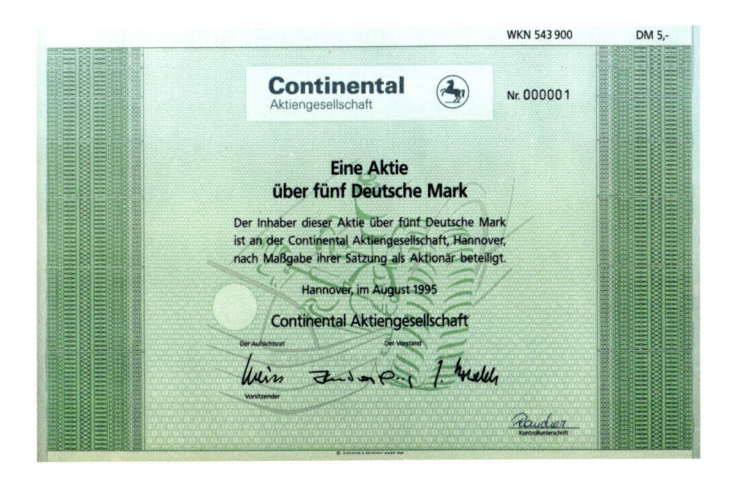

Fig. 95: Continental share with a nominal value of 5 marks from 1995.

The Annual Shareholders' Meeting in June 1996 now saw the abolition of the controversial maximum voting right. Since reforms in capital market legislation had brought in new obligations to report the acquisition of shareholdings in listed companies, it was no longer necessary to limit voting rights. Continental nevertheless remained a potential takeover candidate in the subsequent period. A look at the development of its share price, however, shows that there were probably no new interested parties at that time. After the last trading day price of the equivalent of 9.8 euros per share at the end of 1992, there was a temporary rise until 1994 before a further fall back to 9.5 euros in 1995. With fluctuations, the share price then climbed to the equivalent of 20 euros by the end of 2000, interrupted only by a brief high of 31.8 in 1998. This meant that, in the past 10 years, the value of the shares had doubled, while the DAX index had quadrupled. Continental shares were thus far behind compared with the highly dynamic development of the index. Small shareholders reacted to this with dissatisfaction and criticism, and vented their anger in letters to the chairman of the Executive Board, von Grünberg, and the chairman of the Supervisory Board, Ulrich Weiß. "What distresses me most as a Continental shareholder," one letter-writer told von Grünberg in September 1995, "is the extremely mediocre performance of the Conti share price over a long period of time and the poor image the share has among stock market investors. Your reply will no doubt be that this is dependent on stock market developments and there is little you can do to influence it. But the main blame for the loss of value of Conti shares lies with you, as I will explain below." Even so, since around 1997 at the latest, the company had put much effort into selling Continental as a new "stock market and investment story" and one of the "most innovative partners of the automotive industry." The new company strategy was presented at numerous roadshows in the USA, Switzerland, France and the UK. There was high growth potential in the automotive sector, especially through the new ESP technology, which the company referred to as "unique system and technological know-how." The networking of this system had led to the development of a "30-meter car" after full braking at a speed of 100 km/h and hence a marked improvement in driving safety. "We make individual mobility safer and more comfortable" and "We will be the global technology leader in all our business areas" were the claims made on November 15, 2000, at an analyst's conference in London.

Yet this time, the investor relations efforts proved less successful. "The share price performance in no way reflects the position of Continental as one of the most innovative automotive suppliers," the Executive Board lamented in its annual report for 2000. The many measures had not "led to a reasonable valuation." At the same time, the company was strongly committed to the shareholder value stance that was widely propagated at the time. This also found its way into Continental's newly formulated set of values, or "Basics." In 1999, Continental's share price had already fallen significantly in the wake of a renewed crisis in the automotive industry and a related reduction in profit expectations by the Executive Board. Even so, the company posted an above-average share price performance compared with other listed automotive suppliers such as TRW, Delphi, Denso and Valeo. Its former direct competitors in the tire business, Goodyear and Bridgestone, also saw their share price fall significantly, with the exception being Pirelli. A capital increase of 11.5 million shares at an issue price of 21.5 euros also lowered the price of Continental shares, which financed at least part of the major Teves acquisition. Continental reacted to the low price a year later when it bought back 8.1 million of its own shares, corresponding to 6.1 percent of its share capital. After the share buybacks in the early 1930s, this was the second time in the company's history that this measure was implemented. Later, it would become a common tactic employed by companies as a means of maintaining their share prices. Buying back these shares had little effect on the share price, however. A far greater impact was triggered by news of the withdrawal from circulation of 160,000 tires from General Tire in September 2000, which led to a fall in the share price of 10 percent to 18.9 euros. In the wake of the economic and financial crisis in 2001, the share price fell further and, at 9.2 euros a share, returned to the level of a decade before. For the sixth time in the company's history, dividend payments were canceled. The high level of debt that had accumulated and the reduced earnings meant that the capital base would have been weakened if payments had gone ahead. This was followed by a brief recovery, but Continental shares continued their sideways movement until 2002. At the end of that year, the share was quoted at 14 euros.

Yet the interest of small shareholders in Continental remained high. In June 1998, around 2,000 private shareholders registered for the Annual Shareholders' Meeting. By 2000, this had risen by 48 percent to 2,700. This represented an increase of around 48 percent and compared to other stock corporations was higher than average. The German Protection Association for Share Ownership and the Association for the Protection of Small Shareholders continued to be regular visitors, together making up around 100,000 votes. Also present for the first time were the "Annual Shareholder's Meeting rebels," an organized group of critical shareholders that was feared in the chemical and pharmaceutical industries. However, interest among most shareholders in registering to vote at the Annual Shareholders' Meeting had declined significantly. In June 2000, only 38.4 percent of the share capital was represented. It was only through the involvement of a financial services company that it was possible to stop the downward trend and to achieve capital registrations of over 40 percent. Since July 2002, when the Financial Market Promotion Act came into effect, members of the Supervisory Board and Executive Board of listed companies had also had to notify the state financial services regulator of any acquisition or disposal transactions in shares of their own company.

In 2003, a development began that not only breathed new life into Continental shares but catapulted them to new heights (before, in 2009, the next global financial crisis led to price falls, albeit temporarily.) In the eyes of Continental's Executive Board, only now did the capital markets begin to honor the company's new direction. The phase began with the return of the Continental shares to the DAX on September 22, 2003. After a seven-year absence, the company was again one of the top 30 share values in Germany.

Fig. 96: Chairman of the Continental Executive Board Manfred Wennemer and chief financial officer Alan Hippe (In the background, the Conti share quotation of September 22, 2003).

The return to the top of the stock market brought the shares back into the focus of international financial markets and global investors. "This will create more price potential and new financial flexibility, which we need in order to be able to invest and grow," chief financial officer Alan Hippe said, highlighting the importance of this reentry. "Last but not least, every cent increase in the share price reduces the takeover risk, because it makes us too expensive as a possible acquisition candidate." Deutsche Bank had in fact sold off its last Continental shares a few months beforehand in November 2002. The number of shares was 10 million, at 14.10 euros a share. This did not put too much pressure on the share price, however. The largest single shareholder was now Allianz, and the free float of Continental shares was almost 60 percent. The acquisitions of Teves (1998) and Temic (2001) started the new expansion and growth course. This continued a short time later with the purchases of Phoenix (2004), the automotive electronics business of Motorola (2006) and above all Siemens VDO (2007). This saw share prices reach a new height again, and Continental became the center-point of a new stock exchange and investment success story. Investor relations activities were also stepped up accordingly. In 2003 alone, 11 roadshows and 260 individual meetings with analysts, institutional investors and stock exchange experts took place, in which Continental presented itself as an "innovation leader in the automotive future." Success was not slow in coming: in that year alone, the price of Continental shares rose by more than 100 percent to almost 30 euros and, helped by a general stock exchange boom, climbed to a peak price of 105.40 euros by 2007. The financial media soon celebrated chairman of the Executive Board Manfred Wennemer as "manager strategist of the year" several times over—the same outlets that had once accused him of small-minded austerity instead of bold expansion, and of a strategic U-turn that would set the corporation back significantly. Under his leadership, payments of dividends commenced again, the rate of which climbed from 0.45 cents (2002) to 2 euros per share (2007). In 2003, only 7.2 percent of Continental share owners came from Germany. In contrast, 62.8 percent were investors from abroad: mostly from the USA (32.2 percent), the UK (19.6 percent) and the rest of Europe (11 percent). The biggest shareholders were now French insurance company Axa, the Capital Group and Barclay's Bank. The free float amounted to 77.7 percent. In 2007, the distribution was as follows: 71.3 percent of shareholders came from the USA, Japan and Europe, while Germany again made up 12.4 percent, with 83.6 percent of the share capital now held by institutional investors. Private investors and small shareholders only accounted for 16.4 percent. Within a short space of time, Continental shares had become the new darling of analysts, who predicted further significant price increases for the stock and issued corresponding buy recommendations. Around 40 analysts in Germany and abroad were now following Continental's development continuously, and the investor relations department in Hanover could hardly keep up with the number of inquiries. Soon, the Executive Board chairman and chief financial officer were busy attending investor conferences. They were also closely involved in investor relations communications, which increasingly included product demonstrations too. In September 2005, a presentation of this kind took place during the IAA in Frankfurt with more than 80 international investors and analysts in attendance. Continental shares were receiving more attention than ever before from the general public.

By pursuing a shareholder-friendly course, the Executive Board faced growing criticism from the works councils and the employee representatives on the Supervisory Board. March 2005 and the subsequent year saw fierce debates over Wennemer's proposals for the appropriation of profits and his plans to further increase dividends. The argument was that such a policy could no longer be communicated to the employees, who were suffering because of the harsh cost-cutting measures and financial losses. These protests fell on deaf ears, however, with Wennemer maintaining that there was no direct link between dividends and employee profit-sharing. "Recently, shareholders have had to go without interest on their capital, while employees have always been adequately remunerated for their work," he argued. Surprisingly, no side mentioned employee shares or possible initiatives to relaunch efforts to broaden the circle of shareholding workers and employees at Continental. 2003 had seen a brief attempt to revive this idea before it was again put to bed. Even so, it was impossible to overlook the fact that the stock market price and anticipated capital market reactions now influenced Continental's business policies far more strongly than in the 1990s. The image of Continental and its shares in investor and stock market circles was followed meticulously. The capital market reporting process was looked at, as were any similarities or differences between the self-perception and expectations of the Executive Board on the one hand, and external perceptions of investors and shareholders on the other. Questions were also asked about how such situations were reflected in the undervaluation or overvaluation of Continental shares. The pressure of expectation from the capital market weighed heavily on Wennemer's decision-making. An example of this was how the relevant circles assumed a "normal dividend" between 1.20 and 1.50 euros per share in December 2006, as well as a special payment of 2 to 3 euros per share. In this way, the Executive Board became at times a victim of its own investor relations communication. The decision to pay a dividend of 2 euros per share, thus increasing the dividend by 100 percent compared with 2005, represented a middle ground between external capital market expectations and internal liquidity requirements.

Since returning to the DAX, Continental shares had seen an increase of 411 percent by March 2007. However, from the second half of 2007, the mood on the German capital market deteriorated significantly following the crisis in the US mortgage sector and speculation about an economic and stock market collapse in America. For the first time in many years, the price of Continental shares dropped significantly, and it was only with great effort that the company was able to increase capital that fall by 10 percent of the share capital, with the new shares being issued at a price of 101 euros. This capital increase, which brought in 1.4 billion euros, was necessary to finance part of the 13.5 billion euros needed for the purchase of Siemens VDO, the failure of which would have had unforeseeable consequences. On July 15, 2008, the Schaeffler Group made a public takeover offer to acquire all of Continental's shares for 70.12 euros per share, an offer that was increased to 75 euros a short time later. At a time when Continental shares were trading at a low of 27 euros in November 2008 as a result of the outbreak of the global financial crisis, the takeover bid, which was more than twice as high, therefore offered shareholders a lucrative way out of the general collapse in prices, at least in the case of their Continental shares. At the end of the year, the Schaeffler Group and the two banks involved in the takeover, Sal. Oppenheim and Metzler, together held 89.26 percent of the total share capital. The drama of Schaeffler's Continental takeover and a two-year phase that was accompanied by rumors, company policy information, fragmentary communication, heightened speculation and, ultimately, considerable price drops on the world's stock markets was clearly reflected in the performance of Continental's shares. As a result of the ongoing crisis and speculation that Continental and its new main shareholder Schaeffler were excessively in debt, the price of Continental shares fell to 11.35 euros in 2009. At times, only 11 percent of all Continental shares could be freely traded. In addition, there was speculation about an imminent increase in capital, the apparent need for state aid and personnel changes on the Executive and Supervisory Boards in connection with a drastic downward trend in the automotive industry. Once again, no dividend was paid out—a freeze that would last three years from 2008 to 2010.

While the developments were certainly dramatic, Continental's share price recovered again just as quickly. The new Executive Board chairman and Supervisory Board chairman were also good news for the price development. The capital increase at the start of 2010 proved successful too, lightening the mood despite the tense situation on the financial markets and at Continental. The share capital was increased by 80 million euros to 512 million euros. 31 million shares were issued in several steps at an issue price of 40 euros via private placement to institutional investors, while subscription rights were granted to all other shareholders. The capital increase poured 1.1 billion euros into Continental's coffers and in turn eased the loan burden from the Siemens VDO purchase. The three major shareholders, above all Schaeffler, had explicitly waived the exercise of their subscription rights, so that their portion of the share capital was only 75.1 percent after its increase. The free float of Continental shares thus increased from 10 to 24.9 percent. Even so, the new shareholder structures and the comparatively low number of publicly traded Continental shares meant that the market capitalization criteria of the German stock exchange were no longer fulfilled. At the start of December 2009, after five years, Continental was again relegated from the DAX to the MDAX segment. Nonetheless, Continental's share price had already reached 58.3 euros again by the end of 2010. In 2013, it was at 160 euros (with fluctuations), which was well above the peak price of 2006. Speculation about a rapid return to the DAX after a possible merger with Schaeffler led to jumps in price of up to 20 percent at times. The second reentry into the DAX took place in 2012 after the company's free float had risen to 50.1 percent and its market capitalization to over 16.8 billion euros. Continental was thereby valued more highly than it ever had been in the company's history.

By 2015, the share price had risen even further, surpassing the 200-euro mark for the first time and reaching a new record high of 230 euros, which was then to be improved on again in 2018 at 257 euros. Chief financial officer Wolfgang Schäfer was celebrated in the media as "investor's darling 2014" and "mister 350 percent" (manager magazin). He had been able to completely rewrite the company's stock exchange history and turn the Continental shares (once again) into a new "investment story." Safety, digitalization, high-tech and future mobility were now the focus instead of tires and rubber, promising high margins and growth instead of permanent price pressure, overpowering competition and fluctuating profits. "These are the megatrends driving the automotive industry and from which we will profit for years to come," Schäfer continuously ensured his external creditors and equity investors, as reported by manager magazin. The magazine also named him capital market strategist of the year, while Continental was distinguished as the company with the best capital market communication.

Fig. 97: Continental CFO Wolfgang Schäfer in 2014.

From 2016, however, the rise of Continental shares became much less pronounced and their price performance more volatile. Measuring the company's success by the price of the shares alone proved to be problematic. This was especially true when, in the case of Continental, expectations of investors were by now far beyond the company's actual development—which impacted the share price. For the first time in four years, a negative share price performance was recorded in 2016, with a drop of 18 percent at the end of the year. This was due to growing concerns about a slump in the automotive industry, with analysts significantly lowering their expectations and recommendations for the entire sector and its supplier industry. What only a short time before had been a celebrated showcase industry with groundbreaking innovations for the future of mobility was transformed in the media into a crisis sector facing the greatest challenges and structural upheavals in its history. The change of opinion among analysts and on the financial markets was not without consequences for the share price. By now, 4.25 euros per share were paid as a dividend. Using as an example a 10,000-euro purchase of Continental shares, the long-term development in value over the previous 10 years meant growth in assets to 24,739 euros, i.e. 147 percent or an annual return of 9.5 percent. While impressive, the shares were losing value and during 2018, the upward trend stalled significantly. Several profit warnings, disappointed investor expectations and the deep crisis in the automotive industry caused the share price to halve year-on-year to 120 euros by the end of 2018 and to remain low in 2019. In spring 2020, it was then further hit by the global stock market crash triggered as a result of the coronavirus pandemic. In March 2020, the shares were quoted at 51.40 euros, a level last seen in 2011. During this phase, speculation about a fundamental restructuring of the corporation, rather than profit expectations, repeatedly led to short-lived price jumps of Continental shares, while news of billion-dollar write-downs and losses brought the price back down. So too did massive job losses and a letter sent from the Executive Board to managers which, though intended to serve as a wake-up call about internal quality and earning problems, had a counterintuitive effect. Since the pandemic crash there has been a marked recovery but, as before, the Continental shares reflect the continuing insecurity regarding the further development of the capital market, the supply sector and the company. As well as this, in December 2020, there was another sudden change of CEO due to health reasons.

Yet looking back reveals how patience pays off on the stock market: a buyer of 100 Continental shares in August 1994 at the then nominal value of 5 marks and a price of 11.20 euros (after conversion) would have made 25,000 euros including dividend payments from the initial 1,120 euros at the end of 2017—despite all the fluctuations and three veritable stock exchange crashes. Even at the end of 2020, this sum still stood at around 15,000 euros. The regional distribution of the free float at the end of 2019 shows that, irrespective of all the Continental share life cycles, there is a group of small shareholders who remain loyal to the company. In addition to the 73 percent of foreign institutional investors who held the majority of the free float (54%) of Continental shares, there were 6.6 percent German institutional shareholders and 5.9 percent local small shareholders. Not much expertise is required to forecast that Continental shares will continue to reach new highs, as has so often happened in their life cycle, during the course of the years to come. On the occasion of the company's 175th anniversary in the mid-2040s, it may be that they are quoted at new record prices. Anyone who bought Continental shares in March 2020 (or shortly afterward) at the low price of 55 euros per share can therefore look forward to substantial increases in value. This is provided the person in question possesses the necessary stamina and perseverance, as has been required of Continental shareholders time and again throughout the company's history.

7 From Local Trademark to Global Brand
  The Brand and its Marketing in Continental's History

The Horse's Importance for the "Continental" Brand

At Continental, the horse can be seen everywhere. It appears on Continental products, the employee newsletter, advertising brochures and the annual report. The image used is of a jumping horse. It is either in a word/image symbol combined with the Continental lettering, or an icon inside two circles with the writing "Continental—Since 1871."

Why is the horse used? At first glance, horses have little to do with the company's current or past product portfolios. In order to explain why the horse became the Continental trademark and has remained an important part of its brand image to this day, it is necessary to look back at the early years of the company's history. The first documented connection dates back to 1875—four years after the company was founded. That year, a veterinary surgeon from Hanover by the name of Christian Hartmann published a technical brochure in which he described his latest invention: hoof buffers for horses made of soft rubber. The hoof buffer was attached between the horseshoe and the horse's hoof. The aim was that the complete surface of the hoof (frog, sole and wall) would touch the ground, as was usual in the horse's natural state. When a hoof was shod, only the part with the horseshoe on it (the wall) touched the ground. The hoof buffer now meant that the frog and sole would also do so. This led to less deformities of the hoof, protection from injury and improved sure-footedness, for example on smooth surfaces.

This invention fit well with a time where the horse still played an important role in mobility—as a riding or draft animal that was also sometimes used in cities to pull tram cars. Hanover, with a long tradition in horse breeding, was also an ideal place for the innovative product to make its breakthrough. In his brochure, Hartmann mentioned how Continental had supported his work on the invention and also organized production and sales. All the hoof buffers came with a trademark that showed a jumping horse enclosed by two concentric circles. The lettering "Hartmann-Patent" referred to the inventor, while "Continental-Caoutchouc & Gutta-Percha-Compagnie Hannover" referred to the manufacturer of the new hoof buffer.

In spring 1876, horse hoof buffers made from rubber were registered as a trademark at the Hanover Regional Court. During the 1870s, trademark protection laws had come into force in industrialized countries. Even in ancient times, trademarks had existed, however. These made it possible for consumers to identify with a certain manufacturer and guaranteed a product's quality. The creation of national and international markets in the 19th century during the industrial revolution saw a massive increase in interregional trade. This led to trademarks and their protection becoming much more important. During this time, many brands that are still successful today became established.

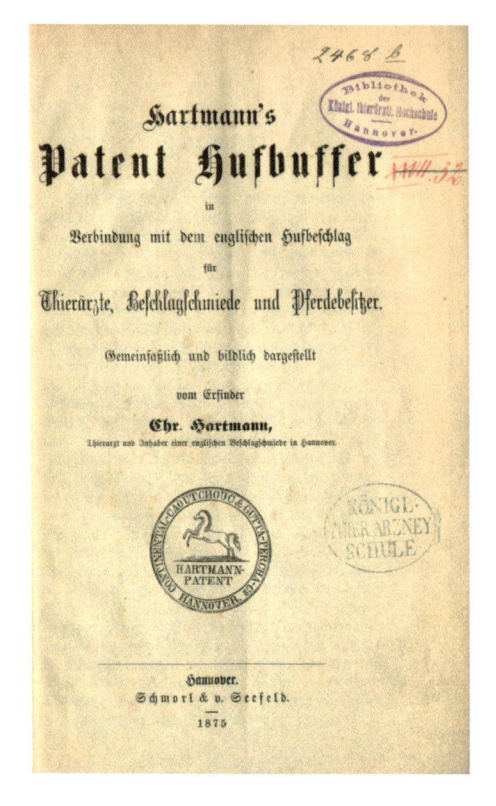

Fig. 98: Technical brochure for horse hoof buffers from 1875.

Continental also tried to secure trademark rights by registering its brands. The trademark showed a slightly modified form, but the essential characteristics were still present. The reference to the Hartmann patent for hoof buffers was also retained. Nonetheless, the logo was gradually also used for other Continental products. In October 1882, all the company's soft rubber products were registered at the Hanover local court. The reference to Hartmann was dropped, the company name was simplified by an abbreviation, and the horse was given a new design. In 1894, a new "imperial law for the protection of product designations" made it possible to protect brand logos throughout Germany. The logo was duly registered on October 1, 1894. With this move, the "horse jumping on a bumpy track" became a permanent feature of Continental's external image. As previously described, pneumatic tires increasingly dominated the product portfolio as the 19th century came to a close. These tires were also given the logo that had originally been introduced for hoof buffers.

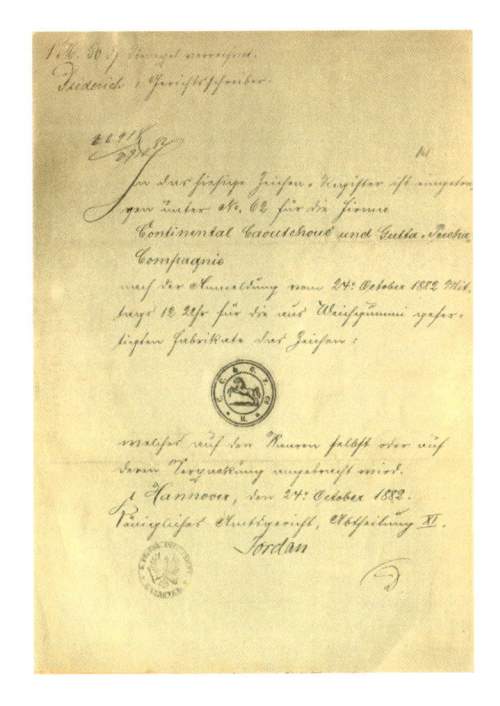

Fig. 99: Certificate of trademark registration from 1882.

The connection to this innovative product from the company's early years thus explains the origin of the horse motif. The relationship is clear, as is the visual similarity. In the surviving business documents from the time, however, there is no explicit explanation of why the horse was used and what motivated this decision. Neither the decision-making process nor the reasons are documented. The same is true for the company name "Continental." All attempts at explaining this today are at best theories.

In addition to the connection with hoof buffers, there may be another reason why Continental chose a horse to represent mobility—which at the end of the 19th century was becoming increasingly motorized. Continental was founded in Hanover on October 8, 1871. In Hanover and the surrounding areas there was a long tradition of using the horse as a symbol. In the 14th century, in order to legitimize their rule, the Dukes of Brunswick and Lüneburg used the horse as a heraldic symbol on their coat of arms. The horse had been a well-known symbol in the early medieval tribal duchy of Saxony. The dukes therefore saw themselves as descendants of this duchy and as upholders of this tradition. Using the horse to symbolize dominance was an important act of communication in a time when only small numbers of people could read and write.

In more recent history, dukes, electoral princes (from 1692) and kings (from 1813) of Hanover used a galloping (and later jumping) horse on their coats of arms and insignia. This tradition continued after the Kingdom of Hanover was annexed by Prussia in 1866. Even today, Lower Saxony's official coat of arms is a jumping white steed. For centuries, the horse has thus been a well-known political symbol in Hanover and the surrounding region. Other companies in Hanover also used this prominent symbol for their products, in the hope of benefiting from its familiarity with consumers. This background may also have played a role at Continental. The consistent use of the jumping horse for early Continental products was a stamp of quality for consumers. It guaranteed recognizability and indicated the regional origin of products.

During the Nazi era, this direct reference to the early medieval Saxon steed was heavily focused on and given a political meaning. The January 1937 issue of the customer magazine *Echo Continental* contains the article "Hanover. The home of Continental." The article describes in detail the traditional closeness of the company to the region. Exaggerated formulations are used for emphasis:

> All this was created by our fathers under the symbol of the Saxon steed: this white horse that once stood for the international fame of a German tribe, and today is the mark of 'Continental,' a tire company that also enjoys global importance. And now, after many years of decline and standstill, that which was created under the symbol of the noble Saxon steed is being continued under the power embodied by the swastika.

At this time, such references can also be found in other articles and texts on Continental's external presentation. The Nazi regime viewed internationality with suspicion, and it was considered politically unreliable. The above remarks can thus be read as an attempt to overlay the company's international character with a politicized local identity. This would then help to counteract any political pressure in advance. In World War I, Continental had already been the target of nationalist critics. At the time, the company was suspected of not only bearing the politically undesirable internationality in its name, but also of being a very foreign company in other respects. The then director, Siegmund Seligmann, took charge personally of this situation in order to prevent decisions that could harm the business. The traditional lineage from the Saxon steed to the Continental horse was an invention of the Nazi era. It can be viewed as a way of conforming to the ideal of Germanness that was being pushed in all areas of society.

Fig. 100: The new illuminated company logo is erected at the warehouse in Hanover-Stöcken, December 1949.

After 1945, the horse was kept on in the Continental logo. The company wanted to quickly forget Continental's role as a model Nazi company and collaborator with the regime. It wanted to leave behind the destruction of World War II. Business was almost at a standstill, both at home and abroad, and the wish now was to rebuild the company. This focus was also visually underscored by a rework of the brand image. In 1929, the Annual Shareholders' Meeting had already changed the name from Continental-Caoutchouc- & Gutta-Percha-Compagnie to the more modern-sounding Continental Gummi-Werke Aktiengesellschaft. In the logo used from late December 1949 , only the name "Continental" appeared, combined with a star. The horse was still present, serving as a symbol of continuity during these changes. In December 1949, the new logo was placed on top of the warehouse in Hanover-Stöcken, making the changes visible from afar. Even today, a Continental logo is positioned at this spot, which can be clearly seen from the nearby autobahn.

The recognition factor of the horse as a logo was also used intensively in advertisements for Continental products. This was not so important for the local market, because everyone in Hanover knew the company. With its factory, Continental was also present as a local manufacturer. Nonetheless, during the 19th century, further national and international markets opened. This meant that a distinctive brand became increasingly important in order to prevail against competitors. Not only that, but using the logo consistently on all products also made it possible to be perceived as a company in the first place. Ideally, consumers would identify with the product and buy more and more items "with the horse."

Fig. 101: Historical advertisement from 1921.

Fig. 102: Brochure 1970.

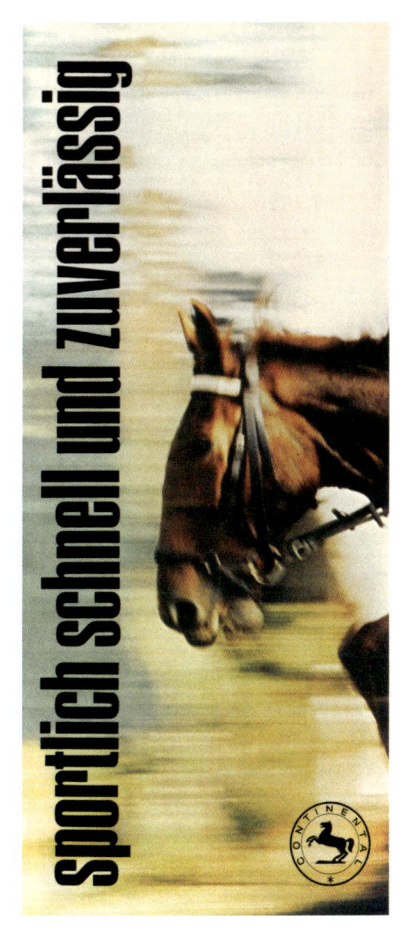

Fig. 103: Versions of the Continental logo from 1979 (top) and 2013 (bottom).

Early advertisements made good use of the contradiction of a horse being used to sell products aimed at motorization. In one campaign from 1921, horses comment on the design of the Continental logo. Reference is not just made to the positive characteristics of horses: "Me as a trademark? Great! I may be a noble animal, but Continental is a fine tire too!" The replacement of the horse as a means of transport was also a recurring theme. In this context, Continental was presented as a pioneer of modern motorization, while at the same time upholding the link to its historical roots: "My picture, always my picture! The gasoline-fueled horses still need me—as a trademark for their Continental tires!" Characteristics generally associated with horses, such as strength and endurance, were also used in Continental advertisements to highlight a product's qualities. The advertising brochure from 1970 illustrated here creates a direct visual link between the horse, its characteristics and the Continental brand. Only inside the flyer is any mention made of the new textile belt tire that is advertised.

In 1979, the logo and entire brand image were revised again. The word "Continental" was now made clearer and appeared twice. Following its latest revision in 2013, a reference was also added in the logo to the company's founding year of 1871. On this occasion, the jumping horse was heavily revised again. The representation is now more abstract, the hooves and mane are less detailed, and the horse's pose is straighter. The basic characteristics though have remained the same since the first version in 1875: the horse jumping on a (no longer quite so) bumpy surface.

So why is the horse used? The question will probably never be conclusively answered as the decision was never documented. Nonetheless, the connection to the innovative hoof buffers and the local relevance of the horse as a political symbol are plausible theories as to why the horse became a part of Continental's corporate identity. The horse has never gone away, regardless of changes to the brand or even the company. It is a strong logo. It stands for almost 150 years of continuity and is perhaps all the more successful because of its apparent contradiction to the company's modern product portfolio.

The Continental Color and Brand Strategy

As well as the Continental name and the horse, the color is also an essential part of the company's corporate identity. Since 1977, Continental has used a warm yellow color, merging into orange. Previously, a combination of blue and yellow had dominated the external presentation of the company and its products since the start of the 20th century. As with the name "Continental," it is not known why these colors were originally chosen. An exhibition from 1936 clearly shows the colors already being used systematically. That year, Continental took Dunlop to court for using the same color combination. The Continental advertising department showed that all poster advertisements at home and abroad had been using the blue and yellow combination since 1907. Even before World War I, Continental was already using this color combination uniformly at racing events. At the opening of the Nürburgring in 1927, Continental even erected a 40-meter-long billboard. In court, Continental's submissions were clearly aimed at convincing the judge that the company had been using blue and yellow for longer than its competitors, and therefore deserved preferential rights. The company's blue and yellow had been registered since May 1934 and were thus also protected by trademark law. The legal dispute with Dunlop ended in 1937 when both companies reached agreement on the use of the colors. "Continental will use yellow for its background, and Dunlop will use blue. This especially applies to the company name. Here, the word 'Continental' can appear in blue on a yellow background, and the word 'Dunlop' in yellow on a blue background."

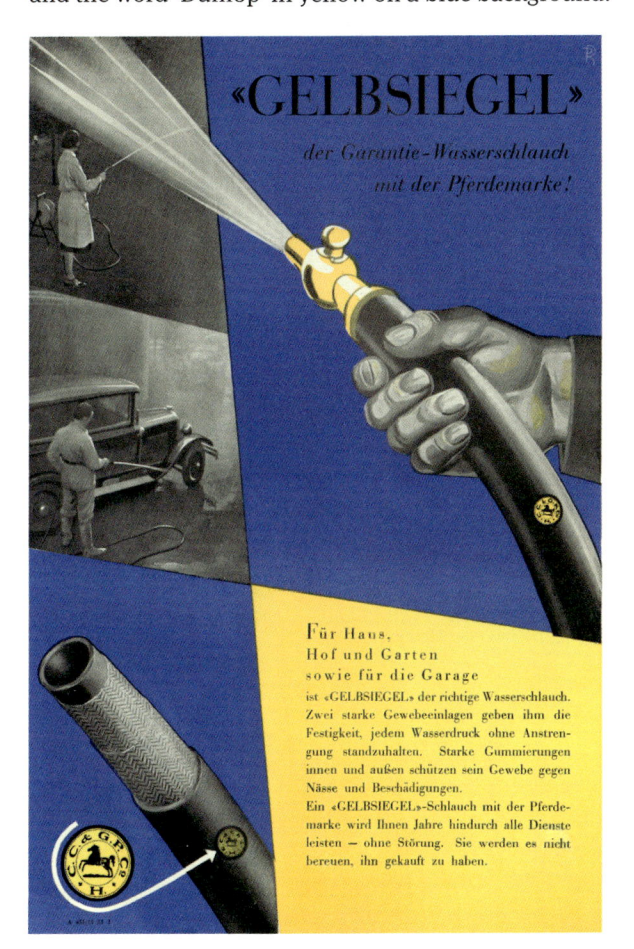

Fig. 104: Historical advertising flier from around 1931.

This color scheme stayed the same until 1977, when the entire brand image was completely revised. "If you look at how we have been presenting ourselves up to now, you quickly see that this was complete chaos," the employee newsletter *conti intern* stated when explaining this new direction. The goal was not just to create uniformity; for the first time, detailed guidelines were also issued that would be mandatory throughout the company. The "Continental" lettering was mostly unchanged. New was the mandatory combination with the jumping horse, which was positioned at the top right next to the lettering. This was meant to symbolize quality and reliability, similar to a copyright symbol. "It is also our guarantee," the new design guidelines stated. This first word and logo are still part of Continental's brand image today. The decades-old color scheme was also revised. "The new Conti yellow is the brightest, warmest yellow ever. [...] It exudes dynamism, activity and confidence."

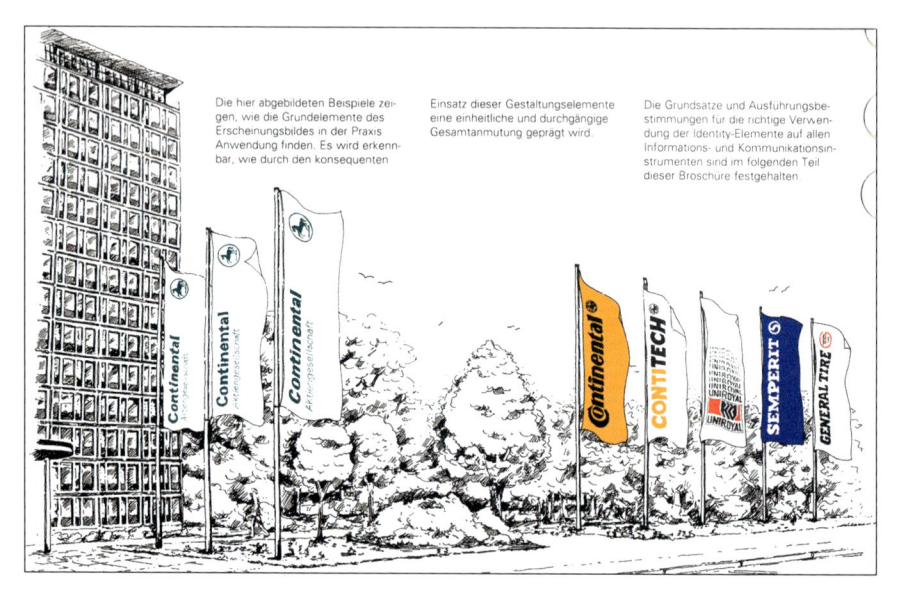

Fig. 105: Extract from Continental's design guidelines in 1988.

The corporate logo introduced in 1988 was a departure from the usual continuity in brand management. The background to this was the development of Continental from a single-brand company to a multiple-brand corporate group. The companies Uniroyal (1979), Semperit (1985) and General Tire (1987) had been acquired, while another new brand—ContiTech (1988)—had been established for the Technical Products division. In May 1988, a management information bulletin stated that it was necessary "to distinguish the company's external appearance from the traditional 'Continental' word and image logo using the color orange." This decision was based on the "branding follows strategy" principle. Continental Aktiengesellschaft had just been renamed at the Annual Shareholders' Meeting. In organizational terms, it was to take on the function of a holding company and give the individual business units more autonomy. The new corporate logo reflected this change. The traditional typography style was modified and "Aktiengesellschaft" was added to the lettering. The decision-makers perceived the new turquoise/green color as radiating "solidity and technical competence without coldness." The horse was also present in this word and image logo. However, it was clearly separated from the lettering, and the design of the circle was modified. The previous word and image logo was not discontinued though. It now stood exclusively for the Continental tire brand.

This separate corporate logo was just a brief episode in the long continuity of the Continental brand image. Separating corporate and product logos was stopped again in 1997. "The 'green' appearance is out and is being replaced by the yellow identity," *conti intern* reported without further explanation. The reason for this step can be found in the design guidelines: "Therefore we are today convinced that the corporation is better presented to the outside by its lead brand 'Continental' (in Conti yellow)." In the annual report, the shareholders were also sold this development as a return to the company's roots. The acquired companies and brands were by now integrated into the company, and it was time to reestablish an identity between the leading brand and the corporation.

The last major revision of the brand image was presented at the 2013 Annual Shareholders' Meeting. In contrast to the previous processes, a detailed description of what the brand should stand for was given for the first time: "Our logo shows what lies behind our products and solutions. It indicates our culture, the way we do things and what we stand for." This reference to values, vision and mission was a departure from the previous policy of modernizing the brand image without much comment. A further difference was how transparently criticism from employees was dealt with. In the past, the brand was revised in a top-down process. Now, explanations were given. "Mare, pony or shying horse?" was the title of an interview in *conti intern*, in which project managers not only responded to critical questions on the horse's design, but also explained the background and relevance of the project.

Continental's brand image has been marked by continuity and transformation for 150 years. The name, the lettering and the horse as logo have survived the many highs and lows of the company's history, even if the design and typography have changed immensely. It is difficult to find radical breaks in this history. The only examples would be the attempt to introduce a separate corporate logo and the change in color tone from blue and yellow to orange. Both examples are a sign of how much value is attributed to the brand. The historical continuity guarantees high recognizability and signals to stakeholders both modernity and a simultaneous awareness of tradition.

The customer magazine *Echo Continental* was a reflection of the company's progressive image

As mentioned previously, since the 19th century, advertising has played an increasingly important role in an expanding company. In the 1920s, advertising became much more important as the automobile changed from being a luxury article to one of daily use. A market for spare tires came into being, as did the necessity of positioning the "Continental" brand on the market. Innumerable media and formats were used to advertise Continental products: from newspaper ads through building facades, cycling jerseys and postcards to even the first animated movies.

Fig. 106: First advertisement for Continental car tires in *Der Motorwagen* from 1898.

At times, considerable effort was put into these advertisements. Published from 1913 to 1941, the customer magazine *Echo Continental* is an example of this. The magazine was published monthly in the first years, and quarterly in later years. 241 issues were brought out in total, and the number of copies rose to over 100,000 in the 1930s. These were sold as subscriptions and reached a wide readership. The editors explained the purpose of the magazine in the first edition from January 1913 as follows:

> For a long time, we have wanted to publish our own monthly review. Our hope was to regularly inform enthusiasts on topics of interest that might be relevant to our products—topics that would range from car tires to car racing and other sports. We are delighted to announce that starting this year, our long-held aspirations will come to fruition. [...] Our first writers from the world of sports are already on board, and we are certain that our readers will be captivated by the content of every 'Echo.' We hope that this first issue will be met with your enthusiasm.

A special editorial team in Continental's advertising department put the issues together with the help of renowned advertising designers, writers and photographers. Erich Maria Remarque, author of *All Quiet on the Western Front*, wrote for *Echo Continental* from 1921 and even served as editor-in-chief between 1923 and 1924. Many other artists, such as Arpad Schmidhammer, Herrmann Schütz or Paul Wolff, are forgotten today apart from their initials on the graphics or names under the photos. Interesting is also the fact that the editorial team strove to involve the impassioned readers in the design of each edition. Especially in the 1920s, lucrative prizes were awarded for the best text on a sporting event, for photos from far-flung countries and remote locations, or even for designs for the "God Pneumos," a figure who regularly appeared in *Echo Continental*.

The magazine was very successful, mainly because the advertisements for Continental products were placed in a context that was interesting or helpful to readers. For example, the authors of *Echo Continental* reported continuously on the latest developments in sport. Articles were written on soccer, tennis, motor racing (then a new sport), bicycle racing and the first aviation competitions, often accompanied by photographs. The sports reporting always contained information on Continental products used in the competitions. Attention was also drawn to solutions provided by the company for the various sports types. Continental placed high importance on its connection to sport at that time. This was because consumer items still accounted for most of the company's sales. The advertisements therefore went to great lengths to document where Continental products had proven themselves in competitions. The hope was to convince amateurs of the quality of tennis or soccer balls, or bicycle tires. Brochures such as *A review of the 1911 lawn tennis season* were elaborately designed. Such material was also created for the regular Prince Heinrich Tour for automobiles, as well as for aviation competitions. This area was also relevant for Continental because at that time the company was supplying materials for covering aircraft wings and the outer hulls of airships.

In the 1920s, women played an important role in *Echo Continental* articles. Articles on "women in sport" or "women as drivers" reported on the increasing visibility of women in these areas, which up to now had been dominated by men. The image painted of women in various articles was progressive for the time, especially with regard to a woman's relationship to her vehicle. In an article from April 1914, female readers were asked to send in photos of themselves at a car's steering wheel, so that they could be published in *Echo Continental*. "Perhaps the photos of these dashing ladies will encourage some male readers to entrust their car into the hands of their wives or daughters." In the 1920s, female readers were already portrayed as very independent, and no longer so reliant on the decisions of their husbands or fathers.

Fig. 107: Image in *Echo Continental* from October 1926.

An article from July 1924 also found appreciative words for women who were proving their worth as car drivers and in motor sport. Nonetheless, wording such as "the delicate sex," "weak female hands," and a "pretty moment" suggested that there was still a distance between women and vehicles. Fashion was very important for women at the wheel, the article stated. And the author enthusiastically drew attention to the great variety of "Continental clothing." The above clichés were less prominent in an article from the November/December issue on female truck drivers in the USA. The author expressed optimism about the future prospects of this job: "Will women be able for it? Experience up to now shows this to be the case."

Fig. 108: Cover page of *Echo Continental* from 1930.

The June 1926 issue of *Echo Continental* dispelled any remaining skepticism: "The modern lady is no longer a member of the 'weaker' sex. She wants to sit behind the wheel herself and steer her car through dangerous city traffic and along race tracks." From the mid-1920s, articles with information addressing women readers directly appeared in almost every issue. Information on how to get a driving license, as well as technical tips on engines and other car parts, were explicitly meant to motivate women to get behind the steering wheel themselves. Ideally, the ladies would wear clothing made of rubberized fabric and drive a car with Continental tires. The authors were generous in their advice on this.

In the December 1925 issue, readers were presented with the fictional portrait of the passionate driver Helga Stoetten in an article entitled "My car—My home." "Delicate," "weak" and "pretty" were no longer the attributes focused on, with the protagonist portrayed as an "ideal of independence in every respect." Educated and with professional experience, she was "one of the first women to decide to drive a car herself." This strengthened her self-reliance and independence, and in this way the car gained symbolic importance: "My car is my castle." In the portrait, driving an automobile is even presented as a requirement for women's emancipation. "If every woman drives her own car and feels the accompanying sense of responsibility, a new female sex will be created." Germany had fallen behind France, Italy and Great Britain in this, and the shortage of female drivers went hand in hand with women being permanently disadvantaged in society. "The deepest desire of the modern woman is a sense of independence and liberation from annoying paternalism. This is why she is so interested in motor racing."

The automobile was a means toward emancipation in the same way as the bicycle was to the generation before. Mobility and the freedom to travel independently and individually were requirements of, and reflected, a modern society. This view can be found in many articles from *Echo Continental*. One article from 1926 asks:

> How was it possible 'once upon a time' for a young lady to travel alone or to stay alone in a hotel. Doubting looks followed her every step. And everyone felt it their right to criticize her inappropriately. Her place in society was not without its drawbacks. Today, when a flashy car driven by a woman pulls up outside a hotel, the guest is greeted with deep devotion. [...] The independence that is the essence of driving silences even the most disrespectful tongue.

In those years, writers for *Echo Continental* made it clear that female drivers were not just potential customers for tires or fashionable clothing made of rubberized fabric. At Continental, mobilization was also seen as a service to society. The emancipation of women was the goal that Continental products helped to achieve.

Testimonials written by well-known women drivers further underscored this stance. Several articles were devoted to Clärenore Stinnes who, between 1927 and 1929, became the first person to drive around the world in a car. Her trip through

24 countries was undertaken in a standard "Adler" car with Continental tires. One of these tires survived the entire journey from Germany to Japan, through South America, the USA and France, and then back to Germany. This tire was honored with its own mention in *Echo Continental*. Noteworthy is that the articles focused on her achievement as a driver and that her gender never played an explicit role.

Fig. 109: Historical advertising postcard from 1928.

Fig. 110: Start of the long distance run at the Avus in Berlin on December 1, 1926.

The readers of *Echo Continental* were introduced to other prominent car drivers: actresses who owned and drove their own automobile, the founder of the Deutsche Damen Automobilclub e. V., or Luise Otto, the first female driving instructor in Germany. Several professional women racing drivers were frequently mentioned in *Echo Continental* and other Continental publications. Direct cooperation with the company is likely to have taken place. Hanni Köhler was an ideal brand ambassador for Continental motorcycle tires after setting 10 world records in 1928. In those years, women were seldom seen in motor sport, and so it stood out all the more when they actually came in winners. Ines Folville did just this at the reliability run in Taunus in 1925. *Echo Continental* noted that she was the only driver in a car equipped with Continental tires. In 1926, Susanne Koerner made it into the domestic and foreign media after her long-distance drive from Berlin to Birmingham. Despite the bad weather it took her only six days to complete the 2,000-kilometer route. Her bike was equipped with Continental tires and she wore Continental clothing made of rubberized fabric. She wrote a travel log for *Echo Continental*. This portrayed how she struggled with the weather conditions and bad roads, and how her intended trip was greeted with skepticism.

The *Echo Continental* of that era was very progressive in its design. The articles on women driving cars or in racing reflected a very modern attitude, which was ahead of its time. It is also possible to get an idea of how Continental viewed its own role and importance. Apart from manufacturing rubber products, the company also saw itself as a pioneer in mobility, freedom and emancipation. What was described above with regard to women applied just as much to sections of society that could not yet afford individual mobility. The progress made in all parts of the supply chain, including tire technology, made mobility affordable for ever larger segments of the population. This was a vision that Continental accepted and supported. *Echo Continental* communicated this vision to tens of thousands of subscribers.

The customer magazine was also very humorous, which helped make it one of the most important advertising formats for Continental at this time. Time and again, caricatures could be found between the reports on current sporting events and the technical guides for ambitious drivers. Some of these drawings were created by famous artists of the era. They show that the Continental advertising department was amazingly open to self-deprecating humor.

Between 1925 and 1929, for example, a series of drawings by the British cartoonist William Heath Robinson was published in *Echo Continental*. Born in 1872, Robinson first made a name for himself as an illustrator of books by Shakespeare

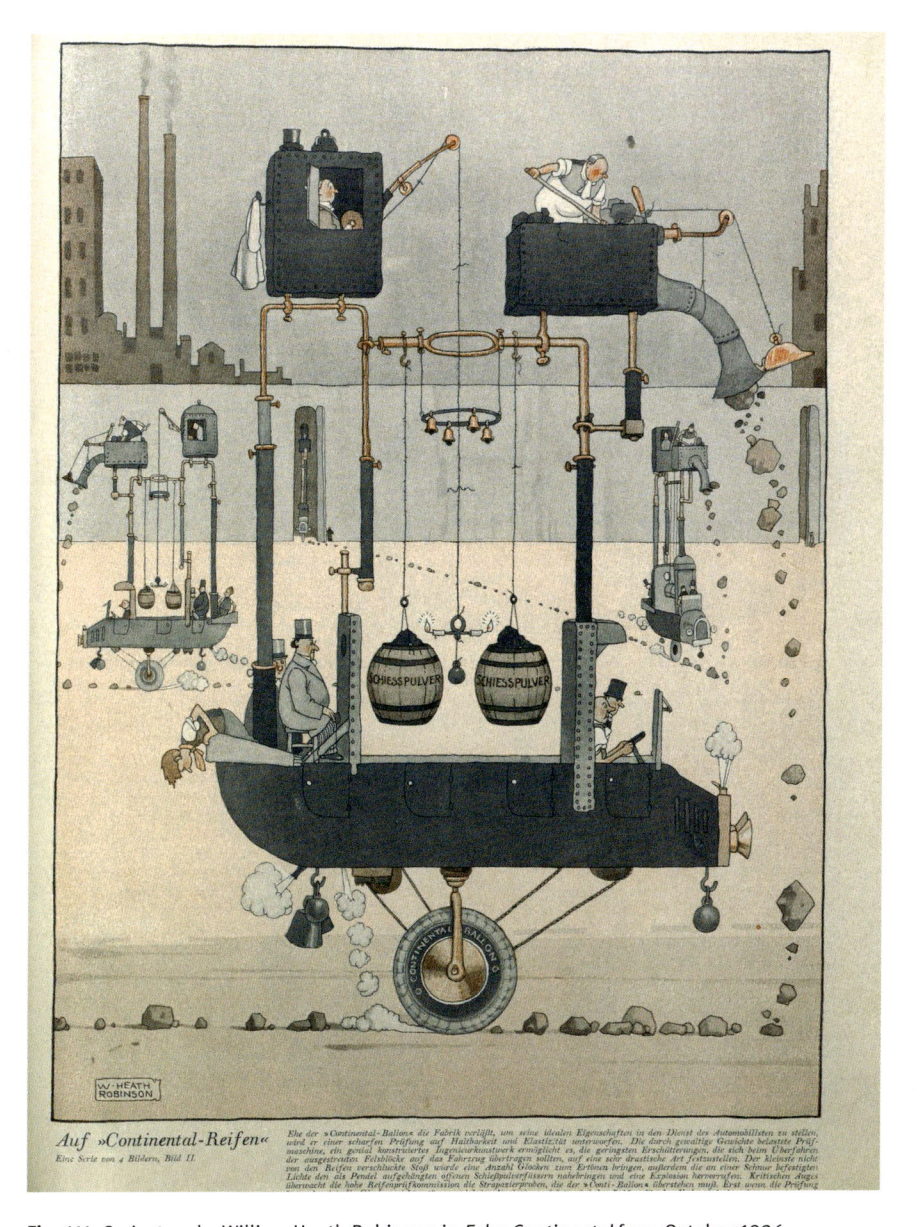

Fig. 111: Caricature by William Heath Robinson in *Echo Continental* from October 1926.

and Edgar Allan Poe. The humor that came to characterize his work first appeared in cartoons published in British magazines during World War I. Robinson countered the horror of war with subtle humor and caricatured above all the German war propaganda. Today, Robinson is still remembered for a genre of drawings that he developed after the war. This genre is hallmarked by extremely complex machines which, despite exaggerated efforts, ultimately produce a banal result. This irony targeted the enthusiasm for technology of the era as well as the accelerated industrialization of Great Britain. The machines were also meant as an ironic metaphor for bureaucracy and the detachment of experts.

For *Echo Continental*, Robinson applied his style to the products and testing processes at Continental. Continental's new innovative product of that time, the "Continental balloon tire," often appeared in his drawings. A caricature from the October 1926 issue gave readers an insight into the elaborate testing procedures established for quality assurance. It showed how every Continental balloon tire was tested for durability and elasticity before delivery, with several employees steering a gigantic "work of engineering genius" across the factory yard. Every time a shock was not absorbed by the tire, two barrels full of gunpowder exploded, indicating the failure of the test. A member of the "high commission for testing tires", dressed in tailcoat and top hat, monitored the testing process on each of these excursions. "Only when the test has passed without an explosion can the tire be released for sale." The new balloon tires also provided vehicles with better protection against impacts and made traveling more comfortable. Low air pressure and larger air cushions enabled these improvements. In his drawings, Robinson portrayed these innovative features with fine irony and exaggeration. A caricature from June 1926 showed a thoroughly positive picture of the current transport system. Thanks to Continental balloon tires, accidents were now a thing of the past. Unimaginable cargoes could be transported, and even your glass of sherry was now safe from falling over from the bumps on the road. "We no longer need any transport police as traffic problems have been done away with. The Conti balloons have seen to this. A new era for motor vehicles has thus begun."

Other drawings by Robinson were also characterized by this humorous exaggeration of the new tire's performance. The increased load-bearing capacity made it possible to move houses and their grounds without needing to interrupt your daily routine. It was now possible to play billiards while crossing cobblestones. Thanks to the new tires, natural obstacles such as deep ravines and steep mountain slopes were no longer a problem for car drivers either. The technical advantages of the new tire were presented and explained to readers in a very matter-of-fact tone in the issues of *Echo Continental*. Right beside this were the caricatures. From today's perspective, this seems like a remarkable level of self-deprecation by Continental and its advertising department. No reader reactions to these drawings have survived. There can be no doubt, however, that they contributed to the great success of *Echo Continental* as an advertising medium. The humor in no way questions the performance of the new balloon tires, rather makes product and manufacturer more accessible and appealing. Because of this witty presentation, these ads proved more effective than conventional ones would have.

The articles on women driving cars or taking part in motor sports, as well as the caricatures by William Heath Robinson, are just a small example of the many areas covered by *Echo Continental* between 1913 and 1941. The 241 issues are full of reports on different sport types, entertaining stories on various topics, poems, technical information and reports on contemporary events. The title pages were often designed by well-known artists, and a wide range of artistic directions were presented over the years. At times, *Echo Continental* was very political. During World War I, many articles reported on the course of the war. As in previous years, Continental products were now also subtly interwoven into the war reporting. Many references were made to the performance of tires and other rubber articles on the front. From 1933, the influence of Nazism's "collective" ideology grew stronger. Publication of *Echo Continental* was then stopped without comment in 1941. The title page of the last issue did not have any artistically pleasing graphics, but showed instead the German army marching into the Balkans.

Talking tires and travelling workers: Characters in Continental advertisements

Despite several attempts, the Continental advertising department was not successful in creating an advertising figure that would permanently capture the public imagination. The French tire manufacturer Michelin, on the other hand, had resounding success with its "Bibendum" figure from 1894. The figure's body and limbs were made from stacks of tires, and soon after its creation, it was used wherever the company was publicly represented. As described above, the Continental horse was designed to be recognized by customers through its uniform presentation. In contrast, numerous variations of the "Bibendum" were doing the rounds. Michelin advertisements, advice literature or the *Michelin Guide* (from 1900) are full of illustrations of "Bibendum" driving, changing tires or selling

Michelin products. The figure is still used today by Michelin, although it has undergone many stylistic revisions.

Fig. 112: Image of "Pneumos" in *Echo Continental* from July 1913. Visible in the background, one of the new Continental signposts.

Continental made various attempts to create a similarly popular advertising figure that could be used flexibly. The results, however, fell well short of "Bibendum's" success, and they were quickly replaced by new figures. One example is the figure "Pneumos" who appeared from 1913, albeit only in *Echo Continental*. This was a guardian angel who helped motorists in distress and defended them against an adversary called "Pannatas." "Pneumos" was portrayed as an old man with a long white beard. All the same, his boots and (Continental) rubber coat were meant to radiate a certain dynamism for car drivers.

In 1926, the artist Otto Schendel (1888–1943) created the figure "Mister Conti," who was similar to Bibendum. "Mister Conti" was a tire that had come to life and had a face, arms and legs. The figure and his clothes were mostly black. This was because of an innovation in tire technology. From around 1926, Continental had integrated carbon black extensively into its rubber mixtures. This lent the tires greater resistance to abrasion and wear and was also responsible for their characteristic black color, which still exists today. The product brand "Continental black" pointed to this new quality feature in its advertising. It was in this vein that "Mister

Conti" was introduced to readers of the January 1927 issue of *Echo Continental*. He promised to accompany readers every step of the way, a promise that he kept. During the following years, "Mister Conti" showed up time and again. He was used in various formats, but usually in an entertainment context, with rhymes and more detailed drawings. Copying "Bibendum," "Mister Conti" also wore many different costumes and had different abilities. Riding motorbikes and helping with breakdowns were no problem for "Mister Conti." In winter, he always had useful tips on Continental products; and if needed, he had the latest manual on hand too. Depending on the time of year, he would turn into the "Carnival Prince" or Santa Claus. All the same, even for enthusiastic drivers and Continental customers, the idea of children receiving presents from a smoking tire was probably not so attractive. In many cases, "Mister Conti" looked more ludicrous than kind. This may have been down to his aristocratic appearance as well. His black clothing, cigar, top hat, shiny shoes and light-colored gloves were symbols of the upper class.

Fig. 113: First appearance of "Mister Conti" in the January 1927 issue of *Echo Continental*.

The French graphic designer Jean-Michel "Mich" Liebeaux (1881–1923) created another less aristocratic advertising figure for Continental. Liebeaux had already made a name for himself in bicycle and motorbike advertising when he started working for Continental's subsidiary in France in 1912. The result of his work was a character who looked like a tramp or vagrant. This figure was perhaps based on Charlie Chaplin in the film "The Tramp," which was well-known around the world after its release in 1915. Liebeaux's version is a man who wears ripped clothes that are way too big for him. He also has a broom with a bindle attached. In some of the early portrayals, the figure is shown on a unicycle and is accompanied by a dog. The steering wheel of the unicycle is an umbrella. A lamp hangs from the bottom of this umbrella, and a bell is attached to the top.

Fig. 114: "Mister Conti" in different contexts.

The figure's poverty did not have negative connotations, however. Through a mixture of humor and romanticizing, these characteristics were rather signs of freedom and independence from social conventions. This tendency can be seen in many tramp representations from that time. Liebeaux's advertising figure did not require luxury or any restrictions to his personal liberty. There was one exception to this rule: "… pourvu que j'aie un pneu-vélo Continental" ("… as long as I have a Continental bicycle tire") was the slogan on one of the advertising posters. In stark contrast to "Mister Conti," the consumer could identify in some way with Liebeaux's advertising figure—be it through humor or in the ideals that the figure represented. This also explains why the figure influenced Continental advertising for such a long time.

Fig. 115: Advertising poster for the French Continental subsidiary from 1912.

The subsidiary, which had been established in Paris in 1904, became intensively involved in advertising during these years. Sometimes, the motifs created in Hanover for the German market were taken over and given French text. Other times, the advertisements were specially created for the French market. Liebeaux's figure is an example of this, and it would prove influential for Continental advertisements for decades to come. After the collapse of Continental's business in France during World War I, Otto Schendel adapted Liebeaux's template to create "Ottokar," a Continental advertising figure that appeared in the early 1930s. For the most part, he copied his template's characteristics and placed his figure in many new situations. Over the next few years, Ottokar turned up in numerous settings and advertised Continental products in a range of different advertising media. This range spanned from advertising brochures, posters and blotting paper for exercise books to postcards and goodie bags for children. At the same time, a further adaptation of "Ottokar" going by the name of "Radolar" was created by Erich A. Meyer and F. Schirrmeister.

Modern advertising formats and repositioning the company as a mobility service provider

Echo Continental shows clearly how creative the Continental advertising department could be when it came to building customer loyalty. In a time where television and the Internet were not yet available, other channels had to be used to address customers. "If an advertising department wants to produce success, it has to be alert and flexible, and to adapt effortlessly to the demands of the day," the *Continental Werknachrichten* (factory newspaper) stated in 1925 in a feature on the department.

Today, the focus is on technologies and services for the sustainable and interconnected mobility of people and goods. In the past, however, the focus was on industrial and consumer goods made of rubber and, above all, on tires. Even in the early stages of its history, Continental was already way ahead when it came to enriching and facilitating people's lives through new forms of mobility. This started with pneumatic tires for bicycles. For the first time ever, large sections of the population could expand their horizons when it came to movement, without needing to spend a lot of money on a horse. Emancipation through mobility was also a major topic for women, and Continental advertisements of the time often portrayed confident women enjoying their newly won freedom—supported by Continental bicycle tires.

Fig. 116: Historical advertising postcard from around 1900.

Step by step, Continental developed more innovations based on its know-how gained from bicycle tires. Pneumatic tire technology was transferred to various other vehicle types in the following years. Automobiles, trucks and tractors initially used solid rubber tires, but these were soon replaced by pneumatic tires. At the start of the 20th century, traveling by automobile was much more arduous and dangerous than today. In many regions, the infrastructure was still designed for carts and small volumes of local traffic. The roads were not suited to fast, heavy cars. Nor were there enough signs with directions or warnings to help drivers unfamiliar with the area. Furthermore, in order to drive a car, you also needed considerable technical know-how. The driver had to be able to solve all the problems that could arise on a journey. These included changing tires and adjusting the engine or chassis. In those days, individual mobility with an automobile was both a challenge and an adventure. More and more people were venturing behind the wheel. It made them feel part of a modern movement that was pushing the boundaries of what an individual could achieve.

As seen earlier with the example of the first women drivers, the new mobility was also perceived as creating a sense of identity. Driving a car was more than simply traveling from A to B: it was a sign of emancipation from past geographical and social restrictions, and it demonstrated a modern and future-oriented affinity to technology. From the very beginning, Continental was a part of this mobility movement. The first issue of *Echo Continental* already proposed the car as a viable alternative to the railway:

> Once upon a time you were just a ticket-holder, a slave who had to submit to the iron constraints of a route and timetable that would never change. And then the car came along! The art of travel has become serious again! The railway was a despot that belittled us, taking away our right to determine a route.

Individual mobility, on the other hand, made possible a free and challenging form of movement. "The car has returned our freedom to decide for ourselves."

Continental supported this development with products and services. The aim was to promote the spread of automobile ownership in other social classes as well. One of the first issues of *Echo Continental* also expressed a wish "to support car tourists in the art of traveling." On the one hand, the task was to convince early car drivers to face the challenges of mobility using Continental products. On the other, an extensive range of advice literature was published with the aim of reducing entry barriers and popularizing driving. The *Continental Handbook for Automobilists* first came out in 1903, and was given free of charge to every owner of a car or motorbike. This "constant and faithful travel companion" provided comprehensive information on planning and executing journeys successfully. The main part of the guide was an index of locations. It listed local gas stations, workshops and tire dealers, as well as places of interest and overnight accommodation options. The guide also provided information on local automobile clubs, traffic regulations, touring and the state of roads. The times of sunset and sunrise, and even when the moon rose in the sky were also given. This was important as street and vehicle lighting were still very under-developed at the start of the 20th century. The *Continental Country Road Atlas for Central Europe* appeared in 1907. Ambitious drivers now had two handy books to help them plan and execute long journeys and tours. Updated editions of the handbook appeared almost annually until it was eventually discontinued in 1937. The Continental atlas was still published until 2008, when digital navigation finally put an end to analog map material.

The publications were supplemented through additional measures for promoting automobile traffic. A Continental "touring office" was opened in 1911 at Continental's headquarters in Hanover. Here, car tourists could have travel itineraries prepared and sent to them free of charge. *Echo Continental* reported that in one year alone, these itineraries covered the distance from the earth to the moon and back. It was also time, the magazine noted, for the municipal authorities to ensure that the road network was provided with adequate signage.

> We have many years of experience in tourism. We also have the expertise to bring out our own touring and travel books, such as the 'Continental Handbook' and the 'Continental Atlases.' We even have our own touring office. All these factors have made it possible for us to create something good. This is how our 'Continental signposts' came into being, which have already become very popular.

Partly on Continental's own initiative, but also in collaboration with local authorities, new signs were erected where none had existed or where the original signs had fallen into disrepair. The aim as noted in *Echo Continental* was to create new signage for the entire German road network. The signs were designed in the Continental color tone and advertised the company. "In this way, we have provided another service to the world of driving that is so close to our hearts." Of course, Continental was serving itself as well. Every driver that looked at a sign in passing was indeed shown the way, but also reminded of the mobility provider from Hanover. By taking the initiative, Continental had created new advertising space in this early example of a public-private partnership. There are no reports of any criticism or conflict regarding this advertising strategy. Indeed, car drivers from out of town must surely have seen the signs as a welcome addition to their travel comfort.

Fig. 117: Extract from *Echo Continental* from 1925.

Why go to so much effort? Why invest so much money in erecting signs, operating travel agencies and updating publications to be handed out free of charge? This strategy only makes sense when a company is striving to do more than just sell products. Today's tagline, "The Future in Motion," could also be applied to Continental's orientation in the early days of the automobile. Continental was then also being positioned as a mobility service provider and holistic partner to motorists.

Tires were the most visible and important product in the portfolio, and today too most people see tires as synonymous with Continental. Nonetheless, a glance at the price lists of the time and *Echo* show that Continental offered a wide range of equipment for individual mobility. If the Continental advertising department had its way, car drivers, motorcyclists and bicyclists would wear clothing made of rubberized materials, use Continental tools and accessories to repair their vehicle, store their boots on special rubber mats, hoot a horn with a Continental rubber ball, and even use the "Continental rubber whip to chase off dogs and rascals" in emergencies. The lists went on and on. Rubber was used in every conceivable form to make driving safer and more comfortable. As always, information rounded off these price lists.

Fig. 118: Extract from a company price list from 1902.

Another area where Continental has actively promoted its products since the 19th century is sports advertising. The 1892 decision to manufacture pneumatic tires for bicycles in Hanover was mostly down to the boom in this means of transport. The new "Pneumatics" were advertised intensively. The advertising brochures that have survived from that time show that a modern form of advertising was used for these innovative and cutting-edge products. Ads with a lot of text and monochrome product sketches were replaced by graphic representations with artistic value. The pneumatic advertisements from the 1890s were thus a precursor of the intensive cooperation with renowned artists and graphic designers who created the magnificent title pages of *Echo Continental* from 1913. Continental was also a pioneer of modern sports marketing. At the start of the 1920s, racing cyclists wore jerseys with the Continental logo for the first time. Before this, ads for Continental were already visible along the perimeters of cycling stadiums.

Now that bicycles were becoming important in people's everyday lives, bicycle sports also became increasingly popular. Bicycle racing tracks were built in many places and lots of European countries held road races. Continental was present with the most modern advertising methods of the time: perimeter advertising, jerseys or a Continental balloon marking the finishing line. Tire storage facilities next to the track provided riders with new material if needed. At that time, competitive cycling had not yet become so professionalized. Only slowly was a uniform set of rules put into place. As in other types of sport, amateurs used to cycle in many of the races at the start. Only gradually would an organized professional sport emerge, with fixed rankings, world championships, and national and international sports federations. Continental supported the stars from professional cycling, regardless of their nationality. It also sponsored amateur cyclists and competitions. Potential customers could identify with both the professional and amateur worlds. If a well-known cyclist became world champion riding on Continental tires, this would make the "Continental" brand and the quality of its products known across many regions. Alternatively, were an unknown rider to win an amateur race for newspaper deliverers say, this engagement was just as likely to show how reliable Continental tires were for this sector.

When automobile ownership started to become more widespread, the Continental advertising department discovered the competitions in this sector too. Speed races, the "reliability runs" held in various countries or even attempts at setting records seemed an ideal advertising medium for Continental products. Until well into the 20th century, only the upper class could afford to own an automobile. Even so, this did not diminish the popularity of the races or of the speed record attempts. The automobile was *the* symbol of the era's enthusiasm for technology. Many people saw themselves at the start of a modern, technology-based era, where the limits of what was technically possible were regarded as new challenges. Continental jumped on this bandwagon and positioned itself as a modern, future-oriented company. A spectacular example of this was its collaboration with Fritz von Opel, grandson of the founder of the Opel car company, Adam Opel. This

Fig. 119: Advertising postcard for the 1925 bicycle racing season with Continental jersey advertising.

Fig. 120: Advertising postcard from 1904 with Continental perimeter advertisements.

era saw the build-up of a close connection between Opel and Continental. In 1922, the von Opel family became shareholders at Continental, and by 1932, they had acquired a majority holding of more than 50 percent of its shares. In 1928, Fritz von Opel designed several versions of a rocket-propelled vehicle. He was helped in his endeavors by rocket technology pioneers Max Valier and Friedrich Wilhelm Sanders. On May 23, 1928, the "Opel RAK 2" reached record speeds of well over 200 km/h in front of thousands of spectators on Berlin's Avus racing track. In the eyes of commentators at the time, this was an almost unimaginable speed for which neither roads nor vehicles were designed. Continental contributed to the success of this record-breaking run by developing a cord tire especially for von Opel's vehicle. The new rocket engine opened up transport possibilities "that up to now were only written about in science fiction novels," enthused *Echo Continental*. While the technology ultimately failed to gain much of a foothold in road traffic, this spectacular cooperation was emblematic of the progressive 1920s, when not only technological but also social boundaries started to fall.

Fig. 121: Fritz von Opel setting a record in Berlin on May 23, 1928, using specially designed Continental tires.

In the decades that followed, attempts were made time and again to reflect the spirit of the age. The style and design of the advertising campaigns always played an important role, as did the question of where exactly was advertised. From today's perspective, there is a certain level of continuity, but also some striking novelties. With regard to advertising, the 1950s and 1960s remained very much in the tradition of previous decades. Color graphics were used extensively, especially for consumer goods, while photography was used only on rare occasions. Racing continued to play a large role as an advertising medium. Continental products were used in numerous car, bicycle, and motorbike races. For a short time between 1954 and 1955, Continental also equipped the first Formula One Mercedes cars with tires.

The usual forms of marketing dominated through the 1970s. The only innovation was an advertising campaign in 1976 that used huge posters so that "all of Germany's 17 million motorists could be reached without taking any detours." The posters were displayed along roads and were not "dry and technological, rather a mix of information, cheekiness and fun."

Fig. 122: Advertising poster for rubber V-belts from 1963.

In the 1980s, the company's advertising presence was given a completely new design. Extensive market research showed that the "Continental" brand had a very conservative image, which was leading to a loss in market share especially in urban areas. The new campaign mostly targeted young drivers. New, colorful advertising images were used to make driving look like fun. The brand was meant to look dynamic and future-oriented: "dynamic, optimistic, successful. This image corresponds to the ideas and feeling of the new generation."

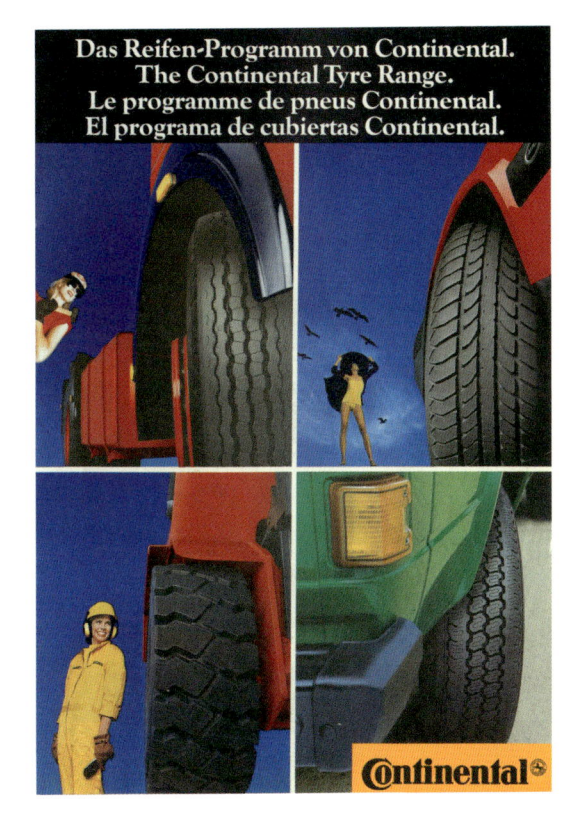

Fig. 123: Tire brochure from 1986.

From the 1990s, Continental started advertising its own products on television for the first time. This was a continuation of a long tradition, for already in the 1920s, Continental commercials had run in cinemas. The focus from the 1950s had been mainly on advertisements in print form. But now a series of spectacular commercials was created to boost sales of Continental products. The message of the commercials was always similar: a Continental tire proves that it can perform in extraordinary situations. The new "ContiSportContact" made possible risky driving maneuvers on a high-rise roof without any barriers. At the same time, the "ContiAquaContact" proved its worth in a slippery swimming pool thanks to its excellent aquaplaning properties. And finally, the "ContiWinterContact" had its braking properties tested on an ice floe in the Arctic. The international direction of these commercials was new: "The televisions ads are shown in France and Spain, as well as in Germany. This is why the slogan used more and more in our international advertisements is: 'Tyres—engineered in Germany'."

conti intern reported in great detail how the new campaign changed the Continental brand image. In 1992, 10 percent of people surveyed agreed with the statement that Continental "made original advertisements," compared with only 4 percent in 1988. 44 percent of respondents now saw Continental as a "likable company," which corresponded to an increase of 10 percentage points.

Fig. 124: Stills from the commercial.

The subsequent campaign in 1999 bravely went on the offensive and highlighted the "well-known emotional relationship that exists between men and cars." TV commercials were combined with print ads (and subtle irony) to tell the story of the attraction of a male driver to his car. Because of their quality, Continental tires played an important role in this relationship. *conti intern* reported openly about the feedback on the commercial. This was mostly positive: "super ad, snappy, full of emotion." Criticism was voiced as well, such as "Conti, never again" or "This is misogynistic macho posturing." Some respondents claimed that the 'affair,' as the relationship between most men and their cars was called, went too far."

Fig. 125: Info brochure on the new ad campaign from 1999.

The ad campaigns are another example of the diverse advertising activities that Continental has deployed in its 150 years of company history. Some of the aspects seem odd and peculiar from today's perspective, while other presentation styles continue to fascinate and have an undiminished aesthetic appeal. The style of Continental advertisements and the media used do not just reflect the company's self-image. They were and remain a mirror for technical and societal developments—which is ultimately one of advertising's key aims.

8 Continental as a Global Company
The Long Road Toward Internationalization

The internationalization at the heart of the company's early strategy

> The company name [Continental], which has remained the same since 1871, was chosen with the intention of having a completely international name that we could give to all our offices, no matter if they were in France, Italy, Russia or beyond.

This quote was taken from a letter from Continental director Siegmund Seligmann on January 11, 1915, and clearly shows how strongly Continental was focused on internationalization even when it was founded. Between 1879 and 1925, Seligmann laid the foundations for Continental's rise from a small rubber factory in Hanover to an internationally active company. At the time of the letter, he saw himself called upon to explain the origin and meaning of the company name, which was being called into question as being too foreign and Romanic. Objectors insisted that it should sound more German. The controversy started with a letter from a shareholder that arrived three weeks after the outbreak of World War I. It demanded that Seligmann change "the annoying name [Continental] into 'Deutsche Gummi-Gesellschaft' (German Rubber Company) or 'Festländische Gummi-Gesellschaft' (Mainland Rubber Company)." "In this difficult yet glorious time, we must purge all that is foreign inside us." In the nationalistic atmosphere of the First World War, such tendencies were not unusual and caused other companies to adapt the brand names of their products.

In this case, the complaint originated from a person with little actual influence. Nonetheless, Seligmann dealt with the matter personally. Members of Continental's management were certainly worried that the authorities would take heed of the complaint and force the company to change the name bestowed on it by its nine founders back in 1871. This concern was justified, as the shareholder in question sent similar letters to the Chamber of Commerce and the Prussian District President in Hanover. In Berlin too, Continental faced similar accusations and challenges. In 1915, the responsible chief of police initiated proceedings that also dealt with the Continental company name. In Hanover, the company then drafted a lengthy statement to refute the allegations. Continental was not a word that had been borrowed from any foreign language, Seligmann argued. "Several millions of marks" had been spent on advertising in Germany and abroad, "with

https://doi.org/10.1515/9783110732375-008

the result that today the word 'Continental' is known in almost every country." It was therefore impossible to change the name. In addition, a large part of the company's business was conducted abroad, which in 1913 accounted for almost 50 percent of total revenue. The letter was not just sent to the chief of police in Berlin, but also to the Chancellor of the German Empire Theobald von Bethmann Hollweg, pointing out "the extraordinary danger to German industry if these Germanization efforts are taken too far." In the end, all attempts at forcing Continental to change its name came to nothing. However, the lengthy and high-level negotiations show how serious the situation was at the time.

Continental's development in the first years and decades of its history illustrate how the above-mentioned focus on exports and international orientation were expedited with great success. Its management—comprised solely of Seligmann (as commercial director) and Adolf Prinzhorn (as technical director) until 1905—endeavored early on to supply the company's innovative soft rubber products beyond Hanover, Prussia and Germany to other European and non-European countries. In today's globalized economy, it is normal for every manager to speak English and for even medium-sized companies to sell and/or manufacture their products abroad. In the second half of the 19th century, however, this was much less common. The dynamic economic situation of Germany's Gründerzeit ("founders' period"—its rapid industrial expansion at the end of the 19th century) led to the creation of innumerable industrial companies, whose innovative products increasingly penetrated the global market. Continental was a child of this era: it was founded in 1871, and right from the start, its focus was on the promising new material called soft rubber. In this context, it is possible that the name "Continental" was intentionally chosen to underline the international ambitions of the founding project.

Today, Continental is not just "continental" in attitude but is active in 59 countries and markets. The above episode from 1915 shows that this internationality has a long history and continues back to the time when the company was founded. Since its foundation, internationalization has shaped Continental's company culture.

It is not known when the first Continental product was exported. The annual report from 1881 states: "Recently, we have especially focused on expanding our export business, and today we can look back on a significant increase in our customer numbers in this sector." It was very likely that innovative products that were successful on the domestic market would soon be offered in other countries too. From 1892 at the latest, with pneumatic tires for bicycles, Continental started manufacturing products that were competitive on other markets. Tires for automobiles followed in 1898.

Seligmann and Prinzhorn relied on the targeted purchase of patents and know-how for more items than just hoof buffers. Numerous other examples have been handed down from the first decades after the company's establishment. After his appointment to the Executive Board, Prinzhorn traveled to the USA in 1876 where he acquired various patents. He undertook many more such trips in the following years, thus enabling the company to further specialize its product portfolio. Coach tires made of solid rubber were produced based on the "Kelly" patent, while the "Swinehart" patent facilitated further diversification in solid rubber tires for heavy carriages and cargo wagons. Licenses acquired from the British tire company Dunlop were used to produce clincher tires, beaded tires and pneumatic tires for bicycles.

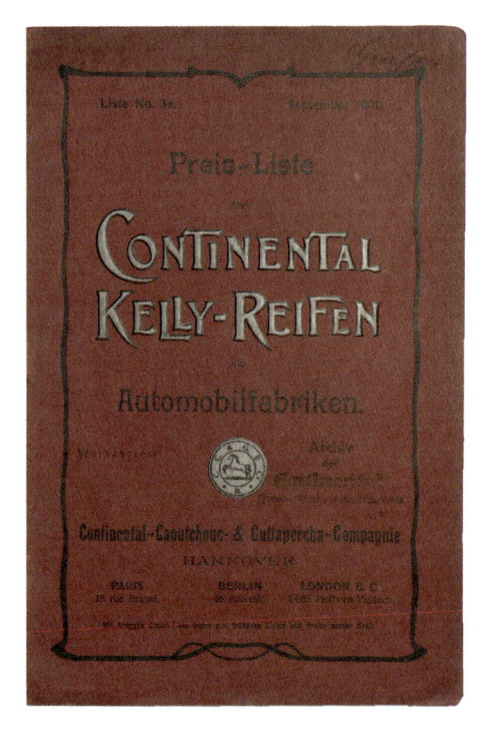

Fig. 126: Price list for "Continental Kelly tires" from 1911. The reference to "Paris-Berlin-London" indicates the company's expansion.

In the early years of its history, Continental itself came up with very few groundbreaking inventions. The company was much more successful in industrializing and perfecting new technologies. Seligmann and Prinzhorn were especially given to cooperating openly with international competitors. Know-how was exchanged, and licenses procured. The US, British and French rubber industries were leaders at this time and thus the preferred cooperation partners for the up-and-coming Hanover-based company. This openness was by no means common. Contacts across the Atlantic were not just an email away. Communication by post and telegram took up a lot of time, while traveling by ocean steamer was almost an adventure. The rise of Continental was to a great extent due to this openness to inventions and innovative developments. It also facilitated the diversification from simple consumer goods made of rubber to highly specialized technical and surgical products and, above all, tires.

In the early days, sales were mostly handled by local agents. These were dealers of tires and other rubber goods who distributed Continental products locally and at their own commercial risk. Gradually, however, a tight network of Continental subsidiaries was built up in Germany and abroad. Before the outbreak of World War I, this network comprised 110 subsidiaries in 53 countries. Continental products were sold on all continents—from Melbourne to St. Petersburg, from Shanghai to Havana, and from Cape Town to Yokohama.

Already in the 19th century, the tendency toward protectionism could be felt, and this caused problems for management. Many countries, including Germany, set up customs barriers to protect their own industries from foreign competition. Competitors were accused of selling at dumping prices without any evidence. Their success, in fact, was often down to more efficient production methods and more technically advanced products. Continental, meanwhile, took a public position on trade policy issues early on. The annual report from 1894 was used to express the critical attitude of Continental's Executive Board toward trade obstacles. A customs agreement concluded with Russia in February of that year was greeted with "joy and satisfaction, because this promises a general revitalization of the declining industrial areas." At that time, Continental was standing on the threshold of further international expansion. Over the next few years, it saw itself repeatedly forced to make public its attitude toward questions on trade policy. In its view, it was high time that innovative pneumatic tires were offered on other markets, and the same was true for a whole range of specialized industrial and consumer rubber goods. The annual reports from the start of the 20th century are full of precise political demands in some cases. In 1902, for example, the report stated:

> The pending negotiations concerning new customs agreements have aroused our great interest. For our industry, it is especially important that the agreements are made for a number of years with precise custom rates. We consider this much more important than high protective duties. Such duties would lead to the risk of states that are party to the agreement demanding their own duties. This could destroy our export business, which has taken on huge significance.

Such statements speak of the increasing success of Continental products on the world market, and of a need for planning security in terms of foreign trade. In 1903, the company even demanded that protective duties for rubber goods be dropped altogether, arguing that the sector (meaning above all Continental) was strong enough to compete with rival products on any market:

> We would like to take this opportunity to highlight that the German rubber goods industry is so powerful that it does not see any value in import duties on rubber products to Germany. On the contrary, we believe it much more important to not increase duties for the states that we export to, than to protect the German rubber goods industry by high import duties.

The annual reports for subsequent years contained similar statements: trade agreements were welcomed, while protectionist measures by individual states were criticized. Time and again, the expectation was expressed that politicians bring about further improvements in trade conditions. By now, Continental's Executive Board was investing considerable sums abroad. It was therefore very keen to protect these investments from the danger of trade wars. The reports also contained a general plea for equal opportunities and rights with regard to global trade. This attitude was quite remarkable at a time when trade policy was increasingly influenced by nationalism and protective duties were experiencing a general renaissance. By rejecting duties, Continental also went against the official stance of the Central Association of German Rubber Goods Producers, many members of which urgently demanded protective tariffs for their products.

Collaborations and establishing an international network (1889–1914)

High import duties barred Continental from entering the market in several European countries. Despite this, the Executive Board continued to drive forward the company's international expansion. It is interesting to note that in these early stages, the company did not resort to the most common instrument to avoid duties, which would have been to build its own plant in the relevant country. Instead, Continental chose a less risky and more pragmatic way for its brand to be imported into and become established in other markets. Despite the small investments involved, this approach proved effective. Extensive cooperation agreements were concluded to this end with local rubber companies in Austria-Hungary (1889), Belgium (1891) Sweden (1902) and the USA (1904). The annual report from 1889 discusses the reasons for the cooperation with the Österreichisch-Amerikanische Gummi-Waaren-Fabrik (Austrian-American Rubber Goods Factory) in Breitensee near Vienna:

> The expansion of our relationships in various European states, especially the Austro-Hungarian Empire, is facing insurmountable difficulties due to high duties. For a long time, starting production there ourselves has seemed desirable. Such a move would lead to the excellent name of our products in this region being utilized in a suitable way.

Continental acquired a share in each of these listed companies, including decision-making rights on the Supervisory Board. A simultaneous transfer of know-how also took place. The knowledge acquired at Hanover and the experience in manufacturing rubber products and tires was passed on to the new cooperation partners. In return, these companies organized the sale of Continental products locally and manufactured the products themselves under license. The cooperation was profitable for both sides. The partners received access to the highly developed know-how regarding product technology and to the latest production processes. Continental, for its part, was given the chance to establish its own products on the respective markets. The prices could remain competitive, and the import duties were avoided.

The managers under Seligmann and Prinzhorn were clearly pragmatic and able to compromise, as shown by their reluctance to force Continental's internationalization at any price. Having its own factory in a foreign country would have suddenly turned the company into a multinational corporation and would have increased the brand name's prestige. In a time of intense competition on the domestic and international markets, such an advantage was not inconsiderable. A factory was solid proof that a business was expanding successfully: more so than any sales company or general representative, no matter how well the cooperation functioned. The company's letterheads were characterized by idealized drawings of the manufacturing facilities, and the factory buildings (some of which were very prestigious) held a high symbolic value. The types of cooperation described did not exactly symbolize a dynamic conquest of new markets by means of the company's own factories. Instead, the focus was on rational and long-term thinking, in which the company's market presence was built up step by step and at reasonable cost and risk. This first phase of international expansion was characterized not so much by its entrepreneurial impact but by sober and pragmatic work for ever more successful value creation.

Fig. 127: Advertising poster from 1906. The degree of internationalization is very clear: an Italian artist created the poster for an Austrian company that was offering a German brand on the French market.

In addition to the investments described above, an international network of branches was set up to organize local sales and marketing, regardless of the sometimes significant customs barriers. From 1904, several of these subsidiaries were upgraded to incorporated companies. This was done to increase the company's ability to act locally, and, ultimately, to make the brand more visible. Within just a few years, Continental-Caoutchouc & Gutta-Percha-Compagnie became a corporation consisting of the parent company in Hanover and subsidiaries in New

York (1904), Paris (1904), London (1905), Melbourne (1905), Stockholm (1906), Copenhagen (1909) and Bucharest (1911). The new subsidiaries not only provided a higher international presence, but were also a starting point for expanding sales activities, in some cases with the company's own local production.

The French market had always been fiercely competitive, and the market leader, Michelin, fought off the competition from Hanover with every means at its disposal. A great many legal disputes from this time have been documented. One example dealt with supposed price dumping on the part of the Germans. Another instance was a conflict lasting many years. It concerned the accusation that the French version of the Continental manual, the Guide Routier Continental, was an unapproved copy of the world-famous Michelin Guide. Both sides heaped fierce accusations upon one another in the media, and even positioned their marketing activities explicitly against their competitor. In order to be able to hold its own in the dispute, the French Continental subsidiary built its own plant in Clichy near Paris. In the annual report for 1906, the shareholders were informed that premises had been acquired at Quai de Clichy 104–112. Production of tires and technical rubber articles began there in 1907 and meant that Continental could assure French customers that its products were not imports but were manufactured in their

Fig. 128: The headquarters of Continental Caoutchouc Co. in Manhattan, New York (43 Warren Street).

own country. In the new plant, around 90 employees produced 30 tires a day. This number increased to approximately 200 by 1913. Continental's involvement in the French market was generally characterized by uncertainty and fear of countermeasures by its competitor. In 1909, the idea was to expand production capacity at Clichy because of increases in French customs duties. In June 1913, however, the Executive Board decided to significantly reduce the investment sums "in consideration of the difficulties and harassment that we face in France." Even so, the plant in Paris was the first time in Continental's history that it had its own factory abroad.

Fig. 129: The Continental plant in Clichy near Paris.

In those years, France, and especially Paris, were very important when it came to finance, art and technology. The World Exhibition in 1900 was just one of many examples of this importance. At this exhibition, Continental was awarded a gold medal, and in Hanover, the company was doing all it could to create a presence on the promising French market too. Motor racing was one of the most popular advertising media used at the time to present the company's products and to prove their superior performance. In 1901, a driver won an international long-distance race for the first time in a German car. The Nice-Salon-Nice race on the French Côte d'Azur was over 392 kilometers long. The winner, driving a Daimler car, required almost seven hours to complete the circuit. The car was also fitted with Continental tires. The victory was testament to the increasing involvement of Continental in racing and of the measures open to increase visibility of the company's products in France. These years saw the start of intense advertising activities, and many of the most notable examples of historical Continental advertising were created for the French market at the start of the 20th century.

With the factory in Clichy/Paris, Continental also became a multinational company in the narrower sense of the term for the first time. Up to World War I, production capacities were also created in other countries. Subsidiaries in the

Fig. 130: French advertising poster for Continental bicycle tires from around 1900.

Netherlands (1906), Italy (1907) and Australia (1913) also served as the starting point for this development. In other cases, local services were significantly expanded to offer customers more than just the product. For the German market, Continental had developed all-round support for cyclists, motorcyclists and car drivers with a wide range of products and services. This was now expanded to Great Britain and France. In the Continental Handbook for Automobilists in Great Britain and Ireland from 1906, British and Irish customers were informed that a larger range would soon be available:

> In consequence of the extension of our English business, we have built a factory in England situated at Hythe Road, Willesden [...]. This factory has been fitted up with the most modern machinery, enabling us to deal with all descriptions of repairs to motor covers and tubes. [...] we shall also manufacture a certain quantity of these tires at this factory in the future.

In addition to its own repair capacities, the company evidently also planned to have its own production facility, although this was not implemented. In the last business year before World War I, Continental exported products to many countries. Of the nearly 58 billion marks in foreign sales, most products were sold to France (22%), Great Britain (20%), Australia (8%), Italy (7%), Argentina (7%) and Russia (6%). The entire annual revenue of the company stood at 119 billion marks.

Collapse of the network abroad and re-internationalization during the 1920s

The outbreak of World War I hit Continental hard. As described above, the importance of exports and foreign sales of subsidiaries had continued to grow until the war. During the war years, the tight network of Continental representative offices was torn apart. In many counties that were now at war with Germany, the company's property was put under forced administration and sometimes even sold off. In several countries, the property could be protected from sale by being taken over by citizens of that country and then reactivated after the war. This was the case, for example, for the Italian subsidiary, where the shares were transferred in time to Swiss and Italian citizens. These individuals then "agreed to act as straw men for [the] shares in Italy" during the general registration of enemy property. The company was managed from Switzerland, where Paul Friedländer, who was head of the company, had fled into exile. A great many letters were sent between Continental headquarters in Hanover and a hotel in Lugano. The letters clearly show both the skepticism and optimism with which the vision of an internationally networked company was greeted. In April 1917, Seligmann wrote less optimistically to Friedländer:

> [...] because you will also be of our view, after all, that in the foreseeable future, even after peace is declared, no business will be possible with our factory in Italy. Under today's conditions, hardly anyone will buy a brand like the Continental pneumatic tire, as everyone knows this to be a German product. I do not think so at least. And those Italian factories which fit Continental pneumatic tires when selling new cars or bicycles will, in my opinion, face serious hostility, and will, for this reason, stop fitting our tires, even if they themselves are quite enthusiastic about our brand.

While Seligmann viewed the prospects of resuming foreign business with considerable skepticism, Friedländer's response was much more positive. In June 1917, he wrote from his Swiss exile that the trade relations with Italy would normalize quickly. After the war, "Germans abroad would have the difficult task of helping to re-establish the good old relationships as quickly as possible." The network of offices, subsidiaries and above all employees who were connected within the countries would in fact later play an important role. After World War I, as the international orientation of Continental was being re-established, its old contacts and structures proved a useful starting point. A much worse situation, however, was faced by the Continental representative office in Australia. Eduard Eichengrün, who called himself Edward Edwards in Australia, had built up the subsidiary from nothing starting in 1905. By 1913, Australia and New Zealand were important sales markets for Continental products. A factory for bicycle and automobile tires was under construction. Despite being a British citizen since 1908, Edwards was interned for five years without a trial when the war broke out. He then lost his citizenship and was deported with his children to Germany. His wife died during his time in prison.

The rampant inflation in Germany, the shortage of raw materials and finally the world economic crisis made it considerably more difficult to rebuild the export business after World War I. In many counties, buildings, manufacturing facilities and even patents and brand rights had been seized. For years, the Continental Executive Board conducted legal proceedings and negotiations to achieve the return of the company's pre-war property. At the same time, as high import duties and other instruments were implemented around the world to supposedly protect each country's own industry, reactivating the old sales structures became increasingly unrealistic. Only in the 1930s was Continental able to achieve its pre-war levels of success in the most important European markets of Great Britain, France and Italy.

Continental Tyre & Rubber Company (Great Britain), Ltd. in London was active again and provided Continental with a re-entry into the British market. In contrast to other countries, the subsidiary was not seized during the war, as a British citizen had been a co-owner since the company started. After a promising start, however, the British government gave in to pressure from the crisis-ridden British tire industry and imposed a high import duty on tires and other rubber products for the first time. After this, Continental withdrew completely from the British market. In July 1927, the managing director of the now inactive subsidiary sent a circular to the dismissed and transferred employees:

> I take this opportunity, gentlemen, to convey to you my and the Company's sincerest thanks for the care and interested manner in which you have looked after the interests of the Company. It is very much to be regretted that circumstances beyond control have spoiled the promising efforts. Maybe someday the Company will restart activities, but at the present time we are unfortunately forced to lose business.

Just like at the start of the 20th century, customs barriers were not helping Continental's international endeavors. In France, even more intensive efforts were undertaken to revitalize business. As previously mentioned, Continental was very active in France prior to the war, with a strong brand, intensive marketing and its own production facility in Clichy near Paris. The position that had been built up needed to be defended in an intense battle against local competitors—a battle that was fought in court and through aggressive advertising campaigns. In addition to a sense of the importance of the French market, the previous experience of successfully establishing a business motivated Continental's Executive Board to work hard to regain the company's former position after the war. The negotiations were hard-fought but in the end came to nothing. For a time, a plan circulated of buying the factory in Clichy, which was now up for sale, via a somewhat dubious French company. The same applied for the old Continental Société Anonyme de Caoutchouc Manufacture that was due to be auctioned in 1921. The resulting organization would then form the nucleus of a new Continental company in France. Siegmund Seligmann and Willy Tischbein were the board members responsible the foreign business. To help with the negotiations, they chose Ernst Loeser, the man in charge when the French subsidiary was first built. Loeser wrote to Hanover with a detailed assessment of the planned cooperation: "It would give me great pleasure to assist you with these tasks so that the company at which I have worked for 15 years will again become viable."

In the end, however, the attempt at taking over the factory in Clichy failed, and it proved impossible to seamlessly return to the pre-war situation. One of the reasons for this was the cooperation agreement that Continental had with the US tire company B. F. Goodrich in these years. Already during the negotiations, Tischbein questioned if the French involvement might disrupt this partnership: "[W]e do not know ourselves how disruptive it could prove for the Goodrich Co. business in France if we [...] started up again in France." The feedback from Akron (Ohio), then center of the US rubber industry, was also negative. The director of Goodrich, Bertram Work, wrote to Tischbein:

> The Russian plan is very interesting but the Paris merger, aside from the sale of your property, does not appeal to me. It sounds like a promotion with nothing real behind it except the promoter's profits. However, we will look into it as the disposal of the Paris plant in itself is worthwhile provided you can get something besides worthless stock certificates.

A little later, he added in another letter that the French cooperation partner was not trustworthy: "Your plant in Clichy is a ruin (I had it examined) and only valuable for the land and buildings." Negotiations were subsequently broken off in April 1922. It has never been ascertained if Goodrich's intervention was the decisive factor. Either way, the fact was that Continental's presence in France was history for now, and at best only rudimentary exports of Continental products took place.

In other countries too, Continental's Executive Board tried during the 1920s to revive the previous international network. The main driving force in this was Willy Tischbein, who was made general director in 1925 after Seligmann's death. Tischbein tried to re-establish the company's pre-war strength while also entering new markets in other countries. Various investment projects were examined for this purpose. In many cases, the old networks could be used alongside the strong position that Continental had acquired with high-quality products and intensive public relations work. These were important advantages in an extremely adverse economic and political environment. In 1921, for example, negotiations started to set up a Continental factory in Manresa (Spain). The project was to be implemented with a local tire manufacturer as cooperation partner. The director of this company was a long-time Continental fan: "Mr. Ciudad was an enthusiastic follower of our brand before the war and used our tires when taking part in car races [...]." The advocates of the project were also local Continental employees who had gained insight into the market through their years of working at the branches or in the subsidiary. Their letters to Hanover often referred to their own worries about the future too. If Continental were to completely withdraw, this could mean immediate dismissals, as the example of the British subsidiary had clearly shown. Nonetheless, the letters regarding the Spanish factory were also full of well-informed warnings of how fragile the market position in Spain was: "If we do not start building a factory in Spain, our Spanish business will completely dry up in the near future. It will get smaller every year until it is no longer worthwhile." A host of European and US competitors were standing ready to enter a market that was new and promising. In the end, this project was not implemented either. "The way the situation is at present, you can probably imagine that we do not want to burden ourselves with the worry of a production company in Spain," Tischbein wrote in April 1923. In Germany at that time, the political and economic situation was extremely difficult. The industrial heartland of the Ruhr valley had been occupied by French and Belgian troops and the economy faced hyperinflation. The time therefore did not seem right to build a new plant abroad.

Further projects were also looked at, such as a factory in Bilbao (Spain) that had been given up by Titan Pollack, a German competitor of Continental. As with Manresa, it was not just the Spanish market that was considered, but also the associated access to the South American sales markets. In 1923, the managers of an Austrian company in Vienna put out feelers to determine whether Continental was interested in starting solid rubber tire production at their subsidiary in Odry, Czechoslovakia. For weeks, careful calculations were made for this potential joint venture, which would certainly have meant a resumption of the previous cooperation strategy. The documents show clearly how complex and discouraging to trade the situation in Europe was at the time. An employee in the accounts department prepared a detailed list of the duties on imports and exports between Germany, Czechoslovakia, Spain and France. The list also contained the possibilities that would result from Continental having a plant in one of these countries. This project failed too because of the unclear prospects and the economic and political turmoil that Continental was confronted with in Germany.

All in all, World War I was a huge setback for Continental in the efforts to internationalize its business that it had been undertaking intensively since 1881. When sales for 1924/25 were compared with the pre-war period of 1913/14, the figures were sobering. Revenue had fallen by more than 92% in France, more than 95% in Italy, and over 70% in Spain. The overview showed that only the revenue in Great Britain was anywhere near where it had been before the war. This also changed in 1927, as described above, when Continental withdrew from the British market. In 1913, exports accounted for 54.5% of Continental's total revenue. In 1926, they made up just 17%.

Fig. 131: Advertisement in Arabic from 1928.

Despite these figures, Continental was in much better shape than many other companies. By the end of the 1920s, it old sales structures had been re-established in many countries, or the process had at least begun. The market share that had been lost was gradually being won back again. In 1923, the Internationale Continental Caoutchouc-Compagnie was founded in Amsterdam. This was a strategic holding company that bundled together the entire foreign business while remaining independent of the extreme inflation in Germany.

Continental survived the economic turbulence of the 1920s and remained comparatively successful during the world economic crisis at the end of the decade. Despite the difficulties on the foreign markets, the 1920s were a phase of new growth, with innovative products such as the cord tire (1921) and the low-pressure balloon tire (1924). The Continental range of industrial products and popular consumer articles made of rubber also became more sophisticated. In 1928/29, after merging with several German competitors, Continental became the main player in the German rubber industry. It was also renamed "Continental Gummi-Werke Aktiengesellschaft."

Fig. 132: Extract from Echo Continental from 1923.

An important factor in this strength lay in the willingness of Continental's managing directors to cooperate with other companies. Similarly to the early phase of international expansion, management was not under any illusions about making up lost ground on its own. US tire and rubber manufacturers were far ahead when it came to product and production technology. In February 1920, negotiations started between Continental and B. F. Goodrich Company, based in Akron (Ohio). These negotiations resulted in a comprehensive friendship and consultation agreement. "I quite agree with you that both of us should benefit largely from a community of interests and that this is one of the strongest features of the proposed plan," Bertram G. Work, managing director of Goodrich, wrote to Seligmann in March 1920.

In the case of Goodrich, Seligmann and Tischbein were also able to fall back on contacts that had been established before the war. A previous agreement between the two companies dated back to April 1911. Then, in return for a license fee and a share of the revenue, Continental made available the know-how in balloon and aircraft materials that it had developed in Hanover. Products manufactured and sold in the USA were labeled with a reference to the Continental brand. After World War I, the situation had reversed. Now, Continental was urgently in need of its counterpart's expertise.

For Continental, this cooperation meant access to the latest cord tire technologies. The company also gained an insight into its US competitor's manufacturing know-how. Over the following years, a continuous learning process ensued as numerous delegations visited the partner's plants. They brought back with them extensive reports on production technology, work processes, procedural techniques and later even accounting methods. The reports on these trips that have survived show how Continental employees inspected almost every corner of the Goodrich factory in Akron. Tire production was just one aspect that was focused on. The visitors also studied the equipment used to make technical hoses, drive belts, conveyor belting, rubber mats, air bags, rubber heels, V-belts and rubber threads. In addition, discussions took place with employees on site, from which the visitors gained a comprehensive insight into their competitor's working methods. Even the smallest of details was included in the reports, such as the type of heating used in the factory halls or how to prevent theft at the plant. These reports show clearly how motivated the visitors were to think deeply about the issues involved. The plants that were visited and the processes inspected were not simply copied. Instead, a precise look was taken at how and where Continental could improve its own approach. In their reports, the technicians often expressed approval of the modernity of the Goodrich production process. Pride in Continental's own achievements shone through as well, however. The company had clearly remained innovative in certain areas despite the war. In one of his reports in 1921, a Continental production technician wrote:

> The next task is to make the production processes of use to Continental. We will not, however, be introducing the Goodrich methods at random and without criticism. Even Goodrich receives complaints, and the company does not always stick firmly to its working methods. [...] On the contrary, Goodrich's entire organization is tailored so that every

company can quickly and very flexibly absorb innovations, or cancel products that are no longer profitable or realistic, such as printing blankets or cover straps. My suggestion is to start with improvements where the greatest problems exist.

Continental profited considerably from this exchange and was able to increase its competitiveness. In the middle of a time of hyperinflation, decisive steps were taken toward modernization and rationalization. This gave the company a major advantage, especially compared to its German and European competitors. The agreement with Goodrich also helped stabilize Continental financially. The US partner took on a 25% share package from a capital increase and granted Continental a loan of 500,000 dollars. In those years, foreign currency was more important than ever. It was needed to import raw materials and at the same time to protect the company's own capital from losing value. The cooperation agreement lasted for nine years, during which time the Continental plant in Hanover underwent a huge transformation based on the exchange with Goodrich. Every piece of technical equipment and every work process was placed under the magnifying glass and checked to see if there was potential for rationalization. In 1925, the above-quoted technician wrote to director Tischbein:

> The Continental factory did not make a bad impression during my first tour after returning from America. In almost all departments, I saw the results of the American trips in the form of machines, mechanical devices and aids for achieving higher output and more straightforward production processes.

The cooperation with Goodrich was also strongly characterized by personal ties between the Executive Board members. For years, Seligmann and Tischbein on the German side and Bertram G. Work (and later David Goodrich) on the American side enjoyed the benefits of very direct communication with one another. In fall 1928, Goodrich signaled that he wished to sell the share package, and negotiations on dissolving the agreement started. These were carried out directly between Tischbein and Goodrich while Goodrich was a guest at Tischbein's estate in Rixförde near Hanover. The tone of the letters between the men over the next few months indicates that the two families had become quite friendly.

Overall, the cooperation was a success and formed an important basis for Continental to regain the competitive position it had enjoyed before World War I. From today's perspective, the collaboration between Continental and Goodrich is significant in two ways. For one, it shows a remarkable willingness to operate transparently on the side of Goodrich. This openness to share experience and know-how with competitors was widespread in the US rubber industry at the time, and was based on a deep conviction that progress would be helped more by such cooperation than by secrecy and aggressive competition. A lot of effort was needed to maintain this attitude so soon after the war, as such close and friendly collaboration with a company from a previously hostile country could trigger criticism. During Germany's phase of high inflation, there was also a widespread fear of the economy being overrun by foreign companies. The German mark was weak, so company shares were a bargain for foreign investors. Seligmann and Tischbein clearly refused to be influenced by this situation. Instead, they seized the opportunities that presented themselves.

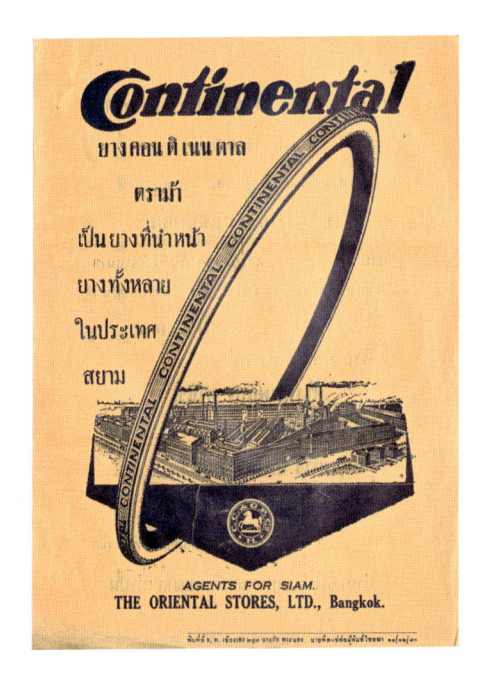

Fig. 133: Advertising brochure of a Continental trader in Bangkok, 1938.

Export strategy in the Nazi era and focussing on the domestic market until well into the 1970s

All the same, Tischbein's re-internationalization in the 1920s was not a great success. Unlike the competition, he did not succeed in building a factory abroad.

New competitors were also building their own factories in Germany, and the effort needed to defend the domestic market against them was too great. Continental tried its best, but it proved very difficult to regain the position enjoyed abroad before World War I. After years of inflation and economic crises, the economic conditions did finally improve. But with Hitler's coming to power in January 1933, the Continental Executive Board faced a regime that totally rejected internationality. The Nazi regime viewed exports and foreign activities merely as a way to acquire urgently needed foreign currency. The top priority was autarky (self-sufficiency), which meant independence from raw material imports, for example. This would reduce Germany's dependence on and interaction with foreign countries.

This political and economic ideology was fundamentally contrary to the orientation of Continental, where internationalism had been an integral part of the corporate culture since 1871. In spite of its ingratiation with the Nazi regime, the Executive Board held onto this culture for a long time and attempted to implement an internationalization strategy that reflected its own interests. The global network before World War I was still a reference point for this. The company's sales figures, however, show how the importance of foreign business continued to decline during the Nazi era. In 1934, exports accounted for just 9.1% of total revenue, a figure that fell to 5.4% by 1938. In 1913, in the last business year before World War I, the figure was 54.5%.

At the same time, the Executive Board member responsible for business abroad, Gustav Schmelz, did everything in his power to intensify the company's export policy and, contrary to Tischbein's strategy in the 1920s, to set up foreign plants. Plans for factories in the USA and Switzerland failed, however, as Nazi economic policy was increasingly implemented by the authorities themselves. The sole successful venture was a tire factory in Torrelavega in Spain, which was built in spring 1936. This meant that Continental had its own factory abroad for the first time since 1914. Even so, just a few months after production started, the project ran into difficulties when Torrelavega came under occupation during the Spanish Civil War. This led to contact with Hanover being broken off for more than a year and a half. At its own subsidiaries, Continental also faced considerable problems in adapting to the new racial policies of the Nazi regime. From 1938, it was forbidden to employ Jewish staff at the company's foreign offices. Continental implemented this rule without protest and dismissed the affected staff members.

Fig. 134: The Continental factory in Torrelavega in March 1936.

During World War II, Continental was part of a large-scale European economy that was controlled and advanced by the Nazi regime. The Executive Board, headed by general director Fritz Könecke, put into place various instruments to align Continental's expansion with the advance of the Wehrmacht. Foreign companies were acquired or invested in, and use was made of cooperative ventures and complex lease and supervision agreements. The German occupying powers controlled these agreements that ensued, such as the transfer of local rubber processing companies to Continental for "supervision." The entire process was aimed at controlling the production processes and integrating them into the Nazi war economy, and was characterized by considerable exploitation. Continental participated in this system and integrated many of these leased and supervised companies into its own production network. These included plants in Posen (Poznań, Poland) and Krainburg (Kranj, Slovenia/Yugoslavia), which were run as fourth and fifth Continental plants. Through these measures, Könecke and the Continental Executive Board tried to ensure an advantageous starting position for the post-war period. The transnational production network also provided some protection against the air raids that became a greater threat in the final years of the war. At the same time, the distribution network in occupied and regime-friendly countries was greatly expanded.

In the last few months of the war, the European network of factories and sales companies collapsed completely. The factories in the occupied and regime-friendly countries had to be hurriedly cleared as the Allies liberated one country after the next from German occupation. Factories in Banloc (Romania), 's-Hertogenbosch (the Netherlands) and Zuen (Belgium) were evacuated, while the Continental plants in Germany were repeatedly subjected to air raids. Just a few weeks before the war ended, the main plant in Hanover was almost completely destroyed in this way. As with the First World War, Continental lost its foreign network when hostilities ended. The "new" plants in Posen and Krainburg now came under the control of the Red Army. As a result, Continental's development was again set back years.

Shortly after the war ended, however, Continental again became a popular cooperation partner for US tire companies. Various companies examined the possibility of reactivating previous business relationships or forming new ones. As after the First World War, pre-war business contacts were the decisive factor here. The plan was to use these contacts to restore the broken links with the most technologically advanced tire manufacturers in the USA. Continental technicians were soon setting off again to visit these companies. This time, however, they were shocked at the backwardness of their own technology and manufacturing processes. "Our impression is that our manufacturing methods have been far surpassed by General [Tire]. Indeed, they must be viewed as partly obsolete," wrote a visitor in the first report from Akron in summer 1948. In March 1949, a comprehensive cooperation agreement was concluded with the US tire company General Tire. As with the agreement with Goodrich from the 1920s, this mainly covered the exchange of know-how. The basis of the cooperation was "to learn without any restrictions about the modern facilities and working methods, in particular in the area of tire manufacturing. For our part, we will provide General Tire with know-how about our production processes, especially in the area of technical and surgical rubber goods." Continental's experience in manufacturing technical rubber products, and the technologies used, were of interest to the US company because a similar production line was planned at Akron. For its part, Continental gained access to the latest tire technologies. Almost more importantly, it acquired knowledge on tire production and the use of machines.

The contract with General Tire ran until 1954 and was then replaced by a comparable agreement with the global market leader, Goodyear. This even included the production of Goodyear tires at Continental and ran until 1961. Both contracts were characterized by Continental technicians visiting the USA and vice versa. One explanation for the frequent travel was the start of the Cold War and the confrontation between the USA and the Soviet Union. Another important factor was that the communication of the 1920s and 1930s had never really been broken off and there was still personal contact. People knew and liked one another and could therefore find a bridge to cooperate again after the war.

Various projects were launched as Continental attempted to regain the international presence it had enjoyed before the war. "Since mid-1948, we have been involved in contractual negotiations with rubber goods producers abroad. In one case, the objective is mutual technical/chemical consultations. The objective of the other instances is technical/chemical assistance from our side." The agreement with General Tire was supplemented by a contract with the Sociedad Argentina Tecnica Industria y Comercial in Buenos Aires (Argentina). This contract involved technical assistance in setting up a factory for technical rubber goods. The contract also contained an option for the licensed production of Continental products. An auxiliary service contract with Mediterranea Gomma SA in San Vittore (Italy) was soon renewed. There were also plans to set up factories in Brazil, Norway and India: "Three of our most important bicycle tire customers from pre-war times have asked Hanover to help them set up and operate a bicycle tire factory in British India."

In June 1949, negotiations were taken up with cooperation partner General Tire to establish a joint tire factory in Denmark. "Continental will take over chemical/technical management and supervision from Hanover; General Tire will transfer its latest experience and methods to the factory." By the end of August 1949, the essential details had already been discussed between both sides. There were agreements ranging from the production program, through price and cost structures, to the salaries of the stenotypists to be employed. The managers responsible reckoned that the Denmark market had considerable potential for renewed activity.

> [...] [W]e can be assured that the name 'Continental' is held in high regard by all the companies in our industry. This good name is based on decades of personal connections to our company, on our continuous high quality, and on our help in the form of goods deliveries during the war.

In the end, however, the plans were aborted. The reason for this was most likely the project's financing, which proved difficult and led to intense discussions between the project partners. In the end, the plans ultimately failed due to the obstacles put in place by customs barriers and foreign currency restrictions.

The factory that was never built is symptomatic of Continental's unsuccessful attempts to re-establish itself in foreign markets. Almost all of the described activities failed or never came near to the strength of Continental's previous position in foreign markets. In the following years, the company focused on the domestic market. Here, Continental faced increased competition following the end of World War II. US, French, British, Italian and Scandinavian tire manufacturers were doing everything to secure their market share as German society increased its mobility at breathtaking speed. Numerous new plants were built during this time, and only with great effort could Continental prevent a substantial fall in its revenue. The fact that many people still trusted the Continental brand, as well as its close ties to successful German automobile manufacturers, provided enough security for the company to hold its position in the original equipment and replacement business. This position gradually crumbled, however. Even the greatest efforts of Continental's Executive Board to at least partially transfer the cartel-like structures that had developed over the past decades to Germany's new "social market economy" ultimately came to nothing.

The focus on the domestic market lasted until the mid-1960s, during which time business in and with foreign countries withered away. This was in strong contrast to the strategy of actively promoting Continental's international expansion that had developed over 70 years of corporate history. As was the case after World War I, the previously established network of branches and sales and production sites had come apart. In many countries, trademark rights and patents were also under public administration. In some cases, proceedings for restitution or compensation ran for many years. This meant that Continental's managers faced a completely unclear situation in many countries that were once very important for exports. The challenges of rebuilding the completely destroyed main plant in Hanover-Vahrenwald and the turmoil of the early post-war years led to the company almost completely neglecting its export business. The one-sided focus on domestic business was not initially noticeable, as sales figures for tires and rubber products continued to reach new record levels. It was not until the end of the economic "miracle years" and international competitors began to acquire more and more market share that the neglected export market was suddenly sorely missed as a means of compensation.

Already in the 1960s, Continental was involved in several cooperation and merger offers. The Executive Board submitted bids to take over the German tire manufacturers Metzeler, Fulda and Veith, but Goodyear and Pirelli got there first. A merger with Dunlop and Pirelli was also rejected for fear of outside interference. When the two companies merged anyway, the Continental Executive Board also rejected an offer to cooperate from Michelin. The company was still strongly convinced of its ability to compete on its own merits. The cooperation with US tire companies was used aggressively, but any further form of merger or takeover was not an option for the Executive Board. At first glance, Continental was already an internationalized company at this time. In 1964, tire production commenced at a new factory in Sarreguemines (France). At the same time, plans were on the table for another tire factory in Brixen (Italy). On top of this came a whole series of minority shareholdings in factories manufacturing technical rubber products in South Africa, Spain, Brazil and Italy. Ultimately, however, these foreign commitments were not indicative of a deeper internationalization strategy, as the Executive Board was far too busy defending its position on the German market. In 1966, the export share of the company's revenue amounted to just 15.2%.

By the time managers at Hanover finally became aware of how important internationalization was for Continental, the company was already in crisis. When it became clear that Michelin's steel belted tire was technologically superior, desperate attempts were undertaken to turn the tide. The overall economic situation also deteriorated after the end of the post-war boom, before the oil price crisis then drove industrialized nations into a severe recession. In this situation, it was no longer possible to achieve organic internationalization by building new plants. This led to the scrapping of plans for a tire factory in Brixen (Italy).

The four phases of internationalization at Continental (1979 to present)

Carl H. Hahn became the new Executive Board chairman in April 1973. Not only did he preside over a tough phase of restructuring, but also pursued a different strategy for internationalization than his predecessors. Building the company's own factories abroad was inconceivable due to the framework conditions. Even so, Hahn resolved to tackle the problem head-on. On January 1, 1974, a cooperation agreement came into effect with the US tire company Uniroyal, which also included an option to buy the latter's European business. Continental was granted access to Uniroyal's production technology for a fee and a share of revenue. Furthermore, a great deal of know-how was exchanged between the two companies. The agreement was part of a restructuring plan initiated by Hahn that would bring the company into the future and help it quickly make up for technological deficits. The contract was supplemented by an agreement on radial ply tires for trucks in spring 1977. "We need to become even more agile and, above all, more international. On the world stage we are a good partner, but still too small," Hahn announced at the Annual Shareholders' Meeting in late 1977. Even so, in that year, Continental generated 25.2% of its revenue through exports.

Fig. 135: Discussions at the press conference to announce the Uniroyal takeover. From left to right: Helmut Werner (Uniroyal), Albert Englebert (Uniroyal), Carl H. Hahn (Continental).

In 1979, Continental then took over the entire Uniroyal European business. The news came as a sensation and heralded the start of the company's first internationalization phase since the Second World War. For years, Continental had been fighting for survival. It had made huge losses and there were serious discussions as to whether to leave the tire business completely. Now, suddenly, the company had a sales network spanning the whole of Europe, with factories in Great Britain (Newbridge), France (Clairoix), Belgium (Herstal), an additional plant in Germany (Aachen), and a factory for textile cord in Steinfort (Luxemburg). Continental had thus again transformed from a company firmly positioned in Germany into a European corporation.

This purchase was far more than just an expansion of production capacities. Through their long association with a US company, the Uniroyal managers were experienced in organizing sales and production in a multinational network. The challenges posed by marketing in different markets and the modern forms of company organization were familiar to Continental's new arrivals. This was in contrast to the at times laborious administration in Hanover, which for many years had been concentrating only on the domestic market and long-established connections with German car manufacturers. This difference in mentality and culture became very noticeable during the integration of the new Uniroyal business unit. At Continental, employees became somewhat fearful of the changes Uniroyal might bring to their workplace. These developments were all a new experience for Continental. Up to now, its internationalization strategy had always focused on either expanding the company's own organization through subsidiaries or plants, or entering into cooperative ventures. A certain distance was always maintained during these collaborations. With the takeover of Uniroyal's European business, Continental was not just going on the offensive, but was also taking a risk in terms of its company culture. This risk paid off in the end, however. The entire organization and its employees were awakened from their Germany-focused comfort zone, and the strong shift in corporate culture encouraged the company to rethink its old ways. Even if comparable resources had been available to build plants and develop sales networks, this would not have had a similar effect. A "not invented here" attitude with regard to product and production technology, marketing strategy and organization principles was now impossible. The new Uniroyal colleagues who suddenly joined Continental's work groups and departments spoke fluent English and were much more confident. This was now truly an international Continental. During the Carl H. Hahn era, the company became geared for ever greater internationalization and was run in this spirit. English courses were offered in the company magazine "Conti intern," and employees were also given the opportunity to work for two to three years at one of Continental's numerous subsidiaries abroad: "A deployment like this will broaden your horizons and help you gain new experience."

The takeover of Uniroyal's European business was supplemented by a series of further cooperation ventures with competitors. For the most part, the collaborations followed a similar pattern. Continental contributed its technical know-how and in return obtained production capacity and distribution channels in the respective countries. An agreement with the Toyo Tire & Rubber Company in Osaka (Japan), for instance, provided access to Japanese automobile manufacturers and enabled Continental to enter the Japanese replacement business. An agreement with General Tire in September 1982 followed similar lines: Continental provided know-how in the truck tire area for a license fee; in return, General Tire produced 500,000 Continental brand tires for the US market. In both cases, the collaboration was hallmarked by mutual gain. In the medium term, contract manufacturing meant that Continental was able to sell its own products and strengthen brand awareness in the Japanese and US markets.

This pragmatic business strategy is comparable with that of the 1900s. Back then, Seligmann and Prinzhorn used very similar agreements to advance Continental's international expansion despite trade obstacles. The course was set for the future in both these phases of relative weakness, when there was little opportunity to independently develop new markets. In 1914, Continental was more or less forced to become international, as the German automobile industry was not yet powerful and would have set narrow limits on company expansion. This predicament was repeated 65 years later under different circumstances. And taking this step proved to be pivotal for the development and even the survival of the company.

Fig. 136: Horst W. Urban and Gilbert H. Neal in Akron (Ohio).

From 1979, Continental advanced its internationalization on a massive scale. In just a few years, the company had its own plants in France, Ireland, Austria, Great Britain, Belgium and Brazil. The final breakthrough to becoming an international and now global company took place in 1987 with the takeover of General Tire in Akron, Ohio. The second internationalization phase after World War II began. All at once, Continental's production network was expanded by six plants in the USA, as well as additional plants in Canada, Morocco and Mexico. The foreign share of company revenue now stood at 65%, reaching the level of 1913—the previous peak of internationalization—after 75 years. By the end of 1988, more than half of Continental's employees worked outside Germany, which was a first in the company's history. In contrast to the previously pursued strategy, General Tire was taken over and integrated as a complete company. For its part, General Tire brought with it a corporate culture that had grown over many years. The tensions that had already arisen in the case of Uniroyal were not always perceived as positive at Continental. Often, they were viewed as a challenge, and some even feared that the company would lose its own identity. In the end though, integration succeeded in every case. The confrontation with other perspectives, business methods and technical approaches always provided the impetus to modernize the company's own approach. This was also the case regarding cooperation with other companies. This was less strong, however, as these partnerships were always temporary. Only when the former competitors and cooperation partners from across the ocean suddenly became colleagues did it become necessary to find a common basis for collaboration. This confrontation with the unknown and the resulting reflection on company culture and identity played a major role in the modernization of both sides and their future success. During this phase, Semperit (1985), Gislaved (1990) and Barum (1993) expanded not only Continental's tire portfolio but also its international production network.

The tendency toward stronger internationalization continued unabated at Continental even after the takeover of General Tire, and has continued up to this day. In a third internationalization phase from the start of the 2000s, production capacities were increasingly relocated to Eastern Europe. This process had already begun in the 1990s and was now continued with more intensity. After the Cold War, Continental entered into various cooperation agreements with local manufacturers in order to secure a share of the new markets that were opening up. The locations in Otrokovice (Czech Republic), Púchov (Slovakia) and Timişoara (Romania) expanded Continental's production network. Today, these are by far the company's largest tire plants. In a second step, more cost-intensive plants in Austria (Traiskirchen), Sweden (Gislaved), Belgium (Herstal) and France (Clairoix) were closed. Tire production was also gradually phased out at the Hanover-Stöcken plant. The background to this was a considerable fall in demand in the entire automotive industry, exacerbated further by the terror attacks of September 11, 2001. "We make these decisions for just one reason: to strengthen Continental again," commented Executive Board chairman Manfred Wennemer on the tough measures taken in 2002.

Other German and numerous international companies were integrated into the Continental corporation at regular intervals. The acquisitions of Phoenix (2004) and Veyance (2015) turned the ContiTech business unit into one of the largest specialists for rubber and plastic technologies worldwide. Since the early 1990s, Continental had pursued an intensive diversification strategy in order to develop from a pure manufacturer of rubber and plastic products into broad-based system supplier. The acquisitions of Teves (1998), Temic (2001) and especially Siemens VDO (2007) transformed Continental into a fully globalized company with plants and sales locations in all parts of the world.

Fig. 137: Image brochure from 2007 about the involvement of the ContiTech division in China.

A fourth internationalization phase in 2010 following the global economic and financial crisis saw a significant stepping up of expansion into Asia. The first activities in this direction had already taken place at the beginning of the decade. On the one hand, the acquisitions of Temic, Phoenix and Siemens VDO brought Asian locations to the company. On the other hand, in the early phase, a series of joint ventures were entered into with Chinese partners. These mostly involved the ContiTech and Automotive Systems divisions. "Increase competitiveness and open up new markets by producing locally: that is Continental's objective in China." Initially, the company went about this in a very reserved fashion, as addressed openly in *conti intern*. The expansion strategy was "characterized by a deliberately cautious search for cooperation partners and smaller purchase opportunities." Nonetheless, by 2010, Continental was represented in the most important local markets in East and Southeast Asia. This was in part through its own plants, but also through sales companies that profited from the successive assertion of free trade policies. At this time, the company already had its own or jointly operated plants in Australia, China, India, Indonesia, Japan, Malaysia, the Philippines, Sri Lanka, South Korea and Thailand. In 2010, *conti intern* wrote: "Continental is investing massively in Asia and will continue to do so. In addition to plans to localize the entire value chain, Continental will also increase its local customer base through joint ventures with local partners." By now there were 41 manufacturing facilities and 27 sales offices in Asia, which employed a staff of 23,000. A total of 14% of company revenue was generated in the region.

Under Elmar Degenhart as Executive Board chairman, the company's expansion into Asia intensified even further. Continental focused specifically on working "in the region for the region" and localizing the entire value chain—from purchasing and marketing through to research & development and production. In an interview, Degenhart stated that the Asian region was "the ideal growth market for our products." From 2010, Degenhart functioned as a "sponsor" for the newly defined key region of China. During his first trip to China in spring 2010, he underlined the importance of the market as well as the opportunities that it created for Continental. "Our task is to seize these opportunities and make the most of them. [...] We should be able to double or triple our sales." The company's foreign revenue climbed from 72.8% (2010) to 81.2% (2019). In the 2019 fiscal year, 22% of sales were generated in Asia, 30% in Europe and 26% in North America. Today, with 595 locations in 59 countries and markets, Continental is more internationally positioned than ever before.

Looking back at this long development, we see that internationalization has been a part of Continental's company culture since its founding in 1871. The founding members, and especially Siegmund Seligmann, recognized the potential to successfully sell Continental products in other markets. At the same time, international expansion has always been a necessary prerequisite for ensuring the company's lasting success. Continental would certainly never have survived for 150 years had courageous steps not been taken to open it up to the world beyond Hanover, Germany and Europe. Its history of internationalization is also a history of successful collaboration. In many situations, it would have been almost impossible to expand successfully or to make up for outdated technologies without outside help. Time and again, an openness to cooperate with competitors allowed both sides to benefit and emerge stronger as a result. Two catastrophic world wars were huge setbacks for Continental in this process. Only the long period of peace in Central Europe after World War II made it possible for Continental to step up its internationalization and globalization. This development does not contradict in any way the previous local limitations of the company. It stands much more for the consistent pursuance of a strategy that started in the 1880s. This strategy was interrupted by two world wars, but is now lived out and continued at Continental. Today, Continental is a truly global company with an ever tighter network of employees all over the world. The obstacles that stood in the way of this development in the past have by no means vanished. Political tendencies toward market foreclosures, distortions of competition and trade wars still exist today, and are even on the rise. Not just in Germany is the globalization of the economy once again coming under critical scrutiny. For Continental, however, it is one of the key foundations of the company's success.

9 Between Vision and Speculation
Continental in 2046, or: The History of Past and Present Expectations for the Future within the Company

Continental's history has always been shaped by the visions of the individuals who led the company and by developments that were unimaginable for contemporaries of the time. This started with Siegmund Seligmann, who saw Continental as a global rubber-processing company even back when the Hanover-based business was still battling with crises. Next in line was Willy Tischbein, who forged the company into a modern tire corporation. Through the decades, these visions evolved and by the 1990s, Continental became a globally active technological leader and integrated supplier whose influence ranged far beyond the tire sector. Today, the company is striving to become an operating system provider for the new software-supported mobility. However, how well the future can be anticipated and imagined is subject to constant change. Sometimes, long-term corporate goals are pursued and grand visions of a company's future role, competitiveness and business model are developed. At other times, corporate plans are limited to following "megatrends" that are apparent to everyone or circumstances make it necessary to "drive by sight" and focus on simply overcoming the challenges of the relevant era. This has also shaped periods in Continental's history. Times of crisis also affect the corporate perspectives of the future, in particular when a company with lofty visions has to come back down to earth and face the realities in the markets. Frequently, a company's plans for the future, its visions and corporate policy goals are not explicitly formulated, yet de facto pursued in its business operations. In other cases, such plans and goals are clearly expressed and widely propagated, but hardly implemented in daily business.

Management's expectations for the future usually correlate with technological developments and technical innovation cycles. In the past, a trip to the laboratories of the R&D departments was the best way to find out more about the future of a company. For a long time, future viability was equated with competence in R&D, and no clear differentiation was made between strategic and technical visions of the future. However, although this purely technological perception of the future is probably still the most powerful, it has lost significance in today's era of (seemingly) constant decreases in technical incubation periods, paired with the growing importance of a holistic future perspective that takes into account ecological, economic, political and social considerations.

For many years, future perspectives and visions were developed within the company itself and converted into corporate strategies. However, increasingly, these are influenced or even practically dictated by external parties, such as investors, analysts and "the markets," who are more interested in a medium-term investment story than in long-term future concepts. Visions for the future have also long become part of the business model of the consulting industry, which has resulted in the future visions of companies becoming standardized to a certain extent. The opposing model propagated by the famous economist Joseph Schumpeter, namely that the basis for innovative action is the intuition, freedom and courage of the entrepreneur to explore new paths, has faded in comparison, without losing its validity. Anniversaries were and are often a good occasion for a company to formulate visions of the future and think about its future market positioning and development. Knowledge of the past future gives historians an advantage over contemporary protagonists. However, this analysis is not aimed at assessing corporate policy in hindsight, but to examine the knowledge and information available to corporate leaders in their time, as well as their experience and expectations. Thus the future can be given its place in a company's history, so to speak. This is done for Continental in the following.

The Invention of New Mobility as a Result of Mastering the Raw Material of the Future. Continental's Long "Rubber Age" (1870s to 1930s)

When Siegmund Seligmann took over the management of the company in 1879, mobility was probably not one of the topics on his mind, and it is likely that he had no clear perception of what shape it would take. In the 1880s, the world of mobility still consisted mainly of the railway, horse-drawn carts and penny-farthings with solid rubber tires. But even after pneumatic tires became available, first for bicycles and a little later also for cars, it was far from foreseeable that this would one day become a high-volume business. What Seligmann did spend time thinking about was how rubber as the material of the future could be mastered. This molded his vision of Continental's development and was the basis for his diversification strategy. Seligmann saw Continental as a global rubber-processing company that could conquer the market with numerous technical rubber products for use in both everyday tasks and leisure activities, with bicycle, motorcycle and car tires being the most prominent Continental products. By the turn of the century, he had already largely succeeded in implementing his vision. The English trade journal *India Rubber World*, which was also regularly read in Hanover, headlined a 1903 article with "The World's Dependence on Rubber" and described the promising rubber age. At that point, Continental was already one step ahead with its operative corporate policy. Continental could be considered to have been a representative of a modern "platform economy" of the day. The company had mastered one of the key materials of the future, and using this know-how

Fig. 138: Laboratories of the future: a look at the R&D departments prior to 1914 and during the 1920s.

and growing expertise as a basis, it had successively opened up new product areas and fields of application. In other words, the real future opportunities lay in the markets that did not yet exist at this time. The central vehicle for this was the rubber laboratory set up in 1874. It was headed by the chemist Adolf Prinzhorn, who started to systematically establish a scientific basis for rubber manufacturing and the processing of raw rubber. Continental was therefore an early adopter of the "scientification" of industry, in other words, the "production of innovation" within a company. This fundamental process was a key factor in the German industry's competitiveness and success on the global markets prior to World War I.

In comparison, Willy Tischbein had more difficulties to cope with after the end of World War I, but also enjoyed an easier situation regarding the future of mobility. In spite of the many adverse circumstances, the arduous return to the global markets and hyperinflation, his actions were not governed by a simple vision of seamlessly continuing the company's pre-war success. Instead, he focused development on transforming Continental into a tire corporation, with the aid of the American tire company Goodrich. Tischbein looked to the USA for inspiration and gathered direct experience during several trips to Akron, Ohio, which had by now become the world's rubber capital. Here he formed a clear and concrete picture of how the future of mobility would look, with mass motorization and the rise of the car as a means of transport for everyone—a scenario that was only vaguely discernible in Germany in the 1920s and did not achieve its breakthrough until the 1950s. When Continental celebrated its 50th anniversary in 1921, there was little sign of grand visions and expectations for the future. "There are few raw materials," stated the commemorative publication,

> that can be processed into as many different things as rubber; it is suitable for countless applications in daily life, traffic and in a multitude of diverse industries. It continues to conquer new areas. What will we have achieved in its application 50 years from now? It is not yet possible to say. What we do know is that we do not want to view the 50th anniversary of our factories as a closing point, but instead as the beginning of the rubber industry's further ascent and of our company's continued success.

This sounded like an afterthought to Seligmann's vision and the goals already largely achieved in the years before. Indeed, the 1918 annual report contained no trace of optimism. "We look to the future with great concern," it stated. "We are at serious risk of not staying competitive on the global markets and even of being unable to fend off foreign competition when the borders are opened again." However, the industry experts of the time gave a favorable prognosis for the German rubber industry and forecast a promising future due to the "replenishment of the German consumer market with diverse rubber goods" alone, in particular in the car tire sector, as the *Berliner Börsen-Courier* stated in mid-1918. Other industry experts were even more forward-thinking regarding future technological developments. In 1922, for example, the Gummi-Zeitung published a fictitious report entitled "Zukunftsbilder der Kautschuk-Industrie" (Visions for the Future of the Rubber Industry), which gave an account of a visit to the "Ideal-Omnium-Rubber Works" in 1940 and described the manufacturing of rubber goods in 1952. Although both articles were presented as speculations that were not to be taken entirely seriously, they contained noteworthy future scenarios and developments, some of which became reality decades later. These included a low-energy vulcanization method, pneumatic tires without inner tubes, indestructible railway rails made of hard rubber instead of brittle steel, rubber surfaces that were warm underfoot thanks to innovative mixing technology and, last but not least, self-regenerating rubber that renewed the worn tire surface with rubber mass flowing through small integrated tubes, eliminating the need to change tires.

Tischbein, however, had other visions. His long-term goal for Continental's future market position was to conquer the European tire market together with Goodrich and to push competitors Michelin, Dunlop and Pirelli into a defensive position. And after that, he probably would have striven to expand globally again. This vision did not become reality, mostly because of the hesitation of the Goodrich Executive Board. After Tischbein's congenial business partner, Goodrich manager Bertram G. Work, suddenly died in August 1927, the board initiated a defensive policy for Europe, without a German junior partner. Increased economic turbulence was also responsible for Tischbein's vision being pushed into the background. The economic slumps in 1926, and in particular between 1929 and 1932, forced Tischbein to concentrate on the urgent operative business and on making Continental crisis-proof by means of radical rationalization and cost-saving measures. He succeeded in this venture, not least by taking over competitors, foremost of which was the neighboring Excelsior AG. In 1932, Continental had grown into a "rubber trust" that dominated the German domestic market by a wide margin. In Tischbein's famous speech in January 1932, he was already venturing a glimpse into the future after the crisis years. At this time, everyone else was still struggling with overcoming the current, immediate crisis, with declines in revenue and massive losses. "I am convinced," said Tischbein,

> that we have never before been in such a favorable position as we are now. Our financial standing is better; the technical facilities of our factory are better and more advanced. Of

course, I do not want to imply that further progress is not possible. Indeed, it is vital. We have also had significant successes in organizing and training our sales force. In summary, I would like to emphasize that 1932 has to be a good year for us if all employees utilize all the strengths I have mentioned. [...] There is always demand, there always will be demand, and it is up to us to secure the share of the market demand that belongs to us and that we can cover.

No Visions, or: The Key to the Future is Managing the Present (1930s to 1970s)

During the Nazi era, the Reich Ministry of Economics and the Reich Office for Economic Development took over the strategic planning for Continental, and the company had to succumb to the plans and goals of the Nazi regime. As part of the "European large-scale economy" envisioned by the National Socialist bureaucrats, Continental was assigned the role of leading rubber corporation to which its French and Italian competitors were to be subordinated. The political power to achieve this lay in German Buna technology. However, at the same time, the Reich Ministry of Economics was careful to not let Continental become too big and powerful and thus put its own corporate objectives above those of the Nazi regime with regard to armament and the war economy. The Nazi bureaucrats played with the thought of dividing the tire world of the 1930s and the future between the German and American corporations. Japanese corporations either did not yet exist or were considered negligible, such as Bridgestone, which had only been founded in 1931. The Continental Executive Board largely complied with these ambitious plans of the Nazi authorities and in many regards integrated the objectives into its corporate policy, even though there was significant internal skepticism toward these aims. By the end of 1943, the company was at the center of a wide, transnational network consisting of lease, support and consulting companies for the rubber industry. Between 1944 and early 1945, this network practically imploded.

After World War II, Continental once again followed the path it took in the 1920s by attempting to reconnect with technology and restore an international market presence with the aid of the American tire companies, and was successful. But instead of far-reaching visions, the company's actions were dominated by short-term reconstruction and a focus on the domestic market. The rubber world of the period directly after the war and the economic "miracle years" was not characterized by a willingness to start afresh or by visions for the future, but instead by firmly established structures. This also determined the considerations of the

Continental Executive Board of the day. In hindsight, one of the later members of Continental's Executive Board described the situation in the 1950s and 1960s as follows: "Technical rubber goods were 90 percent consumer products, the tire world was diagonal, Michelin and Bridgestone were of no significance, Dunlop was a global corporation, and marketing was a means of redistribution. The Executive Board members had lost touch with reality, the term "controller" only called to mind associations with trams, and the range of raw materials and machines was of an unimaginable simplicity." In Hanover, strategic corporate planning had largely wilted into merely facilitating a continuation of the status quo. However, the heads of the corporation were able to point to abundant profits and high profitability as proof that the correct course had been taken. The policy of "no experiments" and defending the company's traditional market power paid off, and it seemed that the convenience of the low-competition, supply-driven tire market had been rewarded.

The members of Continental's Executive Board at the time felt well prepared for the future. They preached the vision of the new Continental also becoming a plastics manufacturer and player in the emerging plastics age, despite the fact that this market was already dominated by overpowering competitors from the chemical industry. And they lulled themselves into a false sense of security, believing that large R&D laboratories with the latest measuring equipment and high R&D investments would ensure that Continental did not miss out on new technologies or future tire developments. In particular, the close technological and scientific ties with the world's leading American tire industry flanked the company's resurgence. By 1961, there was once again talk of the "restored international standing of Continental." The R&D methods were highly modern and ahead of their time in some cases, such as the world's first electronically controlled self-driving car for tire testing in 1968.

But while the researchers at Continental were occupied with optimizing their existing products, their colleagues at Michelin were already working on an entirely new tire concept—which was actually not so new and whose principles Continental engineers had explored in the 1930s. However, these efforts were neither pursued nor later resumed. The company's anticipation skills were not focused on technology, but were limited in 1969 to extrapolating the estimated numbers of cars and trucks that would exist in 1985. Based on this, the future demand for tires was calculated. Together with the forecast average replacement coefficient of 1.4 tires per vehicle and year, the business prospects for the future looked good.

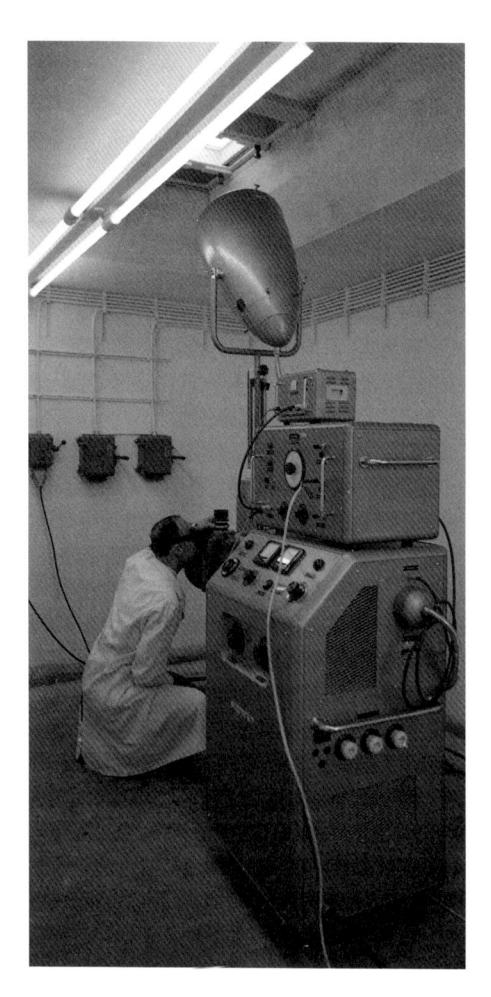

Fig. 139: Laboratories of the future: R&D facility in 1967 (underfloor laboratory with electron stroboscope) for measuring and recording tire grip and rolling behavior during road tests at the Contidrom, the company's testing facility.

On the occasion of its 100-year anniversary in October 1971, Continental surprised customers, employees and the public with a brochure that at first glance seemed to be a strange vision. It presented the "future of deflection," combined with a forecast of the development of traffic and mobility in the years to come. Deflection, it claimed, was rubber's key function that could constantly be improved. This meant deflection in the broadest sense of the term, including absorption of vibrations, impact and noise. In addition, it could act as a "flexible" seal. "Deflection is increasingly needed for all manner of uses, as energy, weight and noise play a growing role in technology. It is not about the rubber items, but instead about the function, a system. As a logical consequence, Continental is becoming a consulting supplier of optimal deflection. Increasingly, the company is not only supplying these deflection products, as 'hardware,' but also consultation and a wealth of services. Continental is not selling tires, but 'tire service life' as a complete system, which encompasses new tires, retreading and constant service as contractual obligations, a kind of 'software,' so to speak. The brochure's conclusion was that, in view of the prediction that traffic and transport would double and triple in the coming years, Continental would have a large role to play in the area of identifying and solving problems.

Fig. 140: Visions of the future on the occasion of the company's 100th anniversary in 1971.

The topic as such was not new: as early as December 1924, the *India Rubber Journal* had published a paper entitled "Der Reifen als ein Teil des Federungssystems" (The Tire as Part of the Suspension System). The engineers in Continental's technical secretariat had it translated from English and studied it in detail. However, in the context of the tire and rubber world of the early 1970s, the topic was revolutionary, as it pointed toward a future of integrated tire systems and "software." In other words, services that would supplement the business areas and activities of the company. Continental's marketing team also presented another anniversary brochure under the heading "Progress as Tradition. The Chances of the Future" and used it to paint a picture of a modern service corporation in the "dynamic style of the future." If it was not known that Continental was at this time already deeply embedded in the crisis of having slept through the radial ply tire revolution and had to fight for survival just a few years later, one could get the impression that an actual forward-looking development forecast and assessment of the future had occurred and had anticipated many of the basic ideas that were to catch on again only 20 years later.

But while Continental's Executive Board members presented themselves as true visionaries and experts on the future, they simultaneously clung to the same previously successful, established paths in operational business. During the company's long crisis from 1970/71 to 1981/82, there was space neither for visionaries nor for defenders of the status quo. Instead, the company needed rescuers capable of solving the problems that were now threatening the company on all fronts. In the era of Alfred Herrhausen and Carl H. Hahn, the company's visions frequently became intertwined with the industry-wide political calculations and plans of Deutsche Bank, which, as major shareholder, dreamed of a large German "rubber corporation" that would include Continental, Phoenix and other rubber companies such as Metzeler, and would be internationally competitive. When these plans failed, Herrhausen saw Continental's future first as a purely non-tire company that only made technical rubber products, then as a subsidiary of the (at the time) large American tire corporations Goodyear or Uniroyal, but these companies were already suffering from massive adjustment problems themselves. Continental became a pawn in the industrial power games and calculations of the major shareholders at the time, which, in addition to Deutsche Bank, included Bayer and Allianz. The future of the company was decided by others. It was to the great credit of Carl H. Hahn, Continental's chairman of the Executive Board at the time, that he restored the company's autonomy and, in spite of the survival struggle and the ongoing crisis, managed to finally develop a vision and implement it in contrast to the desperate back-and-forth planning conducted by Herrhausen. Hahn's vision of Continental was that of an international tire manufacturer formed by taking over and acquiring suitable companies—a vision that must have seemed completely utopian to his contemporaries. However, the vision soon became reality. It was Hahn who also introduced a five-year plan and forecasting instruments at Continental. For decades, the company had been operated and managed cautiously and had frequently fumbled in the dark. The perspective of Continental as an international tire manufacturer renewed the company's future viability and allowed management's stunted anticipation skills to blossom anew.

Visions of an Integrated Supplier and Technology Corporation and of "Intelligent Tires" (1980s to 2001)

In the subsequent years, the company continued on the strategic path toward internationalization. The takeover of the European division of Uniroyal was followed by the acquisition of Semperit and finally General Tire in 1987. But while on this path, several forks in the road that would have steered the company toward a completely different future were either missed or bypassed. In the mid-1980s, Firestone put its European tire activities up for sale; at a later date, there was an opportunity to completely take over Uniroyal-Goodrich, which Michelin then achieved. When General Tire was finally taken over, it turned out to be an expensive and slow restructuring project for Continental. However, as a tire company, Continental found itself at a dead end with restricted future prospects. It was the fourth-largest tire producer in the world, but significantly lagged behind Michelin, Goodyear and Bridgestone, making it too large to exit the sector but too small to successfully bid for a place on the podium. In its search for a solution, Continental's Executive Board once again increased R&D activities. A lot of money was invested in centralizing tire research in Hanover, thus strengthening basic research in particular. In the process, the technical and scientific potential of the existing four development centers of the company, in Hanover, Aachen, Traiskirchen and Akron, was bundled together. The company's sensational acquisition of the fastest computer in the world at the time opened up completely new methods of forecasting and simulation. "Durch Superhirn Cray bessere Reifen für die Zukunft" (Better Tires for the Future Thanks to Superbrain Cray) was the headline of Continental's employee magazine *conti intern* in June 1990. Additionally, the Contidrom tire testing center was expanded to more than double its previous size. The tire engineers and chemists in the development center dreamed of a Continental future in which "it would one day be possible to optimize numerous tire properties with tailor-made rubber types." This wish became reality not even 10 years later. However, the biggest coup was the development of the Conti Tire System (CTS), which the Continental Executive Board soon connected with soaring visions of a future revolution in tire technology, this time triggered by Continental. After the CTS was unable to establish itself on the market, however, the vision was quickly brought back down to earth.

The takeover attempt by Italian competitor Pirelli in 1990/91 then suddenly threatened all other plans and goals of the Executive Board, calling into question the future of Continental as a company. Once again, Continental was confronted with outside industrial policy and strategic planning that attempted to influence and steer its development. Management was convinced that Continental could master the future without Pirelli and succeeded in fending off the takeover, but the close call made everyone aware that the company did not have great future viability and resilience. In December 1991, the new chairman of the Executive Board, Hubertus von Grünberg, presented a 10-point plan that included urgent restructuring efforts, yet lacked visions with broader scope; the goal of entering strategic alliances was an exception, but even this could be considered to be a "poor man's policy" born out of necessity. During this phase, the people at Continental went through an emotional rollercoaster with regard to the company's future prospects and development options. In many cases, this up and down was actually triggered by management itself. But Continental's efforts to create and strengthen the company's sustainability took on a new quality with the strategic decision in 1994 to establish a new automotive division, as a third strategic pillar alongside the tire and technical product units and with the vision of "intelligent tires."

The company now entered into the field of chassis technology, maintaining its core competencies while also acquiring new know-how and beginning to distinguish itself as a system supplier. Numerous "system bridges" between tires and technical products were identified, not only in the traditional tire system (tire plus rim), but also in electronic chassis control, vehicle acoustics, tire pressure control and air spring systems for cars and trucks. The new pillar was not intended to replace the tire business with the sales of modules and components, but instead support and supplement the traditional core business of the corporation. It opened up new earnings potential in a sustainable field in which there was hardly any competition at the time. Back then, it was hard to estimate the growth potential of the new business area. However, it was clear that system technology would be capable of overcoming the strategic impasse and open up new technology and development paths. Not least, the system business was also an attempt to maintain or restore control over the technical content of the tire, which by now was already being largely dictated by the automotive industry. Tire manufacturers who could understood and master chassis technology themselves would be able to identify at an early stage where the development of tire technology would lead in the future. Additionally, Continental was the only large corporation that was also highly diversified in the TP sector, and the complementary expertise of ContiTech gave the company a specific competitive advantage with which it was almost impossible to catch up.

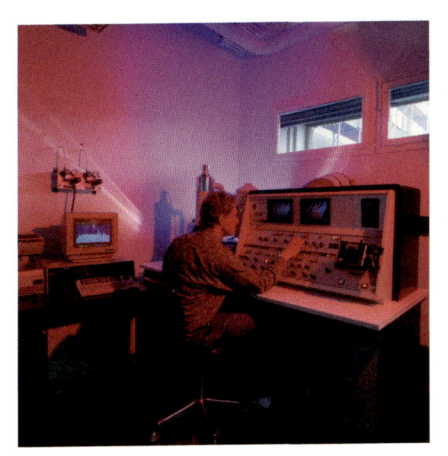

Fig. 141: Laboratories of the future: a view of the new technology center in Hanover in 1996, R&D with electron scanning microscope for tire analysis and computer simulations, as well as testing with a dummy in the sound lab.

On the occasion of its 125th anniversary in 1996, Continental presented itself as an integrated supplier and technology company, as a "global corporation" that placed high hopes on the "small but excellent and future-oriented vehicle systems division." In the tire sector, the objectives were mostly mid-term, but no less ambitious. The targets for the year 2000 included reducing rolling resistance by 30 percent and weight by 35 percent, further increasing mileage and the proportion of renewable raw materials, "and in the long term, perhaps in 25 years, to develop tires with the same lifetime as a car." The real fantasy for the future, however, was associated with the new Automotive Systems division. Here, attempts were made to develop visions for the company as a whole. "From the very beginning, our strategy with Continental Automotive Systems has been to leap as far as possible into the future of automotive technology, without ballast. Less encumbered than others, we can thus provide our customers in the worldwide automotive industry with the perspective of rapid technical progress, innovative products and maximum benefit at attractive prices," announced Hubertus von Grünberg at the Annual Shareholders' Meeting in June 1999.

The company's visions were speeding far ahead of reality. And they were becoming more abstract. The overriding maxim of the newly formulated vision now became "making individual mobility safer and more comfortable." The second maxim was to "strive to be the technology leader in all business areas."

Both of these principles were now implemented into the corporate culture as key components. The boundaries between vision, strategic goals and corporate guidelines for daily operations became blurred. And the perceptions of the future were now explicitly defined in close connection with future mobility. Keywords such as "total chassis management," "global chassis control" or simply the "accident-avoiding car of the future" or "30-meter car" were used to once again describe and consolidate strong, technology-driven visions of the future. This was coupled with a change in the company's self-image. The automotive supplier became a "safety supplier." "The ultimate state of development and, at the same time, the greatest challenge for the future is the intelligent cross-linking of all these active and passive safety systems, which currently function to a large extent independently," stated the 2001 annual report. The fact that these visions of the future were expressed at a time when an economic and financial market crisis was massively affecting the industry and a wave of restructuring and cost-cutting was also sweeping through the corporation made these goals all the more ambitious.

The Future Seems Plannable. Orientation Toward the "Mobility of the Future" (2002 to 2020)

During this phase, the future was debated at Continental more frequently than ever. The future of mobility seemed to be taking on clear contours, with technicians, engineers and management having a relatively transparent idea of what it would entail and society accepting this concept in large part. It involved dramatic technical transformations but was also shaped by political stipulations. The mobility of tomorrow was simultaneously understood to be evolutionary, a "development that is logical, consequential and non-reversible." The protagonists at Continental understood that a new era of mobility was approaching and that it was important to establish the company as an active co-creator of this future, not only by acquiring the necessary knowledge and expertise but also significantly contributing to its realization through innovation. "Technological progress will not only transform the cars of today, but the entire structure of our industry, driven by the development of connected systems," predicted Wolfgang Ziebert, the Executive Board member responsible for the automotive division at Continental, as early as December 2002. He attributed a pioneering role in this process to Continental.

But the strong fixation on and orientation toward the future had its price. The emerging problems in the automotive industry and the imminent economic downturn were detected too late. Moreover, the more concrete the future of mobility became, the more dramatically the visions shrunk, until they were merely strategic goals. The abstract perceptions of the future were broken down into five-year plans with specific objectives. Potential scenarios for the position of the tire sector in this near future were also discussed, for example in 2004. They ranged from selling the American tire business to Bridgestone, to Continental taking over Goodyear. On May 1, 2003, the company's systematic future planning and future management were given an organizational foundation through the creation of a multitudinous new department responsible for "corporate future development."

It is one of the paradoxes of industrial logic that, in this same time period, the R&D department with its workforce of now more than 5,200 and budget of almost 1 billion euros was subjected to massive rationalization measures. All the same, in view of the technological transformation, this department took on a new importance. The proportion of components manufactured in-house by automotive manufacturers, which had amounted to 37.5 percent as recently as 1980, had steadily declined to just over 20 percent—and the downward trend was continuing. The suppliers' share of the value chain was thus increasing, as was their influence on the relationship between suppliers and automotive companies. With the sheer number of technological paths and options that were opening up, in particular in power transmission technology, becoming a leading supplier for all technologies meant tying up a significant amount of resources. Whether there would be one or several drive systems remained—and still remains—completely unclear. In 2012, the Powertrain division created a "Future Map 2020" in which it outlined no less than eight scenarios and technical options to respond appropriately to the developments, opportunities and risks.

The reduction in components manufactured in-house by automobile manufacturers also posed new challenges for the company's internal R&D management. This led to new organizational and innovation processes, such as the creation of a "Cross Divisional Innovation Process for Products & Services" group in 2006. The companies that Continental purchased in this period also brought new technological know-how into the corporation, especially in the fields of telematics and intelligent mobility. However, the gap between the expected near future and the reality of the "new mobility" was growing increasingly bigger. To mark the 100th anniversary of Teves, a brochure was produced in Frankfurt and Hanover in which the future was also discussed in detail. "Continental is ideally positioned as a system supplier to develop solutions for partially automated driving applications and bring them into production by 2016," it said. "Highly automated driving should be possible from 2020, while fully automated driving, even at higher speeds and in more complex driving situations, will be ready for production from around 2025."

Fig. 142: Future visions in the marketing brochure for "100 Years of Teves" dated 2006.

What used to be a vision was now presented as a firm promise: "Telematics will broaden the horizon of automotive electronics," the brochure stated.

> Driving safety and intelligent traffic management have become decisive factors in global mobility. Continental Automotive Systems will bring new impetus to digital car-to-car communication. Connected systems actively and passively support the prevention of accidents, occupant protection and accident assistance. Dynamic and environmentally friendly drive concepts and highly sophisticated convenience functions transform driving into a relaxed, safe and enjoyable experience.

The visions were closely aligned with the clear "megatrends" in the automotive industry: safety and accident-free driving, the environment and zero-emission driving, information and fully connected driving, and cost-effectiveness and affordable mobility for everyone. "Your mobility. Your freedom. Our signature" summarized the corporate vision of 2011, supplemented with the slogan "The future starts earlier with Continental."

The products and applications developed under this slogan by the R&D departments and made ready for production soon included an impressive list of innovations. Examples included the world's first water-cooled turbocharger, the 48-volt Eco Drive module for reduced fuel consumption, the high-resolution

3D Flash Lidar sensor technology for monitoring vehicle surroundings in real time, highly efficient brake systems such as the MK C1, which combined brake actuation, brake booster and the ABS and ESC control systems in a compact, lightweight brake module, as well as an advanced driver assistance system with machine learning, which used radar sensors to help drivers in inner-city traffic assess the traffic situation and make turning maneuvers. Modern digital cameras replaced the old side mirrors made of glass, sensors provided distance monitoring and collision warning functions, and dedicated mobile telecommunication networks allowed vehicles to communicate with each other to prevent accidents and traffic jams. The development finally culminated in a completely new technology for future mobility introduced in 2019: Continental's in-car server CAS1, a high-performance computer on wheels that would act as the heart of digital and connected mobility. The innovative server solution reduced the 70 to 100 control devices in the car and significantly simplified the inner workings of the vehicle.

Fig. 143: Motivational poster with the corporate vision from 2011.

The company's R&D activities had also long been expanded to local development centers, for example to the R&D center in Singapore, which was enlarged in 2014, or to Wuhu, China. At the same time, the High Performance Technology Center at the Korbach plant was launched and a tire development center was opened in Púchov, Slovakia. In Regensburg, a new high-tech laboratory for fuel research was set up, and a global Continental research network for artificial intelligence was established and expanded in cooperation with several universities. 2017 also saw the creation of a new research center for automated driving, connectivity and mobility services in Silicon Valley, where 300 engineers and software developers were recruited to work on the future of mobility. This also included a "future laboratory" for electric mobility, where an innovative, inductive charging technology was developed. At the same time, Continental researchers worked on the transformation of the vehicle into a "connected car" with its very own ecosystem. With the aid of the latest technology, such as the quantum computer IBM Q System One, the R&D laboratories simulated and performed complex calculation models for automated driving and chemical processes. The investments in R&D by now already totaled more than 3.3 billion euros. From 2016, a corporate technology officer (CTO) was put in charge of coordinating the company's extensive research and development activities. The patent statistics clearly showed where the new innovation focus lay: Continental registered a total of 4,172 patents worldwide in 2014, with 3,581 coming from the Automotive Group and 591 from the Rubber Group.

In the meantime, numerous other experts in various departments, and in particular the roughly 450 top-level executives at Continental, were exploring the topic of how the world would look in 10 to 20 years. They formulated their expectations for the future in the company's "Vision 2030."

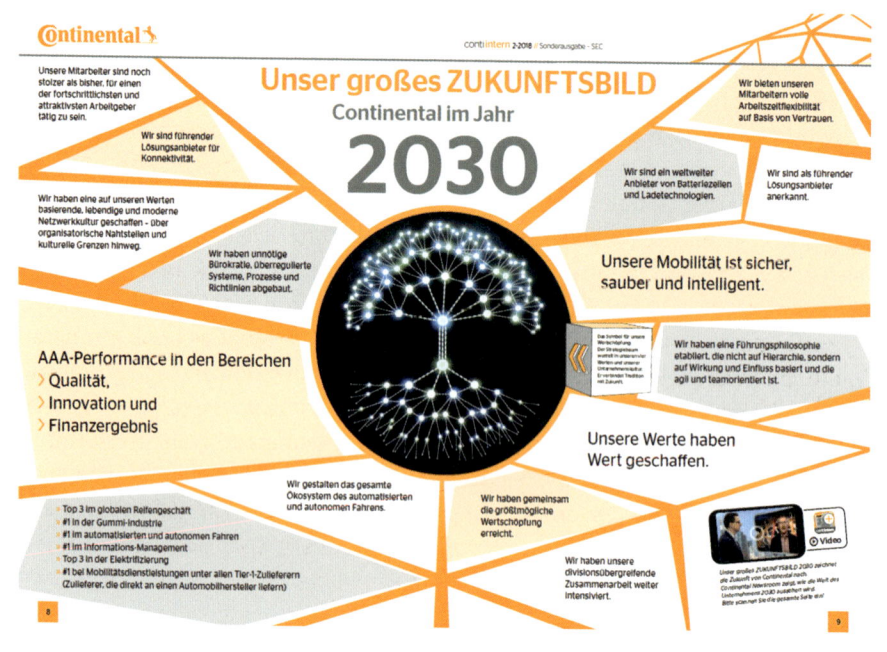

Fig. 144: Continental 2030 future scenario from the staff magazine *conti intern* in 2018.

Cloud-based mobility services and servitization, i.e. supplementing a physical product with software, sensors and services, played a significant role, as did the de facto reinvention of the car as part of the Internet. Whether and to what extent these future mobility scenarios are compatible with actual mobility behavior and habits or deviate significantly from them is examined by experts worldwide in the annual "Continental Mobility Study," which has been conducted since 2009. They discover both skepticism and open-mindedness toward automated driving and point out significant national and regional differences, for example in terms of the willingness to use driverless taxis. The study also makes clear that the new technologies and technical systems need to be explained. Just as the pneumatic tire was once a new technology that had to be explained to users in order to gain acceptance, so today an explanation of the fundamental transformation process of mobility is needed.

In 2017, Elmar Degenhart, then chairman of the Executive Board, summarized his view of future mobility as follows: "Future mobility will be safe, clean, intelligent, and more efficient and ecological than it is today, therefore giving future generations more—not fewer—opportunities to realize their own plans and goals. The boundaries between transport systems will become blurred as a result of their full connectivity, as well as those between the office, living room and car. Mobility is becoming a living space." However, on this journey into the new era of mobility, Continental also experienced ambivalence and asynchronicity with regard to the views of the future and the speed of actual technical, political and social developments. Many visions took longer than expected to reach technical maturity or were slow to gain a foothold in the market. Other developments proceeded much faster. On top of all this, a massive production and sales crisis has been looming over global markets since 2018. In response, Continental launched a transformation program in 2019 with the aim of accelerating technology migration in the field of electric mobility, as well as in digitalization and software-supported mobility. Those responsible in Hanover did not hide the fact that such a transformation not only offered opportunities, but also posed risks. Irrespective of the political guidelines and objectives, the market share of electric and hybrid cars in Germany was still below 10 percent—a negligible amount. Solid-state batteries would not be ready for production before 2030, so that vehicles with the seemingly archaic combustion technology would likely continue to shape the mobility of the future for many years to come. In the case of automated and autonomous driving, too, not only Continental but the entire industry had underestimated its complexity. "We must therefore focus on marketable stages, such as partially automated driving, in spite of the risk that companies from Silicon Valley might succeed in establishing platforms for autonomous driving that the industry will not be able to easily bypass," said Degenhart in an interview. Be that as it may, Continental sees itself positioned for its 150th anniversary in such a way that it will be one of the winners of the great mobility transformation.

Operating System Provider of Software-supported Mobility: Continental in 2046

The remarks that follow have been derived from knowledge about the past and are more speculation than vision; they are an attempt to paint a picture of Continental in the time after the "great mobility transformation." There is no doubt that when the company celebrates its 175th anniversary in 2046, it will once again be a "new Continental." It will have successfully mastered the challenges of the major transformation of the 2020s, with the transition to electric mobility, digitalization, the strict environmental regulations, and the reinvention of the car as a software system and part of the Internet and connected mobility. During a phase of significantly accelerated adaptation, where developments occurred faster than the company could foresee and it lacked the time to manage the profound transformation at its own pace, Continental will have managed to withstand the resulting waves of consolidation unscathed. With the help of its more than 20,000 software developers and IT specialists, acquisitions of innovative start-up companies and cooperative ventures with international IT corporations, it will have rapidly built up and expanded its extensive expertise in the fields of electronics, software and sensor technology, ultimately developing a "platform technology" of software-supported mobility that goes far beyond a mere vehicle computer. Continental will have become a pioneer of the European "software-defined vehicle architecture," an independent software platform for the smart car developed as a response and direct competitor to the corresponding American and Chinese systems, thus becoming one of the world's three leading players in autonomous mobility. Whereas in 2030 the old automotive business will have accounted for three-quarters of revenue, digitization alone will have brought in more than 80% of revenue by 2046. After successfully being a "fast follower" for decades—in the tire business of the 1890s, with Michelin as its main competitor, then almost a hundred years later, in the 1990s, with the automotive business and Bosch—the competition between Continental and these equally technology-driven companies will have created a productive rivalry that puts each other's innovation competence to the test, as opposed to ruinous price wars and market displacement. With its newly developed operating system for software-supported mobility, which will have become the industry standard, it will have set itself apart from its competitors as a pioneer in the industry and built up a set of unique selling points in the global supplier market—just as it did with its tire competitors in the 1990s.

The digital transformation will have also swept through Continental itself. Not only will it have changed the company's business areas and models, its customer structure and prevalent technologies, but also its internal decision-making processes, which will include AI-supported risk and opportunity assessments, as well as automated and computer-optimized controlling and cash management. Software-supported production will have made manufacturing more precise and efficient, while the networking of global activities in real time will have turned the company into a highly flexible and forward-looking organization that gives its employees the freedom they need to develop their skills and creativity. Instead of the separate divisions and departments that hark back to the traditional structures of the technical areas, the company will have reorganized itself into ad-hoc work groups focused on flexible problem-solving, taking interdisciplinary cooperation between hierarchies to an entirely new level. If software is considered as the new raw material of future mobility, with numerous open and unknown business areas, Continental will have actually returned to its roots; to Siegmund Seligmann's strategy of mastering the countless possible technical applications of rubber, the material of the future of his time. In other words, Continental will have come full circle.

The speculative development described above follows the technological and strategic paths that Continental has already embarked upon. But history distrusts extrapolations and teleologies derived from the present. It is aware of the non-intended consequences of change and that the future is open. Managers also know that no strategic path, no matter how well-defined, remains correct for eternity, because there is always the risk of markets and technologies evolving. If the situation of Continental is compared in the context of the 25 years before or after an anniversary of its founding, i.e. 1896 with 1921 and 1996 with 2021, there are completely different corporate identities, internal as well as external, that lie off the technological and strategic paths that were considered promising at the time. Remarkably, there were never any taboos of any kind at Continental against imagining the future and conquering it, whether oriented to its business model, organizational transformations, corporate policy measures or strategic course, as long as the survival, growth, prosperity and autonomy of the company was safeguarded. Everything has been questioned at one time or another and in different forms: the tire sector, the ContiTech business, maintaining traditional locations, the raw materials base, the geographical alignment, as well as some of its corporate leaders. Historical experience also shows that the reality of the future overtakes the imagination of the present (Rödel), and this certainly holds true with regard to Continental. The history of technical developments and visions is also a history of incorrect prognoses and wrong assessments. Visions are generally ambivalent. They can motivate and mobilize, but can also result in fantasies that are rooted in ideology or lose touch with reality. Companies are therefore faced with the question of which mix of fear and hope provides the best preparation for the future (Osterhammel). "From a historical perspective, skepticism is therefore the appropriate form of dealing with seemingly unambiguous contemporary diagnosis and self-assured prognosis." The thoughts and remarks below are plausible from a historical viewpoint, yet of course remain speculative.

First, the mobility of the future will be different than expected or desired. Even now, the state is intervening as never before in the future shape of mobility with legal regulations, drastic, ideologically motivated exhaust emission standards and barely achievable emission ceilings, as well as one-sided subsidies for politically desirable drive concepts. Mobility has become a politicized "living space" characterized by normative concepts of morality. The changes and consequences can be seen simply by comparing Continental's visions of the future of mobility from 2002/03 with those of 2020. And more regulations can be expected in the foreseeable future, from speed limits on the German autobahns and highways to limited, digitally monitored mobility quotas for individual car drivers, as well as other restrictions, for example specified routes for environmental protection reasons, transit bans, special mobility fees and regulated long-distance travel. The supplier and automotive industry is caught in a bind of politically stipulated climate goals, (voluntary) sustainability commitments, eco-moral dictates and a state regulatory regime. Restrictions and governmental or bureaucratic regulations on the mobility of people can also be related to demographic development, such as the rapidly growing number of older car drivers and the growing population density that is taxing the transport infrastructure in cities and popular tourist destinations beyond its capacity. The mobility of the future is thus in the process of changing from an autonomous living space and an expression of individual freedom to a government-regulated commodity. All of this is likely to have serious repercussions for the business model of mobility suppliers and mobility service providers such as Continental—not least with regard to new vehicle concepts, which will also require more "basic" tire technologies—and will increase the industry's vulnerability to decision-making errors.

Second, the supplier sector, like the automotive industry itself, will be subject to erratic changes, especially in Germany. The fundamental transformation of the car as a technical system is sure to affect the German automotive industry, which dominated the sector for more than a century with hardware-related engineering excellence based on the superior inventions of Otto and Diesel. In 10 to 15 years at the latest, the software-dominated electric drives and automotive concepts developed in the USA and China will have conquered the market, and there is no guarantee that the companies we know today will stay independent. A look at the history of Continental shows that OEM companies and automotive manufacturers as customers have come and gone. Initially, Adler-Werke was the largest tire customer. Later, in the 1920s to 1950s, it was Opel, and thereafter the focus was on VW and other carmakers. Ultimately, Continental has always understood that it is important not to be too dependent on a single large automotive company. This principle will also be of value in the future.

Another factor is technical convergence, which is already turning suppliers into the direct competitors of automotive companies in many areas. Mergers and acquisitions between OEMs and suppliers as part of a strategy of backward and forward integration can no longer be ruled out. In the long history of the automotive industry, there have been only two examples of such a combination which either failed or remained insignificant: Ford, which tried to set up its own tire factory, and Michelin, which once held a majority share in Citroen. Mergers, spin-offs and acquisitions in the German and international supplier industry cannot be ruled out. Even the spin-off of drive specialist Vitesco Technologies from Continental in 2021 will be enough to shift the order of the 10 largest automotive suppliers, with Bosch, Continental and ZF Friedrichshafen.

On the tire company level, permanent changes can also not be excluded. At the turn of the millennium, the largest corporations, Michelin, Bridgestone and Goodyear, still controlled around two-thirds of the global market. Today, it is less than half. The reason for this is the penetration of countless Chinese tire manufacturers, which are entering the market primarily with low-cost offers but increasingly also in the high-performance segment of the tire business. For decades, Continental and other large tire companies could be certain that the high barriers to market entry would keep away new competitors and that they could divide the saturated yet expandable tire market between themselves. This has now suddenly changed. On route to its 175th anniversary, Continental might have to fend off a third hostile takeover attempt during the 2030s, this time by financially powerful Chinese tire companies. The fact that Pirelli and Daimler already have financially powerful Chinese major shareholders with a clear industrial policy shows that this is not baseless speculation. In addition, telecommunication, software and other IT companies of the data economy are increasingly entering this market, which in turn are now looking for possible alliances and acquisition targets in the German and international supplier industry in order to quickly obtain the necessary know-how. Apple's planned cooperation, at least temporarily, with the South Korean automobile company Hyundai or the e-vehicle manufacturer Tesla from the USA are only the first examples. The billion-dollar business of future mobility has many new players and, above all, completely new rules of the game compared to the past. For Continental as a supplier, the question is not only: "What are the technologies of tomorrow?" but also "Who are the winners of tomorrow in my business?"

Third, between now and 2046, there will be further economic and financial market crises, and the structure of Continental's major shareholders is not set in stone. One does not have to be clairvoyant to conclude that the ongoing upheavals in global trade, the precarious globalization, the transformation of the financial industry and the inherent instability of global capital market structures will lead to at least one world economic and financial crisis combined with a stock market crash in the next 25 years. Between such crises, however, there will also be long periods of prosperity and global economic growth and expansion. As in the past, Continental is an attractive potential target for financially powerful hedge funds and private equity companies that might succeed in purchasing Continental for an appropriately high price, to then divide the company into parts and sell them off.

Regardless of what the coming years bring, development at Continental has also been shaped by making use of the opportunities offered by the unforeseen. The experience that the company as a social system has collectively acquired during the handling of problems in the past has been condensed into approaches and behaviors in the present that determine its perceptions of and preferences for possible ways of mastering future challenges. In a world in which more and more assistance systems are taking the thinking and foresight out of drivers' hands, it is all the more important for a company to maintain and cultivate an independent ability to anticipate. Superior and successful companies are also characterized by the fact that they think about the future differently than the competition.

Regardless of what the "new Continental" looks like in 2046, it will be an organization that, together with all of its employees, will be self-confident in its resilience and adaptability. This confidence will stem from the experience of having successfully mastered stormy technological developments and transformations, existential crises, changes to its corporate form, as well as political and social challenges. Continental has not only defended its autonomy, but has undergone a dynamic development in terms of growth and innovation. In the world of mobility, it continues to play a decisive role, and throughout all of this, the company has remained acutely aware of its history. "Our confidence in the future is based on our successful past," said Elmar Degenhart, former chairman of the Executive Board, in 2010. This statement will continue to hold true in 2046.

Annex

Annex 1 Member of the Executive Board

	deputy	ordinary	resigned	
Nelles, Philip		01.06.2021		
Wolf, Andreas		03.06.2020		
Kötz, Christian		01.04.2019		
Duensing, Hans-Jürgen		01.05.2015	31.05.2021	
Reinhart, Dr. Ariane		01.10.2014		
Jourdan, Frank		25.09.2013		
Strathmann, Elke		02.01.2012	25.04.2014	
Schäfer, Wolfgang		01.01.2010		
Avila, José A.		01.01.2010	30.09.2018	
Setzer, Nikolai		12.08.2009		Chairman since 01.12.2020
Matschi, Helmut		12.08.2009		
Cramer, Dr. Ralf		12.08.2009	11.08.2017	
Degenhart, Dr. Elmar		12.08.2009	30.11.2020	Chairman since 12.08.2009
Wente, Heinz-Gerhard		03.05.2007	30.04.2015	
Kozyra, William L.		22.02.2006	01.06.2008	
Lerch, Gerhard		30.09.2005	29.09.2008	
Neumann, Karl-Thomas		01.10.2004	12.08.2009	Chairman since 31.08.2008
De Louw, Martien		01.02.2003	12.05.2005	
Sattelberger, Thomas		01.07.2003	02.05.2007	
Hippe, Dr. Alan		01.06.2002	28.02.2009	
Ziebart, Wolfgang		01.10.2000	31.08.2008	
Nikolin, Dr. Hans-Joachim		01.06.1999	31.07.2011	

(continued)

	deputy	ordinary	resigned	
Wennemer, Manfred		01.05.1998	31.08.2008	Chairman since 11.09.2001
Kessel, Dr. Stephan		14.04.1997	11.09.2001	Chairman since 12.04.1999
Friedland, Klaus	01.04.1995	14.04.1997	31.12.2002	
Beller, Hans A.		13.12.1993	12.12.2000	
Ockene, Alan L.		03.05.1991	31.12.1994	
Grünberg, Hubertus von		20.07.1991	01.06.1999	Chairman since 20.07.1991
Fortmann, Heimo	01.01.1990	01.01.1991	12.08.1992	
Röker, Klaus-D.	03.05.1991	01.01.1992	14.04.1997	
Knaup, Ingolf	02.05.1988	01.01.1989	29.02.1992	
Winterstein, Wilhelm P.		01.11.1987	08.06.1994	Vice chairman since 03.05.1991
Sieber, Günter H.		01.11.1987	03.05.1993	
Howaldt, Jens P.	01.01.1982	08.06.1994	07.06.1999	
Frangenberg, Bernd	01.01.1982	01.01.1998	31.03.2002	01.01.1993 til 31.12.1997 President Continental General Tire Inc.
Borgmann, Wilhelm	01.01.1982	01.01.1985	03.05.1991	Vice chairman since 01.01.1987
Werner, Helmut		01.08.1979	31.10.1987	Chairman since 01.01.1982
Kauth, Hans		01.04.1980	31.03.1995	
Haverbeck, Peter	01.05.1978	01.01.1979	30.04.1998	
Dahlström, Norbert		01.04.1976	14.06.1978	
Schäfer, Wilhelm		01.01.1975	02.05.1996	
Wenderoth, Dr. Hans Georg		01.06.1974	31.05.1981	

(continued)

	deputy	ordinary	resigned	
Peter, Dr. Julius		01.06.1974	31.05.1986	
Urban, Horst W.		01.04.1974	09.05.1991	Chairman since 01.11.1987
Hahn, Carl H.		01.04.1973	31.12.1981	Chairman since 01.04.1973
Klein, Werner	01.01.1972	01.04.1973	31.12.1978	
Lohauß, Dr. Gerhard	16.10.1970	02.07.1971	30.09.1980	
Werner, Heinz		28.06.1967	31.05.1974	
Stark, Hans	16.05.1963	01.01.1965	31.12.1973	
Pauck, Hans Christian	16.05.1963	01.01.1965	02.06.1976	
Niemeyer, Adolf D.	01.01.1963	16.05.1963	16.07.1975	Vice chairman since 01.04.1975
Müller, Dr. Oskar	16.05.1961	16.05.1963	02.07.1971	
Beckadolph, Richard	16.05.1961	16.05.1963	28.06.1967	
Braudorn, Karl. H.	28.05.1958	16.05.1963	30.06.1968	
Göbel, Dr. Georg	01.05.1952	12.03.1954	02.07.1971	Speaker of the Board since 01.01.1964
Garbe, Wilhelm	15.02.1951	01.05.1952	31.12.1963	
Jahn, Willy		15.02.1951	31.12.1963	
Hoppmann, Dr. Wilhelm		15.02.1951	31.12.1962	
Loges, Adolf	01.01.1946	01.10.1946	30.06.1963	
Gruppe, Wilhelm	01.09.1945	01.10.1946	31.03.1960	
Odenwald, Dr. Hans	01.10.1942		21.08.1945	
Weber, Dr. Georg	08.11.1938	01.10.1942	21.08.1945	
Fellinger, Ernst	08.11.1938	01.10.1942	20.01.1951	Chairman since 21.08.1945; General Director since 14.12.1949

(continued)

	deputy	ordinary	resigned	
Schmelz, Gustav	07.04.1936	08.03.1938	21.08.1945	
Franz, Hermann	07.04.1936	08.03.1938	21.08.1945	
Könecke, Fritz		31.05.1934	21.08.1945	Chairman since 15.01.1938; Chief executive since 01.12.1942
Schlosshauer, Waldemar		31.05.1934	08.02.1935	
Fey, F. Jakob	10.06.1933		30.06.1936	
Stockhardt, Dr. Paul		17.09.1929	15.01.1938	
Schlosshauer, Waldemar	26.06.1926	18.01.1928	17.09.1929	
Henke, Fritz	26.06.1926	18.01.1928	17.09.1929	
Haupt, Rudolf	26.06.1926		31.12.1927	
Gehrke, Karl	26.06.1926	18.01.1928	15.01.1938	
Blumenberg, Julius	26.06.1926		20.11.1928	
Assbroicher, Heinz	26.06.1926	18.01.1928	21.08.1945	
Volker, Karl	19.04.1921		31.07.1921	
Seligmann, Dr. Edgar	19.04.1921	01.01.1926	21.03.1929	
Oehler, Oswald Erdmann	19.04.1921		08.05.1927	
Köster, August	19.04.1921		31.12.1927	
Tischbein, Willy		01.01.1907	31.12.1934	General Director since 01.01.1926
Gerlach, Dr. Albert		01.07.1905	09.12.1918	
Seligmann, Siegmund		17.07.1879	12.10.1925	
Prinzhorn, Adolf		01.07.1876	31.12.1908	
Abrahamson, S.		1876	1876	
Marquardt, Gustav	30.10.1874	02.03.1875	04.02.1876	
Köhsel, Konrad		08.10.1871	11.10.1874	
Frank, Jacob		08.10.1871	17.04.1879	

Annex 2 Number of Continental Employees

Year	Total	White collar	Blue collar	Year	Total	White collar	Blue collar
2020	236.386			1982	27.631		
2019	241.458			1981	28.640		
2018	243.226			1980	30.727		
2017	235.473			1979	31.340		
2016	220.137			1978	17.928		
2015	207.889			1977	18.173	4.660	13.467
2014	189.168			1976	18.354	4.799	13.875
2013	177.762			1975	18.878	4.903	14.883
2012	169.639			1974	21.528	5.178	16.350
2011	163.788			1973	23.400	5.630	17.770
2010	148.228			1972	24.330	6.034	18.296
2009	134.434			1971	26.467	6.448	20.021
2008	139.155			1970	28.100	6.617	21.227
2007	151.654			1969	27.500	6.463	21.534
2006	85.224			1968	25.700	6.106	20.398
2005	79.849			1967	24.900	5.896	18.918
2004	80.586			1966	26.835	6.050	19.910
2003	68.829			1965	27.562	6.105	21.342
2002	64.379			1964	26.477	5.911	21.113
2001	65.293			1963	25.725	5.612	20.113
2000	63.832			1962	25.488	5.468	20.020
1999	62.155			1961	24.179	5.233	18.946
1998	62.357			1960	24.281	5.107	19.174
1997	44.797			1959	23.551	4.888	18.663
1996	44.767			1958	21.215	4.623	16.592
1995	47.918			1957	20.042	4.457	15.585
1994	48.583			1956	18.325	4.273	14.052
1993	50.974			1955	18.902	4.148	14.754
1992	50.581			1954	17.116	3.934	13.187
1991	49.877			1953	15.260	3.749	11.511
1990	51.064			1952	13.886	3.466	10.420
1989	47.495			1951	12.749	3.261	12.749
1988	45.907			1950	13.662	3.129	10.533
1987	42.263			1949	11.891	2.817	9.074
1986	32.012			1948	11.332	2.313	9.019
1985	31.673			1947	9.538	2.005	7.533
1984	26.401			1946	8.505	1.834	6.671
1983	26.688			1945	6.733	1.537	5.196

(continued)

Year	Total	White collar	Blue collar	Year	Total	White collar	Blue collar
1944*	13.969	2.787	11.182	1919			3.122
1943*	16.176	3.225	12.951	1918	ca. 8000	5.062	2.938
1942**	15.275	3.361	11.914	1917			3.125
1941***	14.871	3.554	11.317	1916			2.612
1940	14.835	3.437	11.398	1915			3.344
1939	13.156	3.444	9.712	1914			7.240
1938	16.476	3.676	12.800	1913	11.590	3.909	7.681
1937	15.254	3.422	11.832	1912	9.795		
1936	13.063	3.394	9.669	1911	9.789		
1935	12.509	3.341	9.168	1910	7.337		
1934	11.992	3.279	8.713	1909	6.850	2.137	4.713
1933	11.006	3.145	7.861	1908	6.144		
1932	10.602	3.125	7.477	1907	5.185		
1931	ca. 11.000			1906	5.556	930	4.626
1930	12.700	4.620	8.100	1905	4.516	693	3.823
1929	16.765	4.765	12.000	1904	3.294	967	2.327
1928	14.897	3.720	11.177	1903	2.741		
1927	14.289	3.550	10.739	1900			1.615
1926	13.306	3.320	9.986	1899	1.537	168	1.369
1925				1894			654
1924	14.483	2.800	11.683	1893			600
1923	11.896	2.350	9.546	1889			498
1922	14.125	2.444	11.681	1884			450
1921			10.000	1879			261
1920			6.749	1874			246

* incl. prisoners of war, incl. Posen and Krainburg
** incl. Posen and Krainburg
*** incl. Posen

Annex 3 Sales Development

Year	Sales (in m.)	Year	Sales (in m.)	Year	Sales (in m.)
2020	37.722,30	1981	3.229,00	1942	241
2019	44.478,40	1980	3.159,70	1941	223
2018	44.404,40	1979*	2.623,40	1940	206
2017	44.009,50	1978	1.555,40	1939	242
2016	40.549,50	1977	1.518,90	1938	262
2015	39.232,00	1976	1.439,00	1937	209
2014	34.505,70	1975	1.369,00	1936	132
2013	33.331,00	1974	1.453,20	1935	117
2012	32.736,20	1973	1.264,00	1934	98
2011	30.504,90	1972	1.174,20	1933	76.4
2010	26.046,90	1971	1.301,70	1932	72.5
2009	20.095,70	1970	1.311,70	1931	96.8 **RM**
2008	24.238,70	1969	1.256,80	1930	145.4 **M**
2007	16.619,40	1968	1.103,80	1929	183.8
2006	14.887,00	1967	1.028	1928	115.5
2005	13.837,20	1966	1.102	1927	109
2004	12.597,40	1965	1.100	1926	98.055
2003	11.534,40	1964	1.045	1925	139.337
2002	11.408,30	1963	976	1924	77.864
2001	11.233,30	1962	941	1923	2052.0
2000	10.115,00	1961	890	1922	1230.0
1999	9.132,20	1960	884	1921	127.7
1998	13.188,60	1959	793	1920	75.6
1997	11.186,10	1958	689	1919	13.5
1996	5.333,10	1957	636	1918	44.1
1995	5.242,00	1956	630	1917	40.0
1994	5.050,00	1955	605	1916	33.59
1993	4.790,30	1954	496	1915	56.3
1992	4.954,30	1953	419	1914	117.99
1991	4.794,30	1952	439	1913	119.33
1990	4.372,1 **EUR**	1951	439	1912	104.76
1989	8.381,9 **DM**	1950	309	1911	93.7
1988	7.905,80	1949	243	1910	81.77
1987	5.097,60	1948	211 **DM**	1909	62.6
1986	4.968,60	1947	45 **RM**	1908	49.99
1985	5.003,30	1946	28	1907	55.5
1984	3.534,00	1945	36.2	1906	48.3
1983	3.387,20	1944	231	1905	35.3
1982	3.248,80	1943	220	1904	23.4

(continued)

Year	Sales (in m.)	Year	Sales (in m.)	Year	Sales (in m.)
1903	21.3	1894	5.88	1885	3.12
1902	18.6	1893	4.66	1884	3.26
1901	16.8	1892	3.80	1883	3.00
1900	15.5	1891	3.65	1882	2.76
1899	14.5	1890	3.60	1881	2.51
1898	12.3	1889	3.45	1880	2.16
1897	10.4	1888	3.30	1879	1.75
1896	8.20	1887	3.09	1878	1.42
1895	7.37	1886	3.08	1877	1.28
				1876	1.37 M

Numbers 1876 to 1923 in D-Mark, 1924 to 1947 in Reichsmark, 1948 to 1989 in D-Mark and since 1990 in Euro. Until 1978, numbers refer to the Continental AG, since 1979 numbers refer to the corporation.

Annex 4a Members of the Supervisory Board (Shareholder Representatives)

Name	Period		
Knauf, Isabel Corinna	26.04.2019		
Khatu, Satish	26.04.2019		
Nonnenmacher, Prof. Rolf	01.10.2014		
Neuß, Sabine	25.04.2014		
Gutzmer, Prof. Peter	04.12.2013	26.04.2019	
Reitzle, Prof. Wolfgang	28.09.2009		Chairman since 19.11.2009
Wolf, Prof. Siegfried	06.12.2010		
Rosenfeld, Klaus	23.04.2009		
Mangold, Prof. Klaus	23.04.2009	26.04.2019	
Dunkel, Dr. Gunther	23.04.2009		
Schaeffler-Thumann, Maria-Elisabeth	05.02.2009		
Schaeffler, Georg F. W.	05.02.2009		
Koerfer, Rolf	05.02.2009	29.11.2010	Chairman since 27.03.2009
Geißinger, Dr. Jürgen	05.02.2009	04.10.2013	
Streiff, Christian	14.10.2005	03.02.2009	
Stockmar, Jürgen	14.05.2004	25.01.2009	
Oosterveld, Jan P.	22.01.2003	26.01.2009	
Flecken, Walter	30.06.2002	20.01.2003	
Wingefeld, Jürgen	01.06.1999	06.10.1999	
Steingraber, Fred G.	01.06.1999	26.01.2009	
Frenzel, Michael	01.06.1999	15.09.2009	
Grünberg, Dr. Hubertus von	01.06.1999	06.03.2009	Chairman since 01.06.1999
Ehrnrooth, Casimir	07.06.1995	01.06.1999	
Garnier, Hans-Detlef von	04.02.1995	07.06.1995	
Voss, Bernd W.	21.01.1994	30.09.2014	
Bodin, Manfred	02.07.1993	23.04.2009	
Breipohl, Diethart	03.07.1992	23.04.2009	
Vita, Giuseppe	10.07.1991	30.06.2002	
Ullsperger, Dieter	10.07.1991	20.01.1994	
Garnier, Hans-Detlef von	23.07.1990	10.07.1991	
Weiss, Ulrich	23.01.1990	01.06.1999	Chairman since 23.01.1990
Henkel, Hans-Olaf	05.07.1989	25.04.2014	
Breitschwerdt, Werner	05.07.1989	14.05.2004	
Angermüller, Hans H.	05.07.1989	01.06.1999	
Schiefer, Friedrich	06.07.1984	03.07.1992	

(continued)

	Period		
Saßmannshausen, Günther	06.07.1984	01.06.1999	
Seelig, Wolfgang	03.07.1981	05.07.1989	
Piltz, Klaus	07.09.1979	10.07.1991	
Pieper, Ernst	07.09.1979	04.02.1995	
Helms, Wilhelm	07.09.1979	02.07.1993	
Fuhrmann, Ernst	07.09.1979	06.07.1984	
Finck von Finckenstein, Karl-Wilhelm Graf	07.09.1979	03.07.1981	
Englebert, Albert	07.09.1979	05.07.1989	
Emcke, Manfred	14.06.1978	23.07.1990	
Merkle, Otto	26.07.1972	14.06.1978	
Meyerheim, Wilhelm	16.11.1971	06.07.1984	
Herrhausen, Dr. Alfred	27.10.1970	30.11.1989	Chairman since 19.11.1970
Janberg, Dr. Hans	30.06.1970	19.09.1970	Chairman since 30.06.1970
Groth, Rudolf	30.06.1970	07.09.1979	
Merkle, Dr. Hans L.	27.06.1966	05.07.1989	Vice chairman 23.10.1969 bis 7.9.1979
Groben, Wilhelm	27.06.1966	26.07.1972	
Timm, Bernhard	19.07.1965	07.09.1979	
Forberg, Prof. Kurt	21.06.1956	30.06.1970	
Klasen, Dr. Karl	10.07.1953	30.06.1970	Chairman since 23.10.1969
Leimer, Margrit	14.08.1950	10.07.1953	
Kessler, Dr. Joachim	13.01.1950	02.11.1951	
Brunswig, Dr. Peter	13.01.1950	22.01.1953	
Uebel, Joseph C.	27.10.1948	14.08.1964	
Nölting, Dr. Ernst	08.05.1946	10.07.1953	
Duerkop, Hellmuth	08.05.1946	10.07.1953	
Pfad, Dr. Bernhard	01.10.1945	10.07.1953	
Menge, Dr. Arthur	01.10.1945	21.06.1956	
von Opel, Dr. Georg	30.09.1939	14.08.1971	Chairman 08.05.1946-12.10.1969
von Opel, Dr. Wilhelm	30.03.1939	08.05.1946	
Lüer, Prof. Carl	30.03.1939	09.08.1945	
Trutz, Karl	19.04.1937	31.10.1950	
Allmers, Dr. Robert	19.04.1937	08.05.1946	
Rösler, Oswald	29.03.1935	08.05.1946	Chairman 29.03.1935-07.04.1936
Uebel, Joseph C.	10.05.1933	08.05.1946	Chairman 07.04.1936-08.05.1946

(continued)

	Period		
Opel, Dr. Fritz	02.05.1932	30.08.1938	
Bahlsen, Hans	02.05.1932	19.04.1937	
Boner, Dr. Franz A.	22.05.1931	29.03.1935	
Seligmann, Dr. Edgar	30.04.1929	10.05.1933	
Schultze, Moritz	30.04.1929	19.04.1937	
Peter, Heinrich	30.04.1929	02.05.1932	
Hirsch, Otto	30.04.1929	02.05.1932	
Bonn, Dr. Paul	30.04.1929	31.12.1930	
Sachs, Dr. Ernst	27.04.1926	02.07.1932	
Oppler, Dr. Sigmund	27.04.1926	02.05.1932	
Work, Bertram G.	12.04.1923	30.08.1927	
Goldschmidt, Dr. Jacob	12.04.1922	10.05.1933	
Caspar, Dr. Julius B.	21.03.1919	27.06.1938	Chairman 27.04.1926–29.03.1935
Coppel, Dr. Alexander	25.03.1915	10.05.1933	
Magnus, Ernst	23.03.1914	10.05.1933	
Lemmermann, Ludwig	23.03.1914	12.11.1925	
Hecht, Hermann	23.09.1909	03.02.1929	
Prinzhorn, Adolf	25.03.1909	28.03.1913	
Tramm, Heinrich	03.04.1903	13.03.1932	Vice chairman since 26.05.1918
Hecht, Ferdinand	10.04.1902	04.01.1909	
von Günzler	29.03.1898	28.07.1902	
Magnus, Eduard	31.03.1897	14.05.1913	
Coppel, Gustav	17.11.1891	25.12.1914	
Arnstädt, Julius	01.01.1887	17.11.1891	
Arnstädt, Emil	01.01.1887	14.11.1908	
Mendel, Julius	22.10.1885	27.04.1926	Chairman since 26.05.1918
Steinsieck, H.	09.04.1885	12.08.1885	
Caspar, Bernhard	12.04.1882	20.05.1918	
Hecht, S. A.	20.03.1876	28.10.1901	
Stockhardt, Paul Otto	28.10.1871	01.05.1897	
Peretz, Hermann	28.10.1871	31.12.1886	
Meyer, Moritz Gerson	28.10.1871	04.03.1879	
Martiny, Joseph Louis	28.10.1871	12.04.1882	
Magnus, Moritz	28.10.1871	11.03.1897	Chairman since 09.11.1888
Köhsel, Otto	28.10.1871	06.09.1874	
Heinemann, Daniel	28.10.1871	14.07.1875	
Meyer, Ferdinand	28.10.1871	02.11.1888	Chairman

Annex 4b Members of the Supervisory Board (Employee representatives)

	Period		
Pfau, Lorenz	26.04.2019		
Allak, Hasan	26.04.2019		
Grioli, Francesco	01.11.2018		
Benner, Christiane	01.03.2018		Vice chairwoman since 01.03.2018
Valten, Gudrun	01.01.2017	26.04.2019	
Scholz, Stefan	30.04.2015		
Volkmann, Elke	25.04.2014		
Vörkel, Kirsten	25.04.2014		
Hausmann, Peter	01.07.2013	31.10.2018	
Otto, Arthur	01.05.2010	30.04.2015	
Köhlinger, Jörg	23.04.2009	24.04.2014	
Fischl, Hans	23.04.2009	31.12.2011	
Iglhaut, Michael	16.03.2006		
Bischoff, Werner	04.07.2005	15.05.2013	Vice chairman since 02.08.2005
Wörle, Erwin	14.05.2004	26.04.2019	
Schustereit, Jörg	14.05.2004	23.04.2009	
Schönfelder, Jörg	14.05.2004		
Nordmann, Dirk	14.05.2004		
Weniger, Dieter	03.06.2003	23.04.2009	
Reese, Dr. Thorsten	03.03.2003	30.04.2010	
Meine, Hartmut	11.07.2001	01.03.2018	Vice chairman since 01.08.2013
Hüttenmeister, Hans-Peter	13.10.1999	30.06.2005	Vice chairman since 14.05.2004
Sumpf, Dirk	11.08.1999	31.05.2003	
Knuth, Gerhard	01.06.1999	15.03.2006	
Hilker, Karl-Heinz	01.06.1999	14.05.2004	
Eickmann, Wilfried	01.06.1999	30.06.2001	
Deister, Michael	01.06.1999	25.04.2014	
Löschner, Hartmut	07.06.1996	28.06.1999	
Sumpf, Dirk	07.06.1995	01.06.1999	
Stark, Rainer	08.06.1994	28.02.2003	
Aschermann, Heidemarie	08.06.1994	14.05.2004	

Annex 4b Members of the Supervisory Board (Employee representatives) — 377

(continued)

	Period		
Hilverkus, Wilfried	11.02.1993	01.06.1999	
Mierswa, Werner	05.07.1989	14.05.2004	
Kölling, Dieter	05.07.1989	01.06.1999	
Keufner, Helmut	05.07.1989	08.06.1994	
Flothow, Friedrich-Karl	05.07.1989	08.06.1994	
Sprätz, Ernst	06.07.1984	05.07.1989	
Schleiermacher, Hugo	06.07.1984	05.07.1989	
Schille, Siegfried	06.07.1984	01.06.1999	
Köhler, Richard	06.07.1984	14.05.2004	Vice chairman since 01.06.1999
Bartels, Adolf	06.07.1984	01.06.1999	Vice chairman since 01.05.1996
Westerhaus, Hermann	07.09.1979	06.07.1984	
Tristram, Heinz	07.09.1979	06.07.1984	
Schultze, Wolfgang	07.09.1979	30.04.1996	Vice chairman since 06.07.1984
Schlesies, Eberhard	07.09.1979	07.06.1995	
Kost, Joachim	07.09.1979	05.07.1989	
Häßler, Rudolf	07.09.1979	06.07.1984	
Goldschald, Willi	07.09.1979	05.07.1989	
Brauns, Siegfried	07.09.1979	06.07.1984	
Alt, Rudolf	07.09.1979	31.12.1992	
Bartilla, Günther	04.07.1973	07.09.1979	
Wessel, Wilhelm	27.06.1966	07.09.1979	
Adams, Benno	27.06.1966	06.07.1984	Vice chairman since 07.09.1979
Appel, Eduard	27.06.1963	04.07.1973	
Diesselmann, Karl	09.07.1953	27.06.1966	
Ziegenbein, Karl	09.07.1953	27.06.1963	
Müller, Hans	09/1933	1934	
Haase, Hermann	05/1933	1934	
Schilling, Georg	11/1930	21.07.1933	
Schlesinger, Hugo	07/1925	30.04.1933	
Kammmann, Albert	10/1924	05/1930	
Leyfeld, Fritz	08/1922	04/1924	
Brinkmann, Karl	08/1922	04/1925	

Image credits

Unless otherwise specified, the source for all images is the Continental company archive in Hanover. Individual images are taken from the photo archive there, the magazines *Echo-Continental*, *Der Continental-Händler*, *conti intern*, etc., company image and advertising brochures, or extracts from business documentation.

Fig. 33: Werknachrichten der Continental Hannover: Belehrung und Aufklärung. - Hannover. BArch, M 1233 (1925, Heft 2, Seite 1)
Fig. 35: https://www.hna.de/lokales/northeim/northeim-ort47320/jahre-conti-northeim-segen-stadt-region-3818139.html
Fig. 48: picture alliance/dpa / Roberto Pfeil
Fig. 95: https://www.manager-magazin.de/magazin/artikel/investors-darling-2014-mister-350-prozent-a-998577.html